CW00419423

Princess Olga
of
Yugoslavia

Her Life and Times

Robert Prentice

Grosvenor House
Publishing Limited

This book is published by
Grosvenor House Publishing Ltd
Link House
140 The Broadway, Tolworth, Surrey, KT6 7HT.
www.grosvenorhousepublishing.co.uk

A CIP record for this book
is available from the British Library

ISBN 978-1-83975-442-5

To the Family of Princess Olga of Yugoslavia,
Greece and Denmark.

Contents

List of Illustrations

Prince Alexander, RAF *(Princess Barbara of Yugoslavia)*

Memorial Service, Winhoring *(Count Toerring)*

Princess Olga, 1950's *(Cecil Beaton/Princess Elizabeth)*

Prince Alexander wedding *(Princess Barbara of Yugoslavia)*

Princess Olga, Vaduz *(Princess Barbara of Yugoslavia)*

Princess Olga, 80th birthday *(Princess Barbara of Yugoslavia)*

Princess Olga and grandsons *(Princess Barbara of Yugoslavia)*

Princess Olga attends Memorial Service, Paris *(Princess Barbara of Yugoslavia)*

Acknowledgements

It would have been impossible to write this biography without the unstinting encouragement and support of many individuals, and I am extremely grateful for their assistance over a prolonged period.

The idea for this biography came about while researching an article on Princess Olga which I had been commissioned to write for Royalty Digest Quarterly. Various family members including Her Royal Highness' daughter, Her Royal Highness Princess Elizabeth of Yugoslavia; her son and daughter-in-law, Their Royal Highness' Prince and Princess Alexander of Yugoslavia; as well as her niece and nephew, Her Imperial and Royal Highness Archduchess Helen of Austria and His Royal Highness, the Duke of Kent were all generous with their time and assistance, at this stage. Princess Olga's grandson, Prince Michel of Yugoslavia, also answered numerous queries by e-mail.

Indeed, it soon became apparent that there was a sufficient depth of material to justify a biography. To this end, Princess Elizabeth subsequently provided me with copies of a wide selection of her mother's private correspondence, pages of Princess Olga's unpublished memoirs and copies of her mother's diaries in her possession. Meanwhile, Prince Alexander of Yugoslavia and his wife Barbara kindly allowed me to read and make copious notes from their extensive holding of Princess Olga's private diaries.

I am also indebted to Her Majesty the Queen for granting me access to, and permitting me to quote from correspondence to and relating to Princess Olga which is held at the Royal Archives in Windsor. I would also like to thank the (since retired) Senior Archivist, Miss Pamela Clark and her staff for their help.

I am particularly grateful to Princess Elizabeth and Princess Barbara of Yugoslavia, Count Hans-Veit Toerring and Hereditary Count Ignaz Toerring for providing me with many of the images used in this book.

Many people agreed to speak to me about Princess Olga. They include her beloved great-niece, Her Imperial and Royal Highness Archduchess Sophie of Austria, Princess of Windisch-Graetz; her former daughter-in-law, Princess Maria Pia of Bourbon-Parma, her former son-in-law Mr Neil Balfour, Mr Vincent Poklewski Koziell, Ms Savina Serpieri and Mr Hugo Vickers. In Athens, Mrs Lila Lalalounis kindly arranged for me to visit Princess Nicholas' former home at Psychiko.

I am also indebted to the staff at the National Archives in Kew who diligently photocopied a large selection of Foreign Office, Dominion Office and Colonial Office papers. I am also grateful to the library staff at Columbia University in New York who arranged for a microfiche of Prince Paul of Yugoslavia's papers to be sent over to Scotland under the Inter-Library Loan Scheme. I wish to acknowledge too the assistance of the staff at Dundee City Library, as well as Anna Petre, Assistant Keeper at the University of Oxford Archives and Ms Judith Curthoys the Archivist at Christ Church College.

Family Tree of Princess Olga of Yugoslavia

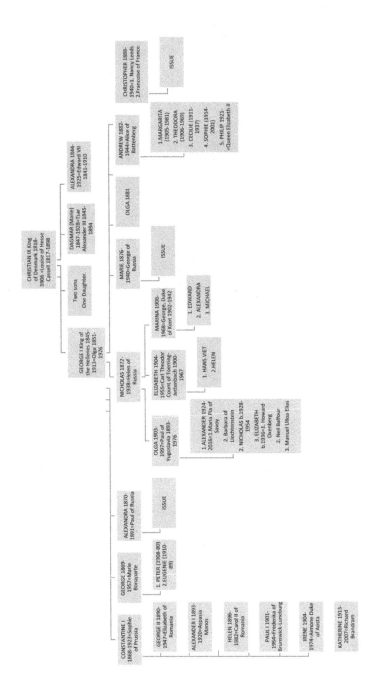

Introduction

Princess Olga of Yugoslavia is largely remembered today as the beautiful, older sister of the equally attractive and much-loved Princess Marina, Duchess of Kent. However, unlike Marina, she has not been the subject of numerous biographies; nor does she have the same "fan following" among those individuals who take a keen interest in royal matters. Indeed, this biography is the first in-depth study of her long life. Nevertheless, Olga or 'The Princess' as I will often refer to her, was to lead a life which was, in many ways, more interesting and involved than that of her younger sister.

The first chapters of this book focus on Olga's dynastic links to the royal families of Europe, particularly those of Imperial Russia and Denmark. They cover too her childhood in Athens, among the 'clannish intimacy' of the Greek royal family, with several detours to the Imperial Court at St Petersburg and the bracing seaside resorts of southern England. This is a vital exercise as it helps the reader to understand Olga's deep love of family, as well as her acute sense of dynastic awareness. These influences underpinned her life.

For the Princess, "family" was not only comprised of her immediate relatives, but also included a large, multi-national group of cousins, aunts and uncles, as well as a non-royal, Miss Kate Fox, Olga's much-loved nurse or 'Nurnie'. Certainly, I find that 'family' provided the Princess with a feeling of security, as well as the freedom to be herself. It was also through 'family' that some of her major character traits were forged: Loyalty, kindness, patriotism, duty, a sense of humour and, above all, a deep Christian faith. It is also fair to say that with such close blood ties, whatever affected a member of her family tended to affect her.

Yet, her sense of dynastic awareness is equally of note and not for nothing has she been referred to as 'the most royal Princess in Europe'. While Olga was proud to be Greek and a Princess of Greece, I determine that she soon acquired a highly distinct 'royal' sense of self, largely thanks to her impeccable Imperial Russian heritage (and to a lesser extent due to her strong links to the Danish House of Sonderburg-Glucksburg). This 'royal' persona undoubtedly had its downsides, for the Princess could often comes across as aloof and haughty. It may also have inclined her to be disapproving of others and their actions. Nonetheless, this dynastic awareness also helped to foster the steeliness and determination which would carry her through the many crises of her adult life.

Indeed, in examining Olga's life in subsequent chapters, I am struck by the extent to which external factors impacted upon her, particularly the political vagaries of 20th century European history. This is amply evidenced by the assassination of King Alexander of Yugoslavia, in 1934, which led to Olga's husband, Paul, being declared Prince Regent, thus propelling the Princess to the exalted position of 'Queen in all but name' of her adopted homeland. Then, in a dreadful volte face, the British backed a coup to remove Paul as Regent and dispatch him and Olga (vilified in the British Parliament as 'a dangerous Royal Enemy') into exile to Kenya as 'political prisoners'. Such happenings caused one relative to rightly reflect that the Princess was actually 'part of history' as opposed to a mere observer of it.

Nevertheless, despite the many challenges that life was to throw at Olga including, in later years, the untimely death of a son, her strength of character and deep religious beliefs helped to sustain her.

Chapter 1 Setting the Scene

Her Royal Highness Princess Olga of Greece and Denmark was born at the Greek royal family's charming country residence, Tatoi at 10.45 am on 11 June 1903. However, the new-born Princess' heritage was anything but Greek: Olga's mother Grand Duchess Elena Vladimirovna, maternal grandfather Grand Duke Vladimir Alexandrovich and paternal grandmother Queen Olga of the Hellenes were Russian and direct descendants of Tsar Nicholas I. Her paternal grandfather King George I of the Hellenes was born in Denmark, the third child of the country's monarch, King Christian IX (often referred to as the "father-in-law of Europe", as many of his children married the heirs of other European royal dynasties). Meanwhile, Olga's maternal grandmother, Grand Duchess Vladimir was born Duchess Marie of Mecklenburg-Schwerin in Ludwigslust, Northern Germany. Indeed, of all her antecedents, only her father Nicholas (born in Athens in 1872, the third son of King George I) and his siblings (except the youngest child Christopher) were actually born in Greece. So how did it come to pass that a minor Danish prince from the ancient Royal House of Oldenburg came to sit on the Hellenic throne?

The story begins in 1821, as Greece fought a valiant War of Independence to end nearly four-hundred years of Turkish Ottoman rule. During their (ultimately successful) eleven-year struggle, the rebels received assistance from Russia, Great Britain and France who, under the Convention of London of 1832, finally recognised Greece as an independent country under their protection. The "Great Powers" favoured a monarchical state. However, since the last Greek sovereign, Emperor Constantine XI, had been killed in the fifteenth century, they settled on a suitable foreign import, Prince Otto Friedrich Ludwig, the 17-year-old second son of King Ludwig I of Bavaria. Sadly, the new King of Greece lacked sound political judgment and this led to regular confrontations with the military. To compound matters, Otto's consort, Queen Amalia, was unable to provide him with a royal heir. Eventually, in 1862, this increasingly unpopular sovereign was overthrown in a military coup and he returned to his native Bavaria, where he died in 1867 at the age of 52.

So once again the Great Powers were faced with the troublesome task of finding a new Greek sovereign. Attention eventually fell on an eighteen-year-old Danish naval cadet, Prince Christian Wilhelm, the second son of Prince Christian of Schleswig-Holstein-Sonderburg-Glucksburg. 'Willi' was in many ways an ideal candidate: Although his father was heir to the Danish throne, the family lived simply in a grace-and-favour burgher's house, the Yellow Palace, on Copenhagen's Amaliegade. Consequently, the young prince remained relatively unspoilt and, as one of a large family of six, was at ease both with himself and with others. Willi was particularly close to his sisters Alexandra ('Alix') and Dagmar ('Minny') and the trio formed 'a still more closely-knit inner circle'[1] within this loving family.

Indeed, it was during a visit to London to visit his older sister Alexandra (who had recently married the heir to British throne, Edward, the Prince of Wales) that the British Prime Minister Lord Palmerston and Foreign Secretary Lord John Russell arranged a meeting with Willi at Marlborough House (the Wales' London residence) to ask him if he would consider becoming the King of Greece. In addition, the British Foreign Office made overtures to the Danish King (Frederick VII), who encouraged his young kinsman to accept the offer. A parliamentary deputation was then sent from Athens to Copenhagen to formally ask the Prince to accept the Greek crown.

Following the ratification of the appointment by the Greek parliament, on 30 March 1863, Willi was proclaimed King George I of the Hellenes (as the previous incumbent, Otto, had never formally abdicated as King of Greece). His accession was bolstered by the welcome news that the British government had decided to cede the Ionian Islands, which were currently a British protectorate under the terms of Treaty of Paris of 1815, to Greece.

The fledgling monarch arrived in Athens in October, a month prior to his father Christian ascending the Danish throne as King Christian IX. King George's adopted homeland was a complete contrast to his birthplace: Greece was barren, sparsely populated (with barely more than a million people), had a low literacy rate, as well as the poorest economy in Europe.[2] Furthermore, the new King's Athenian home, the Royal Palace, had been designed for pomp rather than practical living and was either boiling hot in summer or bitterly cold in winter. Wind (often mixed with dust) continually whistled down the long, draughty corridors while the unsatisfactory sanitary arrangements (there was only one bathroom) did little to alleviate the numerous pungent odours which permeated the interior.[3]

Nevertheless, George was determined to make a success of his new and demanding position. Aided by what the British Minister, Sir Thomas Rumbold, referred to as '[a] considerable firmness of character and personal courage',[4] the young King rose early to deal with his correspondence and initially focused on learning the Greek language (so as to better establish contact with the ordinary people). As George's knowledge of his adopted homeland increased, this shrewd and democratic ruler championed the writing of a new constitution in 1864; this would limit his powers to those of a constitutional monarch. George then dispensed with the services of his Danish advisors, for as he would subsequently emphasise to his sons, 'You must never forget that you are foreigners in this country, *but you must make them [the people] forget it*'.[5]

Having dealt with these matters, the King realised that to truly establish his new dynasty he must find a suitable queen. His gaze soon fell upon the youthful Grand Duchess Olga Constantinovna, a daughter of the Grand Duke Constantine Nikolayevich (the second son of Tsar Nicholas I) and his wife Grand Duchess Alexandra Iosifovna. Given that Olga's father was one of the richest men in Russia (he was variously a 'Great Admiral' in the Imperial Russian Navy and a Viceroy of Poland), this Romanov Grand Duchess was accustomed to the finest things in life: In St Petersburg, she and her family lived in the lavishly appointed Marble Palace; they also owned a vast country estate at Pavlovsk. However, it was not Olga's impressive lineage or wealth which beguiled George, but rather the sixteen-year-old's sweet nature and youthful beauty. The couple were married amid imperial splendour, in October 1867, at St Petersburg's Winter Palace.

When she later disembarked at Piraeus (the harbour near Athens), Queen Olga immediately secured a place in the hearts of the Greek people by wearing a dress in the national colours of blue and white. Nevertheless, unbeknown to the general populace, this shy young bride suffered from homesickness and often resorted to playing with her Russian dolls to lift her spirits. Yet, Olga also possessed a deep sense of duty and soon embraced her much simpler life in Greece: She mastered the language in less than a year and rapidly became acquainted with her public role, founding the Evangelismos Hospital in Athens and an industrial school where girls were taught weaving, lace-making and embroidery.

However, for King George, his wife's greatest achievement was providing him with heirs to secure the future of the Hellenic dynasty: In August 1868, she gave birth to a son Constantine ('Tino') followed at regular intervals over the next twenty years by another seven children (George, Alexandra, Nicholas, Marie, Olga [who died in infancy], Andrew and Christopher). The children were all raised in a relaxed atmosphere akin to that enjoyed by their father in Copenhagen. Consequently, the siblings were rather spirited and regularly upset the palace servants by roller skating through the hallowed State Rooms, often led by the King himself.

In 1871, King George decided to build a country retreat and purchased a 40000-acre plot of land, 35 kilometres north of Athens, at the foot of Mount Parnes. There, he supervised the building of a large house overlooking Phaleron Bay. This residence, known as Tatoi, was said to be an exact replica of a Victorian-style mansion which stood in the grounds of Queen Olga's childhood home at Pavlovsk.[6] A visitor summed up the estate's attraction thus: 'From the balcony [of the main house] one drinks in the pure, light mountain air, perfumed with the firs that grow thickly below'.[7] Predictably, Tatoi would come to be regarded by the royal family as their real home and future generations-including Princess Olga-would develop a very deep and enduring love for the place.

A welcome diversion from life in Greece could be found in the King's homeland of Denmark. Each year, Nicholas' father took his ever-growing family to stay with his parents King Christian IX ('Apapa') and Queen Louise ('Amama') at one of their country homes, the relatively modest Bernstorff or the more imposing Fredensborg Palace. The Greek contingent were invariably joined by King George's sisters Alexandra ('Aunt Alix'), Dagmar ('Aunt Minny', the wife of Tsar Alexander III of Russia) and Thyra ('Aunt Thyra', who was married to Ernest Augustus of Hanover) and their respective families. Olga's father Prince Nicholas was therefore accustomed, from a young age, to mixing happily with his many cousins including Aunt Alix's son George (later King George V of Great Britain) and his younger sister Victoria, as well as Aunt Minny's son Nicholas (from 1894 Tsar Nicholas II of Russia). This "royal mob" of Danish Glucksburg descendants happened to share an enduring passion for practical jokes and frivolity. Indeed, one guest, the Dowager Empress Frederick, complained to her mother Queen Victoria that 'The noise they all made and the wild romps they had were simply indescribable.'[8] Prince Nicholas also developed a deep appreciation of this ancient Nordic Kingdom's history, customs and culture which he subsequently described as 'delightful [and] the height of civilisation'.[9] This is the view he would later pass on to his eldest daughter Olga, who came to regard it as the 'land of my ancestors...'.[10]

As the third son, with no expectations of inheriting the throne, Nicholas had an easier life than his eldest brother Crown Prince Constantine. However, King George was determined to impose a sense of duty and responsibility in all his sons. Keeping to his belief that his family must be identified as Greek, he insisted that the young princes complete their education in Greece. Nevertheless, Nicholas' upbringing seems to have served him well, for he would go on to become a talented all-rounder who could ride, paint, fish, play bridge, golf and sail. On an intellectual level, he enjoyed serious reading and, with a developing interest in the theatre, would subsequently write many plays. Furthermore, Nicholas' wonderful sense of humour was accentuated by 'a devastating aptitude for wickedly accurate mimicry.'[11] Meanwhile, strong moral and religious values were instilled in him by his pious mother, Queen Olga.

In 1897, the King had his first taste of the fickle nature of both Greek politics and the Greek people following the outbreak of the Greco-Turkish War. This conflict had its origins in a struggle over the future status of the Ottoman-controlled island of Crete, where the Christian majority had recently staged rebellions against their Muslim Ottoman rulers and now desired a union with Greece. As the two sides fought to consolidate their grip on power, the King and his government in Athens vacillated and were subsequently accused by the popular National Society (which favoured Greek military intervention against the Turks), of a betrayal of the Christian cause in Crete. Eventually the war spread to the mainland and Greek forces, under the command of Crown Prince Constantine, were sent to fight the Turks. However, the Hellenic forces were greatly outnumbered by Ottoman forces and were eventually defeated at Domokos. A humiliating peace treaty, brokered by the Great Powers, required Greece to pay an indemnity of £4 million to the Turks, in addition to ceding certain border areas of Thessaly.

Although it had been the Greek populace who had campaigned for this war against the Turks, they now rounded on their King and held him solely responsible for entering into the conflict. Furthermore, his son Constantine was denounced as an incompetent military leader.[12] However, amidst the ups and downs that would come to typify the rollercoaster fortunes of the Hellenic royal house, an event then occurred which would dramatically reverse public opinion: In February 1898, the King was returning by carriage from an afternoon outing to Phaleron Bay, accompanied by his daughter Marie, when their carriage was ambushed by two men who tried to assassinate the occupants. Although the assailants failed in their task, this attempt on their sovereign's life infuriated the majority of Greeks. During a subsequent spring tour of the provinces, King George was overwhelmed by the outpouring of sympathy and love from his subjects.[13]

As Prince Nicholas matured, he began to make regular visits to his Aunt Alix and her husband the Prince of Wales ('Uncle Bertie') in England. He particularly enjoyed his forays to the Wales' Norfolk retreat, Sandringham House, where the lavish house parties provided countless opportunities for shooting, fishing and fun (During one stay, an enthusiastic Nicholas was observed encouraging his Aunt Alix to ride her new tricycle down the 'Big House's' long indoor corridors).[14] When, in January 1901, Uncle Bertie ascended the British throne as King Edward

VII, Nicholas' beloved Aunt Alix (now Queen Consort) welcomed the Prince (and subsequently his family) with open arms to Buckingham Palace.

For all these strong Danish and British influences, it was in his mother's Russian homeland that Nicholas would find a bride. Following his first visit, in 1880, the Prince made frequent trips to his maternal grandmother, Grand Duchess Alexandra Iosifovna at Pavlovsk, as well as to his sisters, Alexandra and Marie, who had both married into the Russian Imperial family. He was also, of course, welcome at the homes of his Aunt Minny (Tsarina Marie Feodorovna, as Dagmar was then titled) and her husband Tsar Alexander III. It was through these Imperial connections, that Nicholas first made the acquaintance of Grand Duchess Elena Vladimirovna, the youngest child (and only daughter) of the influential Grand Duke Vladimir Alexandrovich. The latter was the senior Russian Grand Duke at the Imperial Court and derived great power and prestige from his dual roles as Commander of the Imperial Guard Corps and Military Governor of St Petersburg.

Elena's mother Grand Duchess Vladimir (also known in family circles as 'Miechen' or Maria Pavlovna [the Elder]) was equally influential and 'certainly the most brilliant of the women in the Imperial Family.'[15] This eldest daughter of Friedrich Franz II, Grand Duke of Mecklenburg-Schwerin (by his first marriage to Princess Augusta of Reuss), first encountered Grand Duke Vladimir when he was on a visit to Germany in June 1871. The couple were immediately attracted to each other and the ruthless Duchess Marie quickly called off her engagement to Prince Georg of Schwarzburg-Rudolstadt. Nevertheless, her marriage to Vladimir was delayed for nearly two years, due to the Lutheran Duchess' obstinate refusal to convert to the Russian Orthodox faith. Fortunately, Tsar Alexander II eventually consented to the union and the couple married in August 1874.[16] This stance was an early indication that Grand Duchess Vladimir knew her own mind, even at the expense of ruffling some powerful imperial feathers. Thereafter, Maria Pavlovna focused on becoming the driving force of St Petersburg society. Her Salon in the Vladimir Palace, a magnificent granite brick and stucco building, designed in the style of a Florentine palazzo, overlooking the fashionable Dvortsovaya Embankment and the River Neva, regularly attracted those of all nationalities with impeccable social and political connections. She tended to favour those who could amuse over the traditional Russian aristocracy. Furthermore, the Grand Duchess ensured that her guests were treated to the very best: She insisted on serving only the finest wines and black caviar, while her confectionary was the finest Abrikosov and Sons (who specialised in making glacial fruits and chocolate soldiers) could supply. Given that other members of the Imperial family (particularly the new Tsar Nicholas II's consort, Alexandra, who habitually displayed a 'blushing shyness'[17]) preferred not to entertain those from outside their immediate circle, this strategy was to prove most effective in underpinning Miechen's social and political standing.[18]

Given her elevated circumstances (and not forgetting that she was already the apple of her father's eye), Elena ('Helen' or 'Ellen') led a charmed life at the heart of the Imperial court, overseen by her English governesses Miss Millicent Crofts (and later a Mrs Saville). Although devoted to her three older brothers the Grand Dukes Kirill, Boris and Andrei ("the Vladimirovitchi"), she was quite able to hold her own during their spirited recreational activities. Prince Nicholas' Aunt, the (by now) Dowager Tsarina Marie Feodorovna thought Elena 'really quite sweet, but vain and pretty grandiose.'[19] Indeed, she would eventually earn the title of 'La Belle Hélène'[20] as she dined and danced the night away at the fashionable Restaurant Cuba.

This youthful Grand Duchess could also be tempestuous and passionate; her numerous love affairs were well-documented by the international press and included Prince Louis Napoleon. She was betrothed, in October 1898, to Prince Max of Baden. However, the engagement was broken off within the year. Unfortunately, poor Max was of a highly nervous disposition and according to one report '[Elena's] action in jilting him... affected his reason and necessitated his committal to the celebrated Austrian retreat for the insane [at Purkersdorff]'.[21] Such media attention left Elena bereft and vulnerable, while Grand Duchess Vladimir grew increasingly exasperated as polite society speculated over her daughter's inability to settle down with a suitable suitor.

In August 1900, Prince Nicholas made another of his regular visits to St Petersburg. His maternal uncle, Grand Duke Konstantin Konstantinovich mentions approvingly in his diary that, 'Nicky went for a long ride with Elena, whom he likes, as she does him, but Maria Pavlovna rebuked her daughter for this, and told Georgie [the King of Greece] that Nicky could not expect to marry Elena, being neither a future King, nor having any fortune. She and Nicky, however, go together perfectly'.[22] However, Elena's name also continued to be linked with numerous potential suitors including Prince Albert of Schleswig-Holstein (a grandson of Queen Victoria). There was also a most unsuitable romance with a Count Lyoff Loubetskoi. To cap it all, in the spring of 1902 (and now described as the 'greatest Royal flirt in Europe'[23]) Elena eloped with an impecunious student from St Petersburg. The couple managed to reach Warsaw before they were discovered. The spirited Grand Duchess was swiftly escorted back to St Petersburg to face the wrath of her parents.[24]

Meanwhile, Nicholas bided his time and the elopement incident actually worked in his favour, as it forced Maria Pavlovna to adopt a more realistic outlook in her quest for a suitor for her daughter. Fortuitously, in May, the young Prince and the Grand Duke Vladimir were in Madrid to attend the celebrations marking King Alfonso XIII's 16th birthday. This provided the duo with an ideal opportunity to discuss a possible marriage.[25] Elena and Nicholas' engagement was finally announced on 13 June. The young couple were married, on 29 August, in the lavishly gilded church attached to the Imperial family's country residence, the Catherine Palace, at Tsarskoe Selo. Elena looked particularly stunning in the traditional Russian Court dress of silver cloth embossed with lilies and roses, over which she wore the heavy ermine-trimmed ruby robe of an Imperial Grand Duchess. This attire was offset by the splendid Romanov Nuptial Crown.

After honeymooning in Ropcha and Denmark, the bride and groom visited the Tsar at his seaside summer palace at Livadia, in the Crimea, to thank him for his wedding gift of a new home in Athens. They then proceeded to Greece aboard King George's yacht and, on their arrival at Piraeus, Ellen (as she was now invariably referred to) emulated Queen Olga by making her first appearance in her adopted homeland dressed in the Greek national colours. However, the reality of life in Greece must have been a shock to Princess Nicholas (as she was now titled, although her husband would always refer to her as 'the Grand Duchess'): Athens was decidedly 'provincial'[26] when compared to the splendours of St Petersburg and had no aristocracy to speak of, unless you counted the wives of tobacco merchants. In addition, until the newlyweds' new residence was completed (this would take several years), the couple had to make do with a suite of rooms in the Royal Palace. However, Princess Nicholas was not the first royal bride of her generation to arrive in Athens: That privilege had fallen, thirteen years earlier, to Kaiser Wilhelm II's daughter, Princess Sophie of Prussia, following her marriage to Crown Prince Constantine. Like Ellen, this spirited and practical princess had been raised in much grander circumstances, amidst the splendour of Berlin's Kronprinzenpalais. She mainly concerned herself with charitable initiatives involving children and the destitute. Constantine and Sophie currently had four children (George, Alexander, Helen and Paul)[1]-the eldest of King George's grandchildren. They were ably watched over by a Scotch Norland nurse, Catherine 'Gertie' Salmond.

---

[1] Sophie would subsequently give birth to two other children (Irene, born in 1904, and Catherine in 1913).

Fortunately, the redoubtable Princess Nicholas embraced life in her adopted land with a refreshing enthusiasm and quickly became fluent in Greek. However, those who fell under her charm soon learned that it was foolish to misinterpret her good manners for familiarity as this 'austere, beautiful and commanding'[27] Romanov Grand Duchess' eyes could quickly turn ice cold with Imperial anger if someone overstepped the mark. Indeed, Ellen's standards and expectations would forever remain those of Imperial Russia and were backed, in a practical sense, by a considerable dowry of $500,000 as well as an annual allowance from the Apanages, a fund set up by Tsar Paul I for the benefit of the Imperial family.[28]

Chapter 2 A 'Clannish Intimacy'

When it was discovered, in the autumn of 1902, that Princess Nicholas was with child, there was a great rush of activity as Ellen set about organising the acquisition of her future child's layette from a well-known London "Juvenile Outfitter", M. E. Penson. The purchases, made over a six-month period, came to a staggering £188 13s 1d.[1] Further items were also bought in Paris by the Grand Duchess Vladimir who had already decided she would travel to Greece to be present at the birth of her beloved daughter's first child. The King and Queen Olga offered her hospitality at Tatoi, which must have seemed like a country shooting box when compared to the grandeur of her Russian residences.

From the moment that Olga was born on that June morning, Maria Pavlovna was to take an almost proprietorial interest in her eldest Greek granddaughter's upbringing. This would later prove bothersome. Meanwhile, in keeping with the established custom, the infant was suckled by a peasant foster mother and later weaned on to cow's milk from the farm at Tatoi.[2] However, within months, Princess Nicholas discovered that she was again expecting. Troublingly, there were also ongoing concerns over little Olga's physical wellbeing. The child's anxious mother duly contacted Miss Isabel Sharman, the Principal of London's prestigious Norland Institute, who engaged a Miss Kate Fox to come out to Greece on a temporary basis to oversee Olga's care.[3] The latter would later tell this devoted nurse that, 'had it not been for your fateful arrival in Tatoi, my life might have been considerably shortened!'[4] Unsurprisingly, this Middlesex-born spinster soon became an indispensable fixture of household life and, apart from a period from 1913 to 1920, Kate would never leave the bosom of the Nicholas family. Thus, by the time Ellen gave birth to her second daughter, Elisabeth, on 24 May 1904, Miss Fox ('Nurnie' to her charges; 'Foxie' to the adults) was firmly established in post. The short interlude between the birth dates of her younger sister and herself would forever amuse Olga and it later became her habit to write in her diary on Elisabeth's birthday, 'We are twins again for 18 days.'[5]

Following Elisabeth's birth, the Nicholas family moved into their newly-built home, the Nicholas Palace, situated opposite the Royal Gardens on fashionable Sekeri Street. Possessing the atmosphere of an English country house, this white-washed edifice sported a long airy veranda and a cooling fountain in the small front garden to combat the heat. Moreover, unlike the Royal Palace, it was equipped with every modern convenience including central heating and modern bathrooms. A visitor recalled, it was, 'a happy home, the people in it were happy, and so were all the visitors who entered it.'[6] This observation is unsurprising, for Prince and Princess Nicholas were devoted to their children, a fact Olga later acknowledged, 'As I look back over those early years, I realize ...how important their influence has been in my life and what a debt of gratitude I owe them for the happiness and security of our childhood and the meaning of home.'[7]

Although Olga's parents proved frequent visitors, the nurseries were very much Kate Fox's domain: She brooked little interference from anyone, as she imposed a robust English-style discipline. But even the redoubtable Nurnie could not always have her own way: As was the habit at the Greek Court, the children were required to eat lunch at 11am and dinner at 3pm. However, this did not deter Kate from complaining about the 'foreign' food. She was also concerned for Olga's welfare as the toddler was proving to be a particularly slow eater.[8] Foxie's remedy was to introduce traditional English nursery foods such as Robinson's Patent Groats.[9] Fortuitously, the little Princess flourished under this new regime and, by age three, had grown into a fair-haired, blue-eyed child with a rosy complexion.[10]

In the summer of 1905, Olga made her first visit to Russia with her parents and younger sister. The family broke their sea journey at Constantinople (Istanbul) to pay an official visit to the Turkish Sultan Abdul-Hamid at the Yildiz Palace. At the conclusion of this duty call, the Sultan made a "request" to see the little princesses.[11] Abdul-Hamid was duly impressed, embracing both children tenderly and exclaiming expansively in French 'Ces sont des petits anges!'[12] Thereafter, the little group travelled on to Odessa to take the Imperial train north to St Petersburg.

Alarmingly, this excursion north was undertaken against a backdrop of great unrest in Russia. Olga's great-uncle, Grand Duke Sergei Alexandrovich, had been assassinated in February, when a bomb was thrown at his carriage outside his home, the Nikolsky Palace. In June, the crew of the new Imperial Navy battleship *Potemkin* mutinied over the quality of the food. Meanwhile, in Odessa, workers went on strike and the ensuing disturbances would become known as the "1905 Revolution".

The Nicholas' visit also happened to coincide with a time of conflict within the Imperial family. In October, Olga's uncle, the Grand Duke Kirill married-at Tegernsee-his divorced cousin Victoria Melita (the daughter of Grand Duke Vladimir's sister, Marie Alexandrovna), who had previously been married to the Tsarina's brother, Grand Duke Ernst of Hesse (the couple had divorced in 1901). When Kirill subsequently returned alone to St Petersburg to inform his relatives of the marriage, the Tsar's reaction was one of fury: He dispatched his Court Minister, Count Fredericks to Grand Duke Vladimir's home at Tsarskoe Selo to inform him that his eldest son must leave Russia within forty-eight hours; the Tsar also stripped Kirill of his titles and Apanage income.[13] The next day, during a 'strong and disagreeable' audience with Olga's grandfather, Nicholas II resolutely refused to rescind his decision, so Grand Duke Vladimir resigned his position as Commander of the Imperial Guard.[14] The Vladimirs, however, were convinced that the real blame lay with the Tsarina and her 'blind vindictiveness'.[15]

Throughout this dramatic interlude, Kate Fox and her charges initially remained at Tsarskoe Selo, while Prince and Princess Nicholas set out on an autumnal progress via Paris, for stays in London and Sandringham, before proceeding to Windsor for Christmas. Princess Nicholas was in raptures telling Miss Fox, 'England is too delightful for words. I wish I could always live here!'[16] However, Kate had other things on her mind: A dangerous escalation in political turbulence in Russia had obliged Foxie to remove Olga and Elisabeth from Tsarskoe Selo to the safety of Grand Duchess Vladimir's childhood home, Schloss Schwerin, in north Germany. Princess Nicholas seemed unperturbed, merely instructing Kate to, 'Kiss and bless the little darlings from both of us...'[17] However, Ellen should have been concerned for the protests would lead to the adoption of a new Russian Constitution in 1906 and the formation of a legislative assembly, the State Duma. These developments would give the ordinary people a dangerous taste for democracy which would gradually erode the absolute power of the Imperial family.

In the late spring of 1906, Princess Nicholas learned that she was expecting. She gave birth to her third child, a girl (named Marina), on 13 December. Olga remembered this event 'very vividly' and in particular, standing on 'tip-toe to peep into the cradle in our nursery at the tiny pink bundle and thinking it was a new doll'.[18] However, her joy turned quickly to concern: The birth had proved exceptionally difficult (Marina was born with a slightly twisted left foot) and the Princess was informed her mother was 'very ill' and she must 'keep very quiet.'[19] There were to be no more children for Ellen. In due course, a Norland probationer, Grace Gibb, was employed to assist Kate in the nursery.

As Princess Nicholas departed to take a 'treatment' at a health spa in Franzensbad, Olga adopted an almost proprietorial interest in her youngest sister and 'took charge' in her mother's absence.[20] It has been stated that the three sisters would became inseparable and form what has been described as 'a self-sufficient unit adoring each other and their parents with an equal enthusiasm which was never to waver'.[21] This was not entirely accurate: Thenceforth, Olga and Elisabeth would share a bedroom, while baby Marina slept separately in the adjacent night nursery. Moreover, the two eldest sisters were more severely disciplined by their mother than the youngest child,[22] behaviour which was mirrored by Kate Fox who tended to bully and boss the older girls.[23] There seems little doubt that much of this had to do with Marina's minor disability which Ellen emphasised to Kate it was 'important'[24] to hide. However, this would only have been one factor, for Princess Nicholas hated spoilt children, many of whom she encountered on her overseas visits to relatives.

Miss Fox was a great believer in fresh air and encouraged her 'three beauties'[25] to play outdoors (even allowing them to crawl in the sun while attached by a long cord to a tree trunk until they were 'brown as berries'[26]). Visits to the beach at Vouliagmeni and Phaleron were also commonplace, as was Foxie's insistence on sponging her charges down with cold sea water to ward-off the sun's rays. This no-nonsense approach found particular favour with the egalitarian Prince Nicholas, who strove to bring up his children 'on the simple principles of our own [childhood] home life, and to be unpretentious and full of consideration for others.[27] In this he was aided by his parents ('Amama' and 'Apapa' to their grandchildren) who were keen on maintaining a 'clannish intimacy'[28] within their extended (and ever-growing) family. Thus, a tradition emerged whereby the whole royal family would dine each Tuesday at the Nicholas Palace and each Thursday at Crown Prince Constantine's home nearby. Furthermore, following Sunday Mass at the Royal Palace, Olga would stroll with the rest of the family through the English-style gardens. It is therefore not surprising that, aside from her sisters, the young Princess' closest lifelong friendships would be formed from amongst this tight-knit family circle. They included Crown Prince Constantine's daughters Helen ('Sitta'), Irene ('Tim' or 'Tittum') and Catherine ('Baby'); Uncle George's only daughter Eugenie; as well as Uncle Andrew's children Margarita ('Zighoi') Theodora ('Dolla'), Cecilie and Sophie ('Tiny').

For Olga, her siblings and cousins, the time they spent together in the informal setting of Tatoi, during the warm months of late spring and summer, was truly special. From the moment they passed through the double gateposts, with its "Hansel and Gretel" gate lodge, they entered their own private playground that featured visits to the royal dairy-run by a Dane, Miss Petersen-which routinely supplied the King with milk products redolent of his homeland. The nearby home farm also proved a source of endless fascination, for each animal was given its own name and the cattle wore cow bells and ate from white marble troughs. When these attractions palled, the children could visit "The Tower", a tiered edifice filled with an eclectic collection of statues and marble columns unearthed during local excavations.

However, the occasion when Tatoi truly came alive was in late summer, during celebrations for Queen Olga's birthday. A military band would arrive early from Athens to awaken the family, who would then dress in formal attire and process up the hill to attend a Te Deum service at the little church of St Elia. Later, the royals would lunch together in the garden, before welcoming local estate workers and the royal guard for a sort of "peoples' festival" featuring a communal meal, supplemented by copious quantities of local wine. Afterwards, the guests enjoyed some spirited dancing well into the night.

As head of the Hellenic Royal House, King George was venerated by his people. For an impressionable young princess, several events held in his honour would be remembered with particular affection: On the King's name day-23 April-the royal family would embark the royal yacht at Piraeus and sail to a different Greek port each year, to be greeted by local officials and attend a celebratory church service, followed by a reception at the local Town Hall. The King then returned this hospitality at a luncheon aboard his yacht. Again, on King George's birthday, 24 December, the royal family and court would attend a Te Deum service in the palace Chapel and, in the evening, a grand reception was held in the State Apartments.

Princess Nicholas often despaired of the Greek court's informality, not to mention the heritage of some of those marrying into it. She was not afraid to demonstrate this: Ellen insisted on being called Her Imperial and Royal Highness to distinguish her from her sisters-in-law, who now included Andrew's wife Princess Alice of Battenberg and 'Big' George's spouse, Princess Marie Bonaparte. They were *mere* Royal Highnesses. This distinction seems to have the desired effect for Marie Bonaparte admitted to being scared of Princess Nicholas' 'beauty and *her pride*.'[29] Additionally, given the comparatively small size of the Greek royal family, there were frequent displays of pettiness and jockeying for the King and Queen's favour. This rivalry extended to the nursery accommodation at Tatoi, where the ultimate accolade was apparently to be awarded the use of, what Princess Nicholas described as, 'the good nurseries with the big balcony'.[30] With her great wealth, Ellen was also able to ensure that her daughters shone brightly by having the best of everything. During a visit to London she boasted to Foxie of purchasing 'a very smart dress for Olga...all real lace & of course very expensive'.[31] Furthermore, all articles of clothing were embossed with a crown. In addition to these outward manifestations of royalty, Princess Nicholas also made certain that her daughters received rigorous coaching in court etiquette. This included instruction on how to correctly acknowledge the presentation of arms by the Evzone sentries guarding the Nicholas Palace.

Given Queen Olga's devoutness, it comes as no surprise that God and religion played an important part in Olga's life. Ellen too had been raised to respect the liturgies and dogma of the Russian Orthodox Church and thoroughly approved of her mother-in-law's view that services must follow the strict tenets of that Church. Throughout Holy Week and Easter, Olga and her sisters would fast and attend two services each day; one in public at the Metropolitan Cathedral of the Annunciation and another in the Royal Palace's private chapel. On Easter Sunday, Olga joined her contemporaries in the traditional breaking of eggs ("tsougrisma"), which symbolised the opening of the tomb and Christ's resurrection from the dead. To ensure that her granddaughter truly understood the meaning behind such rites, Queen Olga arranged for Olga to receive individual instruction from a Lady-in-Waiting.

Chapter 3 The Russian Influence

As with Prince Nicholas, many of young Olga's character-forming experiences occurred during overseas stays to countries with which she had close family ties, particularly Russia. Ever since that first visit of 1905, the Princess and her sisters would accompany their parents on annual (and sometimes bi-annual) visits to their mother's homeland. These "Imperial" encounters, provided a direct contrast to the relative simplicity of the family's home life in Athens and would imbue the Nicholas' eldest daughter with a sense of dynastic awareness that would never leave her. The experience began as soon as the Nicholas family disembarked their boat in the Crimea and stepped aboard the Imperial train, with its luxurious intercommunicating saloons decorated in palest blue silk.

On reaching the Russian capital, the family were whisked by landau to the Vladimir Palace to savour the heated rooms favoured by their grandmother. The sisters were then led up the magnificent mirrored grand staircase towards the lavish top-floor nursery suite which featured a child-scale house that had once belonged to Princess Nicholas. While Olga later admitted to being frightened of Grand Duke Vladimir and his 'stentorian voice' (which could be heard 'a mile off'[1]), she also recalled that the Grand Duchess ('Gammy') 'spoilt us wildly and we were devoted to her.'[2] Certainly, Maria Pavlovna enjoyed inviting her granddaughters into her Moorish-style boudoir to play and frequently showered them with extravagant presents such as dolls, prams and jewellery. On other occasions, the sisters could not resist the temptation of sliding down the highly-polished banisters of the Palace's Grand Staircase. However, there were drawbacks: Olga recalled that 'Gammy' insisted on personally serving her granddaughter at table and 'heaped' the rich food on her plate, whilst also ensuring that she 'ate every scrap.' Inevitably, this sometimes had 'disastrous effects' on her digestion, a situation which was 'treated by the French doctor with drastic purges...'[3]

Olga was particularly mesmerised by her grandmother's extensive jewellery collection, which consisted of parures of diamonds, emeralds, rubies and sapphires-some as large as pigeon eggs. These were neatly arranged on blue velvet trays and placed in glass cabinets. The collection was under the care of two 'special' maids, who had charge of the keys. As a treat, on most evenings the three sisters would help their grandmother to select her jewellery and they were then permitted to watch as she dressed for dinner or a ball. Adjoining her dressing room, the Grand Duchess had a large bathroom containing a deep tiled square pool. On occasion, she allowed her granddaughters to bathe there, although Olga recounts that, 'After having had more than her share of drenching, [she] would order us out!' Furthermore, 'if it was winter at the time, so we were each carried well-wrapped [back to the nursery] by two tall footmen, the nursery maid following with our night attire.'[4]

But always in the background were simmering tensions between the Grand Duchess Vladimir and Kate Fox, made worse by the latter's 'almost autocratic arrogance'.[5] This occasionally manifested itself in a fraught battle of wills between the two: The Grand Duchess liked the palace's interior kept at a uniform temperature and insisted the windows were kept closed to achieve this. However, Foxie firmly believed that her young charges benefited from the outside air (no matter how cold) and insisted on opening the nursery windows. When she heard of this contravention, Maria Pavlovna immediately proceeded to the nurseries to close the windows. However, to the Grand Duchess' fury Kate later reopened them. Another bone of contention was Miss Fox's belief (shared by Prince and Princess Nicholas) that the children should be spanked for any wrongdoing. This appalled their grandmother, who complained to friends, 'That dreadful woman knocks them about'.[6]

As in Athens, the family environment in Russia could be competitive. Princess Nicholas was certainly keen that her daughters should shine and kept a wary eye on the competition, particularly her brother Kirill's daughter, Marie. From Tsarskoe Selo, she was able to reassure Foxie that 'as far as beauty goes, she [Marie] is not to be mentioned in the same breath as our babies'. Nevertheless, it was more than Ellen could bear to see 'little Marie' paraded around by her Norlander nurse Colinette, after her own daughters had returned to Athens. However, she quickly seized on the competitive advantage of having three daughters, compared to her brother's (then) one, and decided that Marina must have a dress 'like those Mama gave the two others, so now they can all be dressed alike.'[7] This attention-seeking style of couture would be imposed on the young princesses well into their teens.

Olga's maternal grandparents also owned a country residence, the bright and chintzy three-storey Villa Vladimir, adjacent to the Catherine Park at Tsarskoe Selo. To amuse her granddaughters, the Grand Duchess arranged for a little wooden house to be built there featuring a magnificent pink enamel Fabergé doorbell. As with Tatoi, the Catherine Park would prove to be a wonderful playground: It sported a grotto, a Great Pond (bordered by Dutch-style boathouses) and an imposing Chinese Pavilion. However, the chance to jump on the wooden planks of the "Shaking Bridge" (which spanned the Krestovy Canal) probably trumped the other attractions. If the visit happened to take place in winter, the sisters would be transported through the park, wrapped in furs, on a heated droshky (sleigh).

At Tsarskoe, Olga and her sisters enjoyed the company of their mother's family: Grand Duke Kirill and his family lived nearby at the comfortable Cavalier's House, while his younger brother Boris inhabited a commodious English Tudor-style villa. However, the most prestigious neighbours were Tsar Nicholas II and his family, who lived in the nearby Alexander Palace. As Nicholas II had always remained very fond of his cousin Ellen, it was only natural that she and her family would often take tea with the Imperial family in the palace's private wing. Olga would forever remember indulging in the wonderful selection of bon-bons accompanied by steaming glasses of tea flavoured with lemon or a spoonful of jam. The Princess became close to the Tsar's youngest daughters Marie and Anastasia (as well as to their brother Alexei) and they would all spend many happy hours frolicking in the palace's opulent nursery (which boasted a toy puppet theatre).

On occasion, Olga would travel separately from the rest of her family in the company of Miss Fox. After spending the Orthodox Easter of 1908 with her family in St Petersburg, she subsequently joined her Uncle Kirill and his family on a trip to a friend's residence, Haiko Manor at Borga, in the Grand Duchy of Finland. From there, the five-year-old princess wrote a charming letter (probably one of her first) to Princess Nicholas ('Mamma') giving details of her exploits, which included paddling and riding in a hay cart.[8] Given all these experiences, it is not surprising that her experiences in Russia would forever remain etched in Olga's memory and influence her character.

Chapter 4 Turbulent Times

In a young individual's life, there is a moment when the easy acceptance of childhood is finally shattered. For Olga, such an event occurred in February 1909, with the death of her maternal grandfather, the Grand Duke Vladimir. Indeed, the Princess became so upset that she was unable to focus on her lessons.[1] Prince and Princess Nicholas left Athens immediately for St Petersburg and although they missed the funeral, they would remain in Russia until April, to offer comfort to the widowed Grand Duchess. However, Olga kept in touch with her parents through 'remarkably well written' letters which her mother thought was 'quite extraordinary for a child of her age!'[2]

Even as she mourned her father, Ellen arranged for Miss Fox to send on a selection of photographs of her 'chickies' in 'their lovely costumes' to St Petersburg.[3] These she subsequently showed 'to everybody' and was 'particularly pleased' when her brother Boris mentioned that Olga was 'the prettiest' of all his nieces. Princess Nicholas also ensured that, in her absence, her daughters would still attract attention during the forthcoming Orthodox Easter celebrations in Athens. She issued Kate with firm instructions that they should all be attired in white and wear the crosses that their dear, departed Russian grandfather had given to them the previous Easter in Russia.[4]

Thereafter, Prince and Princess Nicholas returned to Athens to spend a long summer at Tatoi, while Kate enjoyed a holiday in England. However, Ellen was dissatisfied with the Greek food and the atmosphere proved far from carefree, for Marina often cried over nothing and the King kept a watchful eye over his family's activities from a well-placed balcony, so it was 'Goodbye to freedom'.[5] However, more worrying, was the deteriorating political situation: In August, a section of the armed forces known as the Military (or Officers') League convened at Athens' Goudi barracks and demanded that the government undertake political reforms and relieve the royal princes of their military commissions. In response, the King dismissed Prime Minister Dimitrios Ralli and asked his sons to resign from their army posts. However, large demonstrations in favour of further change continued throughout September and Olga's grandfather now 'lived from day to day in the pleasant anticipation of being kicked out at any moment...'[6] Unfortunately, Ralli's successor, Kyriakoulis Mavromichalis, resigned in January 1910, following a disagreement with the League, thus creating a dangerous power vacuum. The King feared a civil war but was then assured that the Cretan politician Eleftherios Venizelos could break the current political deadlock. In November, the latter's Liberal Party won 300 out of 362 seats in the parliamentary elections. However, Venizelos would soon prove to be a particularly prickly thorn in the side of the Greek monarchy.

Fortunately, six-year-old Olga was blissfully unaware of these political machinations and spent an 'English Christmas', on 25 December, in the company of Grand Duke Vladimir's widowed sister Marie in Coburg. The three sisters then moved on to St Petersburg to celebrate the Orthodox Christmas, on 7 January 1910, with 'Gammy'. This opportunity to celebrate Christmas twice over was to prove a 'great delight'[7] to the little princesses. In April, the children were reunited with their mother in Frankfurt. However, Ellen became so concerned about the condition of Marina's twisted foot that she arranged with a doctor in Grenoble to style her a special support.[8] In early June, the Nicholas family proceeded to England, initially staying at Buckingham Palace. The recently-widowed Queen Alexandra remained devoted to Prince Nicholas and she was delighted to visit her nephew's daughters each evening in the palace nursery. In addition, Olga received lessons in English history from Marina's godmother, Queen Mary ('Aunt May'). The family then ventured to the bracing seaside resort of Bognor. Out of kindness, Prince Nicholas invited his gossip-loving, spinster cousin Princess Victoria ('Auntie Toria') to join them at Field House, an establishment run by the Norland Institute. Auntie Toria was so delighted by the little princess' playtime antics, that she later asked the girls and Miss Fox to Buckingham Palace for her birthday celebrations.[9]

In the meantime, Ellen and Nicholas had travelled to Tsarskoe Selo, from where Princess Nicholas continued to express anxiety over Marina's foot and enquired of Foxie if 'Baby' had needed to make use of her new support.[10] She was also somewhat perplexed by the behaviour of her mother: Although Maria Pavlovna had initially expressed her pleasure at receiving a 'very well written'[11] letter from Olga, she generally seemed disinterested in her Greek granddaughters. Ellen complained to Foxie that, 'she never asks about them, so I have made a point of always telling her the parts of y[ou]r letters which I think might amuse or interest her'. Unfortunately, Miss Fox's daily letters only served to remind the recently-widowed Grand Duchess Vladimir of the close bond that existed between her daughter and the English nurse. Sadly, Princess Nicholas totally misread the situation and thought that her mother 'seemed rather impressed' by the correspondence.[12] In fact, Maria Pavlovna was inwardly seething for, unknown to Ellen, a letter she had previously written to Kate, in April, advising her on how to behave in her mother's presence, during the earlier spring visit to Cannes, had been delivered in error to Grand Duchess Vladimir who opened and read it.[13] The latter was astounded to find her beloved daughter giving warnings about *her* (an Imperial Highness!) to this mere English servant of whom she had never approved.[14] However, the wily Maria Pavlovna would bide her time before exacting a dreadful revenge on both her daughter and Olga's beloved Nurnie. Meanwhile, unaware of the true state of her mother's feelings, Princess Nicholas returned to chilly Bognor, in late September, to fetch her daughters and take them to Paris for an autumn stay with their beloved Gammy at the Hotel Continental. Tellingly, Miss Fox was obliged to lodge separately at another establishment nearby.[15]

After spending the winter in Athens, the Nicholas family were again reunited with Grand Duchess Vladimir, in May 1911, for a motor tour of Italy. As ever, Gammy indulged Olga by buying her a silver jug and basin before finally bidding the family adieu and travelling on to Contrexéville. The girls then returned to Athens under the care of Foxie, while Prince and Princess Nicholas remained in Italy. In the late summer, Olga and her sisters ventured to Bognor, but were clearly missing their absent parents and tested their Nurnie's tolerance by being 'naughty'.[16] However, they were soon diverted by the arrival of an interesting visitor-their mother's former nurse, Millicent Crofts. 'Milly' came at the invitation of Miss Fox (and with Princess Nicholas' knowledge) and had a salutary tale to impart, which should have served as a warning to Kate: After being employed for ten years as a nurse to the Grand Duchess Vladimir's four children, she had suddenly been dismissed by her employer without being given a chance to say goodbye to her charges. Maria Pavlovna apparently informed Milly that she had favoured her son Boris, to the neglect of his siblings. Naturally, Foxie lost no time in writing to Ellen, in Rome, to impart this news. Princess Nicholas responded with feeling, 'How she must have suffered! I remember perfectly well when she left & how I was told that she would come back & her empty bed next to mine...'[17]

Miss Fox and her charges had now moved on from the autumn chill of Bognor to the equally bracing delights of Westgate-on-Sea where, in mid-November, Kate finally received word from Princess Nicholas (currently in Paris) to say that she and Grand Duchess Vladimir were en route to London for an appointment with an oculist. Foxie was asked to bring the children up to town on the 22nd for a photographic session, after which they would all return together to Paris.[18] In the interim, Ellen had told her brothers all about Millicent Croft's visit and-still blissfully ignorant over the erroneously-opened letter (and her mother's growing resentment)-contrived a meeting (presumably during this visit to London) between Milly and Maria Pavlovna.[19]

However, as 1912 dawned, more pressing problems required to be addressed: Throughout the year there were increased tensions in the Balkans, as the Turks were oppressing the Christian section of the population in Thrace and Macedonia. In October, the situation deteriorated and the Balkan states of Bulgaria, Serbia and Montenegro joined with Greece to take joint military action to put an end to this tyranny, a stance which found great favour amongst the Greek population. As the princes' army commissions had been reinstated, Crown Prince Constantine was able to lead the Greek forces northwards to engage the Ottoman forces, ably assisted by Olga's Lieutenant-General father. Following a determined three-week campaign, Constantine entered Salonika, on 10 November, at the head of his victorious troops. He was joined there, two days later, by a joyful King George.

Meanwhile, just as Olga was concluding another holiday at Westgate-on-Sea, there was a problem with Marina's foot support and Kate Fox rushed her youngest charge to a private clinic at Berck-Plage in France, where her leg was encased in plaster. Princess Nicholas subsequently joined them there, although the elder sisters remained at Westgate under the watchful eye of Millicent Crofts. It is clear from Olga's contemporaneous correspondence with Miss Fox that a remedial procedure took place on Marina's foot in November.[20] Eventually, Olga and Elisabeth joined the others at Berck, although Princess Nicholas was already under pressure to return to Greece to attend to her wartime duties with the army medical services. As Grand Duchess Vladimir happened to be in Paris, she offered to have her granddaughters and Miss Fox to stay with her at the Hotel Continental.[21] Naturally, the Princesses were delighted to see their Gammy who, puffed with Imperial pride, proceeded to introduce her grandchildren to her many Parisian friends. When that delight palled, the Grand Duchess would take the girls for drives in the Bois de Boulogne or to view the Princess' favourite Punch and Judy shows.

However, all good things come to an end and the three Princesses and their Nurnie travelled on with the Grand Duchess to Munich, never realising that they were about to be treated like pawns in a chess game, with their Grandmother acting as the ultimate arbiter. It was during this Bavarian stay that Ellen requested the children be returned to her in Athens. Maria Pavlovna now chose to act on her repressed fury and informed her daughter that, while she was happy to send Olga and Elisabeth back to Athens, Marina must remain under her charge until the troublesome foot had healed.[22] The Grand Duchess had, of course, already calculated that Princess Nicholas would not want her daughters to be parted from each other or their beloved Nurnie. Maria Pavlovna also reasoned that Ellen's current responsibilities in war-torn Greece would prevent her from coming to Munich to intervene.

Thus, the little group travelled on from Munich to St Petersburg where the Grand Duchess, in her public-spirited way, held a Christmas charity bazaar in the Nobility Club, in aid of the children of Greek soldiers killed in the Balkan War. However, as 1913 dawned Maria Pavlovna and Miss Fox clashed (lancing years of pent-up frustration on both parts) after Kate had insisted on bathing Marina, despite the child having a troublesome cough.[23] Miss Fox and her youngest charge were then sent to stay at Harax, in the Crimea, with Prince Nicholas' sister Marie, while Olga and Elisabeth remained in St Petersburg, under the care of a newly-appointed French governess, Mademoiselle Perrin. When Princess Nicholas learned of these developments, she was 'absolutely dumbfounded'[24] and informed Kate that she would 'insist' on the Grand Duchess sending 'the big ones' to the Crimea from where 'it will be easier to get you [all] away'.[25] Ellen also described as 'almost ridiculous' Maria Pavlovna's latest accusation that Foxie had been 'mistreating' her charges and added mockingly, 'It is only <u>now</u>, mind you that the children are being properly looked after and cared for-you and I have never done anything for them and if baby had been left to us, she would have become a cripple.'[26] Yet, it was the three sisters who were suffering most in this drama and Olga would later remember that she and Elisabeth felt 'abandoned to our fate. I did suffer a lot at that time'.[27] The Grand Duchess-clearly with Kate Fox's dismissal from service in mind-also informed Princess Nicholas that 'They [her granddaughters] are old enough to be without a real nurse under the care of their mother who nursed the poor soldiers and <u>will have learnt to take care of her own children</u>.'[28] Unsurprisingly, Ellen was by now 'feeling as if my head was going to burst with all these worries.'[29]

Despite the angst and upheaval around her, Olga wrote a charming letter to her grandfather in Salonika, where her parents were also now based, as Prince Nicholas had been appointed Military Governor. The King touchingly told his daughter-in-law that he been 'delighted' to receive this and had stayed up until 1a.m. to compose a reply.[30] Meanwhile, following a futile telegraphic appeal to her mother, Ellen concluded that it was now 'hopeless' to attempt to reunite her older daughters with Marina and Miss Fox in the Crimea. Instead, she proposed an 'option' whereby Prince Nicholas would request that 'the big ones' go to him in Salonika.[31] Further negotiations must have followed, for by 17 March, Princess Nicholas was setting out for Vienna to collect Olga and Elisabeth. However, these plans were soon to be thwarted by a most dreadful occurrence.

In the late afternoon of 18 March, Prince Nicholas was sitting in the garden of his residence in Salonika, after entertaining his father to lunch, when a soldier ran in shouting, 'They have struck the King'.[32] It transpired that King George had been shot at close range from behind, as he strolled along the pavement and the bullet had pierced his heart. He was immediately rushed to a nearby military hospital, where his son arrived to find him lying lifeless on a bed in a private room. The new King, Constantine, was at army headquarters in Janina when he received a telegram from Nicholas informing him of their father's death. He immediately returned to Athens to take the oath of allegiance to the Constitution and then progressed to Salonika in the royal yacht to bring back the late king's body for burial. It seems especially cruel that King George should be denied his Golden Jubilee at the hands of a cowardly assassin.

Princess Nicholas (en route to Vienna) received the devastating news at Belgrade and immediately returned to Athens. The news also reached St Petersburg before Olga and Elisabeth had departed, so it was left to an 'upset and embarrassed' Grand Duchess Vladimir to break the dreadful news to her granddaughters and make arrangements for their speedy departure southwards under the care of Mademoiselle Perrin. Olga had 'adored' her grandfather and found 'the sorrow of this loss was unbearable'.[33]

After an emotional reunion with their parents in Salonika, Olga and Elisabeth returned to Athens for the funeral at Tatoi on 2 April. Despite this tragedy, Grand Duchess Vladimir remained focused on Marina's health and arranged for her aide, Baron von Offenberg, to accompany her little granddaughter and Miss Fox from Harax to the Institut Orthopédique at Berck-Plage, for further surgery on the troublesome foot. This was undertaken by the eminent orthopaedic surgeon Dr Calot and Maria Pavlovna was presumably paying the bill. The Grand Duchess decided that the time was now ripe to be rid of Miss Fox permanently and she threatened to intercede with the Tsar to cut off Princess Nicholas' Apanage income, unless the nurse was dismissed for inefficiency.[34] Emotional blackmail was also deployed, for Ellen informed Kate that 'The Gd Dchess wants me absolutely to send you away, if not, it means that I love you more than her and things will never be the same again between her & me.' A somewhat cowed Princess Nicholas then made a painful plea, 'Think it all over, put yourself in my position and try to help me through this hard moment...'[35] Unsurprisingly, Foxie seemed slow to react and this caused Ellen to write again and instruct the nurse to take 'a thorough, good long rest' after 'Baby's care in Berck is over'. In the meantime, she would try and find a temporary nurse.[36] The implication was that Kate's departure was to be short-term, although whether the doughty Norlander would have believed this, after recent events, is highly debatable.

In Athens, the Orthodox Easter was approaching and Mrs Caralou (a friend of Queen Olga's) had been charged with giving Olga further religious instruction, prior to her taking Holy Communion on Great Holy Thursday. The priest who took her Confession beforehand, informed her mother, 'that she was such an interesting, serious and dear child!' Tellingly, an increasingly distressed Olga and Elisabeth continued to pray every morning for 'dear Nurnie and Baby and please Jesus bring them back here very quickly.'[37] However, Dr Calot now dropped a bombshell: Marina might have to remain at Berck-Plage for up to a year to recuperate. In the meantime, an increasingly impatient Grand Duchess Vladimir had tired of waiting for her daughter to dismiss Kate and, without Ellen's knowledge, had already interviewed and appointed a replacement nurse, a Yorkshire-born Norlander, Margaret Alison. Princess Nicholas only learned of the change when she received an anguished letter from a distraught Kate Fox detailing how she was forced to hand over her beloved Marina into the care of her successor at Berck-Plage.[38]

Ellen later informed Miss Fox that her mother would pay her a pension of £75 for the first year and £50 per annum thereafter[39] but this was given on condition that Kate did not have any contact with her former charges![40] The children, meanwhile, were told that their beloved Nurnie, whom they last seen in January, was 'going home for a holiday.' However, Olga remained unsettled and displayed such 'grumpy' tendencies that her mother 'gave her a good talking to.'[41] Nevertheless, the child continued to pester her mother about when Miss Fox was due to return.[42] Furthermore, when Princess Nicholas later had to rush off to Berck-Plage to meet the new nurse, her departure seemed to trigger even deeper feelings of insecurity in Olga, for Prince Christopher informed Ellen that her eldest had 'cried bitterly'[43] all the way home after bidding her mother farewell at the station. Such an emotional outpouring is hardly surprising, given that over the past year the child had endured such a long sequence of traumatic experiences. Indeed, she might well have been wondering if she might never see her mother again.

However, regardless of all that had gone before with Foxie, one fact was indisputable: The time had come for the Olga and Elisabeth to have a more settled, organised and robust education. This was now overseen by Mademoiselle Perrin, with additional help from another (Greek) tutor, Kyria Anna. An additional female teacher was also hired to teach Maria Pavlovna's granddaughters her native German tongue, while a Swedish gymnast supervised Elisabeth and Olga's physical education classes. Mademoiselle would eventually be replaced by a Monsieur

Roussel, an emotional Frenchman with a deep and abiding love of French literature.[44] As enlightened parents, Prince and Princess Nicholas also insisted on external cultural activities including visits to museums, art galleries and local archaeological sites.

Meanwhile, the new King's reign inevitably brought changes to family dynamics: Ellen now complained to Foxie that Tatoi was so 'crammed and full'[45] that she was actively seeking an alternative country refuge. Fortunately, by mid-July, the Nicholas' had discovered a bright, airy retreat at Kifissia, although poor Olga was laid low by the combination of a summer fever and a severe reaction to a cholera vaccination. Moreover, she and Elisabeth continued to fret for their Nurnie and implored their mother to tell Kate that they, 'Kiss her with all our heart.'[46]

Back in the harsh world of European politics, relations between Greece and Bulgaria continued to deteriorate. Greece's northern neighbour was convinced that it had a justifiable claim on Salonika and, eschewing diplomatic niceties, suddenly launched an attack on the Greek forces in that city in late June. The Greeks retaliated and defeated the Bulgarians with the aid of Serbia and Romania. The Treaty of Bucharest, signed in August, almost doubled Greece's land area and population. Following such a decisive victory, King Constantine (who had again led his army in battle) was now eulogised as the "Son of the Eagle". The onset of peace meant that Prince Nicholas's post as Military Governor at Salonika was superfluous. He now turned to pursuits of a more aesthetic nature, such as organising the opening of a Byzantine Museum which would display a mixture of classical and modern art. A keen amateur artist himself, the Prince subsequently taught all of his children to draw and paint.

However, for Olga, there was further anguish to endure: At the end of September, Princess Nicholas finally informed her and Elisabeth that their Nurnie was not returning. Although Ellen 'consoled' them, she admitted to Miss Fox that 'it was dreadful to see their grief poor darlings!' Indeed, Olga had gone about 'with a sad little face ever since.'[47] Nevertheless, the sisters were delighted to be reunited with Marina (now wearing what was referred to as an 'apparatus') at Berck-Plage, in mid-October.[48] Touchingly, on her return to Athens, Olga received a recent photograph of her Nurnie which she carefully placed on her bedside table.[49]

As 1914 dawned in wintry Athens, the sisters entertained nineteen of their cousins and friends at a New Year's Day tea party in the Nicholas Palace's dining room.[50] 'The Big Ones' (as Ellen often now described her eldest daughters) commenced riding lessons on a pony which belonged to their cousins Paul and Irene, although a fearful Olga hated this pursuit (as much as Elisabeth adored it). However, she was 'crazy'[51] about babies and loved to pick them up and carry them around. In the summer, the family again escaped the heat of Athens at their villa in Kifissia, where the princesses had a large selection of pets, including a Persian cat (imaginatively called 'Pussy') and a stray mongrel dog named 'Kiffy'. Despite Foxie's absence, the sisters still lived by a set routine: They rose at 7am for baths and then played in the garden till breakfast and once again until lunch, after which they rested. Following tea, they ventured outdoors till bedtime and another bath! On Olga's 11th birthday, she received the gift of a diamond wristwatch which had originally belonged to her maternal great-great grandmother. This keepsake must have whetted the Princess' appetite for family history, as she subsequently asked Ellen to obtain a copy of Captain Walter Christmas' recently-published book "The Life of King George of Greece".[52]

Chapter 5 War and Revolution

It seems fair to assume that none of the royal families in Europe realised the full implications of the assassination of Archduke Franz Ferdinand and his wife Sophie, Duchess of Hohenberg, at the hands of a Bosnian Serb, Gabriel Princip, in Sarajevo on June 28. Tsar Nicholas continued to cruise aboard his yacht *Standart* along the coast of Finland, while the Kaiser set off aboard his yacht *Hohenzollern* for his annual cruise around the coast of Norway. So it was that, on 18 July, Olga and her family commenced a 1500-mile journey to St Petersburg for their customary Russian holiday. They continued to travel onwards to Sebastopol by boat despite Prince Nicholas receiving a warning in Constantinople that there was serious tension in the Balkans.[1] Indeed, by the time the family reached Tsarskoe Selo on 30 July, Austria had declared war on Serbia and St Petersburg grew tense as the Russian Foreign Minister, Sergey Sazonov, convinced the Tsar to order a general mobilisation of Russian forces. However, eleven-year-old Olga was more concerned with visiting her four 'cousins' Olga, Tatiana, Marie and Anastasia at the Alexander Palace and was intrigued to learn they slept in pairs.[2]

On 1 August, Germany declared war on Russia and the Princess' parents were anxious to return to Athens, although they were delayed for several weeks awaiting the issue of a travel permit.[3] In the interim, Great Britain had declared war on Germany. As the streets of St Petersburg trembled to the cadence of men bound for the front marching down the Nevsky Prospect, Olga noticed the worried expressions on her parents' faces and the 'endless discussions and arguments as to the safest way to travel back to Greece.'[4] The family eventually set out for home at the end of August, travelling via Moscow (where they made time to visit the Kremlin), Kiev, Bessarabia and Romania. They reached the latter country just as Russian troops were advancing into Eastern Prussia, only to be routed later at the Battle of Tannenberg. Indeed, the great Imperial Russian Empire of Olga's forefathers was already beginning to crack under the pressure of war and the Princess would never return to her beloved Russia again.

Fortuitously, when they reached Romania, the family found that the ailing King of Romania had thoughtfully sent a special train to transport the little group from Jassy southwards to the resort of Sinaia, where they were again obliged to wait for another travel permit. This gave Olga and her sisters the chance to spend time with 'Aunt Missy' (Crown Princess [later Queen] Marie) and her family at their romantic summer residence, Castle Pelisor. This vivacious and eccentric Englishwoman was a first cousin of Princess Nicholas (both were granddaughters of Tsar Alexander II) and young Olga was immediately captivated by her. However, even in wartime, future dynastic considerations were not forgotten: Marie was 'greatly struck' by Olga's height and seemed keen that she might eventually marry her eldest son Carol (who was ten years the Princess' senior). Ellen was enthusiastic and informed Foxie that 'it would be a splendid marriage.'[5] But for the present, Olga was more interested in visiting Aunt Missy's "Princesses' Nest", a 'most thrilling'[6] tree house built atop a group of pine trees. She also encountered the King of Romania's eccentric wife Queen Elisabeth (also known as the writer Carmen Sylva), 'a fascinating character...oddly dressed in flowing robes with snow white hair',[7] who had arranged a special film performance at the Royal Palace for the children who included Aunt Missy's daughter Marie ('Mignon'). Little could young Olga have realised that 14-year-old Marie would play such a major and, at times, disruptive role in her future life.

After a four-day hiatus, the Nicholas family were finally allowed to proceed by train and car to a little village on the Danube, from where they caught the Orient Express down through Serbia to Salonika. They broke their journey there to view a newly-erected memorial to King George, which Olga recalled was watched over by a Cretan soldier.[8]

On 9 September, the Princesses were relieved to be back in Athens 'to the home we loved'.[9] Olga was now permitted to lunch with her parents' downstairs and, except on the days she played tennis, would join her sisters and cousins at Phaleron Bay to swim. The Princess' favourite playmate was her older cousin Helen whom she deeply 'loved and admired.'[10] Tea was usually taken by the sea, before returning to the city at 6pm to do her "prep". Princess Nicholas was somewhat perplexed by her eldest child who, she informed Foxie, possessed 'a more difficult character [than her siblings]-she is so sensitive and makes life a burden for herself but in the same time she is so sensible and understands the justness of things.'[11]

The outbreak of war contributed further to the existing frictions within the royal family: Ellen felt that Queen Sophie had become 'exclusively German' in her tastes, where previously she had been 'quite English'. Furthermore, the Queen avoided discussing the war's progress with the pro-British Princess Nicholas, although the latter assured Foxie that the rest of the Greek royal family were 'on our side.'[12]Athens too had become a hotbed of division and political intrigue: King Constantine favoured neutrality, feeling that his Kingdom had suffered enough during the Balkan Wars. However, his Prime Minister, Eleftherios Venizelos, wanted Greece to enter the conflict on the side of the Triple Entente powers of Great Britain, France and Russia. Indeed, his supporters now lost no time in accusing Constantine of pro-German sympathies with the pro-Venizelist press gleefully pointing out that the King had received his military training in Germany.[13] Meanwhile, as the sister of the German Kaiser, Queen Sophie was increasingly subject to insults whenever she appeared in public.[14] Fortuitously, Olga remained ignorant of these happenings and, as 1915 dawned, spent much of her time riding at Phaleron. With her love of babies, the Princess also formed a close attachment to one-year-old Sophie, the youngest child of Prince and Princess Andrew.[15] Nevertheless, Olga particularly missed her pre-war seaside visits to Bognor and asked Princess Nicholas, 'if after the war shall we get to England again?'[16]

As was their custom, the family moved up to Kifissia in late June, just as a picture of Princess Nicholas and her dutiful (and beautiful) daughters (taken at a Red Cross charity bazaar) was released for general circulation. Whether this publicity contributed towards the on-going froideur between Queen Sophie and Ellen is unclear, but the latter was 'disappointed' that her daughters were no longer invited up to Tatoi, while the Queen had also seen fit to decline an invitation on behalf of her daughter Irene to join Olga for tea at Kifissia.[17] The situation was doubtless not helped by what Princess Nicholas describes as 'the jealousy of the other nurses for our children ...'[18] It must have been a relief for the family to escape to Spetsai for a month, where for added privacy, Princess Nicholas had rented the entire floor of a hotel. This, despite her admitting to Miss Fox that she was suffering financially from the poor wartime exchange rate on her rouble payments from Russia.[19] However, by December, relations with the Queen must have temporarily thawed, for Olga and her sisters were once again welcomed to Tatoi, just as snow began to fall. All were thrilled when cousin Helen built a snow man and carefully placed a lighted cigarette in its mouth.[20]

Meanwhile, letters sent from the family to Kate Fox were now being routinely opened by the British censor; while relations between the King and Venizelos had deteriorated to the point that the country was now divided into two irreconcilable camps. The allies were keen to take advantage of this "National Schism" and, despite the fact that Greece was officially neutral, they landed a combined party of French and British forces at Salonika, in October, at the invitation of Venizelos. This led to a heated confrontation between Constantine (who was already much weakened from attacks of pneumonia and pleurisy) and his Prime Minister, whom he subsequently dismissed. However, with the Triple Entente powers supporting Venizelos, the King's time was running out.

Following the Christmas break, in January 1916, a by now 'very tall and slim' Olga and her sisters resumed their school studies amid a scarlet fever epidemic which confined them to the gardens of the Nicholas Palace. Surprisingly, sisterly relations were not all they might be: Marina, unlike her more reticent siblings, positively enjoyed being the centre of attention and was particularly unkind to her sisters who complained 'of her nasty little ways.'[21] Matters seemed to improve once Marina and her eldest sister commenced riding lessons together (Elisabeth was already a most accomplished rider).[22]

As she celebrated her 13th birthday, in June, Olga was 'very proud' at having entered her teenage years. Ellen observed that her eldest was 'so distinguished and is beginning to be reasonable but in many ways, she is still quite a child of which I am pleased.'[23] Nonetheless, physically she was 'getting quite formed...'[24] and had excelled academically in her summer examinations. Olga continued to display 'a sort of admiration for Sitta [Helen]'[25] who had become something of a role model for her younger cousin. Helen cared greatly about outward appearances including 'a tidy house, perfect dress, unruffled hair, punctuality, excessive politeness, good manners, form, procedure'.[26] Princess Nicholas accurately predicted that Olga, 'will be very much the style of Sitta but prettier'.[27]

During their summer sojourn at Kifissia, Olga was given the gift of a horse which was stabled at the villa and watched over by the royal family's English groom, Taylor. This development may have been as a result of further tensions between Ellen and the Queen. The former felt that there was now a distinct lack of goodwill 'in higher quarters'[28] about everything- including the borrowing of horses for riding lessons. While Olga and Elisabeth rode out regularly with Prince Andrew's daughters Margarita and Theodora, the same did not apply with the King and Queen's children.[29] Princess Nicholas had already concluded that, 'the more one keeps away from that family the better...'[30] although she had tremendous sympathy for the King's precarious position. Indeed, in July, Constantine had narrowly escaped death when fire had raged through Tatoi, destroying his residence and three-quarters of the estate. Pro-Venizelist supporters were thought to be the culprits, after the police discovered empty petrol cans in three separate locations in the forest; eighteen people lost their lives.[31]

In the autumn, Prince Nicholas made visits to Petrograd[2] and London to attempt to dissuade the Entente powers that his family were biased towards Germany. After an audience with the Tsar, the Prince met

---

[2] As St Petersburg was now called.

the Tsarevich Alexei who sent each of his daughters a kiss; Olga would later describe this forlornly as 'the last contact.'[32] In London, Queen Alexandra informed her beloved nephew that she continued to plead for 'Tino's' cause in letters to her son, King George V.[33] However, by the time Olga's father reached home in November, such family ties seemed irrelevant, as Venizelos had now formed a pro-Entente National Defence Government in Salonika, in direct opposition to Constantine's government in Athens. On 24 November, Venizelos formally declared war on the Central Powers of Germany, Turkey and Bulgaria. Emboldened by this act, the French decided to unseat the Greek King and sent their fleet to blockade the harbour at Piraeus. On 1 December, French ships bombarded Athens. Initially, Olga and her sisters watched the barrage from their top-floor nursery window at the Nicholas Palace. However, when shells later fell around the King's residence nearby, Princess Nicholas shooed her 'frightened' daughters down to the safety of the basement silver vault.[34] Meanwhile, pro-royalist forces were in an increasingly difficult position, as the Entente forces in the north, led by Admiral du Fournet, seized control of the Greek rail network and prevented much-needed artillery and ammunition from reaching Athens. To make matters worse, Ellen's Apanage monies from Russia suddenly stopped and she was forced to make economies.[35]

If events were proving difficult in Greece, they had become impossible in Russia. Over the last decade, the exalted status of the Imperial Family had been gradually undermined amid strikes, protests and calls for political change. Matters reached a critical stage in January 1917, when the Prime Minister, Prince Nicholas Galitzine, decided to postpone the opening of the Duma [Parliament] for a month and this act incited 'widespread and bitter feeling'.[36] In early March, bread riots broke out in Petrograd and the majority of the military garrison mutinied and stormed the Winter Palace. Tsar Nicholas abdicated on 15 March and was placed under house arrest at the Alexander Palace. With the outbreak of revolution in Russia, there was very real concern for the well-being of Olga's grandmothers: Queen Olga had been nursing the wounded at her hospital at Pavlovsk, while Grand Duchess Vladimir was taking a cure at the spa town of Kislovodsk in the northern Caucasus. She had been banished from Petrograd after an altercation with the Tsar over his decision to banish Olga's cousin, the Grand Duke Dimitri, to Persia following his alleged involvement in the death of Rasputin.[37]

Back in Greece, Venizelos continued to rouse revolt and, by May, felt able to inform the international press that, 'It is impossible for King Constantine to maintain his position.'[38] Indeed, the Entente powers threatened to bombard the city if the King did not leave Greece.[39] Constantine's second son, Alexander, was deemed to be an acceptable replacement by the Entente powers as King *pro tem*, the eldest, George, being excluded on the grounds that he had, like his father, undertaken military training in Germany. When word got out that Constantine had stepped down, thousands of people besieged the Royal Palace, where all of the royal family were gathered, to indicate their support for the King. Prince Nicholas met officials and tried to calm the situation. He also asked that the people accept his brother's decision 'without resentment.'[40] However, the crowd steadfastly refused to allow Constantine to leave the Palace and a stand-off lasted overnight. Meanwhile, the landing of Entente troops at Piraeus only served to aggravate the situation. Finally, by indulging in a little deceit, involving decoy cars, the royal family managed to flee the palace. On 14 June, Constantine left Greece by boat from Oropos, north of Athens, to travel onwards to Zurich. All the family, including Olga, were present to wave him off.

King Alexander now turned to his Uncle Nicholas for comfort and he was soon treating the Nicholas Palace as 'a temporary home'.[41] Unfortunately, the Entente Powers newly-appointed High Commissioner, Charles Jonnart, was focused on clearing Athens of all royalist influences, both to facilitate Venizelos' reinstatement (he returned on 27 June) and to isolate the new King. By 25 June, French troops were placed at strategic locations around the city and it became increasingly clear that the time had come for the Nicholas family to leave. On 4 July, the family's servants and an emotional King Alexander gathered on the lawn of the Nicholas Palace to wave them off. In the evening, they departed Greece by sea, a distressed Olga watching as the coast of her homeland gradually receded into the distance.[42]

Chapter 6 Swiss Exile

The Nicholas family initially spent their first months of their exile in St Moritz. The hotel proved too expensive and, in the autumn, they moved to the Savoy Baur en Ville Hotel in Zurich, where Princess Nicholas had managed to secure rooms at a discounted rate. Life was far from luxurious: The three sisters were required to share a bedroom, while a shortage of coal meant that there was only sufficient hot water for a weekly bath. Again, it was Olga, in particular, who seemed most affected by the move, with Ellen complaining to Miss Fox, 'She was dreadful, we didn't know what to do with her...a sweet nature but difficult to understand at times.'[1] The remaining royal family members lived in a more pleasant environment, in the hills above the city, and most days Prince Nicholas and his family would walk up from town to visit, although they always returned "home" in time for tea. Olga and her siblings initially attended a local school, but were unable to follow the lessons which were taught in German. It was then decided they should be educated at home and a tri-lingual, sport-loving, Swiss governess, Mademoiselle Genand, was employed. However, Ellen found exile 'hard to bear...'[2] and confided to Foxie, that 'the jealousy of certain people for our children' remained a pressing problem. Certainly, Princess Nicholas' best efforts to include the other cousins in her daughters' gymnastic classes was met with a curt refusal. She was likewise furious to discover that Olga, Elisabeth and Marina had been excluded from dancing lessons arranged by Princess Alice for her daughters Margarita and Theodora, but to which cousin Irene was also invited. Ellen wished she could get to the bottom of the matter, 'for the children's sake as they feel it dreadfully and are heartily upset.' The 'rumours' initially placed the 'real cause' squarely at the door of Queen Sophie.[3] However, by late December, Princess Nicholas was able to report to Miss Fox that 'things are much better now' and it was all apparently 'simply nastiness and jealousy' on the part of Princess Alice.[4]

As this momentous year drew to a close, further economies (including staff dismissals) were needed as Ellen discovered that her Russian capital had been confiscated.[5] The family observed an 'English Christmas', on 25 December, before leaving Zurich, in January 1918, for the inexpensive Neues Rosatch Hotel at St Moritz. This location proved a particular hit with the three sisters who enjoyed ice skating and learned to ski. It was at this juncture that the family received news of Grand Duchess Vladimir: She was without funds and living with two of her sons in a small villa in the Caucasus. Ellen was incredulous: 'One can't believe it after all that luxury!'[6]

The family moved to the Savoy Hotel at Ouchy in mid-March, where Olga was laid low with chicken pox, just as she attempted to celebrate her 15th birthday, which she deemed 'a very important age!'[7] The Princess was now taller than her mother and, in every sense, a woman. Nevertheless, she continued to be homesick for Greece and was 'very sensitive [and] takes things to heart' which her mother thought 'unfortunate as she will suffer from it all her life.'[8] Nevertheless, Olga's spirits must have been uplifted by the arrival of Queen Olga from Russia, in late June. She brought with her the pleasing news that a Greek student had managed to smuggle her jewels out of the Marble Palace and they had been forwarded to Copenhagen for safekeeping.

In August, the Greek royal family were 'completely devastated'[9] to receive news of the recent murder of Tsar Nicholas and his immediate family at Ekaterinburg in mid-July. Princess Nicholas was verging on denial, informing Foxie, 'We don't know what to think about that dreadful news, *somehow I can't think it is true, it seems too awful*!' When the events of the Tsar's death were eventually confirmed in the press, it filled the Nicholas family with 'unspeakable horror' and the three sisters wept bitterly as they recalled their earlier experiences at Tsarskoe Selo in the company of their Imperial cousins.[10] To add to their woes, the girls were informed that Nurse Margaret was leaving. She had been summoned to the British Consulate and was told in no uncertain terms that if she continued to work for Prince and Princess Nicholas ("Traitors of England") she would be deprived of her British passport.[11] Nevertheless, Ellen tried to make her daughters' lives 'as bright as possible' with dancing lessons on a Saturday morning and attendance at Sunday afternoon tea dances. Tennis, however, remained the girls' 'great pleasure'; Olga and Elisabeth both played in the singles and doubles competitions of the "American Tournament".[12]

The Nicholas' returned to St Moritz's Neues Rosatch Hotel, in late December, this time to celebrate a proper Orthodox Christmas. Olga was delighted to receive a calendar from her Nurnie, and in her letter of thanks, she expressed the hope 'that happy day will come' when they would meet once again and signed herself, 'Yr. ever-devoted Baby Olga.'[13] As 1919 dawned, the Nicholas' agonised over the fate of their Romanov relatives and wondered if the Allied Fleet would be able to rescue Grand Duchess Vladimir from the Caucasus.[14] It was also at this juncture that Ellen began to fret over how the family's changed circumstances might impact on the marriage prospects of her daughters.

This concern was prompted by probing questions from her eldest child for, as Princess Nicholas informed Kate Fox, 'the marriage question seems to preoccupy Olga very much, she wonders whom she will marry and asked me all about it the other day!' It is possible that the young Princess' enquiries might well have been triggered by the forthcoming wedding of her childhood friend, Sofica des Isnards, who was marrying into a rich Dutch family, the Burgens.[15] However, Ellen opined that her fifteen-year-old daughter was far from ready for a serious relationship being still, 'an extraordinary mixture of a big girl and a child.'[16]

In April, the itinerant family moved on to the Hotel Byron at Villeneuve where, to Olga's delight, a baby was born in the hotel.[17] Queen Olga paid another visit and Ellen's Lady-in-Waiting, Mrs Tombazi, taught the girls to make their own summer dresses.[18] When Kate Fox proposed to visit that summer, she was dissuaded from doing so by Princess Nicholas who cited the 'very difficult'[19] attitude of the Swiss Authorities.

In early September, the Nicholas' decided to take a lease on a flat in Montreux's new Riant Château complex. This boasted large, airy rooms and plenty of bathrooms. However, despite moving into this new home, Ellen was perplexed to observe that Olga continued to display 'fits of grumpiness and was snappier and disagreeable and went about with a sullen face!'[20] Fortunately, she recovered her equilibrium in time to lunch with Queen Olga and seemed to enjoy an 'English' style Christmas on 25 December.[21]

As 1920 dawned, the Greek royal family continued to be unpopular with the Swiss and were referred to scathingly in the international press as 'discarded royalty' who could not pay their hotel bills.[22] Prince Nicholas focused on his painting and held an exhibition of his work in Montreux, where he was grateful to be able to sell some pictures at a decent price.[23] The family were also uplifted by the marriage of Prince Christopher to the rich American heiress Mrs Nancy Leeds (the widow of William Leeds the American "Tin Plate King") at the Russian Church at Vevey, on 1 February. Ironically, the *New York Times* would later misreport that seventeen-year-old Olga was betrothed to marry her son William B. Leeds, Jr.[24] The latter would actually go on to marry Olga's cousin, Princess Xenia of Russia, in October 1921.

Around this time, Olga finally enjoyed an emotional reunion with Miss Fox, although this was not widely publicised[25] for fear it would reach the ears of Grand Duchess Vladimir, who was able to pay the Nicholas family a visit in Montreux, in June. Predictably, this determined grand dame had been the last member of the Imperial family to leave Russia. She had sailed, in February, accompanied by her Lady-in-Waiting, Princess Catherine Galitizine ('Turia'), from her final refuge at

Anapa on the Black Sea to Venice aboard an Italian ship, having paid for the journey by selling some jewellery.[26] Olga recalls, 'It was with deep emotion that we all met again. She was much thinner and looked ill. In spite of all she had been through she made plans for our future coming-out ball in the Winter Palace of St Petersburg!!'[27] Interestingly, while en route to Venice, the Grand Duchess' ship had made a stop at Athens, where she disembarked to make a quick tour of the Nicholas Palace and pick bunches of violets from the garden. She later distributed these traditional symbols of good fortune to her family during their reunion.[28]

Unfortunately, the strain and worry had taken its toll on Maria Pavlovna's health and she was now beset with heart problems. She was therefore 'anxious' to rest and take a "cure" at Contrexéville, although the Nicholas' were refused permission to accompany her there. Sadly, the Grand Duchess passed away on 6 September. Princess Nicholas somehow managed to obtain a visa to travel to France for the funeral, where she was reunited with her three brothers, whom she had not seen since prior to the revolution.[29] Maria Pavlovna was buried in the little Orthodox Chapel of Saint Vladimir and Marie-Madeleine at Contrexéville. As her grandmother had been a significant part of Olga's life, the effect of her death, in such reduced circumstances, cannot be over-emphasised.

Given the carnage in post-revolution Russia, it was indeed amazing that the Grand Duchess Vladimir's three sons Kirill, Boris and Andrei survived; they would all subsequently settle in France. Fortuitously, the Grand Duchess left her family a helpful legacy: Just after the revolution, an English friend, Bertie Stopford, disguised himself in the working clothes of an ordinary "comrade" and with the aid of two Gladstone bags, retrieved her jewels from the Vladimir Palace.[30] The gems were subsequently sent by courier to the British Embassy in Berne where, following Maria Pavlovna's death, Princess Nicholas and her brothers met to divide them according to the Grand Duchess' instructions.[31] Ellen was to receive mainly diamonds and a magnificent tiara of fifteen interlaced diamond circles, with a swinging oriental pearl suspended in each. This was subsequently purchased by Queen Mary.[32]

In October, news arrived from Greece that King Alexander had been bitten by a rabid monkey and had developed an infection known as sepsis. Although his mother, Queen Sophie, was denied permission by Venizelos to travel to Athens, his grandmother, Queen Olga, was allowed to make the journey. Delayed by rough seas, she arrived a matter of hours after the King's death, on 25 October.[33] King Alexander had married Aspasia Manos in November 1919 and, although recognised as his legal wife, she was never acknowledged as Queen. At the time of her husband's death, Aspasia was carrying Alexander's child and their daughter, Alexandra, was born in March 1921.

As the weeks passed, Olga fretted about the welfare of Queen Olga, from whom there was no word,[34] and she could only wonder what the future held for the Greek monarchy. Events then took a most unexpected turn, in mid-November, when Venizelos was defeated in the Greek general election. Within days, the fickle Athenians were calling for King Constantine's return. In the interim, Mr Dimitrios Ralli, the new Prime Minister, offered Queen Olga the position of Regent. Constantine now insisted on a plebiscite to reaffirm his position as monarch and this was held on 5 December. Over one million people voted in favour of his return, with only eleven thousand against.[35]

Prince and Princess Nicholas and their family returned to Athens in time to welcome King Constantine home on 19 December. Olga recalled the King's 'deeply moving' arrival, particularly the moment when the royal family gathered on the terrace of the Royal Palace and were 'amazed to see the horses on his carriage being unharnessed and the excited crowd pulling it [the carriage] up the last bit of the road, cheering and crying.' As for the Princess, she found that 'the happiness to be back in our home and find everything as we had left them was indescribable.'[36] Her joy was made complete when Miss Fox re-joined the family in January 1921. Thereafter, Olga travelled to Paris to buy clothes for two forthcoming royal weddings linking the Greek and Romanian royal houses.[37] The first, between Olga's cousin Crown Prince George and Princess Elisabetha of Romania, took place in Bucharest on 27 February. The Princess also attended the nuptials of her favourite cousin Helen to Crown Prince Carol of Romania at the Cathedral in Athens on 10 March.

Meanwhile, as a result of the expansionist policies pursued by Venizelos' government, Constantine had inherited a legacy of war with Turkey. As the summer progressed, this campaign, in Asia Minor, seemed to favour the Greeks, who enjoyed a welcome victory at Eskişehir. Olga, Elisabeth and Marina now undertook an emotional visit to England, their first since before the Great War, and enjoyed an emotional reunion with Queen Alexandra (now deaf and failing) and Queen Mary, both of whom had sent affectionate letters and Christmas gifts during the Nicholas' Swiss exile.[38] In the autumn, the sisters and their Nurnie progressed to Corfu for a month-long stay with Uncle Andrew and his family at Mon Repos. Olga was particularly taken with the family's latest addition, a three-month-old boy named Philip and was happy to take on the special role of godmother-by-proxy (on behalf of Queen Olga) at his christening, on 6 November.[39]

Chapter 7 Bitter Lessons

By September 1921, the war in Asia Minor had reached a stalemate, after Turkish forces halted further Greek advances at Sakarya. As 1922 dawned, the Greek government appealed to the British and French for a diplomatic solution. In February, Princess Nicholas left Athens with her daughters for Cannes at the invitation of her brother-in-law Christopher. Crown Prince Frederick of Denmark ('Rico') was also conveniently in town with his mother Queen Alexandrine (a cousin of Ellen) to visit his ailing maternal grandmother, Grand Duchess Anastasia of Mecklenburg-Schwerin. Olga and Rico subsequently met at Prince Christopher's Villa Kastbeck, although neither the journey to Cannes, nor Olga's encounter with the Crown Prince were accidental: According to the Princess' unpublished memoirs, 'A possible marriage for us had been planned unknown to me, so we [now] met often.' Fortunately, Frederick found the Princess attractive and proposed to her almost immediately, albeit in a rather perfunctory fashion, during a stroll along the promenade. Olga would later reflect on her naivety at this time and admitted, 'I was too bewildered to grasp the full meaning of these words.' Certainly, Princess Nicholas urged caution and 'begged me to be in no haste to be sure that this was really what I wanted in my future life.'[1] However, Olga seemed smitten and informed Miss Fox that Rico 'is such a dear and a real man in every way.' He also proved attentive, writing to her regularly on his journey home to Copenhagen, from where he was able to report that there was 'tremendous joy and ovations for us both!' The Princess was enthralled, 'so thoughtful of him. It is so nice to have the feeling that one means so much to a man...'[2]

The Crown Prince later travelled to Athens, in late March, where he stayed for several weeks at the Nicholas Palace and presented his fiancée with an engagement ring. However, the visit was not a success as Princess Nicholas quickly grasped. The draft of a letter she subsequently wrote to Queen Alexandrine, is particularly illuminating: 'O[lga] has got a very deep and sensitive nature but she is very confermée and doesn't show her feelings easily; she is used to much love and affection and Rico, instead of trying to know and understand her better, was often a little rough and off-handish [sic] with her telling her little things that hurt her feelings...' As a consequence, the Princess became 'silent and seemingly cold till Rico thought she didn't care for him anymore and they both ended by looking cold and indifferent to each other...'. Olga subsequently 'had it out' with Frederick and on the day of his departure, he informed Prince Nicholas bluntly that 'he didn't love Olga anymore and didn't want to marry her!' Rico also spoke separately to Princess Nicholas who was thrown by this 'astonishing news', but asked him 'not to take a rash decision' and talk the matter over first with his parents. Surprisingly, she also asked him to continue to write to her daughter 'as through letters one often come[s] to know each other better than by talking.' Ellen also emphasised 'that he couldn't find a better wife than Olga...' The Crown Prince, meanwhile, asked Prince and Princess Nicholas not to mention their discussions to Olga, to which they readily agreed. But observing the consequences of deliberately keeping their daughter in the dark about the true situation, Princess Nicholas confided to the Danish Queen, was not proving easy as Olga continued to speak of her fiancé in affectionate terms 'as if nothing had happened' and particularly missed his presence. Ellen also informed her cousin that she would not be bringing Olga to Denmark as planned that summer, but still left the door open by indicating that if Frederick wanted to discuss matters with her daughter, it should be done 'quietly in some other place.'[3]

In early May, Princess Nicholas received a sympathetic response from Queen Alexandrine. She reflected on 'how badly he [Rico] has treated your girl,' but added that her son felt 'he has made a mistake and that he does not care enough for her to marry her.' Nevertheless, she agreed with Princess Nicholas' 'excellent' proposal of another meeting between the couple and the hope 'that everything may end well'. At the Danish court the King and Queen were also acting as if nothing was amiss, but felt *'so false'* in doing so.[4]

If there was strain on the Danish royals, the uncertainty surrounding Olga's future would stretch the Princess' normally close bond with her parents to almost breaking point. While Prince Nicholas remained at Tatoi, Olga arrived in France, at the end of July, with her sisters and mother (who was recuperating from an attack of diphtheria) for a stay at the Trianon Palace Hotel at Versailles. Prince Nicholas soon had cause to write to his eldest daughter with stern observations on her recent behaviour: Apparently, during a recent visit by Princess Margaret of Prussia and Hesse ('Aunt Mossy') and her son Christoph to Athens, Olga had got into 'the habit' of 'indulging into sentimental conversation with people [Christoph] you had no business to be on intimate and sentimental terms with!' Indeed, she had 'pushed this relationship [with Christoph] much further than Mummy or I ever thought it possible at the time!' Although, a naïve Olga had subsequently defended her behaviour, saying she had 'no other feelings for him than those of <u>friendly affection!</u>', Prince Nicholas refused to accept this, citing the fact that Aunt Mossy had encouraged Olga to enter into correspondence about Christoph and her feelings for him, which was not something 'an old friend' of the family would have done unless 'you.. made her believe that your feelings were more...' Olga's father felt such behaviour 'was wrong and disloyal, as you were not free and as you were promised (by your own free and independent will) to someone else!' He added, 'Look what trouble you have brought upon yourself and everybody by not being straightforward!'[5] This latter remark seems particularly hypocritical given Olga's parents' recent disingenuous behaviour concerning her engagement to Frederick. However, in a subsequent letter, Prince Nicholas at least felt able to acknowledge his daughter's lack of worldly experience and concluded that with Christoph, she had been 'more foolish than guilty of any serious crime.'[6]

However, Prince Nicholas did not feel that this was the case where Frederick of Denmark was concerned: Whereas, Ellen felt that 'there must have been mistakes and misrepresentations on both sides',[7] her husband took a harsher view and informed Olga, 'The whole business has been entirely your doing!' He cited her 'extremely childish and foolish' behaviour in 'having it out' with Rico, rather than heeding her father's advice, given prior to Frederick's visit, about the need to 'make sacrifices to each other' and consider the other person's feelings. Prince Nicholas' earnest hope was that these 'two bitter lessons....will help you in life and will have taught you the very commonplace sense of the words: Life is duty!'[8] It is not surprising that Prince Nicholas confided to Miss Fox that he was 'simply longing' for the diversions of London, adding: 'I am so miserable about Olga's affairs *which have robbed me of my peace of mind.*'[9]

At Versailles, an equally distressed Princess Nicholas was taking a tonic for her nerves[10] while a guilt-ridden Olga, even prior to receiving her father's forthright epistle about Rico, had taken it upon herself to accept much of the blame for 'this unsettled situation'. Yet, it seems inexcusable that the Princess' parents were still keeping the truth about this relationship from their daughter. Indeed, as far as Olga was concerned, the engagement still seemed to be "on" and she and her parents were simply waiting for word from Copenhagen about a possible meeting between the "couple". She also expressed the hope that 'when that moment comes which will decide matters I may ... think only of others *and try and mend what I have spoiled.*'[11]

In mid-August, the Princess and her mother duly received a 'very nice' letter from King Christian proposing a date around 10 September, by which time Olga had moved into the house of a family friend, Marie-Thérèse de Croisset, in the fashionable Place des Etats-Unis.[12] She was naturally apprehensive: 'If only I knew in what state of mind he [Rico] is in! Is he still bitter and resolved to break off the engagement? I only hope he will listen to me and after that if he still remains the same it means he never really loved me!'[13] The private forty-five-minute meeting between the couple took place on 11 September, at Marie-Thérèse's residence. Unsurprisingly, given his previous attitude in Athens, Rico had decided that the romance could not be salvaged and when Olga tried to reach out to him, he was crushing in his repost and 'said he had no more love for me'.[14] With the decision made, she returned the engagement ring to Frederick[15] and observed philosophically that his love 'couldn't have been very strong while it was there'. However, she remained irritated by the Danish Crown Prince's apparent lack of 'decency and tact' as, prior to the meeting, he had discussed the situation with both her sister Elisabeth and her Uncle Christopher at the Ritz.[16] On reflection, it really does appear to have been a fortuitous parting for both parties. An announcement was made from the Danish Court in Copenhagen, on 24 September, that the engagement had been broken off 'by mutual arrangement'.[17]

In later years Olga remained 'in a way quite proud about [the engagement]'[18] though she had by then somewhat "sanitised" her recollections, maintaining to her relations that the reason the engagement ended was because she was 'horrified' by Rico's tattoos. Furthermore, she implied that the decision had been of her making.[19] This may have been to help her deal with the pain of rejection, for even some fifty-five years later, as she browsed through her 1922 diary, Olga could still clearly recall 'the distress it caused me'.[20] There is a final interesting footnote to this story: Olga's parents apparently 'accused' her cousin Irene of 'spoiling' her chances of marriage with Rico during his stay in Athens! This was something Irene always 'flatly denied'. However, there may have been some truth to this story, as Irene later revealed to Olga 'par hasard one day, that R[ico] had written to her a proposal, after our engagement was broken off, the first time she ever mentioned such a thing to me!'[21]

However, even as Olga's personal crisis was being played out, the Greek royal family was facing a greater problem: Turkish forces, under the brilliant leadership of Mustafa Kemal, had recently mounted a determined counter-offensive against Greek forces and driven them out of Anatolia. When the defeated soldiers returned to Athens, accompanied by fleeing Anatolian Greek refugees, political unrest ensued. Supporters of Venizelos now openly accused the King of having prolonged the war to consolidate his own position. The situation deteriorated so rapidly that, on the advice of the monarchist Chief of the General Staff, General Metaxas, Constantine abdicated on 27 September in order to avoid civil war.[22] The throne now passed to his eldest son George. Almost immediately, the "Athens Revolutionary Committee" ordered ex-King Constantine, Queen Sophie and Prince Nicholas to leave Athens and they departed Greece for Palermo, on 30 September, aboard the battleship *Patris*. In France, Princess Nicholas and her daughters were in a state of shock after being mistakenly informed that Prince Nicholas had been shot during the disturbances in Athens. One can only imagine their relief when he subsequently cabled from Palermo to say he was safe.[23]

Unfortunately, another drama was soon to unfold: Prince Andrew, who had agreed to resign his army post, was lured from his Corfu home on the pretext that he was to give evidence at the trial of seven royalist ex-ministers. Instead, he was detained and held under house arrest on charges of disobeying orders during the recent Asia Minor campaign. While Queen Olga lobbied Britain's King George V and King Alfonso of Spain in the hope that something could be done, Prince Christopher made a brief visit to Athens and managed to "rescue" Princess Nicholas' jewellery and the family cat Pussy, although he was refused permission to visit his brother. Prince Andrew was tried in early December and unanimously found guilty of disobedience and abandoning his post in the face of the enemy. His sentence was to be exiled from his homeland and stripped of his military rank.

All the while, Olga remained in Paris feeling fragile and unsettled from the combined effects of the broken engagement, her mother's illness, the uncertainty over her Uncle Andrew's fate and the demeaning prospect of another exile. She confided to her diary, 'We are just living sur la branche, and one can hardly realise this is the second exile and we are once more like wandering Jews with no home to go to! Oh! It is too awful and I feel so stunned...'[24] The Princess' sense of despair only deepened when her sisters and Miss Fox departed for Chamonix on a short vacation and would continue even after they were all reunited in a shabby hotel at 'dull and depressing' San Remo, at the end of November.[25] However, the arrival of her parents (from Palermo), on 1 December, seemed to cheer her.

Nevertheless, the dawning of a New Year only brought more tragedy: Ex-King Constantine passed away in Palermo after suffering a cerebral haemorrhage on 11 January 1923. Prince and Princess Nicholas travelled to Naples for the funeral. Unfortunately, this latest blow sent Olga into a further spiral of 'awful grief which becomes more acute every day...I feel so crushed, my thoughts are no more my own; sometimes I feel I am going to burst'.[26] Although she did not realise it, events were about to take a turn for the better.

King George I and Queen Olga of the Hellenes.

Grand Duchess Vladimir of Russia

Princess Nicholas with Olga (left) and Elisabeth

L to R Olga, Prince Nicholas, Elisabeth, Princess Nicholas and Marina, Tatoi, circa 1910

The Three Sisters by Lallie Charles featured on a Beagle's Postcard.

Olga (rear, third from right) together with members of the Russian Imperial Family, Tsarskoe Selo.

Three Teenage Sisters L to R Elisabeth, Olga and Marina.

Princess Olga and Prince Paul, Paris, 1920's

Chapter 8 Betrothal and Marriage

After attending the wedding of her friend Marie-Laure de Croisset in Grasse in January, Olga returned to San Remo, with only her Scotch Terrier "Yankee" for company, while the rest of the family holidayed in the Tyrol. However, during a trip to Monte Carlo to consult a dentist, she encountered the Duke of Connaught, a senior and influential member of the British royal family. He seemed taken by both her natural beauty and dignity and sent a positive report back to England and, in due course, the Princess received an invitation to visit London from Princess Victoria (Auntie Toria).

Olga was finally reunited with her family in Merano in mid-March and they all subsequently enjoyed a tour of the castles of the South Tyrol. Fortuitously, Prince Nicholas had recently rented out the Nicholas Palace to Athens' prestigious Hotel Grande Bretagne for use as an annexe. The funds from this enterprise not only enabled his family to travel to London for the Season, but also helped pay for a joint "coming out" party for Olga and Elisabeth.[1] The timing was perfect for Olga admitted to needing, 'a change. I am getting too self-centred.'[2]

Thus, in early June, Prince Nicholas installed his family at the unpretentious Granby Court Hotel in Queen's Gate. Happily, Princess Nicholas' cousin, Princess Beatrice of Edinburgh ('Aunt Bee') and her husband Infante Alfonso ('Uncle Ali'), a cousin of the King of Spain, were in town and made use of their impeccable social connections to arrange invitations for the sisters to attend the various society balls. Always in the background, was the hope that Olga or one of her siblings might capture the eye of the Prince of Wales ('David') or one of his unmarried brothers. The (supposed) high point of the visit was a luncheon with King George V and Queen Mary at Buckingham Palace on 27 June. Yet, Olga seemed underwhelmed by this occasion, noting in her diary: 'Enfin lunch went off all right.'[3]

Nonetheless, the trip to London served to energise Olga and she 'quite enjoyed the novelty of dancing in stately ballrooms ...'[4] where she was certainly turning heads. Indeed, the Infante Alfonso deemed her to be 'the most beautiful of the 3 [sisters].'[5] Unknown to her, the 'change' she so desired was just around the corner and came in the form of the thirty-year-old, Oxford-educated Prince Paul of Serbia, a cousin of King Alexander I of the Serbs, Croats and Slovenes. The Prince first set eyes on the Princess at a ball given by her kinswoman Lady Zia Wernher.[3] Although they were not introduced, Olga clearly made quite an impression, for when Paul returned to his Mayfair flat in Mount Street, he was unable to sleep for thinking about her. However, the Princess was preoccupied that evening by the Prince of Wales' lack of attention towards herself and her sisters.[6]

Paul was persistent and obtained an introduction to the Princess during a Madrid Cup polo match at Roehampton. However, although he received a brief mention (as 'Paul of Serbia') in her diary, Olga's eyes remained focused on the Prince of Wales.[7] A few days later, the Princess attended a dance given by the politician Sir Philip Sassoon, at which Paul also happened to be present. She was touched by his solicitous manner as he engaged her in conversation. By contrast, the British heir-to-the-throne seemed only to have eyes for his long-time mistress Mrs Freda Dudley Ward. Significantly, next day, the Serbian royal was invited to join Olga's party for lunch at Claridge's, followed by a visit to the polo at Ranelagh. This encounter must have been a success for, by the following week, Paul was accompanying the Princess and her family to the Lyric Theatre to see the 'sentimental' musical "Lilac Time".[8] He then kindly arranged for the little group to visit the Shaftesbury Theatre to see Fred and Adele Astaire in "Stop Flirting" (which just happened to be a favourite of Prince Nicholas). Olga was 'delighted' both by the thoughtful gesture and the performance. The Nicholas family and the Prince then proceeded directly to the Duke of Portland's ball, where the Princess was impressed to discover that her admirer was a close friend of the King's second son, Albert ('Bertie'), the Duke of York and his new bride Elizabeth.[9] Thereafter, the relationship seemed to deepen and Olga was particularly pleased that Paul continued to do 'all in his power to make our stay as pleasant and happy as possible.'[10] She now admitted to finding his company stimulating and, during another interminable society ball, eschewed an evening of dancing in favour of sitting quietly talking to the Prince 'the whole of the evening .. and [I] didn't feel a bit bored.'[11] Paul continued his pursuit with a dinner at the Embassy Club, on 27 July, and the Princess found that 'the more I saw of him, the more I felt drawn to him.'[12] Certainly, he was now constantly in her thoughts and the die seemed cast as the duo subsequently made an afternoon visit to the cinema. Yet, there was no whimsical proposal on the Prince's part. Instead, he told Olga 'a little about his sad and lonely childhood' and it was the intuitive Princess who 'suddenly became aware of his true feelings for me'.[13] Seizing the moment, she leaned forward and whispered

---

[3] The elder daughter of Grand Duke Michael Mikhailovich of Russia.

to Paul 'Have you found what you want?' Paul, no doubt relieved that his efforts had not be in vain, replied firmly, 'Yes, at last!'[14] The betrothal was met with approval by the Greek royal family: Indeed, Prince Christopher enthused, 'Paul, brilliantly clever, sensitive, artistic, an idealist, is precisely the right husband for Olga, who is merry, philosophical and practical to the last degree'.[15]

But who exactly was Prince Paul and how did this relatively minor princeling come to be so close to senior members of the British royal family, as well as being à l'aise with all of London society? Paul's story was somewhat heartrending: Born in St Petersburg, on 15 April 1893, he was the only child of Prince Arsène Karageorgević, the younger brother of the late King Peter I of Serbia and a descendent of a wealthy Serbian clan chief and leader George Petrović (also known as "Karadjordje" [Black George] after his dark looks). Fascinatingly, the Karageorgević dynasty was swept back into power in Serbia, following a coup d'état, which saw the murder of the head of a rival dynasty, King Alexander Obrenović and his wife Queen Draga, at the Old Palace in Belgrade on the night of 10/11 June 1903, just as Olga was entering this world at Tatoi. Paul's mother, the vivacious Russian noblewoman Aurora Pavlovna Demidoff, Princess of San Donata, was a member of the fabulously wealthy Demidoff dynasty who owed their fortune to the discovery of rich mineral reserves in the Russian Urals and the supply of arms to the army of Peter the Great. Aurora's grandfather, Nikolay, had served as Court Chamberlain at the Imperial Court in St Petersburg and was later appointed Russian Ambassador to the Court of Tuscany, where he bought a large parcel of land near Florence and built the Villa San Donato. Nikolay was ennobled in 1827 and bore the title of Count of San Donato. In 1840, his younger son Anatole (Aurora's uncle) married Mathilde, a niece of Napoleon Bonaparte, and he was created the first Prince of San Donato. Anatole died without issue in 1870, so the Princely title passed to Aurora's Russian-based father, Paul, who eventually sold the Villa San Donato and focused on restoring the Paggeria (Pages' Lodge) of the Villa Pratolino near Florence, which he had purchased from the Tuscan Grand Ducal family. This villa, often referred to as the Villa Demidoff, would subsequently be inherited by Aurora's younger sister Maria ('Moina').

At the age of one, Paul's parents separated and the Prince, his mother and his Russian nurse left Russia for Nice. By the time of the couple's divorce in 1896, Paul and his nurse had moved to Geneva, to live with his father's widower brother, Peter. Aurora remarried in 1897 and played no further part in her son's upbringing. Sadly, she would die aged 30, in June 1904. Prince Arsène remained an equally remote presence and showed little interest in his shy son. This brash General focused on his military exploits, which Paul later informed Olga were 'his chief concern, [with] wars and duels his passion.'[16] Arsène spent his later life in Paris where he lived in the fashionable 16th arrondissement.

Paul was sent to a boarding school in Lausanne aged seven, where he led a somewhat solitary existence in a room infested with rats and mice. When his Uncle Peter ascended the Serbian throne in 1903, the Prince moved to Belgrade with the King and his family, to live in an attic room of the Old Palace and attend the select Second Belgrade Gymnasium[17]. The Prince was often tormented by King Peter's mentally unstable, eldest son George, who made an attempt to drown Paul by pushing him from a bridge into a lake. However, Paul 'loved and trusted' the King's younger son, Alexander ('Sandro').[18]

Starved of parental affection and feminine tenderness, the teenage Prince Paul took refuge in collecting beautiful objects. He certainly had the means to indulge this habit as he inherited 'a small fortune' at age eighteen.[19] Paul made frequent visits to Italy to visit his Aunt Moina and her wealthy Russian Armenian husband Semyon (who died in 1916) either at the Villa Abamelek in Rome or the Villa Demidoff. The couple later adopted Paul[20], who eventually became heir to their fortune. Almost simultaneously, the Prince developed a close friendship with the Italian royal family and he was particularly devoted to Queen Elena, who was related to the Serbian royal family by marriage. He corresponded regularly with 'Tante Elena' who always showered Paul with 'motherly tenderness'[21] He was also a 'best friend' of her son Umberto, who treated Paul as an elder brother.[22]

After graduating with distinction from the Gymnasium in Belgrade at age 19,[23] in February 1913, Paul went up to Oxford to read classics at Christ Church.[24] He settled into rooms in Peckwater Quadrangle, joined the notorious (but highly exclusive) Bullingdon Club and quickly garnered a circle of influential British aristocratic friends including Walter Dalkeith (the future 8th Duke of Buccleuch) and Robert 'Bobbety' Cranborne (later 5th Marquess of Salisbury). From nearby New College, the Prince also befriended John ('Jock') Balfour (a distant cousin of the former British Prime Minister Arthur Balfour) who would later become a high-flying career diplomat in the British Foreign Office.[25]

However, the Prince's time at Oxford was brief for his studies were interrupted with the outbreak of the First World War in the summer of 1914. He returned home to a country in chaos (as Serbia had been invaded by Austro-Hungarian forces) and served from August 1914 until the spring of 1915 (by which time had developed hepatitis)[26] as a Lieutenant in the Royal Serbian Horse Guards.[27] Paul then spent the summer and autumn holidaying with the Balfour family at their Scottish home, Newton Don, Roxburghshire.

The Prince intended to return to Serbia in November, but suffered a heart attack, en route, in Florence. He convalesced there until the spring of 1916, before travelling to Corfu to be reunited with other members of the Serbian royal family, who were exiled there after German and Austro-Hungarian forces occupied Serbia.[28] Paul then secured a position working with the Red Cross in Geneva,[29] although he would re-join Serbian forces in Salonika, in early 1917, to take part in a spring offensive. Sadly, the Prince's health again deteriorated and he returned to Britain with his digestive system 'in complete disorder.'[30] The doctors eventually established that Paul was suffering from chronic colitis.[31] Meanwhile, as the Austro-Hungarian Empire crumbled, its former South Slavic subjects were focused on achieving self-government. On 29 October 1918, a Croatian Sabor (parliament) in Zagreb declared independence and subsequently indicated a wish to form a union with Serbia and Montenegro. Following negotiations in Geneva, a Unification Proclamation was read by the Serbian Prince Regent (King Peter's son and heir, Alexander) on 1 December, in Belgrade's Terazije Square and the Kingdom of Serbs, Croats and Slovenes was established as a constitutional monarchy with the Karageorgević dynasty at the helm.[32]

In early 1920, Paul returned to Christ Church to complete his studies and met Henry 'Chips' Channon, an immensely rich Chicago-born Anglophile and 'endearing social climber'[33] who was studying French. Channon was particularly fond of Paul,[34] and introduced him to some other influential eccentrics in London Society such as Lady Maud ('Emerald') Cunard. It was also during this period that the Prince made the acquaintance of Prince Albert, who was studying history at nearby Trinity College. However, one of the most important figures in Paul's life was Lady Elizabeth Bowes-Lyon, the youngest daughter of the Earl of Strathmore and Kinghorne. They had recently been introduced through a mutual friend, Lady Doris Gordon-Lennox. Elizabeth visited the Prince in Oxford that spring[35] and Paul was subsequently invited to stay with the Bowes-Lyons family at their country home, St Paul's Walden Bury and at their Scottish home, Glamis Castle. The Prince was certainly smitten by Lady Elizabeth's beauty and many now thought that he was keen to marry her.[36]

Paul concluded his Oxford academic studies in early 1921 with the award of an honour's degree in Modern History.[37] He subsequently shared a flat in Mayfair's Mount Street with Lady Elizabeth's older brother, Michael Bowes-Lyon and another mutual friend, the courtier George 'Grubby' Gage. The Prince was now a regular in aristocratic circles in London and, in September, during another visit to Glamis, he was one of the first to observe the developing romance between Prince Albert and Elizabeth Bowes-Lyon.[38] Although Paul must have been privately disappointed at this development, following the couple's engagement, in mid-January 1923, he kindly hosted a celebratory lunch in their honour at Ciro's, and attended the royal wedding, on 26 April, in Westminster Abbey. Thus, by the time the Prince met Olga in the summer, the time was ripe for romance....

The engagement of Olga and Paul was announced through Reuter's news service on 3 August and widely reported, next day, in the British press. The wedding date (22 October) was chosen by the Royal Court in Belgrade, so as to coincide with the christening of King Alexander and Queen Marie's yet-to-be-born first child. Meanwhile, after a final relaxing summer weekend of tennis and bathing at Brownsea Island in the company of Olga and her parents, Paul hurried back to Belgrade to organise the wedding preparations, while his fiancée returned to Paris to experience the 'novel excitement' of shopping for her trousseau at Jean Patou and ordering a wedding dress based, 'on simple classical lines' in silver lamé.[39] The couple received some wonderful wedding presents: Olga was given a necklace of 26 diamond collets from her grandmother Queen Olga, while Paul's Aunt Moina provided a Boucheron diamond tiara. The bride-to-be was so touched by her generosity, that she paid a visit to Moina at the Villa Demidoff, en route to her nuptials in Belgrade. In the interim, Paul had invited Prince Albert (who had recently been created the Duke of York) to be his best man.

Fortunately, Queen Marie (whom we first encountered as Princess Marie [Mignon] in her native Romania in 1914) obligingly gave birth to a healthy son, Peter, on 6 September, so the wedding arrangements remained firmly on track. On 20 October, Olga and her family arrived in Belgrade aboard King Alexander's private railway carriage, having been greeted earlier at the frontier by Paul. As she alighted the train in Belgrade, King Alexander stepped forward to warmly embrace her and Prince Nicholas noted with satisfaction that the monarch had fallen in love with his daughter 'straightaway'.[40] Olga was then whisked off to the royal palace in an open carriage drawn by white horses. After settling into her rooms, she paid a courtesy call on Queen Marie, who was recovering from an attack of peritonitis and caught a glimpse of little Peter whom she found 'very sweet and not in the least ugly!'[41] It was then time to join a plethora of relatives and friends from all over Europe for tea and dinner, before retiring to bed emotionally drained and physically exhausted.

Olga awoke next morning to find there was a shortage of water in the overcrowded palace. Nevertheless, after breakfasting, she dressed quickly and made her way to the Royal Chapel to attend Peter's christening at 11am. The ceremony was not without incident: When the Duke of York (who was the child's godfather or 'Koom') handed the baby to the Patriarch of Serbia for total immersion (as Orthodox rites required), the priest lost grip of the infant, who promptly fell into the font. Fortunately, the Duke deftly retrieved the distressed baby and returned him to the relieved Patriarch. The christening was followed by a lavish lunch for four-hundred, which to the Princess seemed like 'the whole of Belgrade'.[42] Olga and Paul then escaped to enjoy a sightseeing drive around Belgrade, in the company of the Duke and Duchess of York, followed by afternoon tea aboard the Romanian royal yacht. In the evening, a pre-wedding gala concert was followed by a cold buffet supper.

After a fitful sleep (and doubtless dwelling on the new life which awaited her), the Princess awoke to prepare for her wedding day. While she dressed, Olga was fussed over by Princess Nicholas, Elisabeth, Marina and the ever-faithful Kate Fox. Later, when Prince Nicholas called to collect his daughter for the ceremony, he found her 'quite ready [and] looking perfectly adorable' in her 'simple' wedding dress which was augmented by the gift of a fine lace veil from Turia Campbell (Princess Catherine Galitzine). There followed a brief, but touching moment when Olga's parents' blessed her with 'a lovely icon' which Ellen had purchased specially in Paris. Finally, at noon, it was time for the bride-to-be and her family to walk through the palace corridors, which were lined by 'an admiring crowd of courtiers' to the Royal Chapel. The Princess wore 'an angelic expression of purity' as she joined Paul at the altar for the marriage which was solemnized by the Patriarch. In keeping with Serbian tradition, the bride stepped over a strip of cloth, scattered corn and kissed a new-born baby (Peter). Touchingly, at the conclusion of the ceremony, the newlyweds went over to Olga's parents and embraced them tenderly. Prince Nicholas was moved to find that his eldest child, 'had made such an extraordinary impression on everybody.'[43]

During the wedding lunch, Olga 'had a smile and kind word'[44] for each of her hundred guests, before embarking with Paul on a short ceremonial drive through the principal streets of the city. Thereafter, the newlyweds departed for the station and as their *wagon lit* pulled out of the platform, Olga confided thankfully to her diary, 'On our own life à deux!'[45] Meanwhile, a thankful Prince Nicholas informed his mother, 'at least we know that she loves her husband and that he simply worships her.'[46] However, the perceptive Duchess of York, reflecting on her Balkan visit, noted 'how odd' the bride's new in-laws were. [47] As Olga would soon discover, they were indeed a far cry from the close, loving family unit she had just left behind.

After spending the first few days of their honeymoon in Venice, Olga and Paul moved on to Florence to visit Aunt Moina. However, the main part of this five-week romantic sojourn was spent in Rome, at the Villa

Abamalek, from where the couple made an excursion to the Villa Savoia, to be entertained by the King and Queen of Italy and their family. Olga enthused to her diary, 'Our happiness, mine at least, increases daily and time seems to fly'.[48]

Meanwhile, in Paris, the Nicholas' had rented an airy apartment at 4 Square Trocadero and the newlyweds joined them for Christmas, although the celebrations were somewhat tempered by the news that King George had been forced to leave Greece, on 19 December, following a failed royalist coup. In March 1924, a Second Hellenic Republic would be declared.

Chapter 9 Belgrade, Bohinj and Beyond

In early January 1924, Olga returned to her adopted homeland with her husband to settle into their apartments on the upper floor of the New Palace, adjacent to those of Peter and his nurse. It proved to be a difficult adjustment: Of Belgrade, the Princess informed Marina: 'I fear there is not much to say in its favour as it is not precisely a very beautiful or elegant town ...'[1] She was finding life 'a dreadful bore and a monotony..' and blamed this on the 'queer unhomely atmosphere in the house' and lack of family life.[2] Inevitably, the two people the newlyweds came in closest contact with were the King and Queen. Unfortunately, they enjoyed a rather mercurial relationship and had recently had a terrible row. Thus, for the next two weeks, Alexander and Paul ate their meals together in one room, while Olga dined separately with Mignon in another. Otherwise, the Queen sulked in her room.[3] Unfortunately, Alexander's marriage to Marie had not come about as the result of a passionate love affair, but rather as 'the practical matter of building a dynasty'.[4] It also did not help that the Queen and her husband were totally different in character and outlook: Marie was of large build (Alexander called her "La Grosse"), spoke with a guttural German accent, dressed simply and had a distinctly un-regal manner. Furthermore, she was far more interested in racing motorcars, than dealing with the minutiae of court life.[5] Additionally, unlike the King, she was a staunch Anglophile, having been raised by her English-born mother, Marie, and an English nurse, Mary 'Nana' Green.

By contrast, the King was a highly intelligent man of charm and polish, but prone to 'changeable moods'.[6] A Francophile like his late father King Peter, he served in the Corps des Pages at the Russian Imperial Court and received his military training at the École Spéciale Militaire de Saint-Cyr. Alexander spoke wonderful French (though no English) and this was the language spoken at court. Although 'very much the soldier and commander,'[7] he also possessed an appealing manner which made people feel more at ease speaking to him than to the Queen. Indeed, Olga subsequently admitted, 'I grew very fond of Sandro...'[8]

Olga and Paul left Belgrade by train, in early February, for a two-day visit to Zagreb. This offered the duo a chance to prove themselves, with the added incentive that the Prince might eventually be asked to return there as Governor of Croatia. The couple were received at the station with full honours and later attended an evening engagement at the University which required them to kick-off the proceedings by dancing the local folk dance, the Kolo. Later, while Olga made small talk in German with the ladies, Paul spoke to the menfolk. However, neither slept well and next morning the Princess felt 'too tired' to accompany Paul on a tour of the local Museum and Library. However, she felt able to re-join the official schedule after lunch and was pleased to find that the city possessed 'a less provincial air than Belgrade!'[9] With their future prospects in mind, the royal couple ensured that they 'praised Zagreb up to the skies'[10] prior to their departure and were 'so thankful it all went off successfully...'[11]

The Prince and Princess dutifully returned to dreary Belgrade to attend a rather stilted Charity Ball in aid of the Navy at the Casino des Officiers. The following morning, the Princess was astonished to discover that while she and Paul dutifully attended church, the King and Queen preferred to languish in bed.[12] Yet, the King and Queen actively sought out their company: Mignon particularly enjoyed listening to Olga read aloud from "The Admirable Crichton", while the King might join the couple after dinner for a game of cards, although his attempts at teaching the Princess the 'rather complicated'[13] game of bridge were met with polite indifference. To her delight, Olga discovered that there was a sizeable White Russian community in Belgrade. Most of the doctors were Russian, while the best boot maker in town was a retired White Russian Colonel.

However, one aspect of life in her adopted homeland was very familiar to this Greek Princess: The country was a political minefield. The mainly Roman Catholic Croats and Slovenes (who had previously formed part of the Austro-Hungarian Empire) regarded themselves as a cut above the Orthodox Serbs and Montenegrins. Furthermore, the Croats-led by Stjepan Radić and his Croatian People's Peasant People's Party-felt (with some justification) that the balance of power was in favour of the Serbs and wanted a move towards a more autonomous, federal union. The Serbs, meanwhile, favoured the current centralisation of power in Belgrade. Worryingly, there was also still considerable opposition towards the Serbian Karageorgević dynasty from the Croats.[14]

With time on her hands, Olga was soon keen to improve standards at Court. She confided to her mother that 'I have seldom seen a household worse organised than this; everything goes as it likes with no one at the head'. The proactive Princess started by asking the Queen what she was going to do about the highly unsuitable housemaids' clothes. Unaccustomed to such zeal, Mignon at first seemed undecided but soon 'begged' Olga to obtain a catalogue from a servant's outfitter.[15]

Sadly, Alexander remained 'very cold' towards his wife and another row soon ensued that left Mignon in tears. It was all a 'rather a painful and sad experience' for Olga who confessed to Princess Nicholas that the main problem was 'that special thing has not happened for very nearly a year now.' She was particularly concerned too for little Peter, 'because if things get worse it has a charming life before it, poor little thing.'[16] According to Olga, the King was now determined to send Queen Marie back to Romania with their small son and was even contemplating asking the Patriarch to dissolve the marriage, on the grounds of his wife's laziness and incompetence. However, the horrified Princess 'begged' the King to give the Queen another chance for Peter's sake[17]. All this made Olga, 'thank God for my own happiness, we get greater friends every day and have everything in common...'[18] Olga's 'happiness' was now compounded by the wonderful news that she was expecting her first child and this explained her morning tiredness during the Zagreb trip. Unfortunately, Alexander had made no effort to pursue the matter of Paul's appointment as Governor in Croatia: He was simply informed that it was 'unsuitable at that period.'[19]

When the Queen returned from a long visit to Paris in April, the Princess observed empathetically, 'Poor thing, how sad she must be to come back. Like beginning lessons on Monday morning, only worse!'[20] Olga focused on dealing with her voluminous correspondence and receiving daily Serbian language lessons from a 'dear old' Professor Zdravković.[21] However, the lessons were increasingly interrupted by bouts of morning sickness. It was also during this period that the Princess learned about the practicalities of political life. Much of this information was gleaned during the many post-dinner chats she and Paul enjoyed with the King, when topics discussed would include tantalising snippets of the latest domestic political gossip and intrigues, although they also touched on world affairs.[22]

Naturally, Olga wanted to be nearer her own family during the latter stages of her pregnancy, while Paul wished for his first child to be born in England. The couple therefore took out a short lease on a small country house at Bisham Grange, which fronted on to the River Thames. Despite being heavily pregnant, the Princess joined her husband on a nostalgic visit to Oxford, where she inspected Paul's former rooms in Christ Church College's Peckwater Quadrant. On occasion, Paul would travel up to London to escort Marina and Elisabeth (who were staying with their parents at the Granby Court Hotel) to the various society balls. During Royal Ascot week, the Prince encountered his friend the Duchess of York, who kindly offered the couple the use of her London home, White Lodge at Richmond, for the forthcoming confinement. It was there, on 13 August, that Olga gave birth to a nine-and-a-three quarter pound boy. Olga and Paul named their firstborn Alexander and he was christened, in the presence of his great-grandmother Queen Olga, according to the rites of the Greek Orthodox Church at White Lodge, on 6 September; his godparents included King Alexander and the Duke of York.

Unlike many mothers of her generation, Olga was a great believer in breast feeding and insisted on nursing the child herself for the first eight months.[23] However, she was also greatly concerned about finding somewhere to raise her new-born. With nothing urgent to draw them back to Belgrade, the little family initially took a small suite of rooms at Claridge's, although they eventually found a modest French abode to rent at Grasse-the Villa Otrada-which Olga thought 'very small.'[24] Fortunately, Prince Paul won his wife over when he agreed to hire an excellent French cook and an English valet. Meanwhile, the Princess was 'proud of my large son ... a happy smiling infant admired by all'[25] and delighted when her parents and sisters settled into a nearby villa in time for Christmas. Nor was Olga forgotten by her Demidoff in-laws: Aunt Moina kindly sent her a generous gift of Fr.5000 as a Festive gift.[26]

This Riviera interlude also allowed the Princess to become acquainted with her father-in-law, Prince Arsène, who often came over to lunch at the Villa Otrada from nearby Nice. Sadly, these visits were interrupted when baby Alexander was struck down with bronchitis. However, always in the background was the question of finding suitable employment for Paul, as well as a permanent family home. Unfortunately, there was no offer of either from King Alexander, although Aunt Moina offered to rent the family a house at Fiesole. This gesture drew a caustic response from a frustrated Olga, 'Why not give us one of the twenty she possesses around Pratolino?'[27] Furthermore, the Yugoslav King and Queen's lack of concern over Paul's need for accommodation caused the Princess to note indignantly, 'So that settles it! They don't seem to want us ever to come back...'[28]

In need of a change, on 21 May 1925, the Prince and Princess left Alexander in the care of his nurse and set out for Paris, with the intention of renting an apartment. However, the delights of the London Season soon beckoned and, by early June, they had moved on to England. Eventually, a telegram arrived from Alexander and Mignon inviting the duo to their Slovenian summer residence at Bled. However, when the Prince and Princess arrived in Slovenia, there was neither the offer of a house, nor a job for Paul. It was a thus a rather dejected Olga who returned to Grasse to help her son celebrate his first birthday on 13 August, while Paul remained at Bled. This proved to be a wise move, as King Alexander decided to offer his cousin the exclusive use of a house at Bohinjsko-Jezero, an hour's drive from Bled. The Princess was overjoyed by the news and quickly joined Paul in Ljubljana (the main city in Slovenia) for a tour of inspection of their new residence.[29]

She was not to be disappointed: After motoring through the ravines of the mountainous Sava Valley, Olga and Paul espied a chalet-style house set on a hill and with views extending over a nearby lake. Their new home was set out over three levels: The top floor contained two nurseries, while immediately below was a master bedroom with en suite bathroom and a separate dressing room. Of equal importance to Olga were the two spacious guest bedrooms, which would accommodate visiting family and friends.[30] An added bonus was that the house could be easily (and thriftily) decorated using swathes of chintz and white-wash on the walls.

Unfortunately, there was not a lot of time to admire their new home, as the couple soon proceeded to Italy to attend the wedding of Princess Mafalda of Savoy to Prince Philip of Hesse. This gathering offered Olga the chance for a reunion with her sister Elisabeth and her Greek cousins, including King George. It must have been a splendid occasion, for the Princess recalled that, 'we all wore tiaras and as many jewels as we had'[31], while the men were attired in full uniform. Olga was led into the Castle of Racconigi's candlelit Chapel by the Austrian Archduke Franz-Joseph. A fellow guest was the young Italian Prime Minister Benito Mussolini. The latter clearly caught the Princess' eye for she mentions his presence in her account of the wedding to Miss Fox.[32]

Thereafter, Olga and Paul left for Turin in the company of her cousin Irene. The Princess informed Foxie that, 'We had a gay time together ...and relaxed our good manners a bit!' Their sojourn included 'an interesting visit' to the famous Fiat car factory, where the group were taken for a spin on the rooftop test track and Olga spotted a 'delicious little two-seater' which 'was just what I have been raving about for months!!'[33] After the Princess had taken the car for a spin, Paul took the hint and quickly purchased one for his wife for £160.[34] The Prince and Princess then ventured to Florence where they lunched on several occasions with Aunt Moina.

On their return to Cannes, the duo shopped for furniture for the new Slovenian retreat. Thereafter, with the King's blessing, Paul journeyed to England to source some works of modern art which would form the nucleus of a collection to be displayed at a new gallery in Belgrade. Olga, meanwhile, returned to Belgrade with their 'beloved tiny'.[35] Although this was little Alexander's first visit to the land of his Karageorgević ancestors, the Princess must have been taken aback by the King's reaction to her young son: Not only was Sandro at the station to meet them, but in a display of great affection, he immediately scooped up the little child 'and carried him in his arms all the way back to the palace.'[36] On their arrival there, the King then rushed in to introduce the swarthy infant to his wife. What the Queen thought of all this is not recorded but, given the diffident relationship Alexander had with his son Peter, such overt displays of devotion can hardly have endeared Olga or her young child to Mignon. Nevertheless, this bond between the two Alexander's would grow stronger with the years.[37]

When Prince Paul returned to Belgrade from London, the Princess threw herself into preparations for the Festive season at the New Palace. Her efforts soon caught the attention of the King who helped her to decorate the Christmas Tree and even climbed up a ladder to fix the star to the top.[38] Then, as the 'English' Christmas Day (December 25) was celebrated as Mother's Day in Serbia, she attended a party for children and their mothers in the ballroom of the Old Palace which featured games, singing and dancing.

Thereafter, Olga was distressed to learn that Crown Prince Carol of Romania had renounced his rights to the throne and deserted her cousin Helen to live outside Paris with a Romanian apothecary's daughter, Elena 'Magda' Lupescu. Sitta's marriage seems to have deteriorated quickly after the birth of their son Michael, in October 1921, and it certainly had not helped that the couple were temperamentally different: Helen was level-headed and reserved, while Carol was impetuous and possessed of a hot temper.[39] On 4 January 1926, Carol and Helen's son Michael was officially designated Heir Apparent to the Romanian throne.

On the Orthodox Christmas Eve (January 6), the Princess was intrigued to observe another Slav convention, the arrival of the badnjak (Yule log). The latter was delivered by a Guards Brigade to the head of the household, King Alexander, who subsequently showered his troops with spices and sweets from a basket. The log was then taken inside the Palace and placed in a large fire place, where it was left to smoulder throughout the Christmas period.

Miss Fox, meanwhile, was taking on a new role in her former charge's life, dealing enthusiastically and promptly with numerous requests from Olga, mostly of a practical household nature, including the provision of fabric samples for Bohinj. The Princess was also tentatively dipping her toe into public life in Belgrade, becoming patron to several child welfare charities, a role which she found 'mostly interesting and creative.'[40] In addition, she was keen to foster closer ties between Alexander and Peter, although her efforts did not find favour with Paul, who thought the Crown Prince was 'dreadfully spoilt and is only good when amused.' By contrast Mignon was becoming increasingly fond of young Alexander, giving him a gift of Beatrix Potter books and praising his 'sweet, even sunny nature!'[41]

In late March, the Prince and Princess paid a visit to Rome and took tea with Queen Olga who was 'in high spirits and most amusing'[42], although her eye-sight was poor. After a brief visit to Queen Sophie in Florence, the couple returned to Rome, to spend the Orthodox Easter with the Nicholas family at the Hotel Eden, before rushing off to Paris for some 'necessary household shopping' for Bohinj[43]. It is small wonder that the Princess complained to Foxie that she had 'never been so rushed in my life'.[44]

Returning to Belgrade in late May, Olga found the King and Queen ('our hosts')[45] were absent. However, she focused on preparations for the forthcoming (first) summer season at Bohinj, where a household staff of four had already been assembled, overseen by a new butler, Doušan. When Olga, Paul and Alexander arrived in Slovenia in mid-June, they were given 'a touching reception' by the inhabitants of the local village and accompanied to their house by half a dozen farmers, sporting helmets and swords, mounted on cart horses. Olga enthused, 'it's too good to be true to be in our own house surrounded by our things!'[46] Yet, within days, her joy was to turn to sorrow following the news that Queen Olga had died. The Prince and Princess attended both the funeral service in Rome, on 22 June, and the interment the following day at the Russian Orthodox Church in Florence.

Back at Bohinj, Olga supervised the laying of a tennis court before welcoming their first guests, the King and Queen ('the Masters from Bled')[47] who came to lunch and remained to tea. Shortly thereafter, Kate Fox arrived by train at nearby Bistrica to be met by the Princess in her little Fiat car. With Nurnie safely installed, the Prince and Princess felt able to make a brief visit to Munich to attend the opera. Olga then joined the King and Queen on a holiday to the Dalmatian Coast, but was shocked to find that little Peter was 'half again as thin' as before. She soon discovered the reason: The poor child was being fed ten raw figs each day at teatime by his nurse.[48]

In mid-September, the Princess was pleased to welcome her parents and Marina to Bohinj. They enjoyed games of tennis, although Prince Nicholas preferred to go fishing. Sadly, a much-anticipated visit by Olga's sister Elisabeth failed to materialise, causing the Princess to complain to Foxie that, 'I had prepared everything for her and miss her fearfully as she would have taken so much more interest in my house than Marina does; she [Marina] is sweet of course, but it's not the same.'[49] Clearly, neither sister had succeeded in impressing their eldest sister, although for rather different reasons.

Olga admitted to missing Bohinj 'frightfully', on her return to Belgrade's New Palace at the end of October, particularly 'our liberty'. Another problem was that little Alexander was served 'tasteless' food prepared in the unhygienic palace kitchens.[50] Nor was it proving easy with two sets of nursery staff working in such close quarters: Peter's nurse, 'Nana' Bell, was apparently 'a dangerous old gossip' and Olga warned Alexander's nurse, Ethel Roberts, to be 'more careful' with what information she shared, 'as it's important the children should be friends *for more reasons than one.*' This was a tacit acknowledgment by the Princess that her family were reliant on the King and Queen's largesse. Interestingly, Olga was already beginning to lose faith in Miss Roberts and confessed to Kate Fox that the nurse was deliberately undermining her position by being rude and seeking 'to take advantage of me... [51] Worse still, she had proven to be untruthful which to her upright employer was 'a blow after I had trusted her so much.'[52] Miss Fox was eventually assigned the task of interviewing suitable replacements in London (aided by an exhaustive list of requirements from her former charge). Foxie concluded that a Miss Wilson might prove suitable and she duly arrived in Belgrade on 3 December. Fortunately, the new nurse was an immediate hit with Alexander and the Princess now relished the 'pleasant atmosphere'in the nursery. [53] Conversely, and despite everything, Olga did not enjoy saying goodbye to Miss Roberts and she personally supervised the arrangements for Ethel's homeward journey to Cheshire.[54]

Queen Marie, meanwhile, was currently in Bucharest, where her father, King Ferdinand, was dying from cancer. That there was an interfering side to Mignon was exposed in an American newspaper: The Queen was said to have 'hustled home to her [Romanian] people' in order to get involved with 'meddling in matters concerning the succession to the throne'. More specifically, she and her sister Elisabetha were apparently advancing the cause of their exiled brother Carol by 'trying to discredit the Regency' provisions that had been put in place for the now rightful heir, Michael, in the event of King Ferdinand's incapacity or death.[55] Naturally, such reports can have done little to endear Mignon to Olga, who later telephoned Michael's mother Helen to offer some words of support.[56]

In January 1927, Olga and Paul left Belgrade for Cannes to spend the early winter months with the Princess' family, while Alexander remained in Belgrade under Miss Wilson's tender care. During their absence, Miss Wilson and Miss Bell muddled along 'very well' together and Alexander and Peter now met 'all the time...' On her return to Belgrade, Olga informed her mother that Paul's museum was nearing completion, while she was due to preside at a concert, in the Old Palace, in honour of the three hundred delegates who were attending the 20th International Congress of Byzantine Studies. The Princess also acknowledged that Belgrade, 'feels rather like in a prison...and it takes a

little while to get [back] into the [official] life and readjust ones ideas...'[57]
She also complained to Foxie that she was 'dreading' the Orthodox
Easter, as the correct religious traditions were not properly observed at
the Belgrade Court.[58]

Olga was also keen to raise little Alexander's public profile by
having some pictures published in a magazine. She seems to have been
spurred on by a recent article about Peter in the *Nursery World Magazine*.
However, it was the editor of the *Woman's Pictorial* who responded to
Olga's enquiry, indicating her publication would be 'delighted' to publish
Alexander's photograph.[59] For good measure, the Princess also enclosed
a small note, 'about the way he spends his days, his nurseries etc.' [60]
doubtless in the hope that this information would be used in an article to
accompany the picture.

The Princess then made arrangements to visit London with Paul and
Marina. The main purpose of this spring trip was to try and advance
Marina's marital prospects with the Prince of Wales.[61] However, no
sooner had Paul splashed out 160 guineas to rent Lord Ednam's house,
in fashionable Cheyne Walk[62] than there as an unfortunate development:
The person the Prince was counting on to act as a "fixer" for Marina had
departed for the United States the previous week. Nevertheless, Olga
remained determined that her sister would make an impression and sent
an urgent plea to Princess Nicholas asking to borrow a diamond rivière
necklace.[63] Within a week, the Princess was able to report to her mother
that the trio had spent most of the previous evening in the Prince of
Wales' company at the home of society hostess, Mrs. Audrey Coates. She
observed too that, 'all is in God's Hands and now we have, so to speak,
entered this door, it will be interesting to see how events will shape
themselves.'[64]

However, although Paul, Olga and Marina would bump into the
Prince of Wales most evenings at the Ritz or Ciro's night club (where he
often danced with Marina whose 'thoughts are certainly very much filled
with him') Queen Mary did not ask the persistent trio to stay at Windsor
Castle for Ascot week.[65] Indeed, by the end of June, when the Prince of
Wales had failed to acknowledge their presence at the Sutherland's
costume ball, Olga was in fits of despair, telling Kate Fox that, 'Things
have not been going very satisfactorily lately.' Fortunately, Marina was
less bothered and 'took it in a philosophical way and managed to amuse
herself without him.'[66]

However, there was still hope: On 11 July, Olga informed Foxie that
things, 'seem to have suddenly taken a turn for the better', as Paul and
Marina were dining with the Prince of Wales at York House that evening.
The Princess had apparently received an explanation for David's past
behaviour: 'He was very much attracted by [Marina] but wished to do

away with gossip by not seeing her!'[67] However, the outcome was to prove less than pleasing, which is hardly surprising given that David was still currently involved in a passionate relationship with Mrs Freda Dudley Ward.

Olga and Paul subsequently accompanied Marina back to Paris, where they had been given the use of Lord Derby's flat on the Avenue d'Iéna. In the interim, King Alexander had purchased a Rolls Royce motorcar for Olga as a gift and this was driven back to Bohinj from Paris by a manservant, with Paul and Marina as passengers.[68] The Princess and her sister Elisabeth followed on by train to Slovenia, where the weather was so pleasant that the family spent most of the time in bathing costumes. Meanwhile, Olga heard rumours from 'all sides' that Mignon was pregnant, with the baby due in January.[69]

As autumn took hold, young Peter returned to Bled following a trip to the seaside with Miss Bell. The Princess again noted with dismay that he was 'looking thinner than ever.' When King Alexander later discovered that the nurse had allowed his son outdoors without adequate sun protection, 'Nana' was summarily dismissed. While Olga believed that this action was long overdue, she was also sympathetic: 'I think it is a cruel way of sending the poor woman away instead of at least preparing her a little beforehand!' Nor did the royal nursery purge there: A maid and a military officer (who had been Peter's constant companion) were also sacked. The Princess felt these concurrent departures were 'cruel' on the child, who was 'sure to feel deeply, being sensitive and highly strung...' She also doubted that Mignon (who confided to Olga that she now wished to have Peter more to herself) could 'be of much help' as she knew 'very little about his life, diet and habits.'[70]

Olga continued to be concerned too for the welfare of her cousin Helen. Her husband Carol was threatening to return to Romania, only months after their son Michael had ascended the throne, following King Ferdinand's death in July. Indeed, Sitta was now feeling so depressed that she 'begged' Olga to visit her.[71] Around this time, the Princess was also involved in a contretemps with Mignon, who was currently at Topola: The palace director had prepared an apartment for her sister, Elisabeth, downstairs and not on the upper floor as Olga had instructed. Apparently, the swap over was done on the Queen's express orders, as the room the Princess had earmarked was being 'completely rearranged' for Mignon's 'accouchement'. An irate Olga telephoned Queen Marie, but she refused to back down, so the defiant Princess simply arranged for a divan-bed to be placed in her sitting room instead.[72] The King too was proving difficult: Olga told her mother that he had suddenly left for Topola 'without a word' one Sunday, despite having previously asked the Princess to accompany him to church.[73]

Chapter 10 Finding One's Feet

Throughout November, Olga had been feeling decidedly queasy and to her joy learned that she was pregnant, with the baby due the following June. She informed Miss Fox triumphantly that she had a unique antidote for morning sickness: Sneezing twice allayed the feelings of nausea! The Prince and Princess subsequently made a conciliatory visit to Topola for lunch with Mignon and found that Peter had acquired a new English nurse, Miss Sylvia Crowther. The child was coping well with the change being, 'perfectly happy, much less jumpy and nervous'.[1]

Olga then liaised with Miss Fox over purchasing some Christmas gifts in London. One present she was not distributing was her psychoanalyst Aunt, Marie Bonaparte's 'filthy book'[4] which she informed Princess Nicholas was 'too disgusting' adding, 'If she must write such obscene things why on earth can't she take on a nom de plume!'[2] Heeding the earlier plea from Helen to visit Bucharest, Olga, Paul and Elisabeth then departed Yugoslavia for a two-week stay in Romania. Inevitably, there were protracted discussions about Sitta's impending divorce from Carol and Olga was grateful that Paul was able to offer her cousin some good advice as 'he saw the situation very clearly.'[3]

The Prince and Princess returned to Belgrade well in advance of 1928's Orthodox Christmas celebrations. Olga had thoughtfully cancelled a visit to her parents in Paris, as she felt it would be 'undiplomatic' if they were to leave Yugoslavia again 'practically on the eve' of Queen Marie giving birth.[4] Instead, Paul and his family dutifully joined the King and Queen at the Palace for the traditional Christmas Eve celebrations, during which Peter and Alexander played contentedly with toy cars sent to them by Princess Nicholas. Olga thought it 'a blessing' that the future heir and her son were 'both the best of friends...' although this was a somewhat rosy viewpoint, as Alexander was a swarthy child and could be 'a bit rough' at times with the more fragile Peter.[5]

Although, for the moment, all eyes were on the Queen, the Princess was now in regular correspondence with her London obstetrician, Mr Gilliat. He encouraged Olga to travel to England for the birth of her

---

[4] Probably "A Childhood Memory of Leonardo da Vinci." Paris, Gallimard, 1927.

second child and she planned to arrive in London around mid-May.[6] Meanwhile, on 19 January, Mignon gave birth to a boy who was named Tomislav. Olga thought this an 'awful name', but acknowledged that it was politically expedient as it 'flattered the Croatians' having been the name of the first Croatian King[7].

In early May, Olga, Paul and Alexander departed Belgrade. The couple had rented a house in London's Manchester Square for the confinement, although the Princess found that the sultry weather disturbed her sleep. Furthermore, she was often left exhausted by visits from a steady stream of royal relatives, including Queen Sophie and her daughter Irene, who journeyed up from Birchington in Kent. The Greek royals enthused so much about the 'champagne' air at their seaside resort,[8] that the Princess subsequently journeyed down to Birchington by train, accompanied by Alexander, to inspect the facilities. She was so impressed by what she found, that she decided to leave her son there, under Irene's care.[9]

Even amid her own impending happiness, Olga was still focused on Marina's marriage prospects and wrote to Foxie, 'May God grant this year to be more satisfactory for Marina than last'.[10] However, with the Princess indisposed, it fell to Prince Paul to chaperon his sister-in-law to the Season's events and he complained of feeling 'like an old dowager chaperoning her grandchildren'.[11]

On 29 June, Olga gave birth to a second son, Nicholas, who weighed just over nine pounds. Both parents were delighted, although his mother later recalled she 'had longed for a daughter but he was so adorable I wouldn't have changed him for the whole world.'[12] Within weeks, the Princess and Paul journeyed down to Birchington with their new-born, to be reunited with Alexander at the Beresford Hotel. Olga must still have been rather frail for she was forced to lie down for most of the journey and, on her arrival, required to be carried up to her hotel room in a chair.[13] Unfortunately, the Beresford was infested with vermin which proved 'sheer agony' for the Prince, who diplomatically departed for a visit to friends in London and Portland.[14]

In mid-August, the family returned to Slovenia. On a visit to the King and Queen at Bled, the Princess was upset by the appalling behaviour of Miss Crowther, who 'gives herself fearful airs of importance, smokes [and] sits crossed-legged during the cinemas in the evening.' However, what truly horrified the responsible mother in Olga, was that on one occasion, 'Crowdie' left little Tomislav ('Tommy') alone atop her bed and he had subsequently fallen to the floor. The nurse apparently laughed this incident off, as did Mignon who was, 'completely under her charm, [and] even offers her [Crowther] cigarettes...'[15] For a Queen to behave in such a familiar way with a servant was simply not done.

However, the problem went deeper: Olga was fed up living in the New Palace where her 'hosts' were 'always very difficult' over the most trivial of requests. Her main solace was 'my precious Nicky-boy'.[16] Fortuitously, in January 1929, the King and Queen moved to a new Byzantine-style palace at Dedinje and this provided Olga with at least a small measure of the independence she craved. However, always in the background were mounting political problems: On 6 January, King Alexander suspended the 1921 Vidovdan constitution, banned national political parties, assumed full executive powers and renamed the country Yugoslavia, all in the hope that this might curb separatist tendencies, particularly in Croatia.

The Prince and Princess travelled to Palermo, in February, to attend the wedding of Olga's widowed Uncle Christopher[5] to Princess Francoise of Orléans ('Fattie'). Thereafter, they moved on to Rome and were soon 'living grandly' at the Quirinale Palace at the invitation of Queen Elena.[17] On their return to Belgrade, the couple celebrated the opening of Paul's Museum of Contemporary Art. Touchingly, the inaugural spring exhibition featured a recent portrait of Olga by Jacques Blanche. The Princess then journeyed to Bucharest, at the end of March, with her sons and sister Elisabeth to once again enjoy the 'cosy' family camaraderie of the recently-divorced Sitta's home.[18] Thereafter, she joined Paul on a trip to the Clinique Valmont in Glion. Although the purpose of the visit was to attempt to find a cure for the Prince's ongoing digestive problems, it eventually transpired that Olga had a stomach abscess and needed total bed rest. She embroidered 'with a vengeance' to pass the long days. [19]

In August, Paul and Olga returned to Slovenia, where Queen Marie had given birth to her third child, a boy named Andrej ('Andy') on 28 June. Life at Bohinj was 'somewhat hectic'[20] but at least it followed an established pattern, with walks in the morning, afternoon sunbathing sessions and tennis after tea. For added fun, the Princess had recently purchased an India rubber boat from Hamleys and quickly established that "shooting the rapids" made her bathing sessions 'more attractive!'[21] Although this all made for a contented family picture, Olga was currently in despair over a sudden lack of interaction between the King's children and her own. She placed the blame for this firmly at the door of the 'aggressively modern' Miss Crowther. [22]

Back in Belgrade, the Princess continued to do her best to support the King by undertaking official duties. Her exertions did not go unnoticed: Milan Stojadinović, a well-known Serbian politician and future Prime Minister, was clearly entranced by the Princess and, in his

---

[5] Prince Christopher's first wife died of cancer in London on 29 August 1923

memoirs, he recalls attending a reception in the Grand Salle of the New Palace to raise funds for the establishment of a Red Cross hospital. As Patron of the project, Olga hosted the event and it fell to Stojadinović to make a speech thanking her for her input and thus 'assuring the project's success in advance'. Despite Olga's 'sincere gratitude' for his words, the politician dismissed the occasion as something to nourish the 'petty and naïve ambition of a Princess who wished to assume the function of a queen even if only for a few hours'. The wily politician was clearly aware of the ongoing friction between Olga and Mignon, for he noted that if the Queen (who was absent from Belgrade) had known of the event, '[she] would not have permitted it out of jealousy of Olga'.[23] Stojadinović also lambasted the Princess for being 'ambitious' and indicated that she was not popular in Yugoslavia due to her haughty manner and foreign birth.[24] Nevertheless, by the same token, he conceded that she had garnered an increasing 'hold' over Belgrade society and court life.[25] Which begs the question that if she was so unpopular, how did she manage to achieve such a dominance?

However, in general, life at the New Palace was now lived at a far more relaxed pace. Olga and Paul loved nothing better than taking Nicholas for an afternoon stroll in the country in his folding pram; Alexander often accompanied them, riding happily alongside on his bicycle. Indeed, all-in-all, the Princess much preferred a quiet, domestic routine and, in January 1930, when she and Paul were required to travel to Rome for the wedding of Italy's Crown Prince Umberto to Princess Marie-José of Belgium, Olga made no attempt to conceal her displeasure, informing the Duke of York that she was 'very envious' of his wife Elizabeth who had remained at home.[26]

The following month, Olga was in the midst of a busy schedule of official duties when Miss Wilson 'calmly' announced that she was leaving; she gave no reason nor did the Princess seek one. Olga had come to the view that 'Binson' did not approve of her[27] although the real issue was similar to that with the previous incumbent: The Princess had lost confidence in the nurse, who had only a 'half-hearted interest in the children' as they were '...just a means of earning her living.'[28] It was left to Binson to arrange for her replacement and, although the salary was a not ungenerous £150 per annum,[29] Olga later learned that Miss Wilson had unhelpfully advised potential applicants that Belgrade was a 'lonely and desolate' place. The Princess also revealed to Foxie that many of the applicants had not 'the foggiest idea as to who "Princess Paul of Yugoslavia" can possibly be.'[30] In the interim, a temporary nurse, Miss Susan Roberts, was appointed, but only after being carefully vetted in England beforehand by Miss Fox.[31] Once again, this latest addition to the household found great favour as she was 'just the type of person

I wanted-cheerful, smiling, yet very firm...' and blessed with 'common sense'.[32] Olga soon reached an agreement with Roberts ('Bobbie') that she would remain in post for a year.[33] Duly reassured, Olga departed for Paris to inspect her parents' new flat on the Avenue Jules Sandeau and later joined Paul in Munich for the Oberammergau Festival. On her return to Bohinj, there was the usual stream of guests including Sir Nevile Henderson, the newly-appointed British Minister in Belgrade with whom she enjoyed the word-game playing Lexicon.[34]

In mid-October, the Prince and Princess returned to snowy Belgrade and the exciting news that Olga's younger cousin Sophie had fallen in love with Prince Christoph of Hesse; the couple were subsequently married, at Kronberg, on 15 December. Tiny was to be the first of Uncle Andrew and Aunt Alice's children to marry, although their remaining daughters would all marry the following year. However, the Hesse wedding took place against the backdrop of a deepening political crisis in Germany, with Adolf Hitler and his National Socialist Party already ensconced as the main party of opposition in the Reichstag.

As the New Year of 1931 dawned, Olga paid a Christmas visit to 'her' Home for Russian Children to distribute toys. She also found time to go sledging and, for the first time since her Swiss exile, tried her hand at skiing. Yet, there was one blot on the festive celebrations: Olga was distressed to discover that her gold evening bag, containing a favourite diamond-studded jade cigarette case (a gift from King Alexander), had been stolen during a New Year party at the American Legation.[35] Despite suffering from a bad cold, the Princess' winter schedule remained busy: She stoically opened her Serbian Crèche's Charity Bazaar, before rushing off to Darmstadt, to attend the wedding of her cousin Cecilie to George Donatus, Hereditary Grand Duke of Hesse.

A most welcome development domestically was an improvement in relations, at nursery level, between Olga's staff and those of the King. This change permeated right to the top as King Alexander-to the Princess' amazement-now proposed a sea trip down the Dalmatian Coast for both nurseries. Although this was subsequently arranged for May, Olga remained wary of any backlash from Queen Marie, as the King lavished 'too much attention' on Alexander and Nicholas.[36]

Throughout the spring, the Princess continued to fret over her cousin Helen's future: Her ex-husband Carol had, as predicted, succeeded in returning to Romania (soon followed by Madam Lupescu) and seized the crown from his son Michael. He also surrounded Helen's home with a police guard and prohibited her from appearing in public.[37] Sitta made a brief visit to Yugoslavia, in early May, to discuss financial matters and Olga rushed to the frontier 'to meet her and cheer her up' as she 'seemed so broken'.[38] After reaching agreements on financial and child access matters with Carol, Helen decided to leave Bucharest to start a new life in Italy.[39] Olga had clearly played a significant role in this outcome, for King Alexander praised her to Paul for being 'full of wisdom and good sense on the question of Sitta and I attribute to her the largest part for succeeding in convincing poor Sitta to make the break which I think to be the best course for her future...'[40]

The Prince and Princess left Belgrade, in early June, for a trip to Paris to celebrate Olga's birthday followed by visit to London for Royal Ascot week. Thereafter, in mid-July, the Princess joined her children and Miss Roberts at Bohinj and was soon firing off another batch of requests to Foxie, which included sending out 'the very best <u>York Ham</u>' for Paul's delectation via the Orient Express.[41] Olga had then to rush to Paris to visit her mother who was struck down with conjunctivitis. She was therefore unable to attend her cousin Theodora's marriage to Berthold, Margrave of Baden at the Neues Schloss on 17 August. However, the recent weddings of Prince Andrew's daughters only served to underline to Olga and a 'worried' Princess Nicholas that there was now a pressing need to find 'suitable' suitors for Elisabeth and Marina, who were 27 and 24 respectively.[42]

In mid-October, Olga and Paul arrived in Scotland for a stay at Abbotsford, the ancestral home of the renowned Victorian novelist, Sir Walter Scott. The Princess loved Scotland noting, 'I can't get over the beauty of this country.'[43] The days were spent motoring through the countryside and visiting Walter Dalkeith and his wife Molly at their nearby home, Eildon Hall. However, the visit was not all about pleasure: The Princess had earlier visited Clydebank to launch the Yugoslavian Navy's Flotilla Leader *Dubrovnik* and she informed a delighted Miss Fox that the occasion had been 'a wonderful success'. [44]

Olga then departed for London to interview applicants selected by the Carnegie House Agency for a post as nurse/governess in Belgrade, to commence in January 1932. This was to replace Miss Roberts, who was due to return to England. The Princess was particularly impressed by Ethel Smith, a 'very sensible' forty-nine-year-old clergyman's daughter. Before finally agreeing to employ her, this increasingly cautious employer made enquiries through an intermediary, to clarify if Ethel was able to knit and sew and would be prepared to wear a uniform. Having passed these hurdles, Miss Smith was then required to agree to Olga's employment terms in writing prior to her service commencing.[45]

In the interim, Paul had consulted the Italian bacteriologist Dr Aldo Castellani and he had finally identified the microbe which was causing the Prince's stomach troubles. In late October, Paul entered Castellani's Putney nursing home for a course of treatment.[46] When Olga came to London, at the end of November, she expected to find her husband fully-recovered but instead found Paul to be 'very weak and painfully thin.' Following discussions with the doctor, it was decided to extend his treatment for a further ten days. In fact, the Princess was so dismayed by the extent of her husband's suffering, that she attended a 'moving' spiritual healing service, taken by a Mr James Hickson.[47]

Paul was discharged from the clinic on 10 December; he and Olga then travelled to Paris for a short stay at the Ritz. Unfortunately their return to Belgrade was postponed as King Alexander and Queen Marie-with whom they were due to travel home-delayed their departure to allow the King to consult with his Parisian doctors and attend a lunch with the French President. The Princess bemoaned to Miss Fox, who was currently holding the fort in Belgrade, 'It's too maddening for words.'[48] Nevertheless, she had an interesting piece of gossip to impart: While in Paris, Mignon had hired a new Norwegian nurse, Ellen Matzow, to assist Miss Crowther.

On the couple's return to Belgrade, the King generously gave Paul a valuable Oriental vase, while the Princess received a 'huge envelope' stuffed with French bank notes.[49] However, the King's relationship with his wife remained fraught and Olga informed Marina that Sandro would sometimes be, 'in one of his teasing moods' when he would talk 'nonsense to Mignon...comparing her with one of his ministers [and] screaming with laughter at his own jokes...'· He also seemed lonely and would often call on the Prince and Princess, at the New Palace, in the afternoons. On other occasions, they would come across him walking in solitary silence out at Dedinje.[50]

Fortunately, young Alexander was doing 'very well' with his schooling thanks to Miss Smith's efforts. By contrast, the Princess cast a rather disapproving eye over Peter's education, or rather the lack of it. According to Miss Crowther, the nine-year-old Crown Prince had not undertaken any lessons for four months and was still read to at bedtime 'like a child of 5'. This led Olga to conclude that, 'They [The King and Queen] seem to be bent on making a half-wit out of him, poor child.'[51]

Regrettably, Paul's health continued to remain a source of concern: After representing the King at the funeral of the assassinated French President Paul Doumer in May, the Prince and his supportive wife journeyed to London for a further two-month course of treatment under Dr Castellani. His digestive problems were probably exacerbated by money worries for an investment in a Swedish match firm had gobbled up much of his capital.[52]

Paul's treatment completed, the couple returned to Slovenia, with the Princess increasingly focused on finding a suitable husband for her sisters. It therefore seems doubtful that the arrival at Bohinj, in September, of the wealthy Bavarian aristocrat (and nephew of the Queen of the

Belgians), Count Karl Theodor ('Toto') Toerring-Jettenbach was simply a coincidence. Indeed, Olga was soon reporting enthusiastically to Marina that Karl Theodor was adopting 'a teasing attitude' with 'Woolly' [Elisabeth] when they were alone together.[53] A few weeks later, Elisabeth joined Olga and Paul on a trip to Munich for the Oktoberfest. Although the trio lunched with Toto and he proved 'awfully nice and friendly', the Princess lamented to Marina that he had not shown 'any special or marked attention to Woolly.'[54]

Subsequently, Olga busied herself with the children and preparations for the Christmas celebrations in Belgrade. As 1933 dawned, she attended a New Year's Day Anglican service at the Anglo-American Club, where she encountered the Sitters, an English couple who ran the local YMCA. They would go to become long-standing friends of both the Prince and Princess. Unfortunately, Miss Crowther's conduct continued to be problematic and she had recently been 'rude' to the King. The latter now asked Olga if Marina-who seemed to be on friendly terms with the Queen-would speak to his wife about 'Crowdie's' behaviour during a forthcoming visit[55]. Olga and Aunt Missy both blamed Mignon's 'lack of dignity' for the current state of affairs.[56]

The Princess' diary remained as busy as ever: She attended the Russian Invalids Ball and paid a visit to the local Srpska Majka (Mothers of Serbia) offices to open the organisation's annual Charity Bazaar. She was also present at a ceremony at which Prince Paul received the Legion d'honneur from the French Minister. Although Olga continued to strike an imposing figure as she carried out these official engagements, she confessed to Marina that she often felt ill-at-ease when she opened some event, 'with a few words and a thumping heart and all eyes glued on me! Ghastly!'[57]

Troublingly, political matters in and around Yugoslavia were again proving difficult. When the King returned home from a visit to Romania, Olga and Paul were taken aback when he informed them that he was 'nervous' over a possible attack by the Italians.[58] The Prince, meanwhile, was 'v[ery] worried' over Alexander's inconsistency on matters of internal policy, as well as the quality of advice he was receiving.[59] Recent attacks on the Catholic church had not gone down well in Croatia, where the Peasant Party leader Vladko Maček was proving a vociferous opponent of the King's autocratic style. Maček was also determined that Croatia should receive a greater degree of autonomy. Other non-Serbian political leaders including Anton Korošec of the Slovenian Peoples' Party and Mehmed Spaho of the Bosnian Moslem Organisation concurred. Unfortunately, all three were arrested in April and sentenced to three years in jail for treason.[60] This was a grave error and reflected the King's inability to keep on top of the political situation. Indeed, Alexander subsequently admitted to an astounded Olga that '[he] doesn't know what to do!!'[61] Matters were not helped by the fact that the King was still living in a 'crushing home atmosphere'[62] for Miss Crowther remained firmly in situ, despite various appeals to Mignon to get 'rid' of her for the sake of the children.[63] It is no wonder the increasingly detached monarch sought refuge alone at Topola, which the Princess thought 'folly.'[64]

The King's actions could also impact on Olga's home life. "Uncle" had recently given Alexander an electric car (known affectionately as a "Bug") which he had 'not really deserved' as his school marks were poor.[65] This apparent award for failure seems to have sent out the wrong message and Miss Smith was at her 'wit's end' in trying to get her charge to focus on his lessons. [66] The "Bug" was eventually taken away but when matters still did not improve, Alexander's 'persistent defiance' earned him a spanking.[67] His rebelliousness continued long into the summer, as did the traditional punishment.

In March, Count Toerring invited Olga, Paul, Elisabeth and Marina to Munich. Unfortunately, the Princess continued to find her host 'v[ery] shy'[68] while Elisabeth was forced to admit that she knew 'nothing of his real feelings.'[69] However, the little group drew solace from the fact that Toto seemed sorry to see them depart.

Back in Belgrade, the Princess often walked up to Kosh, as the view in spring reminded her of Greece. This caused her to wonder 'When will I see it again?'[70] Olga seemed buoyed by recent-if premature-press reports that the Greek monarchy would soon be restored following the re-election of the royalist Panagis Tsaldaris as Prime Minister. She had also heard rumours that Eleftherios Venizelos ('the Devil') [71] was to be court martialled.

The Princess celebrated her 30th birthday, on 11 June, and found it, 'unbelievable to have left the twenties behind for ever.'[72] As Paul was on a visit to England, the celebrations were low-key. On his return, the Prince paid a visit to the King at Dedinje and found him in a 'bad mood.'[73] A few days later, Olga learned that the Palace Director had given Paul, 'the cheerful news that S[andro] has given this house [the New Palace] over to the town for a museum.'[74] By coincidence, Paul and Olga had already been searching for a new home, but it was proving impossible to find anything large enough for their needs, which explains the Princess' terse comment, 'so we must clear out-abroad...as no house suitable here!!'[75] By the next day, her feelings had intensified, '[I] felt knocked on the head all day...[76] The astute Olga also observed, 'It is so hard on poor Pacey [Paul] *who is by far the best friend S[andro] will ever have.*'[77] Was it possible that others were conspiring to get rid of this 'best friend' and his family from Belgrade, in order to promote their own agenda with the increasingly mercurial King?

There was certainly a campaign aimed at discrediting the Princess: The King usually held her in the highest regard and, as we have seen, often confided in her. However, in another talk with Paul on 30 June, Alexander suddenly accused her of being "une intriguante" and "gaffeuse" [a miscaller]. Olga fumed that 'Someone must be telling him lies he believes.'[78] The following day, the distraught Princess called on the King at Dedinje. However, rather than clear the air, the audience seems to have descended into a heated exchange, 'Nothing would persuade him. [He] said we were ungrateful after all he had done for us...'[79] Even after she and Paul had withdrawn to Bohinj, Olga continued to rail against the injustice of the falsehoods that were being propagated against her and noted, 'Still feel stunned.... All illusions about him [the King] gone. [I] can never feel the same [about him] again'. Mignon, she now believed, 'could only be an enemy.'[80] Unsurprisingly, Paul's digestive system was not reacting well to all these pressures and by early July he had lost four kilos in weight.[81]

A few weeks later, the Prince and Princess met the King at Bled for the first time since his previous outburst. He seemed 'v[ery] amiable' and, intriguingly, Mignon claimed 'to know nothing'[82] of the contretemps. Perhaps having tired of all the machinations surrounding her, Olga suddenly longed for a visit to the sea and ventured alone to Trieste for the day by rail, on 1 August, and a welcome reunion with Aunt Bee, Uncle Ali and their sons. They were all currently staying with Amedeo, the Duke of Aosta aboard his yacht at Miramare. The Princess found Amedeo ('Bouby') to be, 'awfully nice and affect[ionate]' as they lunched on a terrace and bathed. Many of Olga's relations feel she had a 'crush' on the Oxford-educated Duke who was tall, cultivated and handsome. Indeed, she lingered so long that she missed her train home, so Paul had to arrange for 'a special one' to transport his wife back to Bohinj.[83]

Chapter 11 Two Weddings and A Funeral

During a late summer visit to Munich, Paul gleaned some 'v[ery] interesting news', which caused him and his wife to take the view that it might be expedient to take Marina with them to England during their autumn visit to settle Alexander into his new boarding school, Ludgrove. The target this time was George V's youngest son, Prince George, as there was now apparently 'no hope' of a romantic match between Marina and the Prince of Wales. However, the Princess was concerned to learn that her cousin Irene was already in London, 'No doubt to catch George too!'[1] Before their departure, Paul was required to travel to Belgrade with the King on official business. The visit went well and Alexander gave the Prince and Princess a 'v[ery] generous sum'[2] as a gift for their forthcoming tenth wedding anniversary. In another volte face, he also announced that he had decided to build another residence at Dedinje, which would be made available for Paul and Olga's use. The couple were even to have a say in the design and layout.[3]

Tantalisingly, on 9 September, a wire arrived from Count Toerring to say he would arrive with his cousin Albrecht the following day at Bohinj. Although the harassed Princess was the perfect hostess, she was ever-watchful for any romantic developments between Elisabeth and the Count. After lunch, on the second day of the visit, she observed: 'Toto quite amiable, [he] sat beside Fael [Elisabeth] in the garden-[he] seems attracted but no further.' With the clock for her own departure for London already ticking, she wondered impatiently, 'What can be the cause?' Somehow, Olga found time to take Alexander out for a drive and 'spoke of a few facts of life to prepare him...'[4] for the start of his schooldays.

Olga, Paul, Marina and Alexander departed Bohinj by train on 12 September and subsequently arrived at London's Brown's Hotel. A week later, the Prince and Princess took Alexander down to Ludlow, where they were introduced to their son's housemaster, Mr Henley, and his 'charming' wife. Although Olga was 'miserable at the parting,'[5] Mr Henley wrote on several occasions to reassure her that Alexander was happy. Nevertheless, before returning to Belgrade, the anxious Princess paid another visit to the school, just to be sure.

Meanwhile, Elisabeth and Count Toerring had remained at Bohinj in the company of Prince and Princess Nicholas, always with the hope of a further romantic development. Finally, on 21 September, while out stalking chamois, the couple realised that they were in love. That evening, Toto acted on these feelings and proposed to Elisabeth in the drawing room.[6] Olga was delighted to receive a telegram, next morning, informing her of the news and noted, 'It has come at last. We could hardly believe it'.[7] Sadly, there was nothing positive to report where Marina and Prince George were concerned.

On 10 October, Olga, Paul and Marina proceeded by rail to Munich where a 'radiant' Elisabeth (who was on a visit to her future in-laws) was waiting to greet them at their hotel.[8] After much family discussion, it was decided that the wedding should take place in January at Schloss Seefeld, the home of Toto's brother Hans Heribert. However, as she prepared to leave Munich, the Princess could not help but notice that the city was 'draped' in Swastika banners as the new German Chancellor, Adolf Hitler, was due to visit the city to open the new Glaspalast.[9] On returning to Bohinj, there was worrying news from Henry Channon in England: Prince George was 'almost certain[ly]' on the verge of becoming engaged to a Lady Ann Wood, a cousin of his wife, Honor! Olga was aghast at this disparate union, writing witheringly, 'What are we coming to?'[10]

The Prince and Princess celebrated their tenth wedding anniversary on 22 October at Bohinj. Touchingly, Paul had bought Princess Nicholas' diamond crown brooch as an anniversary gift for Olga, thus providing his parents-in-law with some vital funds with which to buy Elisabeth's trousseau.[11] Unfortunately, the Prince's ongoing digestive problems then necessitated his departure for treatment in Paris, causing his wife to declare in exasperation, 'If only he was well and strong and less nervous.'[12]

Olga decided to prolong her stay in Slovenia into November. Thereafter, she travelled to Paris to find that Paul's Parisian doctor had 'hit on the microbe' which was making him unwell. The Princess' relief was palpable: 'God give.'[13] She was now able to focus on Elisabeth and accompanied the bride-to-be to the couturier Jean Patou to select her wedding dress and trousseau. Unfortunately, King Alexander made a last-minute request that Olga and Paul should return to Belgrade to help him entertain King Boris and Queen Giovanna of Bulgaria. The Princess was displeased noting it, 'bores us to death...'[14] Nevertheless, she played her role as a co-host to perfection and was rewarded with the gift of a gold and ruby bracelet at the end of the visit by King Boris.

The Prince and Princess returned to Paris in time to join Olga's family for an 'English' Christmas on 25 December. Although Nicholas remained in Belgrade, Alexander joined them from Ludgrove bearing a 'reasonable report' from his headmaster. The latter also indicated that their son 'was a rather more than averagely intelligent boy'.[15] Nonetheless, Olga was somewhat frustrated by her elder child's reticence, and confessed to Foxie, 'I _do_ long sometimes to know his inner feelings and impressions...'[16]

As 1933 drew to a close, Olga and Paul were shocked to learn of a foiled assassination attempt against King Alexander in Zagreb, orchestrated by the Croatian Ustaše revolutionary movement. It was a sign that the simmering pot that was Yugoslavia was now reaching boiling point. Olga ended the year by questioning, 'Why this bad luck?'[17]

In early January, the family travelled by train to a cold and wintry Munich for Elisabeth's nuptials. During the marriage ceremony in the private chapel at Schloss Seefeld, Olga was moved by the singing of the Bavarian choristers and the sight of her 'radiant' sister looking '[so] confident in the future' with a husband who was 'such a dear and adores her.'[18]

By contrast, during a subsequent stopover in Paris en route to London, the Princess experienced, at first hand, the continuing plight of her exiled Russian relatives. A 'gentleman' called on Princess Nicholas with a message from her brother Kirill informing her that he and his family were 'desperate and on the brink of ruin.'[19] Olga made an approach to Lady Zia Wernher, in an attempt to obtain financial assistance for Uncle Kirill. Unfortunately, she felt unable to help.[20]

The Princess was then consumed with worry of her son Alexander's health, as mastoiditis was feared. She spent a whole day sitting at her son's bedside at Ludlow before receiving the relatively good diagnosis that it was actually a swelling in the gland from a chill.[21] Although Olga and Paul left London for Paris on 7 February, Miss Fox was drafted in to look after the boy while he recovered. A concerned Ethel Smith wrote a line to Kate from the King's residence at Dedinje which provides an interesting insight into the contrast in characters of Olga's two sons: 'It has always been difficult to get [Alexander] to express himself' while 'Nicky can do this to the smallest detail.' However, Nicholas required 'very careful handling' for although 'intelligent' he was 'wilful and very impatient of control.'[22]

In Paris, Olga took the chance to make a rare visit to her father's art studio with Marina, while Paul stocked up on some gold bought through Morgan's Bank which he would later send to London for safekeeping.[23] Was he already planning for a future life outside of a troubled Yugoslavia? On their return to Belgrade, the Prince and Princess found the King intent on securing Yugoslavia's borders: In February, a defensive alliance-the Balkan Entente-was signed in Athens by Yugoslavia, Romania, Greece and Turkey. This Pact sought to guarantee the signatories' political independence, as well as curbing the expansionist ambitions of Hungary, Italy, Bulgaria and the Soviet Union. Sadly, Alexander had now become 'the object of fierce hatred' in Croatia and stood accused of treating it as 'a Serbian province administered by bureaucrats from Belgrade and patrolled by Serbian gendarmes'.[24] Indeed, the international press went further and described him as a 'tyrant'.[25]

Meanwhile, Olga was occupied with her own domestic battles: She was furious to discover that, during her absence, Miss Crowther had been 'horrid'[26] to Nicholas on several occasions; while Paul was pressed into hours of conversation by an increasingly fraught King Alexander. There was no escape from these tensions, even over Easter, as the Prince and Princess were living temporarily under the King's roof at Dedinje. Nevertheless, Olga believed that her husband took 'things too much to heart'.[27]

In May, Olga and Paul accompanied Marina to London. The Princess' eyes were still firmly on the ultimate prize-a marriage between her youngest sister and the Prince of Wales.[28] However, she was soon in despair when, after a week, there was still no word from Sir Godfrey Thomas, the Prince of Wales' Private Secretary.[29] Fortuitously, the next day, following lunch with the Channons, Olga, Paul and Marina called on Emerald Cunard, where they found Prince George who proved 'very amiable'.[30] From Paris, Princess Nicholas continued to ramp up the pressure on her eldest daughter by telephone: She was 'very worried' over the lack of contact with the Prince of Wales and informed Olga that she 'ought to ring him up and not try to see him through 3rd people.' However, Paul later consulted Sir Godfrey Thomas who asked them not to do this as 'he'd see to it.'[31] He was good as his word, for next day they received an invitation to Sunday lunch with the Prince at his Sunningdale home, Fort Belvedere. By now, Olga was almost beside herself: 'It's in God's hands and tomorrow will decide us [whether] to stay or leave...'[32] The trio duly ventured to 'the Fort' on 13 May where they found their host 'with some queer friends (2 couples, 2 Americans). Very sociable and nice.' David later took them on a post-prandial tour of his garden, although the Princess observed that, 'He paid no special attention to Marina as we feared' adding ominously, 'He seems to be settled in his life.'[33] It seems likely that one of the Americans was Mrs Wallis Simpson who was already establishing herself as the 'reigning lady'[34] of the Prince's circle, having successfully seen off a previous paramour, Lady Thelma Furness.

Olga now redirected her focus on David's youngest brother, George. On 15 May, she, Paul and Marina attended the opera where they sat in Emerald Cunard's box. Conveniently, Prince George was a fellow guest and promised to lunch with them next day.[35] He proved to be a 'v[ery] nice and quite funny' companion[36] and the little party later went on to tour the National Gallery. While walking through this venerable institution, Prince George casually mentioned that he might make a visit to Yugoslavia in the summer. Marina was delighted to hear this and suddenly became 'anxious' to attend an Evening Court at the Palace that night.[37] An equally enthusiastic Olga immediately contacted Queen Mary who 'arranged it at once.'[38]

The happy trio returned to Paris the following day. However, Princess Nicholas admonished her eldest daughter for not remaining in London with Marina, to pursue matters further with the Prince of Wales. The Princess was surprised at her mother's reaction noting, 'I don't think we could have done more'.[39] Ellen's steely attitude may have been partly dictated by the fact she and Prince Nicholas were being forced to make 'drastic changes' to their lifestyle as their income had lately been much reduced.[40] While Marina ventured to a French spa in the Savoie in an attempt to lose weight, Olga and Paul made a visit to Munich and received the 'wonderful news' that Elisabeth was pregnant.[41] The Princess would subsequently admit to Foxie that '[I] long to be in the same state!'[42]

Back in Slovenia, Olga learned that during her absence Yugoslavia had signed commercial agreement with Nazi Germany and King Alexander had employed a tutor from England, Cecil Parrot, to oversee Peter's education. Worryingly, Parrot considered his charge to be at least two years behind with his schoolwork[43] and it was subsequently decided that Peter should attend an English preparatory school at Cobham, Sandroyd, which the Princess felt was 'sure to do him some good.'[44]

At the end of July, in neighbouring Austria a political crisis arose when the Chancellor, Engelbert Dollfuss, was assassinated by National Socialists in a failed coup attempt. This event set alarm bells ringing in Belgrade, whilst it also irritated Mussolini sufficiently to deploy part of the Italian army along the Austrian border (and threaten Germany with war should it attempt to invade Austria). As if on cue, on 2 August, Hindenburg, the German President died and Olga rightly predicted that Hitler, 'will be more powerful than ever.'[45]

In the meantime, a wire was received at Bohinj, on 5 August, from Prince George asking if he might come out to Slovenia around the 15th. Olga seems to have been wrong-footed, confiding to her diary that, 'We never thought he would.'[46] The plane carrying Prince George and his aide Major Humphrey Butler arrived at Ljubljana late on the afternoon of 16 August, with the exhausted duo reaching Bohinj just in time for dinner. Over the next few days, 'Georgy' passed his time shooting and fishing, but there was no sign of an impending engagement! However, Olga's Uncle Christopher found that 'The atmosphere grew more and more electric'.[47] On the evening of 20 August, after all the guests-save Marina and George-had retired, Prince Christopher discovered he had left his cigarette case downstairs. When he went to retrieve it, the Prince noticed through the open drawing room door that Marina and George were seated close together on the sofa and he decided to beat a hasty retreat upstairs. Apparently, this had been the crucial moment when Georgy proposed to Marina.[48] The latter was soon rushing upstairs to impart her news to an overjoyed Olga who later admitted that 'my mind reels to think of all it means.'[49]

Subsequently, Olga and Paul accompanied Marina and George to the Salzburg Music Festival where the couple's betrothal was confirmed by Prince George during an impromptu press conference at the Hotel de l'Europe on 29 August. Back at Bohinj, an exhausted Olga informed Miss Fox that they were 'completely submerged' by congratulatory telegrams and her brain was 'in a whirl'. However, she was happy with the match, as George and Marina-who were already en route to King George V's Scottish summer residence at Balmoral-were 'made for each other.' Nevertheless, the Princess admitted that she was in 'despair' not to be joining her sister in Scotland, 'as we have always shared so much together and now it seems so sad, we can't'.[50]

In late September, Marina wrote to Olga from Balmoral with the news that the wedding would take place on 29 November. The Princess replied immediately and, as she had already been pondering the possibility that Nicholas might be asked to be a pageboy, she now planted the seed with the bride-to-be noting, 'It would be rather sweet [him] between the 2 York girls, besides being the nearest on your side...'[51] However, soon thereafter, familial relations became somewhat tense: While closing up Bohinj for the winter, Olga received a telephone call from Paul in Belgrade saying that he had just received a letter from Princess Nicholas which left him 'v[ery] upset.' It mentioned the 'various' relations who were to be accommodated at Buckingham Palace for the wedding; however, the list did not include Olga or Paul or their children. Indeed, Paul felt so aggrieved that he indicated he would not attend the event.[52] The Princess immediately wrote to her mother to say that she felt 'sad, hurt and very disappointed' to be 'treated like outsiders!'[53]

Olga returned to Belgrade on 30 September to set up home in a modest villa in Tolstojeva Ulica. This would serve as the family's residence until the move to the new residence at Dedinje in the spring of 1936. However, the matter of the wedding arrangements continued to fester and Olga's longtime friend, Lilia Ralli 'promised' to speak to Marina about the matter.[54] She was as good as her word and soon 'everything was arranged' for the extended family to be housed together at Buckingham Palace.[55] However, Marina too was determined to have her say and informed Olga that she had been distressed by the tone of her recent letter to their mother. The Princess responded to her youngest sister in a conciliatory tone indicating she was 'frightfully sorry to have upset you...'[56]

In the interim, King Alexander had asked Olga and Paul to join him and Mignon on an overnight trip to Kotor prior to his departure, on 6 October, for a five-day State Visit to France. He was leaving at a time of intense Ustaše guerrilla activity and security around him had recently been tightened.[57] The little party left Belgrade on 5 October and motored to Kotor where they embarked the *Dubrovnik*. That evening, Olga sat on deck chatting with the King about his forthcoming visit and begged him to take a bullet-proof vest. Alexander joked, 'For Bulgaria yes, but surely not for France?'[58] Next morning, after the group visited an old coastal church dedicated to St Sava, the King re-embarked the *Dubrovnik* to sail to Marseille, while Olga, Paul and Queen Marie returned to Belgrade by train. As Mignon had recently been debilitated by a gallbladder complaint, she decided to seek treatment in Paris prior to rendezvousing with the King in Marseille. She left Belgrade on 8 October.[59]

On 9 October, Prince Nicholas' younger sister Marie ('Aunt Minny') and a friend arrived in Belgrade; Olga took them on a visit to Avala, while Paul busied himself at his museum. Meanwhile, in Marseilles, the King had disembarked the *Dubrovnik* to be greeted at the Quai des Belges by the French Foreign Minister, Louis Barthou. During the ceremonial drive into the city, a man ran out of the crowd at Stock Exchange Square and with a cry of 'Vive Le Roi' leapt onto the running board of the car and fired several shots at the King's chest. Alexander was rushed to the police prefecture, and although doctors were summoned, he died within the hour.[60]

In Belgrade, Olga and Paul were taking tea in the drawing room of their villa, when a servant entered at 6.35pm and told the Prince that there was a telephone call from Marseilles. When Paul returned, he relayed the news that an assassination attempt had been made on 'our beloved Sandro's' life and he was 'mortally wounded'. One can only imagine the atmosphere in the room. Fortunately, the King had left stipulations in his will for the appointment of a Regency Council composed of three Regents: Paul was named as Head Regent and he was to be joined by Ivo Perović, the Governor of Croatia and Radenko Stanković, a Professor of Medicine at Belgrade University. The Regency Council would act until the new King, 11-year-old Peter, reached his majority at the age of 18, in September 1941. Olga found it 'impossible to grasp the immensity of this tragedy'[61] as she joined her husband at the King's home at Dedinje, but was reassured by Paul's 'wonderfully calm and strong' demeanour.[62]

Henceforth, Paul would be known as the Prince Regent and now became the tangible symbol of the monarchy, both in Yugoslavia and overseas. Olga also had an important role to play as his Consort; indeed, she would effectively become Queen in all but name. However, for the moment, in Mignon's absence, it was left to the Princess to undertake the delicate task of breaking the news of their father's death to his sons Andy and Tommy.[63] Thereafter, as she awaited the arrival of King Peter and the (now) Dowager Queen by train from France, the Princess focused on preparing the ballroom of the Old Palace for the late King's Lying-in-State. Meanwhile, the international press now laid the blame for the assassination firmly at the door of Ante Pavelić and the Ustaše.[64] The assassin was later identified as a Bulgarian, Vlado Chernozemski, who had close links with the Internal Macedonian Revolutionary Organization (IMRO) and Ustaše training camps in Italy.[65] However, as far as Prince Paul was concerned, King Alexander had been 'murdered by Mussolini.'[66]

King Peter and his party arrived in Belgrade by train at 9 am on 13 October, to a city where the buildings and lampposts were draped in black. As she stepped forward to offer her condolences, the Princess noted that 'the poor Queen' was 'wonderfully brave and resigned.'[67] She also found it 'heart-breaking' to observe 'little Peter' standing 'in his father's place'.[68] However, by the time the late King's mortal remains reached Belgrade two days later, Olga was beginning to grasp the enormity of the task facing Paul and herself. She informed Foxie that 'It is like a hideous nightmare from which alas there is no awakening, only God in his mercy can uphold us'. While King Peter and the Prince Regent remained heavily guarded, the Princess welcomed the arriving dignitaries, who included her parents and Marina, along with her fiancé Prince George (who was representing his father King George V). Their presence provided the beleaguered Princess with some much-needed support and she confided to Miss Fox that she was 'so happy to have them.'[69] Following a moving funeral service conducted by Patriarch Varnava at the Cathedral on 18 October, Alexander's coffin was taken by train to Oplenac from where it was carried aloft by military veterans to the Karageorgević mausoleum in St George's Church for burial.

An array of family challenges now faced the Prince and Princess: Although the new King and the Dowager Queen remained at the Royal Palace at Dedinje with their respective households, there was the added complication that the real authority lay elsewhere, with Paul and the other Regents. Another difficulty was the continued presence of Queen Marie of Romania; she had formed the opinion that her daughter Mignon seemed incapable of acting on her own and was keen to dispense matriarchal advice.[70] Perhaps at her mother's prompting, the Dowager Queen soon presented the Prince Regent with a list titled, "Queen

Marie's Requests".[71] Although Mignon received 'a generous allowance'[72] King Peter's finances were 'in a very confused state' due to the on-going construction of new residences at Dedinje, Miločer and Bled.[73] There also appears to have been friction over the new King's education: According to contemporary press reports, Peter and his mother were in favour of him returning to school in England. However, the Regency Council decided that he should be educated in Belgrade,[74] for in these increasingly dangerous times it would be impossible to guarantee the King's safety over such a long and exposed route. The late King's sister Helen ('Tabé') was also proving troublesome: According to Philip of Hesse, she was creating 'an atmosphere of poison' against Paul and Olga by presenting herself as 'the poor innocent martyr hunted to death by her wicked relations.'[75]

Fortunately, there was at least one bit of welcome news: Mignon had finally agreed to Miss Crowther's departure. In her diary entry, Olga was blunt: 'Our private opinion is that she has neglected Peter in favour of Tommy and Andy...'[76] Temporarily buoyed by this news, she departed for Paris by train, on 4 November, to assist Marina with her wedding preparations. The Princess admitted to Kate Fox that she 'simply hated leaving Paul at this moment but it has to be...'[77] On her arrival in Paris, the Princess was taken aback by the presence of 'heaps of detectives' tasked with guarding her.[78] There was also a stark reminder of Alexander's assassination when she attended a 'very impressive' Memorial Service in the late King's memory at the Arc de Triomphe on 10 November.[79] However, overall, the Princess felt it had been a 'cosy' time 'being all together again for the last time before Marina flies away.'[80] Meanwhile, the Princess' new position in Yugoslavia was already being acknowledged in the international press, with one publication headlining a feature, 'Beauty Ranks High in Yugoslavia,' below which was a prominent photograph of Olga who is described as 'the wife of Regent Prince Paul who really rules Yugoslavia for the boy king Peter'.[81]

On the morning of 21 November, the bridal party left Paris by special train and were greeted by Prince George on their arrival at Dover. Olga subsequently visited St James' Palace to inspect the wedding gifts and marvelled at the 'incredible quantity' of furniture, silver, china and pictures on display.[82] However, when Paul arrived from Belgrade, a few days later, the Princess was immediately struck by his gaunt appearance.[83] The wedding day found Olga in 'a highly emotional state' which is unsurprising given that word had just been received of a plot to assassinate her husband. The authorities were taking no chances and two swarthy Serbian bodyguards, as well as the Head of the British Special Branch, were immediately assigned to guard the Prince Regent.[84]

Interestingly, the couple had already discussed such an eventuality, as Paul revealed in a letter, dated 3 November, to his friend Jock Balfour: 'Should anything happen to me-it would be a wonder if it didn't-I beg of you to look after Olga and the children. *I've already told her to consult you on every occasion where she needs sound and reliable advice...*'[85] Meanwhile, from her front row seat in the Sanctuary, the Princess looked on, as to the hymn "Gracious Spirit, Holy Ghost", her beloved Marina, looking adorable in a silver and white Molyneux dress and diamond fringe tiara, processed up the Nave of the Abbey on the arm of a proud Prince Nicholas. The marriage was solemnised by the Archbishop of Canterbury, Cosmo Lang and, henceforth, Marina would hold the title of Her Royal Highness the Duchess of Kent (Prince George having recently been created Duke of Kent).

Chapter 12 Queen in all but Name

When Olga and Paul returned to Belgrade on 8 December, the Princess fretted that her husband had 'so much to cope with.'[1] This included 'a very unpleasant' meeting with the Dowager Queen at Dedinje, on 15 December, during which she demanded 'to have a say in the Regency [Council]'. To his credit, Paul stood firm to the wishes of King Alexander's will.[2] This altercation must have taken its toll on the harassed Regent as his ongoing stomach problems flared up again. Olga did her best to smooth the troubled waters and escorted Mignon to Topola, on what would have been her late husband's forty-sixth birthday, to lay flowers on his grave. She also tried to help her husband relax by accompanying him on long walks after lunch or organising shooting trips with Sir Nevile Henderson.[3]

On 19 December, Prince and Princess Nicholas arrived from Paris with Alexander who was on his Christmas school break. He informed his mother that he was not enjoying his time at school and this was reflected in a poor academic report. The Princess proved empathetic and made 'allowances for the various events which lately upset him'.[4] Thereafter, Mignon's sister Elisabetha arrived for a two-week stay, Olga noting coldly, 'I can't say we rejoice to see her.'[5] The Greek Queen was now separated from King George and living on an estate in Romania.

The Prince Regent, meanwhile, faced his first political test: In late December 1934, the Yugoslav cabinet resigned after disagreements between Prime Minister Uzonović and Foreign Minister Jevtić, (the so-called 'strong men' of Yugoslav politics[6]). It was Jevtić whom Paul would subsequently appoint as Prime Minister following consultations with the Slovenian Clerical Party leader, Father Anton Koroshetz and Dr Mehmed Spaho, who represented Yugoslavia's Moslem population. In addition, Olga was annoyed to receive a letter from Marina stating that she and Prince George were not being allowed to come to Belgrade for the Orthodox Christmas celebrations for 'political reasons,'[7] this despite Sir Nevile Henderson assuring her that the British Foreign office were 'all for it.'[8]

As 1935 dawned, Prince Paul continued to find the change of pace exacting. It did not help that their current residence, a suburban villa, was too small 'and always full of people'.[9] Furthermore, Paul was 'depressed and pessimistic for now and [the] future' causing the Princess to ponder,

'How can I help him?'[10] However, within days, the Prince received a flattering letter from Philip of Hesse stating that the Regent's deft handling of King Alexander's funeral had impressed the Third Reich's representative, the Luftwaffe Commander-in-Chief, Hermann Goering. Indeed, the Prince had 'made a good friend' in Goering whose 'greatest wish' was that the Regent should visit the 'new' Germany so that he and Hitler would 'be able to prove their friendship.'[11]

In the interim, the Princess was 'thrilled' by the news that her sister Elisabeth had given birth to a son, Hans-Veit, on 11 January. Olga subsequently attended the christening of her new-born nephew in Munich and informed Miss Fox that 'the joy of seeing Woolly and her baby ... was indescribable.'[12] On her return to Belgrade, the Princess had cause to reflect on her relationship with Nicholas and noted that while Paul was 'apt to spoil' the child, 'he knows there's no nonsense with me.'[13] Otherwise, Olga was much occupied with her growing round of official duties which included daily audiences and hosting state lunches for visiting diplomats. Fortunately, she benefited greatly from the assistance provided by her faithful Lady-in-Waiting, Stanka Lozanić ('Loz'), who had recently become engaged to the British journalist Patrick Maitland. Furthermore, the Princess gradually made use of her position as Consort to effect some changes at Court: She organised new liveries for the chauffeurs and footmen and asked Dr Slavko Gruitch, the Court Marshall, to arrange for the introduction of the traditional Orthodox Lenten services she had so missed since arriving in Belgrade.

By mid-January, Paul had arranged for the release of most of the interned political leaders including Vladko Maček, in the hope that this might encourage dialogue and, eventually, an agreement between the Serbs, Croats and Slovenes. This was all the more pressing given that Parliamentary elections were due to be held in May. However, the run-up to these was marred by violence which an exasperated Prince Regent roundly condemned.[14] The Princess noted forlornly that even after a 'heavy day' her exhausted husband slept badly.[15] Matters were not helped by the news that Sir Nevile Henderson was due to be replaced as British Minister, in the late summer. Nevertheless, this change would be somewhat tempered by the arrival of Paul's friend, Jock Balfour, as the British Chargé d'affaires.

Another concern for Olga, in the spring, was the fluid political situation in Greece. She noted there had been 'serious revolution' against the People's Party government of Panagis Tsaldaris with most of the Greek naval fleet backing 'the fiend'[16], Venizelos. Happily, the Tsaldaris government was able to quell the revolt and later purged the armed forces of Venizelist and Republican forces. The Princess also continued to take a keen interest in Soviet affairs: A Yugoslav violinist and his wife, who had recently worked in the Soviet Union, called on her to give an account of conditions there, the details of which were 'enough to drive me insane.'[17]

Olga was overjoyed to receive a letter from Marina, in late March, informing her that she was pregnant. This was news that she was soon able to share with Princess Nicholas who arrived in early April from Cannes for the Easter celebrations. The Princess continued to reach out to King Peter, who was 'delighted' to be invited regularly for Sunday lunch with her family.[18] She also remained keen to foster the friendship between the King and Alexander through joint riding and gymnastic lessons. Nevertheless, the education of King Peter and his brothers was proving troublesome: Cecil Parrott informed the beleaguered Regent that he felt totally ignored by Peter's new Governor.[19]

As devoted Anglophiles, the Prince and Princess celebrated the Silver Jubilee of Britain's King George V at a celebratory Te Deum at the Cathedral on 6 May, followed by dinner at the British Legation. Thereafter, Olga threw herself into welcoming the French Fleet who were on a "Friendship Visit" to Yugoslavia, under the command of Admiral Mouget. Fortuitously, the French visit happened to coincide with the Princess' four-day solo visit down the Dalmatian Coast, which included the christening and a tour of 'her' ship, the *Princesa Olga,* in Split, on 23 May. This duty completed, Olga then embarked the French naval vessel *Tartu* for the much-anticipated courtesy call during which she posed happily with the ship's company for a group photograph and proposed a rousing toast 'to the glory of the French navy (!)'[20]

Olga also spent much of the early summer with sittings for a bust by the prominent Croatian sculptor Toma Rosandić. She continued to worry over the difficulties of Paul's situation, but felt 'incapable of helping him' as it was 'all so complicated.'[21] The Princess was underselling herself for, through her regular post-dinner chats with the late King and her husband, she had gained a clear understanding of the vagaries of the Yugoslav political environment. Certainly, she was the one person who was ideally placed to provide the Prince Regent with a sympathetic-and totally confidential-ear. Jock Balfour too proved understanding and, when time permitted, Paul and Olga would escape to his house for tea. Indeed, the British colony would continue to remain the Princess' natural milieu as she attended lectures at the English Club or met up with the Sitters.

In early June, Elisabeth and her son Hans-Veit arrived in Belgrade. Her visit happened to coincide with that of Hermann Goering, who was accompanied by his new wife Emmy and Philip of Hesse.[22] Germany was following up on the earlier overtures made by the Hessian Prince, particularly in relation to developing trade and political links with

Yugoslavia. While Paul received Goering for a reassuring 'long and important talk', Olga and Elisabeth entertained his 'very nice' wife and later attended a lavish party at the German Legation.[23] Thereafter, while the rest of the German party departed for Poland and Hungary, Philip of Hesse flew to Athens, arriving just in time for the Greek elections on 9 June. These were won by an alliance of the pro-royalist Peoples' Party and National Radical Party. It would be safe to assume that Philip had discussed his solo visit beforehand with Olga (who remained totally focused on the restoration of the Greek monarchy). Indeed, during a subsequent stopover in Belgrade, on 19 June, he was invited to lunch with the Princess who noted, tantalisingly, that he 'saw and heard a lot down there.'[24] Hesse would return to Belgrade the following month bringing 'some messages' from Hitler and toys from Goering for Alexander and Nicholas.[25] For Paul, Philip, with his close links to the German political elite, was clearly a useful contact to have. Furthermore, as a son-in-law of the King of Italy, he was also ideally placed to know of any developments in the fluid Italian political situation. This information could be passed on to the Yugoslav government who were rightly wary of Italy's expansionist ambitions along the Dalmatian Coast.

In the Yugoslav May elections, Jevtić's government held on to power, although there was considerable support for Maček's United Opposition Party. The latter refused to take their places in the Skupština (Parliament), as they felt the electoral system was "weighted" in favour of the government. The Prince Regent faced this latest challenge robustly and, on 21 June, held a meeting with Maček, who emphasised the need for a change to the Yugoslav constitution so as to allow Croatia greater autonomy. Although Paul was empathetic, he stressed that as a "caretaker" of the country on behalf of King Peter, he was unwilling to support any major constitutional change.[26] Olga took the view that Maček was 'full of good intentions.'[27] Shortly thereafter, the Jevtić government fell and Milan Stojadinović's newly-formed Yugoslav Radical Union won the next general election on a platform of introducing liberal reforms.

The family now travelled to Bohinj for a much-needed summer holiday. However, the Princess was dismayed to find their retreat was, 'All the same yet somehow changed.'[28] With the recent elevation in the couple's status, security was much tighter and a large wooden fence had been erected around the whole property and was patrolled by sentries. Furthermore, the house had lost its homely feel, as the family were always surrounded by a large official entourage. Meanwhile, news came through that King George's divorce from Elisabetha of Romania had finally been granted. The Princess, with an eye to the imminent restoration of the Greek monarchy, felt it was 'much better' to happen 'now than later.'[29] Indeed, Olga continued to canvas effectively on behalf of 'Georgie' from Slovenia and, on 15 July, held a lunch in honour of the Greek Royalist politician, Georgios Kondylis. He subsequently enthused to King George about the 'wonderful reception' he had received at Bohinj from Olga and indicated this had 'strengthened his determination to serve the cause of the restoration.'[30] However, the biggest prize was left until last: On 3 August, the Greek Prime Minister, Panagis Tsaldaris, joined the family for lunch. Until now, Tsaldaris had seemed to lack enthusiasm over the restoration issue, but his encounter with this charming, yet steely Greek Princess clearly focused his mind for he was soon making 'amiable remarks' to the Greek press about Olga and now agreed to hold a plebiscite on the monarchy's future.[31]

As July drew to a close, the Princess was much weakened from constant attacks of nausea. However, she was preoccupied by worries over Paul who was suffering from painful myolysis[6] in one of his arms. An operation to provide the Prince with some relief was undertaken in the bathroom at Bohinj on 19 August. Milan Stojadinović would later claim that the Princess had informed him that the arm problem had been caused by Mignon striking the Prince in the course of a heated argument.[32]

In late August, Olga learned that she was pregnant with her third child. The Princess confided to Foxie that she was, 'deeply grateful for this wonderful blessing and even if it's late it is all the more welcome and will be a great comfort to me in many ways.'[33] After hosting a Session of the Petite Entente powers at Bled, Olga bid farewell to Miss Smith, who was returning to London to work in Marina's household. While Ethel became 'very upset' as she took her leave of a 'tearful' Nicholas, the Princess was by now reconciled to such staff changes, noting briskly in her diary, 'another chapter of life closed.'[34] Fortunately, Miss Peters, the new governess, seemed 'nice and sensible'.[35] However, Olga was concerned to learn that Alexander remained unhappy at Ludgrove, despite his housemaster's best efforts.[36]

The 'serious' European political situation continued to trouble the Princess and when Italy invaded Abyssinia on 3 October, Yugoslavia joined other members of the League of Nations in imposing sanctions against the aggressor which, until now, had been the country's main trading partner. Indeed, the Slavs were now so wary of Italy's territorial ambitions (and apparent desire to 'dismember'[37] their country), that those in power were increasingly of the view that closer economic ties with Germany might put a check on Mussolini's aspirations. This suited

---

[6] A break down in muscle tissue.

Hitler and by mid-1936, Yugoslavia's import and export trade had largely passed into German hands.

Despite these external pressures, Olga and Paul tried to relax and picnicked together by a castle at a lovely spot called Brdo. They were so enchanted that the Prince Regent later purchased the residence using his own private funds. Anyway, Paul had felt obliged to relinquish Bohinj as, although King Alexander had gifted the property to his cousin, the title deeds had never been formally transferred into the Prince's name.[38] From Athens came the troubling news that the Tsaldaris government had been overthrown in a coup organised by Georgios Kondylis. With the plebiscite on the monarchy's future due on 3 November, the Princess was concerned to learn, on 10 October, that martial law had been declared. Nevertheless, she continued to canvas for the Greek monarchy's restoration from Belgrade, resolutely receiving a deputation of loyal Greeks who had travelled north from Salonika.[39]

The Prince and Princess visited London in late October. Olga rushed to the Kent's London home in Belgrave Square to see Marina's new-born son, Edward, and then paid a visit to her obstetrician, Mr Gilliat, who was 'v[ery] satisfied' with the progress of her pregnancy.[40] During this visit, the Princess dined with the Prince of Wales and Mrs Simpson at Fort Belvedere. While familiarity did not exactly breed contempt, it caused Olga to form the opinion that David was 'rather pathetic.'[41] She fretted too that Paul was often left 'completely dead' following long discussions with British officials at the Foreign Office.[42]

On 3 November, Greece's King George came to dine with the Princess at Belgrave Square and informed his delighted cousin that 85%[7] of the Greek people had voted for his return. She delayed her own departure for Yugoslavia in order to attend an 'awfully moving' thanksgiving service for the Hellenic monarchy's restoration at the Greek Orthodox Church.[43] She later joined the Prince of Wales at Victoria Station to bid Georgie and his brother Paul farewell as they set off on their journey homewards to Athens.

Back home in Belgrade, a sleep-deprived Paul continued to be beset by 'awful worries'[44] while Olga was astonished to learn that her cousin Georgie was contemplating pardoning the former Greek Prime Minister Eleftherios Venizelos and equally horrified to discover that Konstantinos Demertzis ('a Venizelist Professor') had been appointed as the next Prime Minister.[45] When she later watched a film of the King's return to Athens, rather than be happy, she felt 'so upset.'[46] Meanwhile, in England, Auntie Toria died after suffering a gastric haemorrhage. Olga rightly felt

---

[7] The final tally was 97.9% in favour.

that her brother King George V, 'would mind it awfully.'[47] Touchingly, the old spinster left her home, Coppins, to the Duke of Kent in her will.

Although the practical-minded Princess continued to oversee works at the new house at Dedinje, a persistent pain in one of her legs forced her to cancel official engagements.[48] The political ramifications of Italy's recent invasion of Abyssinia continued to unfold and, on 18 December, the British Foreign Secretary, Sir Samuel Hoare, resigned following his failure to reach a negotiated settlement. He was replaced by Anthony Eden, who had studied alongside Paul at Christ Church. Unfortunately, these two individuals 'entertained a strong mutual dislike'[49] which did not bode well for future Anglo-Yugoslav relations.

To the Princess' delight, Alexander ('Quiss') arrived home on 21 December for his Christmas holiday break. His presence helped to ease relations with Mignon as the two continued to enjoy a good rapport.[50] As 1936 dawned, the Toerrings arrived to join in the Orthodox Christmas festivities and the Princess noted that her baby was, 'getting very lively and active'.[51] Olga then happened to read a newspaper report which stated that King George V was ill with bronchitis; this was later confirmed by the Duke of Kent who added that, 'there was no hope.'[52] The King died two days later and the Princess seemed stunned: 'One can't grasp all it means nor that David is now Edward VIII!'[53] Paul left Belgrade, on 24 January, to attend the funeral while his wife had to content herself with listening to the service on the radio. In the Prince's absence, Olga received Prime Minister Stojadinović: The wily politician was all sugar and the Princess learned that 'Pacey's journey [to England] has lifted his prestige enormously here.'[54]

On Paul's return, Olga observed with anxiety that her husband was increasingly worried over 'exterior politics.'[55] Of particular concern, was the German occupation of the Rhineland in violation of the 1919 Treaty of Versailles. Equally disturbing, was an attempt on the Yugoslav Prime Minister's life whilst he was delivering a speech in parliament. Stojadinović would subsequently allege that the Princess informed him that she was convinced-as was Prince Paul-that the shooting was an attempt to start a coup, led by the Army Minister, General Pierre Jivković, but with the tacit approval of the Dowager Queen.[56]

After giving her final audience on 9 March, Olga focused on moving to her new home at Dedinje in time for the birth of her third child. She had already arranged for a priest to bless Beli Dvor [The White Palace], in advance of the family taking up residence on 15 March. Fittingly, Jock Balfour and his wife were the couple's first guests. They thought the neo-Palladian residence, which was furnished with Adam-style chandeliers, a delicate collection of late 18th century parcel-gilt chairs, tilt-top tea tables, Sèvres porcelain and Savonnerie tapestries, 'lovely.' However,

Olga felt Paul was being denied the chance to fully enjoy his new home, as he was 'devoured with worry and bitterness' over the news that France had failed to react militarily against Germany, following the recent remilitarisation of the Rhineland. [57] The Prince had probably concluded that Hitler would now feel free to continue with his dangerous expansionist policies elsewhere on the Continent.

Princess Nicholas arrived in Belgrade, on 19 March, to be by her daughter's side for the accouchement. However, as April dawned, the baby had still not arrived and the doctor refused to induce the birth.[58] Finally, on the evening of 6 April, Olga went into labour and, aided by her mother, gave birth, in the early hours of 7 April, to a girl, who weighed-in at 7 pounds 6 ounces. The Princess was filled with 'such heavenly joy' at the birth of 'my little daughter' and calmly looked on from her bed as Ethel Roberts, who had been recalled temporarily to Belgrade, gave the new-born her first bath in front of the bedroom fire. Thereafter, a priest arrived to bless both mother and daughter.[59] Olga remained in bed over Easter, but was soon up and about and making regular visits to the nursery to breastfeed the infant, as she was determined not to use 'artificial' products.[60] The baby was christened Elizabeth (Jelisaveta) by the Patriarch in Beli Dvor's impressive Main Salon. 'Pixie' would prove to be a welcome distraction for her harassed father.[61]

On 11 June, Dr Hjalmar Schacht, the President of the German Reichsbank, paid a two-day visit to Belgrade, in an attempt to foster closer relations with Yugoslavia through the provision of increased German economic aid. Schacht also brought a thought-provoking message from Goering, which Stojadinović passed on to Paul, 'Germany is willing to furnish us [with] complete security against Hungary and Italy.'[62]

On the domestic front, there were continuing problems over Alexander's education at Ludgrove. Mr Parrott (currently in England), eventually arranged for the boy to be moved to a new preparatory school, Chartridge Hill, news which the Princess found 'such a relief'.[63] Olga was also concerned about Nicholas' education, as she felt that his governess lacked 'authority with him.'[64] Miss Peters conceded that her intelligent charge would now benefit from being sent to boarding school in England.[65]

In late June, the family moved to Bled to stay at King Peter's Villa Suvobor until their new residence at Brdo was completed. This coincided with the arrival of Elizabeth's new nurse, Miss Ede, from England. Olga therefore had to bid goodbye to the faithful Miss Roberts and, on this occasion, they both 'sobbed.'[66] Indeed, the combination of house moves, staff changes and the physical demands of a new baby had left Olga exhausted and susceptible to severe headaches. Fortuitously, Miss Fox arrived on 1 July and, of course, she and the Princess 'talked without end.'[67] It helped too that Kate approved of Miss Ede and was happy to relieve the nurse as required. However, there was no such respite for the Prince: To Olga's chagrin, even when on holiday, her husband was subject to constant interruptions by officials (or 'his daily bores'[68] as she came to refer to them).

The family relocated to Brdo on 1 August and within days were receiving their first guests, Prince and Princess Nicholas. However, Olga 'trembled' for a week over the possibility that King Edward VIII and his paramour Mrs Simpson 'might descend on us' en route to a cruise holiday departing from Šibenik.[69] Her worst fears were realised when the duo arrived at the Yugoslav border, on 9 August, aboard a private railway car (provided by Mussolini) which was attached to the rear of the Orient Express. The Prince Regent greeted them and brought the couple by car to Brdo for a brief visit. While the Princess noted that David and his party, 'all admired the place hugely'[70] she was also subtly able to indicate her displeasure at Mrs Simpson's presence by not receiving her as the King's lady.[71] Nonetheless, next day, 'a v[ery] amiable wire of thanks...' arrived from the British monarch. [72]

In late August, Olga and Paul held a housewarming party for some of their closest friends including Lilia Ralli, the Channons and the Balfours. Thereafter, Paul and Georgy Kent left for Munich, the former 'happy as a schoolboy on holiday' at his brief release from duty.[73] On 19 September, Alexander departed by rail for England, accompanied by his guard, Captain Prosen. Although Quiss was enjoying his new school, his mother remained concerned about the poor quality of the dental treatment her son was receiving in London. A new dentist was found in Harley Street but Miss Fox was instructed to inform him that 'On no account must he alter or take out anything'. The Princess added for emphasis, 'I hope I have made myself clear...'[74] Whilst Olga certainly appears to have been demanding of her old Nurnie, she was also incredibly kind and made substantial bi-annual contributions towards the running costs of Miss Fox's London flat.[75] Fortuitously, Elizabeth was proving to be a welcome salve and the besotted Princess admitted to Miss Fox that, 'She always comes to my room after tea to kick on the sofa and I simply can't tear myself away from her...' [76]

Just as the Prince and Princess were preparing to leave for London to attend a charity concert at the Yugoslav Legation, the Duke of Kent telephoned to forewarn them that Mrs Simpson's recent divorce from her husband Ernest was 'much spoken of, and that if the King now chose to marry her, the marriage would be morganatic.' Queen Mary, he added, was 'ill about it.'[77] Prior to their departure, Olga and Paul bid farewell to

Prince and Princess Nicholas, who were returning to Greece for the first time in fourteen years to attend the reinterment at Tatoi, on 22 November, of the mortal remains of the various royal family members, including Queen Olga, who had died while in exile. The Princess was 'in despair not to be able to go down myself...'[78]

Paul departed Belgrade first, bound for Brdo where he had arranged to meet Maček. According to the latter's memoirs, the two men mostly discussed art and other matters unrelated to Yugoslavia' internal political situation. Nevertheless, the meeting was a success in so far as Maček found the Prince Regent to be cultivated and, from his perspective as a Croat, devoid of the zealous Serb patriotism of King Alexander.[79] Meanwhile, Olga's latest charity bazaar proved to be a great success, in part due to the fact that 'everyone' wanted copies of a fund-raising postcard which featured a photograph of Elizabeth with her mother.[80] It was therefore a contented Olga who left Belgrade by rail, on 9 November, to rendezvous with Paul at Kranj.

In London, the Princess was delighted to be by her sister's side again, especially since Marina was now heavily pregnant with her second child. However, Olga remained anxious about the growing influence of Mrs Simpson over the King which was the talk of a cocktail party at the Channon's on 12 November. What she thought of Mrs Simpson's attendance, the following evening, at the charity concert at the Yugoslav Legation in aid of Dr Katherine MacPhail's English-Yugoslav Hospital at Sremska Kamenica (described in the American press as Wallis' 'debut in London diplomatic society'[81]) might best be left to the imagination. The Princess was certainly out of sorts that evening and complained in her diary of, 'crowds and heat and my tiara was agony'.[82] It must have been a relief to escape with the Kents to 'comfy' Coppins for the weekend, although even here there was no avoiding the problem for, on the Sunday afternoon, the King brought his American paramour over from Fort Belvedere to tea.[83] Mrs Simpson was also present at a dinner, a few days later, at Emerald Cunard's house and everyone was keen to keep the conversation on safe ground, with tiaras being chosen as the topic. Olga-perhaps recalling her earlier experience at the Legation-innocently remarked that her tiara gave her a headache. Wallis laughed and opined, 'Well, anyway, a tiara is one of the things I shall never have.' This remark was followed by 'an embarrassed pause'.[84] Paul, meanwhile, took the chance to speak with David and found him to be 'adamant' where 'she' is concerned.[85]

On 19 November, Olga learned that Aunt Bee's second son Alonso, an air force pilot in Spain, had been killed after making a forced landing in Madrid. She immediately dashed over to comfort Princess Beatrice, whom she found 'quite calm and so brave'[86] As a result, the Princess was late in arriving at a dinner party being held by Henry Channon in the King's honour. Paul later went to ask Wallis if she would persuade the 'jolly, gay' King to telephone his sympathy to the Infanta. The Prince and Olga then looked on incredulously as Mrs Simpson-in the face of the King's attempts to procrastinate-firmly instructed her lover to do it, 'now to please me, sir'.[87] The King's jovial spirits, although somewhat insensitive in the circumstances, were doubtless due to his relief at having informed the Duke of Kent, earlier that evening, that he had made up his mind to marry Mrs Simpson.[88] When Prince George later related this conversation to a stunned Olga, she pondered, 'Will they want her as Queen or the Yorks?'[89] Within a few days, Georgy was also able to inform his sister-in-law that Queen Mary believed the King would 'have to abdicate for Bertie...' which the Princess thought 'too tragic.'[90]

As December dawned, the Kents were cancelling engagements and Olga's attention now turned to providing a caring shoulder for her sister Marina and the British royal family. On 3 December, the news of the King's love affair was trumpeted across the front pages of *The Times*, with the newspaper appealing to His Majesty to provide 'some authoritative act or statement'[91] to quash the uncertainty surrounding the throne. That same day, the Prince and Princess were obliged to attend a luncheon with Sir Samuel and Lady Hoare at the Admiralty. The meal seemed 'endless' and the guests 'distrait.' During a subsequent tour of the building with their host, Olga pinched Henry Channon, doubtless for him to make some excuse to hasten their departure.[92] That evening, as the Princess dined with the Kents, Chips called-by to say that the Abdication had been delayed as the King was fighting on, although Mrs Simpson had already left for France in the King's Buick.[93] The following afternoon, Olga notes that Bertie and Elizabeth came to Belgrave Square after tea, 'for a wander, he mute and broken...'[94] while Paul had postponed his departure as the feeling now within the royal family was 'that [the King] had better go as he can't be trusted to play the game'.[95]

During a weekend visit to the Yorks at Royal Lodge, a sympathetic Olga found Bertie 'in an awful state of worry' and ignorant of developments as the King refused to see him or even speak to him over the telephone.[96] The Princess was not taken-in by Mrs Simpson's statement, on 7 December, that she would give up the King and observed sceptically, 'no doubt to get him back after'.[97] Unfortunately, a 'heavy-hearted' Prince Paul had to leave London on 8 December, just as the Duke of Kent was motoring down to Fort Belvedere to spend the night. That evening, Georgy informed Olga and Marina by telephone that the King was 'quite decided to go!' Olga's thoughts immediately turned to the Duke of York: 'What a calamity and what an inheritance for Bertie!'

She also deplored David's actions, 'How can he let down the Empire like this and not mind!'[98]

On the evening of 11 December, Olga listened at Belgrave Square to (the now) Prince Edward's abdication broadcast from Windsor Castle and found it 'so pathetic',[99] a not unsurprising reaction given that her own grandfather and uncle had fought so hard to retain their thrones. After motoring down to Coppins to help Marina celebrate her 30th birthday, the Princess and Alexander departed for Belgrade. Olga hated leaving Marina so near to her confinement, but fortunately Lilia Ralli had arrived to be with her. Meanwhile, the Duke of Kent wrote to Paul to acknowledge the Princess' 'enormous help' to Marina during such a difficult period. [100]

It was a somewhat exhausted Olga who reached Belgrade on the morning of 23 December, after a long, cold journey. She immediately rushed up to see Elizabeth, but her thoughts also remained very much with Marina and, on Christmas Day, the 'incredible' news came through from London that her sister had been safely delivered of a daughter at 11am. Olga immediately rang up the Duke of Kent to congratulate him and observed in her diary, 'What a lovely Xmas present.'[101] The infant would subsequently be christened Alexandra Helen Elizabeth Olga Christabel and the Princess was named as one of her niece's godparents. By contrast, the Prince and Princess also received a steely letter from Queen Mary asking them to refrain from seeing Lady Cunard as, 'It certainly would make it difficult if you did so while staying with [Prince] George', who had already agreed not to meet the American socialite again, at the new King's request.[102] Nevertheless, despite the abdication, Olga and Paul sent the ex-King a letter of festive greetings. Prince Edward was touched and subsequently wrote to the Regent, from his temporary home at Schloss Enzesfeld in Austria to say, 'I do thank you and Olga very much for thinking of me'.[103] Paul would subsequently invite the ex-King to Slovenia, although the latter rejected this 'kind invitation', as his plans were 'still uncertain.'[104]

The Princess saw in the New Year of 1937 quietly at home and indulged in some ice-skating with her sons. She continued to dwell on the Soviet threat to Europe and thought it 'so stupid and blind' of the British government to forbid its citizens from fighting in the Spanish civil war and believed that Germany, Italy and Japan were the 'only countries awake to the Soviet danger.'[105] Olga also remained concerned over her fatigued husband's 'dark outlook'[106] which was hardly alleviated by the 'alarming news' of 'terrorists let loose' who were 'aiming' to harm him. Disturbingly, there was also now 'a certain risk' to Alexander as he travelled to and from school in England.[107]

In the spring, the Princess acted as hostess to a number of top-level foreign dignitaries. The first to visit was the Italian Foreign Minister, Count Ciano, who was in Belgrade to finalise an economic and political agreement between his country and Yugoslavia. Over lunch at Beli Dvor, Olga was surprised to find that, 'He seemed quite nice and natural without the "highness" we expected!'[108] Thereafter, she was preoccupied with arrangements for the State Visit of President Eduard Benes of Czechoslovakia. Although 'quite exhausted'[109] from these exertions, Olga then departed Belgrade for Paris to spend the Orthodox Easter with her parents and purchase a gold lamé dress from Molyneux for the upcoming Coronation in London. However, she was soon distracted by news of her husband's dissatisfaction over his 'placement' at the event, which he felt was not in keeping with his position as Prince Regent.[110] Indeed, it took a full week of negotiations-and the intervention of the Duke of Kent-before matters were resolved to Paul's satisfaction.[111] Nevertheless, even then the Princess remained anxious, noting, 'If only all is well in London *and there is no sourness with Pacey*.'[112]

Olga left Paris with her father and her cousin Eugenie, on 9 May, and they rendezvoused with Paul at Boulogne. Fortunately, the negotiations over precedence were all forgotten as the Kents welcomed the Prince and Princess at Victoria railway station and whisked them straight to Buckingham Palace, where the King and Queen called on them in their suite. The following afternoon, the Princess took tea at Belgrave Square with Marina, during which she looked in on the babies. Her first impression of her niece Alexandra was that she resembled her mother and had 'the same blue eyes.'[113] Olga subsequently accompanied Paul to Oxford to attend a ceremony at Balliol College during which the Prince Regent was awarded an Honorary Degree of Doctor of Civil Law.

The day of the coronation, 12 May, dawned 'rainy and wet' and the Princess was awoken at 5.30am by the noise of the crowds outside. She dressed and put-on Queen Olga's magnificent ruby parure borrowed from Princess Nicholas for the occasion. Ironically, after all the fuss over the placement, she and Paul were seated in the Quire directly behind the throne, so 'saw little.' Nevertheless, Olga found the ceremonial 'too beautiful for words' and thought the new Queen 'very sweet and demure, he [The King] very racé and dignified.'[114] A week later, the Princess received the glad news that her sister Elisabeth had given birth to a daughter in Bavaria following a difficult delivery. She planned to visit of course, but first indulged in several increasingly rare evenings of escapism with Paul and the Kents at Ciro's nightclub.

Nevertheless, all too soon, Paul and Olga once again boarded the boat train to France, accompanied by the ever-present security detail. Word had recently been received at the British Embassy in Paris that the

Prince Regent was to be the first victim of a new terrorist campaign against the Yugoslav government,[115] so on their arrival in the French capital, the couple were greeted by 'millions of police' and a motor-cycle escort rushed them to the Ritz.[116] Fortunately the visit, which included an official luncheon with President Le Brun at the Elysée Palace, passed off without incident.

En route home, the couple stopped off in Bavaria. While Paul remained in Munich, Olga made her way to Winhöring to finally meet her new-born niece, Helen, whom she described as having 'long dark hair and blue eyes and sweet features like Fael.'[117] The caring Princess encouraged her exhausted sister to rest on a sofa in her sitting room, while the infant slept nearby at an open window. After attending the child's christening, the Prince and Princess returned to Brdo, on 3 June, and Olga suddenly remembered that this was the wedding day of Prince Edward (now newly-created Duke of Windsor) to Wallis at the Château de Candé near Tours. She held out little hope for this 'pathetic' union.[118]

The Princess now focused on enjoying some precious time with her children. She admitted to Marina that, 'I spend every spare moment I can with my Tiny-Ling [Elizabeth]'[119] who now 'talked without end' and 'crawls about like lightening...'[120] However, she was uneasy about the suitability of Miss Ede who displayed, 'reserve and [a] queer dry mentality' and she had already decided that if the nurse proved to be a negative influence on Elizabeth, 'I won't hesitate in parting from her.'[121] Olga also adopted an enlightened approach with the 'highly inquisitive' Nicholas concerning the facts of life; she read him excerpts from a book entitled, "How I Began".[122] Unfortunately, Paul's responsibilities continued apace: On 14 June, Vladko Maček arrived at Brdo for discussions but the encounter only seemed to plunge the Regent into deeper despair with the Princess noting, 'He doesn't see how much longer he can stand it as no one is really to be trusted...'[123]

Inevitably, the summer visitors soon started to arrive. The first, on 21 June, was Prince Nicholas' sister Marie who proved a wonderful source of interesting stories, particularly about the outbreak of the Russian revolution. As Olga waved her off at the end of her stay, she admitted, 'I shall miss her awfully.[124] Grand Duchess Marie's presence was certainly a welcome antidote to the various official lunches held throughout July in honour of the German, British and French Ministers. Thereafter, Paul became 'v[ery] depressed' following a debate in the Skupština relating to the formal Ratification of a Concordat with the Vatican.[125] Although supported by the Prince Regent, the agreement was heavily opposed by Serbian Orthodox clergy who feared it would place the Croatian Catholics in a dominant position. It did not help that the Orthodox Patriarch Varnava Rosić died suddenly, just as the Skupština finally endorsed the Concordat by one single vote. The Princess feared this would turn the priest into 'a martyr'. She agonised too that 'Our people who are not [normally] religious have suddenly become fanatics'[126] and might possibly be on the verge of tearing the country apart over the issue.[127]

At the end of July, Alexander arrived from school in England. He had now left Chartridge Hill school and was due to start at Eton after the summer break. His return coincided with an overnight visit from Olga's dear friend Amedeo of Aosta. Bouby swam with the Princess and the boys and generally 'made all kinds of nonsense which was great fun.'[128] Less welcome, was the 'pompous'[129] King Carol of Romania who remained for two days and tired Paul with 'lengthy weighty talks.'[130] Olga fretted too that the on-going fallout from the Concordat debacle had left the Regent 'exhausted and unnerved.'[131] Indeed, Henry Channon, visiting Brdo in late August, questioned, 'whether he will stay the course...'[132] The Princess was particularly furious at the attitude of Stojadinović who seemed to prefer vacationing on the coast, 'and takes it all as a joke.'[133]

Certainly, Paul was nearing the end of his rope with his Prime Minister whom he felt, 'had shown a remarkable lack of foresight' in continuing to block any agreement with Maček and the Croats.[134] Nevertheless, the resolute Regent again reached out to Maček during 'important talks' at Brdo on 9 September.[135] Paul's determination would pay off as the Croat politician would go on to form alliances with other (opposition) Serbian parties to form a broad-based Bloc of National Agreement, while Stojadinović was eventually forced to withdraw from the controversial Concordat.[136]

Thereafter, the departure of Alexander (to attend Eton), young Nicholas (to commence his school studies at Sandroyd boarding school) and Miss Peters (to a new posting), left Olga feeling 'crushed.'[137] In October, she travelled to London to undergo a routine gynaecological procedure and an appendectomy at the Carnarvon Nursing Home. The Princess would remain hospitalised for four weeks under the expert care of a Sister Rice, to whom she would later present a brooch bearing her chiffre, as a token of her thanks.[138]

Countess Toerring also happened to be in London and the three sisters had some wonderful fun being photographed by a leading society photographer.[139] However, the trio were soon to be left stunned by news of a most dreadful loss: On 16 November, their cousin Cecilie (pregnant with her fourth child), her husband Grand Duke George Donatus ('Don'), their two sons Ludgwig and Alexander and Cecilie's mother-in-law, Grand Duchess Eleonore, were all killed when their Sabena airplane hit a chimney in heavy fog near Ostend's Steene Aerodrome. The party had been en route to London for the wedding of Cecilie's brother-in-law Ludwig ('Lu') to the Honourable Margaret Campbell-Geddes ('Peg'). Cecilie's little daughter Johanna was not on board the plane. The first the sisters knew of it was via a message left for Marina at Belgrave Square. They immediately 'dashed off' to Kensington Palace to see Cecilie's maternal grandmother, Victoria, the Dowager Duchess of Milford Haven, who was 'dazed with grief'.[140] Next morning, the Princess' joined other 'near relations' at St Peter's, Eaton Square for Lu and Peg's wedding service. Olga found it 'the most ghastly [sic] ceremony in the world, the poor little bride in black...' adding, 'For us it was like a funeral.'[141] The Princess later learned that it had fallen to her father to inform his brother Andrew of the tragedy that had befallen his favourite daughter and her family.[142]

At the end of November, the Princess travelled to Paris to finish her recuperation at her parent's flat. The parting with Marina and Elisabeth had been particularly heartfelt given the recent tragedy and left her 'in despair'.[143] Olga's time in France also included an emotional meeting at St Cloud with her Uncle Andrew, who arrived fresh from his daughter Cecilie's funeral at Darmstadt.[144] As the Princess subsequently travelled home by train via Italy, she was heartened when Prince Amedeo of Aosta and his wife Anne ('Mo') kindly came aboard at Trieste to greet her as she passed through. Indeed, the dashing Duke (who had just been appointed Italy's Viceroy in Abyssinia) later insisted on accompanying Olga as far as Postumia. She seemed entranced observing, 'He is such a dear it's a pity he must go so far.'[145] The Princess would later keep a special eye on Bouby's movements overseas via diplomatic channels.[146]

Olga arrived back in Belgrade, on 11 December, after an absence of nearly three months. This most perceptive of mothers was able to make use of her recent long sojourn to observe her daughter through fresh eyes: Elizabeth she concluded, 'Has a will of her own and needs careful managing.'[147] She also learned that Mignon had a new English "companion", a Mrs Rosemary Creswell. With still vivid memories of the Queen's unorthodox previous affiliation with Miss Crowther, the Princess was wary of this new arrival, particularly when she established that 'Rosemary' had been given a bedroom adjoining that of the Dowager Queen.[148] On 22 December, Alexander and Nicholas returned from school and Olga dashed around arranging the guest rooms for the arrival of her parents. She was concerned over the state of her father's health, particularly his persistent coughing fits. Meanwhile, Mignon had to rush off to Romania as her mother Queen Marie-who had been in poor health for many months-had suffered a haemorrhage.

As 1938 began, Olga continued to provide support to her husband who was growing increasingly unhappy with Stojadinović's right-wing government. One would have thought, therefore, that the Princess would have been glad of the diversion of attending her cousin Crown Prince Paul's wedding to Princess Frederika of Hanover in Athens. However, so anxious did Olga become over her return to Athens after an absence of sixteen years, that she was unable to eat. The Princess also began to refer to Greece in her diary as, 'what used to be home' and felt keenly that she and Marina were returning to Athens as 'foreigners.' By the same token, she was also excited, in an almost childlike way, and made sure to keep awake so as to catch sight of the '1st Greek soldier' as she crossed the frontier by train.[149] Her mercurial state-of-mind would certainly not have been helped by continuing worries over Prince Nicholas, who was already installed at the Hotel Grande Bretagne in Athens and complaining about his swollen legs.

The Prince Regent and his Consort arrived in Athens, on 7 January, to a full ceremonial welcome as befitted their new status. Olga admitted in her diary that 'My knees were trembling' while 'to hear the [Greek] Anthem finished me.' She was immediately struck by how much the city had grown, and her sense of disconnection continued when she attended a reception at the Royal Palace and found that many of the guests were 'unknown' to her.[150] A visit to Tatoi did little to comfort her: The main house was being rebuilt, following years of neglect, and the unfamiliar new interiors left her feeling 'like a ghost.'[151] The Princess was also far from gushing about Frederika, describing her as, 'angelic tho' not pretty'.[152] Moreover, on the eve of the wedding, Prince Nicholas was taken unwell and the doctor diagnosed heart problems.[153] Nevertheless, as she drove to the Cathedral for the Orthodox wedding ceremony next day, Olga was moved by the 'touching ovations' of the 'enthusiastic crowds' who greeted her.[154]

No sooner had the Princess returned to Belgrade than she received news from her mother that there had been a marked deterioration in her father's condition. Indeed, the doctors in Athens were keen to send for a heart specialist from Berlin. When she later discovered that Prince Nicholas was 'barely conscious' Paul 'urged' his wife to leave immediately for Greece.[155] On reaching Athens' Grand Bretagne Hotel, Olga found her father 'so changed and thin',[156] although he seemed to recognise her. Sadly, 'the past and present seemed confused in his mind.'[157] Marina and Elisabeth were currently on holiday in St Anton with their husbands, and the Princess wrote to warn them that their father was, 'no more the Vuzzie we knew before.'[158] On 7 February, Prince Nicholas' breathing became irregular and his condition deteriorated further, so Olga and her mother maintained a bedside vigil. The Prince died at 11.50 the following morning, his eldest child noting that, 'our sweetest most beloved Vuzzie passed away peacefully without pain.' Later, she would observe, 'I heard his voice in my heart saying "Take care of Mummy-my sweet one."'[159]

On 9 February, the Toerrings, the Kents and the ever-solicitous Prince Regent arrived in Athens. Next day, as crowds lined the streets, Prince Nicholas' mortal remains were moved from the Grand Bretagne to the Cathedral by gun carriage for the Lying-in-State. On 12 February, following an emotional funeral service, he was finally laid to rest amidst the cypress trees at Tatoi. A concerned Marina confided to Foxie that Olga, 'looks quite exhausted.'[160] However, only once did this faithful daughter leave Princess Nicholas' side; on 18 February, Olga ventured with Lilia Ralli to her favourite beach at Phaleron to enjoy the bracing air. There was at least one positive outcome to this devastating episode: The Princess had again come to realise that 'My love for the country of my birth is stronger than ever.'[161] Nor would it ever waver again...

The three Princesses and their mother left Athens, on 23 February, to travel to Belgrade. Olga had decided that, for the moment, Ellen should remain with her at Beli Dvor. Although the Princess drew comfort from playing with Elizabeth ('my precious baby'[162]) she unfortunately had a contretemps with Queen Marie over Alexander's care in England: He had been unwell and Miss Fox had arranged for the teenager to be treated by a specialist, Dr Crookes. Mignon happened to be in London and, doubtless trying to be helpful, made the grave error of attempting to involve another doctor. Olga was determined to nip this in the bud and telephoned the Dowager Queen on two separate occasions to explain that she and Paul, 'were perfectly satisfied with the specialist treatment and did not want any other doctor to be consulted'.[163] This episode can hardly have endeared the Princess to Marie, but perhaps the latter should have been more concerned for the welfare of her own son, Peter, whom the Princess felt was leading such an 'unnatural' life in Belgrade.[164]

As spring dawned, Olga grew increasingly interested in the work of the Red Cross and realised its importance 'more than ever now',[165] an oblique reference to the deteriorating political situation in Europe. She was also aware of growing anti-Semitism in the continent: Following the annexation of Austria by Nazi Germany (the *Anschluss*) on 12 March, she noted in her diary that 'all the Jews are being expelled.'[166] What the Princess does not mention was that this new "Greater Germany" now extended right up to Yugoslavia's border. In Bavaria, Elisabeth Toerring was growing anxious as Toto had been called-up[167] although Olga was equally concerned by the situation in the Soviet Union where 'arrests and trials and condemnations' were being routinely ignored by the outside world.[168] Meanwhile, the American press were displaying gloomy headlines declaring, 'War Clouds over Europe'[169] and Anthony Eden had already resigned over the British Prime Minster, Neville Chamberlain's policy of appeasement towards the Fascist powers. Naturally, the Prince and Princess kept a close eye on the deteriorating international situation and subsequently listened on the radio to speeches made by Mussolini and Hitler during a State Banquet in the latter's honour in Rome.

Despite the unsettled international situation, the Princess and her mother made a two-week visit to Athens to sort out some business affairs and attend the traditional Orthodox 40-day memorial service at Prince Nicholas' grave. On their return to Belgrade, Mignon-who had by now returned from England-visited Beli Dvor, but further blotted her copy book by offering no words of condolence to Princess Nicholas.[170] Miss Fox then arrived on a spring visit, but her presence proved to be a mixed blessing, as she and Ellen talked 'by the hour' late into the evening, which Olga found exhausting.[171] There was a brief respite, in early May, when Princess Nicholas returned to Athens with her daughter Elisabeth to view a house. However, this led to a frisson of friction between the sisters, as Countess Toerring was keen to be back at Winhöring in time for her daughter Helen's first birthday on 20 May. Olga emphasised to her sister, 'that she must try not to make M[ummy] feel rushed...'[172]

In the interim, the Princess had agreed to travel to Paris to empty her parents' flat. This proved a daunting experience as she could feel her father's, 'beloved presence everywhere'.[173] However, although she stoically got on with the task in hand, she admitted to Foxie that, 'so much upsets me', particularly sorting through the private correspondence in her father's desk which, 'made me feel I was committing an indiscretion.'[174] Fortunately, there was an interlude when Olga attended a large Sunday family lunch at Uncle George's house at St Cloud in honour of her cousin Eugenie, who was marrying a Polish aristocrat, Dominik Radziwill.

The Duchess of Kent then flew over from London and the Princess was particularly glad of her help disassembling Prince Nicholas' artist studio. The sister's final day together was spent taking tea with a friend, Germaine Montebello, followed by dinner and a ciné film of Eugenie's wedding at Uncle George's house. Olga undoubtedly erred in travelling out to Le Bourget Aerodrome to bid Marina farewell, for she later confided to Foxie that, 'it upset me frightfully...'[175] This is understandable given that the Hesse family's air accident was still very much on her mind.

The Princess celebrated her 35th birthday at Winhöring on 11 June, where she was reunited with her mother. The duo returned to Brdo to the welcome news that Alexander had been doing 'much better' at school; while Nicholas had come top in Latin.[176] Olga was soon enjoying the novel experience of filming Elizabeth using a new ciné camera, while her 'exhausted' husband endured an 'endless' meeting with Maček, in an attempt to resolve the continuing impasse between the opposition and Stojadinović's government.[177]

111

Princess Nicholas and Olga spent the first half of July in Athens where they viewed a large villa situated on a corner site in the up-market suburb of Psychiko. The family lawyer, Mr Philon, advised Ellen to buy it. With the business side of the visit almost completed, Olga celebrated her name day on 11 July (when friends sent the traditional gifts of sweets and flowers to her hotel at Kifissia) and subsequently attended the christening of her Godson Fernand ('Freddy') Serpieri, the son of her close friend Pénélope Julie 'Diddie' Serpieri (née Vlasto) and her husband Johnny.

Back at Brdo, a telegram arrived from King Carol of Romania, on 18 July, bearing the news that his mother Queen Marie had died at Castle Pele□. The Princess steeled herself to receive news of the arrangements for the funeral in Bucharest, 'to which I expect I must go with Pacey.'[178] Olga, Paul and Princess Nicholas duly joined the large party of royal mourners in Bucharest who included the Kents. Many non-royal dignitaries, including Goering, Ribbentrop and Mussolini were also in attendance. After viewing the Lying-in-State in the White Hall of the Cotroceni Palace, Ellen and her family could only marvel at, 'the amount of theatrical emotion on display.'[179] Following the funeral service, all the gathered royals accompanied Queen Marie's mortal remains, as they were transported by train across the Wallachian Plains to be interred alongside her late husband in the Monastery of Curtea de Argeş. On their return to Slovenia, the Prince and Princess received word from King Carol that his mother had left 'indications' in her will-Olga was to receive 'a small cristal [sic] box mounted in white enamel worked with [a] golden pattern' which had been in Aunt Missy's bedroom.[180]

Shortly thereafter, Alexander, Nicholas and their summer tutor, a Scotsman, Mr Caldwell arrived at Brdo. Olga bathed with her sons in the nearby lake and played tennis with their tutor whom she soon discovered could serve, 'real cannon ball shots which reduced me to pulp!'[181] However, official life soon intruded, with the Princess co-hosting a lunch for representatives of the Petite Entente powers who were holding a summit at nearby Bled. Fortunately, Olga, her sons and Mr Caldwell were then able to escape to join the Kents on a ten-day cruise to Cavtat. The harassed Prince Regent, alas, was 'too busy' to join them, as he had to travel to Belgrade for a parade.[182] He returned to Brdo consumed with worry over the possibility of a war between Germany and Czechoslovakia in the Sudetenland.

The Prince and Princess travelled to Winhöring on 12 September. Their brief visit coincided with a speech by Hitler at Nuremberg in which he denounced Czechoslovakia as a 'fraudulent state' out to subdue the Sudeten Germans.[183] Although the flustered Regent travelled into Munich to hold consultations with one of his Ministers, Olga seemed relatively unruffled noting, 'So far, the situation, though serious, is the same.'[184] However, when it was later announced over the radio that Chamberlain was flying out to Bavaria for a meeting with Hitler, the Princess realised that the situation was becoming serious.[185] It was certainly a worrying time to be sending the boys back to England.

On 19 September, Paul received news that his father Prince Arsène was dying, just as Princess Nicholas learned that her brother Kirill had been taken ill with cardiovascular problems. As the Regent was already committed to a meeting with King Boris of Bulgaria at Brdo, it was left to Olga to travel to Paris to attend to her father-in-law. Princess Nicholas decided to accompany her. However, as they passed through Munich, on 21 September, the duo were alarmed to learn from Elisabeth that Toto had been called-up and was already at the Czech frontier.[186] In Paris, the Princesses installed themselves at the Lancaster Hotel, from where Ellen rushed to be with her ailing brother at the American Hospital, while Olga hurried over to Avenue Montaigne to find Prince Arsène looking 'ghastly'.[187] Fortunately, his manservant Bandelać was in constant attendance. As the situation between Germany and Czechoslovakia deteriorated, Purić, the Yugoslav Minister in Paris, called on the Princess and advised her to leave for Belgrade, 'as soon as possible.' Nevertheless, she demurred[188] possibly because Miss Fox had arrived in Paris en route to Munich, although Kate quickly abandoned her plans on Prince Paul's advice and returned to England. Meanwhile, when Olga learned of the 'conditions' Hitler wished to impose on the Czechs over the Sudetenland, she queried, '[he] asks for rather much and will they give in?'[189] The Princess became aware too of a growing sense of panic around her, with trains out of Paris now filled to capacity. Indeed, the Regent urged his wife to leave and even mentioned the possibility of recalling their sons back to Yugoslavia.[190] Fortunately, the British Prime Minister would soon come to Olga's rescue, playing a major role in the peace talks between Britain, Germany, France and Italy, which resulted in the Munich Agreement of 30 September. This accord allowed for Germany's annexation of the Sudetenland and, importantly, also forestalled war in Europe. The Princess believed that Chamberlain, 'Probably will get the Garter for this and deserves it.'[191] By contrast, she branded Duff Cooper 'a fool' for denouncing the Agreement and resigning as First Sea Lord in protest.[192]

Grand Duke Kirill died on 12 October with Ellen and Olga at his bedside. They both attended his funeral service at the Russian Orthodox Church in Paris and his interment at the Ducal Mausoleum in Glockenburg, on 18 October. However, the following day, the Princess received the sad news from Paul (who was currently in Munich) that Prince Arsène had died and that the funeral would take place at Topola in four days' time. Olga immediately set out from Coburg for Munich to be with her husband, and they travelled onwards together to Ljubljana to rendezvous with the Simplon Express, which was conveying Paul's father's mortal remains back to Yugoslavia. Following an impressive funeral ceremony conducted by the Patriarch, Prince Arsène was laid to rest in the crypt of the Royal Mausoleum at Topola.

On 25 October, it was officially announced, from London, that the Duke of Kent had been appointed Governor-General of Australia. The thought of Marina living at the other side of the world for up to five years was a daunting prospect for Olga who observed, 'So far for so long!'[193] It was also at this time that the Princess endured the 'awful' experience of bidding farewell to her mother as she returned to Athens to build a new life for herself.[194] In the meantime, there was another ongoing political crisis in Belgrade: On 10 October, Stojadinović's government resigned and fresh elections were held in December. Although Stojadinović won, with 54% of the vote, Maček's coalition polled a healthy 45%. Moreover, in Croatia, the coalition actually gained 70% of the vote,[195] thus signalling a clear mandate for political change. Paul now faced the considerable challenge of keeping Maček from throwing his lot in with the Italians, who were actively seeking to tear Catholic Croatia away from Yugoslavia.

After attending a Congress of the Srpska Majka (Mothers of Serbia) at the Old Palace on 14 November, the Princess travelled to Paris and found that her train was full of Jewish refugees.[196] This exodus could hardly have come as a surprise, as she had recently confided to her diary that the persecution of the Jews in Germany was now 'more violent than ever.'[197] Lilia Ralli was Olga's hostess in the French capital, where much of her time was spent finalising Prince Arsène affairs on behalf of her harassed husband. On 21 November, the Princess met up with Paul at Calais and they travelled on to London for a stay at Buckingham Palace. As their arrival coincided with the sudden death, in a London nursing home, of Olga's kinswoman Queen Maud of Norway, the Princess and the Regent immediately rushed upstairs to offer their condolences to her widower, King Haakon. Paul later held important discussions with the British government for he was anxious to obtain military aid from Britain, as well as subsidised trade terms for Yugoslavia in order to reduce its economic dependence on Germany.[198] However, in general, Chamberlain's government showed little inclination to proceed with either.

Thereafter, Chips Channon hosted a cocktail party for the Yugoslav royals, and found Olga to be, 'very royal'.[199] Yet, the Prince and Princess were also quite happy to mix with Marina and George's outré social circle, including the American film star Douglas Fairbanks Junior, whom

Olga thought, 'very good looking and full of charm.'[200] On 6 December, Paul departed London's Victoria Station for Paris (and a meeting with the Foreign Minister Georges Bonnet) amidst rumours of another Croat terrorist plot against him.[201] Naturally, these reports unnerved Olga and she admitted to being 'scared' by this 'beastly news.'[202]

The Prince Regent was now at the forefront of international press attention: He was currently featured on the cover of *Time Magazine*, while the *New York Times* predicted there was 'political turmoil' awaiting him back in Belgrade following the recent elections.[203] Certainly, when Olga finally had the chance to speak to Paul at Beli Dvor, from the exiled Queen of Spain's London home, on 11 December, he sounded 'so flat' from all the work and worry.[204] By contrast, the Kents encouraged the Princess to let her hair down, attending a Cecily Courtneidge review (during which they 'all cried with laughter') and dancing the night away at the "400 Club" until 3am.[205]

However, the realities of everyday life soon intervened: With Nicholas and Alexander's school terms now finished, the Princess and her sons left London, arriving in Belgrade in time to celebrate 'English' Christmas. Unfortunately, the Prince Regent continued to feel 'worried and low'[206] over Stojadinović's failure to reach out to the Croats, while the recent resignation of the respected Slovene Populist Party leader (and Minister of the Interior), Father Anton Korosec only served to inflame matters. As the year ended, Olga's final diary entry read, 'Last day of this sad year. God give 1939 brings Peace and understanding to this troubled world.'[207] If only she knew...

King Alexander of Yugoslavia

Queen Marie of Yugoslavia

Family group on holiday in Slovenia L to R Marina, Alexander, Elisabeth, Olga and Nicholas, early 1930's

L to R Princesses Elisabeth, Nicholas and Olga in mourning for King Alexander, 1934.

King Peter of Yugoslavia (mid-1930's)

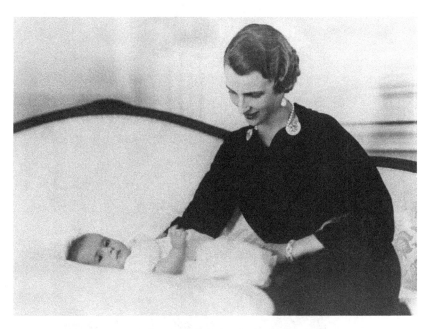

Princess Olga with baby Elizabeth (1936)

Princess Olga (left) and Princess Elisabeth in the Salon of Beli Dvor, late 1930's

A newly-widowed Princess Nicholas in mourning, 1938.

Princess Marina (late 1930's)

State Reception, Reich Chancellery, Berlin, June 1939, L to R (front) Hitler, Princess Olga (talking to Magda Goebbels) with to rear (right) Field Marshal Goering (talking to Princess Mafalda of Hesse).

Princess Olga and Prince Paul on a visit to Zagreb, Croatia in January 1940

The TATLER

Vol. CLV. No. 2017. London, February 21, 1940   POSTAGE: Inland 1½d.; Canada and Newfoundland 1¼d.; Foreign 9d.   Price One Shilling

H.R.H. PRINCESS PAUL OF YUGOSLAVIA

A beautiful portrait study of the Consort of the Regent of Yugoslavia.   H.R.H., the former Princess Olga, is a sister of H.R.H. the Duchess of Kent and the eldest of the three daughters of Prince Nicholas of Greece.   She was married to Prince Paul in 1923.   It was in 1934 that Prince Paul was appointed Regent of Yugoslavia during the minority of the young King Peter who succeeded on the assassination of King Alexander in Marseilles in 1934

Princess Olga features on Tatler magazine's front cover, February 1940

125

Chapter 13 Troubled Times

In February 1939, as the political situation deteriorated further, Olga had a welcome visit from Marina. Paul then discovered that Stojadinović, while holding discussions over the future of Albania with Count Ciano, had gone beyond the agreed remit and entered into some form of "hazy" agreement to divide up that country between Italy and Yugoslavia. Worse still, the Prime Minister later failed to inform the Prince of this arrangement during his report on the talks. Paul only learned of its existence when Ciano later alluded to the matter in conversation.[1] The outraged Regent forced Stojadinović's resignation, on 4 February, by refusing to allow him to form a new cabinet. Dragiša Cvetković, who had previously served as Minister of Social Policy and Public Health, was appointed Prime Minister and given the delicate task of reaching a settlement with Maček and the Croats. This was becoming all the more pressing given that, following upon Stojadinović's dismissal, Italy put an end to its policy of rapprochement with Yugoslavia. Mussolini now wanted an independent Croatia but linked closely to Italy in a confederation.[2]

In the spring, Elizabeth was sent to Athens to visit her grandmother, while the Princess was kept busy with her correspondence, holding audiences and attending charity events. She remained unfazed by her eventful life and informed Foxie, 'It's all interesting if one puts one's heart into it and helps to pass the time.'[3] Unfortunately, an increasingly restless Cecil Parrot had resigned his post as Peter's tutor and accused the hard-pressed Prince Regent of neglecting King Peter's education.[4] The royal tutor's perspective seems to have been rather self-serving for his charge would later complain that Parrot 'would not realise that I was not a child anymore but a youth with my own ideas.'[5] Paul was naturally hurt by Parrot's allegation, although Olga 'tried to be fair in this matter'.[6] Fortunately, the tutor agreed to remain in post until the Dowager Queen returned to Belgrade.[7] Meanwhile, the Prince Regent soon had more pressing matters to deal with as Germany invaded Czechoslovakia in mid-March in direct contravention of the Munich Agreement. Britain was now forced to abandon its policy of appeasement.

Mignon arrived back in Belgrade in time for Easter. She was now spending most of her time with her companion, Mrs Cresswell, between a flat in London and a cottage at Gransden, Cambridgeshire. Olga felt this would be an opportune moment to make a quick dash to Athens to fetch Elizabeth, and as she explained to Marina, 'I desperately need to get away and relax after this awful time of tension and taught nerves...' With Parrot still determined to leave Belgrade, the Princess asked for Marina's assistance in finding him a post at the BBC in London.[8] His departure would only serve to tighten the already close bond that existed between Olga and King Peter.

On Good Friday, 7 April, Italy invaded Albania. Yugoslavia was left increasingly vulnerable as it now shared two borders with Italy-in the North West and the South. Olga-now returned from Athens-was growing increasingly concerned for her husband's wellbeing as he broke down and wept,[9] for Italy's recent actions had only served to underline that the weight of Yugoslavia's uncertain future rested squarely on his shoulders. Another contributory factor was that the Regent had no real opportunity to unwind-what little exercise he was able to undertake was limited to a walk along the same stretch of road with his wife. Furthermore, the detectives who accompanied them only served to remind Paul of the perils of the post he held. The Princess was suffering too: She confided to Marina that 'my head is completely incoherent' and she was heartbroken over the recent departure of Nicholas and Alexander to school in England, as it had been decided that, 'they are safer there [rather] than staying here and adding to our worries and responsibilities...'[10]

Interestingly, Mrs Creswell (who accompanied the boys back to London) had taken with her various pieces of Olga's jewellery, accompanied by a list of the items for Marina's attention. The jewels were to be lodged with Coutts bank for safekeeping.[11] By the same token, it is clear from the Princess' correspondence that she had already discussed with Marina the possibility of finding a house to rent in Britain in case she and Paul had to flee Yugoslavia. However, frustrated over the lack of sisterly progress, Olga now placed her faith in the reliable Miss Fox to whom she stressed that any house 'must be ready at a moment's notice'. The Princess preferred Scotland as the location and emphasised 'if we come it would not be just on a short visit.'[12]

Fortuitously, the Duke of Kent empathized with his in-law's plight in Yugoslavia and observed that, 'living on top of a volcano is appalling & one can't settle to anything.' Unfortunately, divided loyalties were already emerging, even in this close family: The Toerrings had recently spent two weeks at Coppins over Easter and Prince George noted, '[They] enjoyed themselves I think-tho' arguments never ceased! But it did them good to get away and see the other point of view.'[13]

In addition to dealing with Yugoslavia's political problems, the Prince Regent was also required to undertake a series of important State Visits to Italy, Germany and Great Britain in May, June and July respectively. This is where Olga, with her ample attributes of beauty, grace, poise, intelligence and linguistic skills, was most able to help ease her husband's troublesome diplomatic path. The couple, accompanied by the Yugoslav Foreign Minister Cincar-Marković, left Belgrade for Rome on the evening of 8 May.

Unfortunately, the Princess had been beset with problems over her wardrobe for the trip (the items had only arrived in Belgrade from Paris on the morning of her departure) and this had left her feeling on edge. However, the main focus of Olga's concern continued to lie with Paul, who prior to the visit had been unable to either sleep or eat and frequently felt faint. It was for his sake that the Princess tried to remain upbeat, telling Foxie, 'I pray for confidence and calm and simply <u>cannot</u> believe that the worse is likely to happen'.[14] The Yugoslav party arrived in Rome on 10 May and, as they drew into the station, the Prince looked decidedly apprehensive. He was probably already aware that Count Ciano was currently involved in negotiations with Maček to back an Italian-funded Croat revolt.[15] The reception for the Prince Regent and his wife was 'warm and cordial'[16] and led by Paul's beloved 'Oncle' and 'Tante', King Victor Emanuele and Queen Elena. After lunch at the Quirinale Palace, the Regent held talks with Mussolini (as did Ciano with Cincar-Marković), the British press having already noted that, 'it is being left to the Italians [by Germany] to tighten the screw on Yugoslavia so that her foreign policy will be brought into conformity with German and Italian wishes.'[17]

Next day, while Olga lunched with Prince Christopher and his wife in Rome, Paul ventured to Naples to attend a Naval Review. During the proceedings, a Yugoslav Cadet training ship passed-by and sent him greetings by cable. However, the vessel was actually on a clandestine mission to transport the vast majority of Yugoslavia's gold reserves to Britain for safe keeping.[18] On 12 May, the royal couple and Cincar-Marković were received in Private Audience at the Vatican by Pope Pius. During a subsequent call on Cardinal Maglione, the Vatican's Secretary of State, Olga was given a miniature depicting the Madonna and child.[19] The Princess summed-up the State Visit in a letter to Kate Fox, 'All together everyone was charming from the King and Queen down to the man in the street!'[20] However, hardly had the couple returned to Belgrade than Ciano signed a military and political alliance with Germany, commonly referred to as the "Pact of Steel".

Olga then prepared for the State Visit to Germany and was pleased to learn that the Toerrings had been invited to an official dinner. The Prince and Princess arrived in Berlin on the afternoon of June 1 and were greeted at the station by Herr Hitler who presented Olga with a huge bouquet of flowers, an extravagant gesture which was to set the tone for the visit. Goering was much in evidence, which was hardly surprising given that part of his 'foreign political task' was 'to cultivate' relations 'especially' with the Prince Regent.[21] Furthermore, since Hitler was unmarried, Frau Goering was to act as the official hostess during the visit. Olga and Paul quickly settled into their quarters at the Bellevue Palace and later attended a State Banquet at the Reich Chancellery. The Princess looked on engagingly as her husband stressed in his speech that the visit was an indication of Yugoslavia's determination to work with the German people in peace and friendship. Hitler, for his part, vowed to respect Yugoslavia's territorial rights.[22] Olga subsequently wrote to Marina with her first impressions of the Führer, '[He] is charming and v[ery] gentle-perfect manners.'[23]

The following day there was an impressive grand military parade by 25000 troops and featuring a fly-past by 300 aircraft. It was during this event that Olga first began to see past the veneer being propagated by her hosts for she became increasingly suspicious that some of the tanks seemed remarkably familiar. She quietly arranged for her A.D.C. to take a quick look behind the scenes. He confirmed her chariness was justified; the same military hardware was indeed making several circuits.[24] In the evening, Olga and Paul sat through a five-hour, three-act performance of the Wagner opera Die Meistersinger von Nürnberg at the Prussian State Opera House. The Princess, however, was somewhat distracted by the antics of her neighbour, Herr Hitler, whom she noted had the habit of 'shutting his eyes as though he were in a trance.'[25] Furthermore, the Führer's eyes would well-up with tears if he discussed anything pertaining to children.[26]

On 3 June, the Prince and Princess undertook a trip to Potsdam to attend a lunch hosted by the German Foreign Minister Ribbentrop at the Neues Palais. Next day, they were given a tour of Berlin, and in the evening, the couple attended a candlelit dinner and ballet display at the Charlottenburg Palace. The scale of the entertainments and the use of so many former royal palaces were doubtless intended to impress the Yugoslav royals. Intriguingly, a family lunch at the Bellevue Palace (attended by Olga's cousins Sophie, Theodora and Margarita and their husbands) had to be eaten alfresco after it was discovered that the palace's rooms had been bugged.[27] This avoidance action was to prove fortuitous, as it was during this luncheon that Prince Paul informed another guest, Infante Alfonso (Uncle Ali), that he thought Hitler was mad and that war was imminent.[28]

On 5 June, over a farewell lunch at the Chancellery, Hitler informed the Princess that he wished relations between Great Britain and Germany could be 'restored', while adding for good measure that he suffered from a split personality![29] Unsurprisingly, Olga's initial favourable impression of the Führer had changed; her daughter Elizabeth recalls that her mother 'was disgusted by Hitler. She thought [he] was raving mad.'[30] The final two days of the royal couple's time in Germany were spent as guests of Goering and his wife at their country estate, Carinhall, in the Schorfheide Forest, some 60 kilometres north east of Berlin. However, the Princess' sangfroid was to be sorely tested when Goering appeared at dinner dressed as William Tell.[31] Interestingly, Olga would later tell her daughter-in-law Barbara that Frau Goering 'was the only nice person' among the official German party.[32]

Although the American press observed that Yugoslavia was 'now accounted as tied to [the] Anti-Comintern Front'[33] the reality was somewhat different: The Führer apparently left Berlin for his summer break in Obersalzberg in disgust, as the State Visit had not achieved the outcome that he wished for; that is to say, a firm commitment on the part of Yugoslavia to side with the Axis powers. Hitler duly vented his frustrations on his departed guests: The Prince Regent had proved 'slippery as an eel' during talks, while Olga was peremptorily dismissed as a 'typical ice-cold Englishwoman only concerned with high-living'.[34]

The Prince and Princess arrived back in Brdo to the sad news that little Johanna of Hesse, her late cousin Cecilie's only surviving child, had died from meningitis. Olga's heart 'ached' for 'poor Lu [of Hesse]' who, along with his wife Peg, had adopted his orphaned niece.[35] Thereafter, given the increasingly troubled times, the Princess focused on the need to find a more secure means of communicating with family and friends overseas. She informed Miss Fox that sending correspondence by diplomatic bag was 'safest', particularly where it concerned details of Kate's (still) continuing efforts to find a "safe" house for her family. An Edwardian shooting lodge, Monksford House, at Newton St Boswells in the Scottish borders, was currently deemed, 'by far the most suitable'.[36] What is certainly clear is that should the family be required to flee Yugoslavia, their destination of choice was Britain.

There was a brief touch of normality, when Olga and Princess Nicholas travelled to Florence for the wedding of her cousin Irene to Prince Aimone, the Duke of Spoleto on 1 July. Olga and Paul then began preparations for a two-week visit to England. The couple arrived in London, on 17 July, and were greeted, at Victoria Station, by Alexander and the Kents. The following evening, the King and Queen hosted a magnificent ball in the Yugoslavs' honour, attended by eight hundred guests who danced till dawn to the music of the Jack Jackson Orchestra. Thereafter, the Prince Regent was invested with the Order of the Garter, Britain's oldest and highest Order of Chivalry. Sir Nevile Henderson wrote from Berlin to proffer his congratulations, but warned Paul that war was inevitable.[37] The Prince was also keen to issue his own words of caution: During a lunch with Chamberlain at 10 Downing Street, Paul impressed on his host that Germany was committed to forming an alliance with Russia and that negotiations were already under way.[38] At the end of the visit, Henry Channon was at Victoria Station to bid Olga and Paul farewell and admitted to 'a gulp of misery' as he contemplated the couple's uncertain future.[39] Still, the Prince was praised in the press for, 'bearing a heavy burden and bearing it very well'. It was also acknowledged that the Regent primarily saw himself as a 'trustee' for King Peter and would do nothing which might 'jeopardise' the latter's position.[40]

At Brdo, Olga and Paul were joined by Miss Fox, the Kents, the Toerrings and Princess Nicholas. Unsurprisingly, the atmosphere was somewhat strained and since Yugoslavia intended to remain neutral in any conflict, it seemed increasingly likely that Olga would become Marina and Elisabeth's mutual point of contact. Events now moved surprisingly quickly: On 23 August, it was announced-as Paul had earlier predicted to Chamberlain-that Germany and Russia had signed a Treaty of Non-Aggression. To this Treaty was appended a secret protocol which divided eastern Europe into German and Soviet spheres of influence; this effectively gave the green light for further German territorial gains. On receiving this news, the Duke of Kent and Count Toerring both left Brdo for their respective homelands.

Olga now concentrated on helping to ease Paul's burden, as he continued to oversee negotiations for a settlement between the Serbs and Croats. Eventually, on 26 August, Prime Minister Cvetković and Maček signed a *Sporazum* (Agreement) which created the Banate (Banovina) of Croatia, a semi-autonomous entity which encompassed Croatia and large sections of Bosnia and Herzegovina. In addition, the Croat Peasant Party agreed to take their seats in the Skupština in Belgrade and participate in a coalition government, in which Maček would serve as Deputy Prime Minister. This Agreement was a major coup for the Prince Regent, as well as a severe blow to the Italian government, who had been under the impression that they already had Croatia "in the bag".[41]

At the end of August, as the European crisis deepened, Marina, Miss Fox, Alexander and Nicholas all returned to England. On 1 September, Germany invaded Poland and Elisabeth Toerring immediately set out for Munich. However, Princess Nicholas decided to remain at Brdo for the moment. On 3 September, Britain declared war on Germany. For devoted Anglophiles like the Prince and Princess, this was a dreadful blow. Indeed, as she returned to Belgrade next day, Olga wrote from the train to Marina to say she had listened the previous evening, 'to poor Bertie's broadcast followed by the [national] anthem-more than I could bare [sic]... and why all this? And how and when will it end?' She also admitted to being 'mad with worry', particularly for their sister Elisabeth who 'must be in such agony about Toto. So far, we don't know if he has been called up!' However, the Princess was also keen to reassure Marina that Paul, 'is amazingly calm and level-headed as always in such moments and has taken every precaution.'[42] Olga's chief desire was that Yugoslavia, 'keep out of it!' [43] She finished her long letter by entrusting the care of her sons to Marina and George, adding, 'I know I can count on you my sweet F'al to keep me somehow in touch with them.'[44]

Initially, the Princess was able to communicate with Countess Toerring, both in Munich and Winhöring, by telephone although they had to converse 'with care', as the German authorities, 'listen to every word.'[45] Unfortunately, Olga was unable to telephone Marina in England and she missed their regular chats. She now invariably concluded any correspondence with the Duchess of Kent (sent via the weekly diplomatic bag to London) with the heartfelt entreaty, 'I miss you so terribly and hug you with all my heart'. However, Queen Marie continued to irritate Olga by never asking after Alexander and Nicholas' welfare in England and generally behaved 'as though they don't exist!' Nevertheless, she tried to remain philosophical and informed Marina, 'Strange person *and what a world apart from our way of seeing things*-but I won't let it upset me, life is too full to get oneself embittered by what one can't help.'[46]

In due course, the Princess was diverted by the 'horrors in Poland'[8] and noted that 'with Russia coming in they haven't a chance.'[47] When she subsequently learned from refugees that Polish aristocrats were routinely being rounded up and shot by Soviet forces,[48] Olga must have realised that her ongoing antipathy towards this communist regime was justified. Another casualty of this war was her friend, Sir Nevile Henderson, who admitted to feeling 'broken in mind and body at the failure of my efforts and the tragic consequences of that failure.'[49] The former British Ambassador to Germany had been forced to leave Berlin in haste without most of his possessions, including his dog which was now being cared for by the Embassy's butler. His plight must have served as a salutary reminder to the Yugoslav royals of their own, equally precarious situation. The Princess' new role as the President of the Yugoslav Red Cross, ('a colossal business'[50]) left her with little time for self-reflection, as the organisation were now deeply involved in dealing with the floods of refugees who were arriving in Belgrade on a daily basis.

---

[8] On 17 September, Soviet troops invaded Poland via the country's undefended Eastern border.

In early October, Britain's Queen Elizabeth wrote a particularly positive fifteen-page letter to Paul: 'Humanity' she wrote '*must fight* against bad things if we are to survive' adding that 'This country has settled down grimly, quietly and <u>with the utmost determination</u> to try and rid the world of this evil thing that has been let loose by those idiotic Germans. It is truly a struggle of the spirit...' The subtext was clear: Yugoslavia should join Britain in this fight for 'the ultimate victory of good.' The letter ended with some wonderfully stirring words which reflected the esteem in which the Prince and Princess were held: 'Bertie thinks so often of you and Olga and all you have to bear. HOW LUCKY YUGOSLAVIA IS TO HAVE YOU.'[51]

The Duke of Kent was currently stationed in Scotland, at Admiralty House in North Queensferry. Paul had recently asked Prince George to act as Guardian to Alexander and Nicholas which he was 'very glad' to do.[52] Marina, meanwhile, was liaising with Miss Fox in an attempt to find suitable accommodation for Alexander and Nicholas for the Christmas holiday period. There was also a possibility that Elisabeth and her children might visit Belgrade from Bavaria, where food rationing was becoming more severe.[53] When, in late October, a censor in Berlin tersely informed Olga that all private phone calls to Germany from abroad were now forbidden, she came to the view that if Count Toerring was again called back to the Front, it would be safer if the Countess and her children remained in neutral Belgrade during their next visit.[54]

Unfortunately, there had lately been some unhelpful publicity about Quiss having joined Eton's Officer Training Corps. Paul-no doubt mindful of Yugoslavia's neutrality-was trying, with the aid of Henry Channon, to keep this news out of the British press.[55] The Prince and Princess were growing increasingly concerned about their eldest child: He had twice broken house rules at Eton and according to his housemaster had 'a casual outlook on life.' This view, however, was not shared by all of his teachers, some of whom felt that Alexander had promise and all were agreed that he was 'a very nice boy.' Nevertheless, his exasperated mother pondered in a letter to Miss Fox 'Why is it, I wonder, that he must always be our greatest source of worry?' Unfavourable comparisons with Nicholas inevitably began to emerge: 'Nicky has such a good report and writes to his father that he [is] trying for a scholarship.'[56]

On 6 November, Countess Toerring and her children finally arrived in Belgrade. Initially, there were the inevitable conversations about wartime shortages but soon there was a noticeable strain in relations between Elisabeth and Paul, with the under-pressure Regent proving particularly prickly. Indeed, Olga informed Marina, 'Occasionally the discussions border on violence but she [Elisabeth] tactfully keeps within limits, you know how Dicky [Paul] can be!'[57] Doubtless, Olga meant violent outbursts, not physical harm! Perhaps, out of tact, the Prince left for Brdo for three days to rest. It is also clear from Olga's correspondence that there was also a 'tragic gulf' between Countess Toerring and Marina[58]. Count Toerring then paid a short visit to Belgrade but remained 'buttoned up and silent'.[59] He and his wife returned to Munich on 4 December, leaving their children temporarily under Olga's care, although the children's nurses were soon 'getting on each other's nerves'[60] while Elizabeth sometimes became jealous when her mother played with little Helen.[61] However, the Princess was mainly preoccupied with her official duties, which now included presiding over a Committee entrusted with organising the evacuation of children from Belgrade, should that prove necessary.

With Christmas fast approaching, the Princess made a determined effort to celebrate, including ordering red candles and table decorations from Fortnum and Mason. However, she was somewhat thwarted by the poor choice of gifts available in Belgrade and complained to Foxie that this made it 'impossible to *compete* from here' with the wonderful gifts sent by Marina from England. In an uncharacteristic fit of petulance, she dismissed a new Kent family photograph as 'not good at all.'[62] However, the real issue was the absence of her sons without whom Christmas seemed, 'so unnatural somehow...'[63] She fretted too over Alexander's continuing lack of academic prowess and felt keenly that he should 'give more of himself' and 'grasp things in both hands'.[64]

As the New Year of 1940 dawned, the Princess tried to remain optimistic. She informed Marina, 'The future looks dark I must admit-but I <u>know</u> the light is there behind it all the time.'[65] Shortly thereafter, the Count of Paris and his sister Françoise, the second wife of Prince Christopher, overnighted at Beli Dvor, en route to Athens where the latter was 'seriously ill'.[66] Uncle Christopher died on 21 January, by which time divisions in the Princess' extended family were escalating: The Duke of Kent, after hearing that an enemy plane had strafed an unarmed fishing boat off the British coast, wrote to Paul decrying the Germans as, 'swine's' who 'really deserve to be exterminated.'[67]

On the diplomatic front, Raymond Brugère, the French Minister in Belgrade, now felt sure that the Prince Regent was aiming to have Yugoslavia enter the war on the Allied side, as soon as Allied forces had seized Salonika (Yugoslavia's only outlet to the Mediterranean) and cleared the Adriatic and Mediterranean of Axis forces.[68] The international press, meanwhile, was increasingly fascinated by the growing dilemma facing both Paul and Yugoslavia, with the *New York Times* alluding to the presence of, 'a German wolf and a Russian bear prowling around hungrily, while off at a distance the British lion is showing signs of irritability'.[69] Even Anthony Eden (now Secretary of State for Dominion Affairs) sympathised with Paul over his unenviable situation writing, 'I can well imagine how responsible and anxious your task must be in these difficult days.'[70]

In the middle of these escalating tensions, Paul and Olga paid a four-day visit to Zagreb to celebrate the *Sporazum* which the Prince Regent had worked so hard to secure. Although the stoical Princess managed to sit through a dinner at the Governor's residence with a temperature of 38.4 Celsius ('I suppose by sheer force of will'), the following morning she was forced to consult a doctor who gave her 'some very good stuff' which enabled her to attend an afternoon reception for eight hundred guests. Olga was temporarily buoyed-up by the visit and thought it 'a great success...'[71] The British Minister, Ronald Ian Campbell, was also impressed and informed his Foreign Secretary, Lord Halifax, that 'Prince Paul and Princess Olga played their parts magnificently, their prestige and popularity increasing visibly as their stay proceeded...'[72]

Back at Beli Dvor, the Princess was 'in despair'[73] over her sister Elisabeth's decision to take her children back to Germany. She then decided to travel to Athens for the funeral of Prince Christopher on 26 January. Although Olga originally planned to stay only two days, a bridge collapse near Salonika delayed her return to Belgrade for several weeks. Meanwhile, in Bulgaria, the pro-German politician, Bogdan Filov was appointed Prime Minister, further adding to the Prince Regent's woes. A concerned Olga informed Foxie that Paul was 'very run down & nervous & sleeps badly.'[74] She almost immediately regretted sending Elizabeth and Miss Ede off to Athens for a two-week holiday, in early March, as the house felt 'so sad and empty' in the 'depressing' weather.[75] In addition, relations between the Prince and Princess were tense as Olga had discovered that, during her earlier absence in Greece, Paul had opened some letters addressed to her from Marina.[76] The Princess also complained to her mother that during telephone conversations between Belgrade and Athens she had to leave, 'so much unsaid and unasked' as Paul, 'would sit there the whole time, soit disant plunged in a book but I could see he followed every word I said-*quite paralyzing*.'[77]

In late March, Henry Channon (with Churchill's approval) visited Belgrade and was immediately entranced by Beli Dvor which he described as 'grande luxe' with 'glorious food and silent sullen bowing Serbs, sentries and heel clicking A.D.C.'s everywhere.'[78] Chips was equally impressed by Paul noting, 'up to now his instinct has been unerring, *and he is surely one of the most astute diplomats and statesmen of our time*.'[79] The visit clearly had an important purpose as the Duke of Kent would later write to the Regent, '*I hope you got all the information you wanted from him...*'[80] Channon took his leave, on the evening of

29 March, filled with deep misgivings and feared that the Nazis might 'swoop down upon him [the Prince Regent] and destroy his haven and his people.'[81] Meanwhile, from her home in England, Mignon made it crystal clear in letters to Paul that she was now very content to leave 'my Peter boy'[82] under his and Olga's charge having, 'made up my mind that the question of my travelling for some time to come is out of the question.'[83] Indeed, it would soon become almost impossible.

Just as Olga was preparing to travel to England to spend the Easter school break at Coppins, her departure was delayed by the German invasion of Denmark and Norway on 9 April. The Princess was naturally anxious about leaving Paul at such a difficult time, but she also realised that her sons and the Kents (who had opened-up Coppins specially for the holidays) were keen to see her. She eventually departed Belgrade by train, on 11 April, accompanied by her sister Elisabeth who had been spending a short holiday in Belgrade. The sisters parted at Ljubljana and Olga informed her mother that, 'It was beastly saying good-bye to Fael... and to see her go off alone...She cried a lot when we parted poor darling- it's awful being so suddenly cut off from her!' Reaching Paris on 13 April, the Princess spent the morning with her friend Sofica des Isnards before boarding an Air France flight for the final leg of her journey to England–her first experience of flying in an aeroplane. As a special wartime precaution the flight was given a military air escort to Heston Aerodrome, where Marina was waiting to greet her sister. Olga had decided to take a suite at the Dorchester for convenience and the sisters were soon enjoying a 'cosy tea together [and] talking our heads off ...', while Miss Fox 'sobbed with emotion' on being reunited with her former charge.[84]

The following morning, the Princess travelled down to Coppins with Nicholas and noticed that Prince George was, 'not looking very well, with blotchy and pale patches on his face.' Olga must have mentioned this to Marina, who informed her that, 'he has not been well lately and seems to rather resent his inactivity at [a desk job at] the Admiralty and [the] lack of exercise.' That evening, Georgy sat crocheting ('a killing sight') and the Princess sensed that he, 'seemed to want me to talk to him', so she 'gave up' on her attempts at letter writing. But there were light-hearted moments too: Olga informed Princess Nicholas that, 'the children insisted that he [Prince George] and I should bath them, so we draped ourselves in aprons and did one each amidst a pandemonium of splashing and laughter!'[85]

After lunching with the King and Queen and Queen Mary at Buckingham Palace, on 15 April, the Princess' skills as a nurse were soon put into use when Nicholas caught mumps.[86] Alexander too was in need of maternal reassurance, following an earlier attack of German measles.

He was currently recuperating with the Buccleuchs in Scotland and when Olga joined him there, she was delighted to discover that 'my Quissy' had 'at last' received 'a really good [school report] and full of praise.'[87] Nevertheless, according to Prince George, Alexander was experiencing problems with Miss Fox; he had 'outgrown her' and was not enjoying 'being ordered about by an old woman.'[88] The Princess, however, was distracted by worrying news from Paul: He had decided to send Elizabeth to Lausanne, in neutral Switzerland, under the care of Miss Ede, as he feared an attack on Yugoslavia by the Italians was imminent. Clearly, the Regent still continued to view Britain as the ultimate refuge for he informed his wife that if things were not 'normal' by the time she was due to return home, Elizabeth 'will be taken to Paris and from there you can arrange about her joining you [in England].' He took the very sensible view that, 'at least, you'll [then] have all three children under your wing...'[89]

In the interim, Olga, Alexander and Marina lunched with Mignon who later informed Paul it was, '[a] joy to see them.'[90] Princess Olga also received 'unanimous praise' for her husband's neutral stance from her British friends and discovered that, 'many agree [with me] that they [the British government] are too slow here to make decisions.'[91] This was a viewpoint shared by the Prince Regent who complained that, 'one nation perishes after another before they even begin to move'.[92]

Elizabeth and Miss Ede arrived in London by air from Paris on 9 May. It is a mercy that they had not tarried long in Switzerland, as next day German forces advanced into the Low Countries. Paul had already informed his wife to do as she, 'thought best as he could not foresee the future.' The Princess had briefly wondered about sending Elizabeth to Coppins but feared that she and her cousin Edward might clash as they both possessed 'decided' characters. Furthermore, Olga was also wary of Prince George, who was not proving to be as malleable as Marina over future accommodation arrangements.[93]

The Princess then unwittingly found herself on the edges of a political drama, when she lunched with the Prime Minister Neville Chamberlain and Lord Halifax at the Dorchester, on 10 May, for immediately thereafter Chamberlain left to tender his resignation to the King at Buckingham Palace. Although Bertie favoured Halifax as Chamberlain's successor, the latter was not keen to accept the post. The King subsequently invited Winston Churchill to form a unified National Government. The Princess wondered 'What will it mean?' but almost answered herself by noting, 'At this moment many think that the new P.M. is the right person, *being more ruthless and unscrupulous*. On verra.'[94]Indeed.

Certainly, Olga was now prepared for exile and informed Miss Fox that she and her husband would probably be 'kicked out [of Yugoslavia] and abroad' by the year's end.[95] However, with the war literally on Britain's doorstep, she urgently needed to contact Paul for further instructions. A coded telegram was duly sent to Belgrade by the Yugoslav Minister in London and the Prince Regent replied on 15 May (just as the Germans advanced across the River Meuse into France), to say that the Princess should either leave immediately or not at all. Fortunately, the Duke of Kent-who had just been appointed a staff officer at RAF Training Command-came to the rescue and arranged for her to fly to Le Bourget in the King's plane. Olga then boarded the Simplon Express in Paris and reached Belgrade (and an emotional reunion with a Paul) on 19 May.[96] It had proved difficult for her to leave the children behind in England, but she realised that they would be well looked after by the Kents and Miss Fox. However, at the end of May, as German forces advanced through northern France and British troops were being evacuated from the beaches at Dunkirk, the Prince and Princess arranged for Elizabeth to return to Yugoslavia. Otherwise, Olga resolutely resumed her official duties, although she was clearly preparing for impending trouble. She informed Foxie that she had, 'put order' in her papers and 'been through all my drawers *and burnt heaps, which is often wise.*'[97]

On 14 June, German forces advanced into Paris and met with no resistance. The fall of France can hardly have instilled much confidence in either Olga or Paul, for if the Germans were able to achieve such an easy victory against a major power, what chance did Yugoslavia have? To make matters worse, on 10 June Mussolini took the "plunge" and sided with Germany. Although, Il Duce rushed to reassure the countries of the Balkans that they were in no danger from invasion, the cynical Allied press observed that the Italian dictator was merely, 'aping his [German] Master' as similar assurances had been given by Hitler to the Low Countries.[98] On 24 June, the Yugoslav government formally recognised the Soviet Union from whom it now hoped to buy some much-needed armaments. This diplomatic development had personal repercussions for Olga, who noted indignantly in her diary, 'I had the ordeal of having the Soviet Minister and wife at 11! I wore a cross around my neck which I held all the time.'[99] Nevertheless, the Soviet Union could prove to be a useful ally, as it was opposed to Italy's expansionist policies in the Balkans and could act as a check on a move by Mussolini against Yugoslavia.

Chapter 14 Yugoslavia in Crisis

With most of its allies now under German occupation and an invasion by Hitler's forces imminent, the Foreign Office in London belatedly turned its attention to the Balkans. Paul received an impersonal political letter from George VI on 3 July (actually written by a Whitehall mandarin) in which the King admired 'the firm and independent lines you have chosen.'[1] The purpose of the letter was apparently aimed at 'stiffening the attitude of the Regent'[2] so that Yugoslavia would maintain this stance. There was also some amusing news of Queen Marie from the Duke of Kent: Apparently, she possessed, 'an arsenal of guns and expects to protect herself from all comers.'[3]

By early July, Olga had moved to Brdo accompanied by Elizabeth and Miss Ede. The Princess lamented to Miss Fox that correspondence with England had now dropped to a trickle, adding that she was anxious for her sons to return home as, 'we dread what lies in the future...'[4] The increasing external pressures on Olga and Paul were again impacting on their personal lives and causing matters to be blown out of all proportion. The Princess confessed to her mother (in a letter dated 16 July) that, since her return from England, there had been a 'change of mood' on Paul's part towards her. Eventually, she had tackled him, 'quietly (because I've found that a grand hurt tone goes nowhere with him) *why we seem to have become strangers...*' Apparently, the Prince had earlier 'discovered' and read a letter Olga had been in the course of writing to a friend in response to one of theirs. She had previously 'slipped' this, along with some other letters, between the pages of a book in her bathroom. The Princess was astounded to learn that Paul felt the tone of this letter, 'was proof enough that I had a feeling ... more than friendship, a "love letter" in other words!!' But why had Paul gone into and searched through his wife's bathroom, in the first place? Was it because he did not trust his wife? Such a motivation was perfectly plausible for he now informed a, *'stunned and bewildered'* Olga, *'that he had swallowed a lot of things on my part which had made him miserable before...'* but *'...this was the last straw and we couldn't possibly go on living together...'* as *'he could never have the same feeling for me again.'* The Princess admitted to Princess Nicholas that she, 'could not deny that the letter had some affectionate silly phrases in it as I was replying in the same spirit..., *but which certainly did not mean any deeper feeling'*. Olga had even 'tried to explain [to Paul] the essence of my fondness' for the friend, which was 'in all sincerity-a mixture of [my] loneliness' and the friend's 'enthusiasm and love of Greece which had fired my own...' That night the couple slept apart, the Princess *'feeling quite broken.'* Fortunately, she subsequently succeeded in convincing her husband, 'that there was nothing in the whole thing, enough to wreck our lives.' However, Olga also confided to her mother that the whole episode had, 'been very shattering and nerve-racking as you can imagine and a horrid experience.'[5]

On 21 July, Alexander and Nicholas left England to begin the perilous sea and land journey home via Lisbon and Vichy just as Germany commenced air attacks over the south of England. Unsurprisingly, the Princess was glad beyond words when they arrived at Brdo on 3 August. Providentially, the boys' presence helped to lighten the mood as they busied themselves playing tennis and swimming. Another welcome visitor was Princess Ileana of Romania. Disturbingly, her Austrian castle at Sonnberg had recently been searched room by room by the Nazi Schutzstaffel (SS).[6]

It was this juncture that Britain created the Special Operations Executive (SOE), under the directorship of Hugh Dalton, the Minister for Economic Warfare. The SOE's aim was to provide support to resistance movements abroad through sabotage and subversion. The organisation relied mainly on the collusion of key members of the local population, under the supervision of British operatives.[7] Throughout the second half of 1940, as Yugoslavia became of increasing strategic interest to the British, the SOE focused on developing a united Serbian front which would oppose any attempt to offer concessions to the Axis powers. Tom Masterson led the SOE operations from an office in Belgrade.[8]

Although the Kents were absent, the Toerrings were still able to make an autumn visit to Brdo in September, as did a very worried Princess Nicholas. The latter rightly feared that Italy had designs on Greece and there was invariably a distinct froideur towards Toto and Elisabeth whenever politics was mentioned, for as Olga acknowledged, 'so much we see with different eyes.'[9] Unfortunately, the Prince Regent was unable to take a good rest in Slovenia, as there was the usual procession of co-regents, government officials and diplomats seeking to confer with him.

Inevitably, the recent defeats sustained by the Allies were weighing heavily on Paul and Olga's mind, and when news came through, on 7 September, of the first intense German air raids on London, the Princess agonised over the safety of the Kents and Kate Fox.[10] The Prince and Princess were further shaken when Romania's King Carol was forced to abdicate on 6 September, leaving his country under the control of the

Fascist Conducător (dictator) Ion Antonescu and his brutal Iron Guard. Paul came to Carol and his mistress, Magda Lupescu's, aid by arranging for their safe passage through Yugoslavia to Italy.[11] However, Olga's main concern was again for her cousin Helen: Following Carol's abdication, Sitta's son Michael was once again proclaimed King of Romania and Antonescu permitted Helen to return from exile in Florence to be with him. Although Sitta subsequently telephoned Olga to tell her of the wonderful reception she had received from the people[12] the Queen Mother and Michael were watched over by Antonescu's spies and their movements severely restricted.

Around this time, King Peter received his commission as a second lieutenant in the Yugoslav forces. The Princess was happy to observe that Paul made time to sit with Peter after dinner, when they would discuss events and listen to the radio bulletins. However, the Prince Regent was soon filled with apprehension by the signature, on 27 September, of a Tripartite Pact between Italy, Germany and Japan. This was designed 'to establish and maintain a new order of things'[13] and provide mutual support militarily, politically and economically between the signatories. As if on cue, German troops then advanced into Romania and Yugoslavia found itself having to share yet another border with an Axis-controlled country. However, Hitler had lately grown tired of Mussolini 'ramming the Yugoslav issue down the Nazi throat' and now made it clear to the Italians that their troops would not be permitted to conduct operations against the Slavs from German-controlled territories[14]. Italy, therefore, turned its attentions towards Greece, as it provided an ideal location from which to establish aero-naval bases for use against British operations in the Near and Middle East. Olga was thus forced to look on helplessly as Italian forces invaded the north-west of her homeland from bases in Albania at the end of October. She scoffed too, over Italy's 'open excuses' that the subsequent bombing of the Macedonian city of Bitoli, by three Italian Royal Air Force planes, had been 'by mistake'.[15] However, the Princess was at least able to channel her anger into practical deeds by liaising with the Director of the Yugoslav Red Cross to provide some welfare assistance to Greece.[16] Meanwhile, Paul met with his War Minister, General Petar Pešić, who was subsequently able to offer the Greek High Command expert advice on organising a counter-attack against the Italians. This offensive campaign proved particularly successful and, throughout November, Greek forces under the command of General Papagos made significant advances into Southern Albania. The Princess was naturally pleased at 'such wonderful results' from 'our brave little [Greek] soldiers' which, she informed Miss Fox, 'fill me with pride and thankfulness to God who surely protects the cause of justice and liberty.'[17]

Following upon this progress, Churchill was keen to forge a Balkan bulwark against Axis advances and provide further support to the Greeks. Thus, another stilted missive, dated 14 November, arrived from King George VI urging Paul 'to talk with your courageous neighbour Greece, and also to Turkey on the subject of closer cooperation...' In addition, the British were keen to ensure that Yugoslavia maintained a neutral stance and did not engage Italians forces in Albania, as this might draw the Germans directly into the conflict. Nevertheless, the King's official note conceded that '*you may have to make concessions to the Axis on non-essential matters. At the same time, I am sure you will never give way where the sovereignty of your country is concerned...*'[18] Was this an acknowledgement that Yugoslavia might have to work with the Axis powers, so long as this did not involve surrendering its neutrality? If so, what was to be the scope of any such 'concessions'? Tellingly, there was no British offer of much-needed armaments for the increasingly besieged Regent and his country.

But events were already spiralling out of control: Hungary and Romania signed the Tripartite Pact on 20 and 23 November respectively, just as Lord Halifax was informing the British War Cabinet that Bulgaria might also join the Axis side under pressure from Ribbentrop.[19] The British Minister in Belgrade now realised that a progressively ringfenced Yugoslavia risked facing 'the immediate possibility of most severe Axis pressure' and sent a telegram to the Foreign Office in London, on 23 November, pleading for something 'to strengthen the hands of the Prince Regent' against opposition rumblings.[20] Unfortunately, a subsequent memorandum by the British Chiefs of Staff indicated that they could only offer 'highly limited'[21] naval and air support to the Yugoslavs which may account for the British Foreign Office's vague response to Campbell in Belgrade: If Yugoslavia had to act to defend its freedom and independence, 'they may rest assured that H[er] M[ajesty's] G[overnment] will make a common cause with them.'[22] With such indefinite words, it is hardly surprising that Paul, on logical reflection, favoured maintaining a neutral stance, whilst also attempting to build up Yugoslav military forces.

However, the British government would soon require much more from the Prince Regent and his country. Following Italy's 'botching up'[23] of the invasion of Greece, an impatient Hitler was initially focused on a Peripheral Strategy, which would transfer the war to the Eastern Mediterranean, so as to shift the balance of power there in favour of the Axis. Any German assault on Greece was to come from the north through Bulgaria[24] and Hitler was immediately faced with a dilemma over which route should be used by his forces: One possibility was via Hungary and Romania, while the other traversed Austria and Yugoslavia. The latter choice was much preferable, as it would enable German troops to be transported from Vienna and Klagenfurt right through to Belgrade and onward to Sofia. The route also avoided crossing the Danube and cut the distance German forces would have to cover by half. However, this option would require the Yugoslav government to grant Germany rights of transit or, at the very least, maintain a 'benevolent neutrality'[25] as the German route through Bulgaria made use of a railway which skirted along Yugoslavia's Eastern border.

As the British Minister in Belgrade had predicted, the first of many "invitations" now arrived from Berlin seeking Paul's presence for talks.[26] The Prince Regent, however, decided to send his Foreign Minister, with strict instructions to commit to nothing.[27] Cincar-Marković met with Hitler at Fuschl in Austria, on 28 November. The Führer by-passed the rights of transit question and instead requested that Yugoslavia should sign a non-aggression pact with Germany and Italy. This came with the added taster of an offer to grant the vital seaport of Salonika to Yugoslavia.[28] The Princess was aware of this development and, on 5 December, observed that Paul had presided over a 'long counsel [sic]' of Ministers to discuss the matter. [29] Eventually, on 7 December, the Belgrade government informed the German Minister in Belgrade, von Heeren, that it was 'willing to discuss' the possibility of signing such a pact.[30] However, the Princess admitted to Kate Fox that, in general, she tried not to 'dwell upon' the war 'too much' and had learned to relax by reading extracts from her father's memoirs to Nicholas (who displayed a keen interest in his ancestors) or making fabric-covered hangars for a forthcoming charity bazaar.[31] To have 'plenty to do', she informed Marina, was 'a blessing'.[32] Meanwhile, to the consternation of Ronald Ian Campbell, the SOE were currently arming potential opponents of the Prince Regent and his government with rifles and grenades (sent out to Belgrade by diplomatic courier from London, as well as through the British Military Mission in Athens).[33]

On 21 December, the German Foreign Minister, Ribbentrop informed von Heeren-to the initial bewilderment of the Yugoslavs-that the non-aggression pact option was no longer viable, 'for the strengthening of Yugoslavia's relations with the Axis powers'.[34] It transpired that Hitler had decided to shelve his Peripheral Strategy in favour of an attack on the Soviet Union ("Operation Barbarossa") in the spring of 1941. This volte face was in part due to the Soviet Foreign Minister Vyacheslav Molotov pronouncing, during a recent visit to Berlin, that his country would resist any attempts by Germany to penetrate the Balkans.[35] To help achieve this new objective, Hitler now sought a much quicker preliminary defensive attack on Greece to secure his southern flank ("Operation Marita") prior to mounting Operation Barbarossa. In addition, he also needed to obtain the aforementioned

German military transit rights across Yugoslavia to Sofia, as this would shorten the period of this first interdependent phase of the new campaign from ten weeks to six weeks.[36] The Germans, however, would soon discover that the Yugoslavs, led by the Prince Regent, could be 'tough bargainers.'[37]

As the year drew to a close, Olga admitted to feeling a little tired, for in addition to her other duties, she had also been caring for Elizabeth, as Miss Ede had succumbed to a bad cold. Nevertheless, she stoically entertained the Bishop of Gibraltar to tea and, on 24 December, took a welcome call from her cousin George in Athens, who telephoned to thank Paul for the food that Yugoslavia had provided to the Greek army.[38] Olga's belief in God continued to provide her with a firm anchor during these troubled times and she prayed regularly for friends and family.[39] Nevertheless, she was unnerved to learn from Prince George that a 'whole load' of bombs had been dropped near Coppins,[40] and she later wrote to Marina to express her concern at the 'risks' she was taking in making tours of England's worst bomb-damaged areas.[41] The Princess ended 1940 by making her first radio appeal on behalf of her Winter Help charity.

As 1941 dawned-the last period of Paul's Regency as Peter would attain his majority in September-Olga hoped that the war would soon end.[42] The exhausted Prince Regent (who had briefly considered resigning as Head of State at the end of December) was currently concerned that Cvetković was struggling to maintain support in Belgrade for the *Sporazum*.[43] During another telephone call to Belgrade on 6 January, Greece's King George spoke to Paul of his concern about German troop movements in Romania and his fear that Nazi forces would soon move into Bulgaria to join with the Italians in mounting an attack on Greece. The thought of such a 'dirty trick' being perpetuated against her homeland infuriated Olga.[44] The Princess noted too that Paul had received a 'long letter' from General Metaxas 'explaining his fears' that Axis troops would be permitted to pass through Yugoslavia so as to invade Greece.[45] The Regent replied that while Yugoslavia was, 'not in a position to take an offensive attitude unless actually attacked ourselves', German troops would not be allowed to pass through Yugoslavia and that his forces would 'maintain our [current] mobilisation so as not to be caught unprepared.'[46]

The Toerrings arrived in Belgrade on 10 January, followed two days later by Henry Channon. For Olga, Chips' presence was 'like a bit of the old days' and provided 'a link with F'al [Marina].'[47]After lunch Channon had a chance to talk to the Regent whom he found 'violently anti-German' and 'playing for time; until we [the British] are more powerful.' Paul therefore 'prayed' that 'England would not do anything rash like sending troops to Greece, which would only bring the Germans southwards into the Balkans'.[48] His hopes were soon to be dashed for that very evening the British Minister called on the Prince and informed him that Churchill had approved the sending of British forces into Greece to form a united Balkan front.[49] Paul subsequently stressed to Ronald Ian Campbell during a 'heated' audience, [50] that such an action could provoke Hitler into mounting a 'strong' German attack on Salonika[51] and thus precipitate a full-scale Balkan war at a time when Yugoslavia was 'quite unprepared'.[52] When Campbell duly reported Paul's fears in a ciphered telegram to London, Churchill, knowing that General Wavell had already arrived in Athens for consultations with the Greeks, simply brushed the Regent's protests aside. In a Minute to Anthony Eden[9] he noted, 'In the face of it Prince Paul's attitude looks like that of an unfortunate man in a cage with a tiger, hoping not to provoke him, while dinner-time steadily approaches.'[53] Nevertheless, the British Minister in Belgrade was a staunch supporter of the Regent and subsequently implored Chips, over lunch, to try and persuade Paul to stay on at the end of his Regency, rather than hand over the reins of power to a young boy with war threatening.[54]

The Princess' diaries and correspondence were now increasingly concerned with the deteriorating situation on Yugoslavia's border and she was particularly disturbed to learn, on 17 January, that civilian train transport had been suspended in Hungary so as to focus on troop transportation[55] (with the unwritten fear that Hungarian forces might soon be heading in these trains towards Belgrade). The Princess even indicated to Miss Fox that they might both be enjoying 'those lovely, cosy teas round your table' perhaps 'sooner than we think!' (Did she already feel her days in Belgrade were numbered?) Certainly, Olga lamented to Foxie that, 'The outlook all round us looks pretty black & for P[aul] it's like walking on live wire more than ever'. She also acknowledged that, 'one must be prepared for the worse if it must come'.[56]

On 19 January, the Princess helped Henry Channon to pack in anticipation of his departure for Athens. Chips remained concerned for his friends and noted, 'I have the curious empty vacuum sensation of being on the edge of a volcano which may erupt tonight'.[57] Next morning, as Channon prepared to leave for Greece (armed with a pile of letters and parcels from Olga for Princess Nicholas), Olga observed forlornly, 'how I envy him.'[58] Chips saw 'tears come into Princess Olga's fine eyes' which troubled him as 'she is usually so undemonstrative'. Paul seemed equally

---

[9] Anthony Eden was reappointed British Foreign Secretary on 22 December 1940.

downhearted and murmured, 'Goodbye Chips, I fear I may never see you again'.[59] Ironically, the British cabinet were now informed that the Greek government were currently refusing to allow the deployment of British forces in their country[60] (and echoing Paul's fears) reasoning that the arrival of the rather limited British contingent available would merely precipitate a German attack, without offering Greece any meaningful assistance.[61]

Even at this juncture, the diplomatic round continued: The Princess acted as hostess at a lunch, on 23 January, in honour of President Roosevelt's European envoy, Colonel William Donovan, who subsequently had a long talk with Paul. He issued an ultimatum, indicating that if Yugoslavia permitted the German military rights of transit, the United States would not 'interfere on her behalf' at any subsequent peace talks.[62] The Regent assured Donovan that Yugoslavia would fight rather than allow German troops to cross her country.[63] On 29 January, news of the death of Greece's esteemed General Metaxas so unsettled the Princess that she sent for the Greek Minister, Raoul Bibica-Rosetti, to discuss its implications. He sought to reassure her that the Greek forces, 'will continue to fight even harder in his memory.'[64]

Within days Olga was observing that, 'Pacey had more very disquieting and threatening news from Germany'.[65] With Axis pressure mounting, Cvetković indicated that he and Cincar-Marković would be prepared to visit Germany for talks. A Crown Council was held on 8 February to discuss the upcoming meeting with Hitler, which was arranged for 14 February at Berchtesgaden. Although the Princess found her husband 'very depressed'[66] about the impending talks as well as, 'harassed & anxious for the future'[67] she, by contrast, remained remarkably resolute, 'One must be prepared to face it [war] if it comes our way, with God's help.'[68] Olga's political sympathies continued to lie both with her homeland and the British: In a response to Princess Nicholas she observed, 'If only we could join hands and fight the common danger together. Our position just now is so angoissant...'[69] The Princess wrote to Kate Fox in a similar vein noting, 'how earnestly I pray for our brave little [Greek] soldiers and that all their sacrifices [against the Italians in Albania] should not be in vain.' She also praised the recent, 'sensational' Allied successes at Benghazi in North Africa.[70] However, the latter victory was to have serious repercussions for Yugoslavia as, despite Athens' earlier misgivings, Churchill was now focused on sending British troops to provide 'speedy succour' to Greece against a possible German attack and help counter any threat to Britain's position in the Near East.[71] To help achieve this goal, Britain now expected Yugoslavia to discard the neutrality policy and fight alongside

British and Turkish forces, to defend the southern Balkan peninsula from German forces.

In the meantime, Yugoslav officials put up a determined stand at the Berchtesgaden meetings, with Cvetković emphasising to Ribbentrop that Yugoslavia was only interested in maintaining peace in the Balkans. The German Foreign Minister's response was to try and sweet talk his guests into committing Yugoslavia to sign the Tripartite Pact by emphasising that this accord was aimed at 'preventing the extension of the war' and 'did not represent a treaty of alliance against England.'[72] When Cvetković subsequently met with Hitler, later in the day, he emphasised the need for a diplomatic solution and, intent on gaining valuable time, proposed that the Prince Regent and the Fuhrer should meet at a later date to discuss matters further.[73]

No sooner had Olga been informed by her mother that news of the Berchtesgaden talks had been badly received in Greece,[74] than the pressure on Yugoslavia continued to gather momentum with the announcement, on 17 February, that Turkey and Bulgaria had signed a non-aggression pact. The Princess thought this move, 'folly' as it left 'the way clear for the Germans to march [unchallenged] through to Thrace!'[75] She also noted in exasperation that Paul was trying to plot a way forward diplomatically but was still awaiting a response to a note sent to her cousin Georgie in Athens asking, 'some vital questions for future moves.'[76] When the King's response finally arrived, it proved 'rather vague.'[77]

A few days later, Olga was again tearing up, 'heaps more papers'[78] as German troops were 'massing' on the Romanian border with Bulgaria which, she noted, 'can only be with one object...'[79] Indeed, for the Yugoslav government, this menacing military build-up on its doorstep, now 'spoke a stronger language than moral exhortations from England's friends'.[80] Nonetheless, the Princess carried on with her duties and attended a charity art auction in aid of impoverished artists.

On 22 February, Anthony Eden arrived in Athens to hold discussions with the Hellenic government over possible British military aid to Greece. The British were now of the view that, 'it would not be safe' to count on Yugoslavia in any forthcoming conflict. Nevertheless, an approach was made through Campbell in Belgrade to ascertain the Yugoslav government's current stance.[81] On 27 February, Yugoslavia's 'attitude' was relayed through their Ambassador in Turkey to Eden at the British Embassy in Ankara: Yugoslavia would defend itself against any aggression and would not allow foreign troops to pass through its territory.[82]

The Princess was by now keenly aware of rising tensions within Yugoslavia: While giving tea to Dr Katherine MacPhail on 26 February, she observed that the Scotswoman appeared 'v[ery] worried' and was even considering evacuating her children's hospital at Sremska Kamenica.[83] A few days later, Olga received the Minister for Public Health in order, 'to make concrete decisions' for a general medical evacuation scheme.[84] Troublingly, on 1 March, Bulgaria's Filov government signed the Tripartite Pact in Vienna and, as the Princess had predicted, troops of the German Twelfth Army subsequently marched into Bulgaria from Romania, closing the Axis ring around Yugoslavia and putting intense pressure on the Prince Regent and his government.

Having already spent nearly £100,000 on SOE operations in Yugoslavia at this juncture, the British now sent out a new official, Major George Taylor, from London as Chief Representative to coordinate the SOE's Balkan operations. These were increasingly focused on 'encouraging' the Yugoslav opposition to put pressure on Cvetković's government not to side with the Axis powers. Taylor discovered that the organisation, under Masterson, had already established a considerable network of contacts including Milos Tupanjanin of the Serbian Peasant Party (SPP) and Ilija Trifunović, President of the Serbian National Associations and Chairman of the Narodna Odbrana (an SOE-funded Serbian patriotic organisation).[85] In addition, the SOE were also actively bribing army personnel in order to facilitate a regime change.[86]

Following upon Bulgaria's ascension to the Tripartite Pact, the chief members of the Yugoslav government (including the Prime Minister and Maček) 'insisted' that the Prince Regent meet with Hitler.[87] Thus, after dinner on 2 March, Olga bid her husband an emotional farewell as he departed by train for Brdo, en route to Berchtesgaden, 'in a very depressed condition'. She felt helpless and observed, 'I long to help him and share his worries'.[88] The following day, the apprehensive Regent rang his wife twice from Slovenia, doubtless for some much-needed support. However, in her husbands' absence, the Princess was feeling increasingly isolated in Belgrade, particularly when she learned that Eden was currently being feted, 'amid wild enthusiasm' in her native Athens.[89]

On 4 March, the Prince Regent arrived at Berchtesgaden for the meeting with Hitler which lasted for several hours. The Fuhrer tried to intimidate Paul by inferring that once British forces had been cleared from Greece, the Germans would not remain in the Balkans indefinitely, thus creating a power vacuum which might allow Salonika, so strategically important to the Yugoslavs, to fall to the Italians or Bulgarians. The Regent parried by explaining, 'how difficult for him the decision was' given, *the Greek descent of his wife [and] his personal sympathies for England...*'[90] Hitler then asked Paul 'point blank to join the Tripartite Pact on the grounds that he needed a strong independent

Yugoslavia '"aus egoitischen grunden" *and that he could no longer protect us [Yugoslavia] unless the signature of Mussolini was on the same document next to his.'* The Regent countered that he did not believe there could be peace in Europe without an 'Anglo-German understanding' and added that it would be impossible for Yugoslavia to sign the Pact due to the clauses which required each signatory to assist one another militarily. Surprisingly, the Fuhrer indicated that these 'might be avoided'.[91] Despite significant pressure from Hitler-and the latter's promise that Salonika would be ceded to Yugoslavia at the end of the war-the Prince 'reserved' any decision on signing the pact and indicated that it was for the Yugoslav government to consider the path offered by Germany.[92] The Regent left Berchtesgaden, 'convinced that war was inevitable but that we had to gain time to be able to mobilize.'[93] Although Olga made no direct reference to the Berchtesgaden meeting, in her diary entry for 4 March, she did write, 'Think so much of Paul today.'[94] On the same day, she wrote to Foxie that, *'so much hangs in the balance...'*[95]

British government policy was by now firmly directed towards preventing Yugoslavia signing the Pact: While the Prince was holding his discussions with Hitler, Campbell returned to Belgrade from a meeting in Athens with Eden, armed with another of the Foreign Minister's pleading letters to Paul, as well as instructions, 'to make a determined attempt to check the deterioration in the Prince Regent's attitude.' The British Minister was also told to 'outline' British plans in Greece and make a request that Yugoslav staff officer(s) should be sent to Athens at once to discuss future tactics, in the hope of persuading the Slavs to become involved.[96]

On 5 March, as British troops landed in Greece, Olga met with the Court Minister, Milan Antić, and pressed him about her cousin Georgie's need for further clarification of Yugoslavia's position vis-à-vis her homeland. However, the Court Minister said that they must await Paul's arrival. The Prince duly returned at 10.20 that evening to be met at the station by Olga and Ronald Ian Campbell (who handed over Eden's latest letter). The British Foreign Secretary now wrote urging the Regent to, 'join with us' at a time the Germans had designs on Salonika, thus leaving Yugoslavia 'at Germany's mercy' such that 'bit by bit her independent national life would be choked out of her', and 'then Italy would take her pound of flesh from the helpless victim'.[97] The contents of Eden's letter certainly seemed to strike a chord with Olga who noted, *'It makes me go back to my 1st & real feeling-not to stay passive.'*[98] Clearly, if the decision had been hers alone to make (and with no other considerations on which to deliberate), Yugoslavia would have come to her homeland's aid and fought the Germans.

The Prince summoned a Crown Council for 6 March during which he gave an account of his conversation with Hitler and Cincar-Marković. He followed this up with an analysis of Yugoslavia's current position with respect to Germany.[99] However, the Princess noted that despite the majority of the Council being 'for fighting', at the request of Maček, the War Minister, General Pešić, then gave an assessment of Yugoslavia's ability to defend itself in the event of war. His conclusions, she observed, were damning: 'It would be a disaster after 2 weeks as we have not enough ammunition and would lack food'. Olga was all too aware that the current food shortage in Yugoslavia was, ironically, in part due to 'heaps' of food being sent to fortify the Greek army.[100] The War Minister also warned that, in the event of war, the Germans would quickly overrun the entire northern part of Yugoslavia (including the three main cities of Belgrade, Zagreb and Llubljana) and the retreating Yugoslav army would be forced to hide out in the Herzegovinian mountains.[101] Pešić therefore favoured reaching favourable terms with Germany, a view which was shared by General Kosić, the Yugoslav Chief of Staff.[102] Maček's response was equally robust: He 'insisted' on Yugoslavia signing the pact, while his Slovene colleague, Father Kulovec, was 'solidaire' with him.[103] By contrast, despite the gloomy military assessment, the Princess continued to have strong misgivings and noted, 'if we sign the pact, we cannot help Greece and [it] would be slowly paralized [sic]. Meanwhile the Germ[ans] will march on Salonika, Turkey won't move and all the sacrifices are in vain and Italy is compensated.'[104]

A Yugoslav Draft Agreement, containing onerous conditions which required to be guaranteed by Germany, before a final decision could be taken on the signing (or not) of the Pact, was presented by Cvetković to von Heeren, for transmission to Berlin on 7 March. The first condition was that the sovereignty and territorial integrity of Yugoslavia would be respected. Secondly, no military assistance or collaboration would be required from Yugoslavia (nor would the passage or transportation of German troops be permitted through its territory during the war). Finally, Yugoslavia's interest in a free outlet to the Aegean Sea through Salonika would be taken into account in any reorganisation of Europe.[105] In the meantime, Cvetković told Olga he was against signing the Pact[106] while the Princess' Lady-in-Waiting informed her mistress that, 'one and all want to fight & make any sacrifice rather than become slaves.'[107]

The Yugoslav government, meanwhile, decided to take up Eden's offer of sending a Staff Officer to Athens to consult with the British and Greek General Staff. During these discussions, held on 8 and 9 March, the Yugoslavs sought a clear indication of what practical aid they might expect, for they continued to be short of military equipment. Sadly, the discussions proved 'inconclusive', with vague assurances that if

Yugoslavia joined the Allied cause, 'she would have a call on the common pool of supplies...'[108] Again, this can hardly have filled Paul (or his government) with confidence.

On 8 March, Olga fretted that her husband was 'harassed all day' by opposition politicians whom she felt would be better involved in 'sinking' their differences 'in such a serious moment.'[109] After dinner, the Prince and Princess watched a documentary film with their friends, the Sitters. The subject matter of the film, titled *Pastor Hall,* was hardly guaranteed to reassure, for it told the story of the arrest and torture of a protestant pastor in a Nazi concentration camp. Olga later informed Princess Nicholas that it was, 'beyond all words-we were sick-in fact Weezie [Paul] couldn't sit through it.'[110]

Hitler now decided to assent to most of Yugoslav's demands, and on 9 March, von Heeren communicated Germany's response to the Yugoslav government. The Axis partners would agree to guarantee Yugoslavia's sovereignty and territorial integrity; they would not, however, require passage of Axis troops through its territory nor would any military assistance against Greece be asked for. Finally, Salonika would be awarded to the Slavs. However, Yugoslavia could not be released from article 3 of the Pact, as regards the rendering of military support by signatories of the treaty in such cases as it applied.[111] That evening, Olga and Paul both spoke to the King of Greece: Georgie wanted to know if Yugoslavia was now going to fight on the Allied side. The Princess was clearly becoming increasingly riled by Greece's, as well as her mother's, lack of understanding of Yugoslavia's perilous position, noting, 'everyone there [in Athens] speaks of nothing but our attitude. If only our risks of helping them were not so great!'[112]

A second Crown Council was held on 11 March to consider the German response and von Heeren subsequently reported back to Berlin that the Slavs were stoically holding out against accepting any military clause which might oblige them to become involved in a war against the United States or Soviet Union.[113] Olga informed Princess Nicholas that this continuation of negotiations was aimed at 'trying to gain time'[114] for Paul still hoped to persuade Maček and Kuloveć to change their positions.[115] However, the Princess confided to her diary that she was concerned that her husband was, 'worn out with worry as to what to do'.[116]

While Berlin deliberated on a further response to the Yugoslav government, a concerned von Heeren sent his superiors a report of 'strong agitation' among the public and the army in Belgrade concerning 'an alleged German ultimatum' on the signing of the Pact.[117] On 12 March, Hitler, perhaps prompted by von Heeren's missive, finally agreed to accede to Yugoslavia's demands. Nonetheless, the Slavs still pushed for more: For 'compelling [domestic] reasons' they wished to publicise the declaration that Italy and Germany would not make any demands for military assistance from Yugoslavia.[118] This audacious request was soon declined by an exasperated Ribbentrop who feared that if this clause was made public, other newly-acceding countries to the Pact might expect similar 'exceptions' and the whole structure would be 'watered down'.[119] The Yugoslavs must now have realised that they had wrung out the maximum obtainable concessions from Germany, for Olga noted that the prevailing outlook of the Crown Council, which met again on the morning of 15 March, was that everything possible should be done to avoid 'the madness' of war with the Axis powers.[120] Furthermore, as Maček and Kuloveć now insisted that Yugoslavia sign the Pact, Paul realised that if this was not done, he faced losing the support of the Croats and Slovenes, and the country 'of which I was, so to speak, the trustee for my King' would then be split.[121] Churchill, however, informed President Roosevelt that he was still determined to get Yugoslavia into the war at all costs, so they could attack-and crush-Italian forces in Albania and free-up Greek troops for an offensive against the Germans.[122]

Meanwhile, Olga continued to be frustrated at her Greek family's failure to fully appreciate the difficult situation she, Paul and Yugoslavia now faced. She decided to write 'a detailed letter' to Princess Nicholas 'to give her an idea of the agony of mind we are living through.'[123] In this she emphasised that her own '[personal] feelings must not and cannot count' and that while both she and Paul personally longed 'to put ourselves openly on the side we believe to be the winning one [the Allies]' the present military superiority of German and Italian forces made this impossible. Furthermore, she stressed that Yugoslavia had already obtained 'exceptional promises and guarantees of no occupation whatever... if we promise to keep *neutral*' and 'stay out of the struggle temporarily'. The Princess also pointed out that as Paul was only in power for another six months, this 'doesn't give him the right to plunge the country into war on his own conviction and responsibility' and other opinions had to be taken into account. She did, however, concede that, 'the ordinary people are all for fighting to have done with the constant pressure and demands of Kitty [Germany]-but it's not enough to rely upon'. However, she emphasised to her mother that, '*it's certainly not lack of physical courage* but the country's position on the map is so desperate, hemmed in on all sides with so little outlet.'[124]

Nonetheless, Olga was privately buoyed by the recent 'splendid successes' of Greece's 'brave beloved little soldiers' against Italy's army in Albania [125] and confided to Marina of, 'the longing to help them [Greece] in their hour of need-[so as] to be able to prove what one believes in...'

She also admitted to feelings of loneliness and particularly missed, 'a friend for a cosy talk [and] to whom I could express all I feel'. She certainly did not unburden herself to Paul, preferring to 'spare' him and be 'as helpful as possible in any small way...'[126] This sense of separation was further intensified by the Princess' belief that, as a Greek, she was viewed by some in Belgrade with suspicion. Indeed, Paul would later recall that the opposition politician Trifunović told him bluntly, 'that if I signed the pact, I would be declared a pro-German and if I didn't "We'll say that you plunged us into war on account of that Greek wife of yours."'[127]

On 18 March, the British Foreign Minister again wrote at length to Paul urging the Yugoslavs not to sign the Pact and to 'fight rather than submit.'[128] This was delivered by hand to the Regent at Beli Dvor, that evening, by Terence Shone, the British Minister Plenipotentiary at Cairo. He was regarded by the British Foreign office as, 'a close personal friend of Prince Paul'[129], based on his previous posting as First Secretary of the British Legation in Belgrade and thus ideally placed to 'reinforce' the message contained in Eden's letter.[130] Olga was both surprised and delighted to see Shone and noted, 'We kept him to dinner-so nice to talk to, brings England so near.'[131]

19 March would prove to be an eventful day: Following on his dinner with the Prince and Princess, Shone reported back to Eden that the Regent remained in 'an undecided frame of mind.'[132] Germany, meanwhile, upped the pressure on Yugoslavia by imposing a deadline for the signing of the Pact,[133] while at the British Legation, a joint meeting was held between the diplomatic staff and operatives from the SOE and Secret Intelligence Service (SIS). This gathering has been identified by historians as the crucial moment when the British acknowledged the need to form an alternative Yugoslav government via a coup, should the current Yugoslav administration sign the Tripartite Pact.[134]

The following day, Cincar-Marković gave a detailed account of the terms of the Pact to the full cabinet. After 'a full and frank discussion'[135] it was then agreed by an overwhelming majority of the Crown Council that, as Hitler had agreed to the necessary concessions, the Pact should be signed. However, the three ministers who voted against signing (Budisavljevtić, Cubrilović and Konstantinović) later resigned in protest. Apparently, their resignations were at the instigation of the SOE, in close co-ordination with Milos Tupanjanin of the SPP,[136] in an attempt to precipitate a political crisis. Nevertheless, Paul would subsequently convince Konstantinović to withdraw his resignation and Cvetković was soon able to fill the other ministerial posts. Meanwhile, the international press was impressed by the *published* terms negotiated by the Yugoslavs with the *New York Times* noting: 'If [Yugoslavia] is now forced to yield it will be reluctantly, *with concessions which the other Balkans were unable to obtain'*.[137] And that was the vital point.

On the evening of 20 March, Olga and Paul dined with the American Minister, Arthur Lane at the United States Legation. Terence Shone was a fellow guest and engaged the Princess in conversation. She recalled, '[He] implores us to gain time and not commit ourselves yet [so as] to give them [the Allies] time to prepare...'[138] However, the American press were already reporting that the pro-British elements in Belgrade were now ready to rebel,[139] a view shared by Ronald Ian Campbell who now asked his Foreign Office masters for permission to put the necessary measures in motion for a coup d'état against the government.[140]

On 21 March, Olga observed that Paul was still 'making every effort to put off signing [the Pact].' When she later spoke to her mother, she was informed that 'they were all in a panic in Athens as it was said we had [already] signed [the Pact].' The Princess was maddened at this misinformation ('I said not yet') and emphasised to Princess Nicholas that no matter what happened King George 'could count on no [German] troops or arms passing here.'[141] In other respects, Ellen seemed remarkably well-informed for, next day, she was able to tell her somewhat surprised daughter, 'that there might be a revolution here any moment and feared for us-the army might rise.' This 'alarming news' had apparently been telephoned through to Athens by the British and Greek Ministers in Belgrade. Olga openly deplored these 'rumours spread by foreign propaganda' which she felt were responsible for sending the local population 'off their heads.'[142]

On the evening of 22 March, Terence Shone had a meeting with Prince Paul at Beli Dvor during which the Regent explained that he 'was doing all he could to delay matters,' but also pointed out to the Englishman that, 'if he did not sign the agreement and his country was involved in the horrors of war, many of his people, and not only Croats, would blame him for having failed to take the chance which the agreement offered of peace.' When the Prince was asked by Shone what he would do if the Germans demanded that their troops be permitted to pass through South Serbia, he immediately replied 'then we shall fight'.[143]

The following day, Paul informed the British Minister that the Germans had given the Yugoslav government until midnight to agree to sign the Pact, after which time the favourable terms would no longer be open to them.[144] In the interim, pleading cables arrived from the United States and King George VI. Bertie's offering ended with the stark words, 'We Count on You'.[145] Olga, meanwhile, noted that the Orthodox Patriarch had unhelpfully 'took upon himself' to issue a warning to the nation to fight rather than sign the pact.[146]

After another Crown Council meeting, Cincar-Marković informed von Heeren, just prior to the midnight deadline, that the Yugoslavs would sign.[147] Now that the decision had been made, Paul and the Princess had little option but to await the reactions both in Yugoslavia and overseas. Ominously, during an Audience with the Regent that evening, the Head of the Air Force, General Dušan Simović indicated that 'he could not answer for the discipline of the fighting services if the Tripartite Pact was signed,' adding threateningly that airmen might even bomb Beli Dvor.[148] When Olga later informed a sceptical Princess Nicholas of the Yugoslav government's decision, she noted, 'M[ummy] does not see how we can trust to any written promises [and] that if we sign it will make a disastrous impression on Greece and England.'[149] Worryingly, the situation in Greece was also growing increasingly serious: German troops from the Twelve Army, Eight Air Corps and numerous Mountain Divisions were massing from West to East on the country's borders.[150]

On 24 March, as Cvetković and Cincar-Marković left for Vienna to sign the Pact, Olga's already tense mood was not improved by her Lady-in-Waiting imparting the unwelcome news that public opinion was firmly 'against any terms signed.' The Princess later noted somewhat defensively in her diary, 'yet she knows how loyally P[aul] is trying to protect the country.'[151] The SOE had by now concluded that a change of regime was the only way forward and Ronald Ian Campbell was given full authority by Eden to progress matters.[152] Although the coup would be formally led by the General Dušan Simović (who also agreed to form a government following the rebellion), the planning and organisation was actually conducted by a group of anti-Axis Serb-nationalist officers who included Brigadier-General Borivoje Mirković of the Royal Yugoslav Air Force and Major Živan Knežević of the Royal Guard.[153]

Yugoslavia's representatives signed the Tripartite Pact on 25 March, in a ceremony at the Belvedere Palace in Vienna. It is unfortunate that the Yugoslavs were unable to secure Hitler's consent to the publication of the secret clauses which stipulated the Axis governments would 'not demand' the transportation of their troops through Yugoslavia nor make 'any request whatsoever' regarding military assistance[154] for this may have softened public opinion and perhaps have caused the Allies to reconsider their strategy in Yugoslavia. However, for Olga and Paul, the signing was certainly not an occasion for rejoicing. Rather, it was 'a heavy sad day for us both specially the thought that Greece and England might look upon us as enemies.' Indeed, the Princess seems to have no inkling of any impending trouble and noted in her diary that, *the country is calm, ready to defend to the utmost any violation of the treaty.*' Princess Nicholas informed her beleaguered daughter that, in Athens, 'they are all stunned and horrified' by this turn of events,[155] while Henry Channon reflected that, 'The Regent's name is mud in this London which he so loves; he is stamped as a traitor.'[156]

On 26 March, as she listened to negative radio reports from Athens and London, Olga experienced 'a sick heartache.'[157] Meanwhile, the international press was already reporting violent anti-Pact riots in Belgrade, Sarajevo and Centinje.[158] That afternoon, Olga noticed her husband was 'worn out' as he received Cvetković on his return from Vienna.[159] Paul later decided to travel by train to Brdo for a few days' rest and, after informing King Peter of his plans,[160] he departed Belgrade at 9pm in the Royal Train and retired to his sleeping compartment. This development initially caused consternation among the coup organisers, who feared that the Prince Regent had got wind of their scheme and was fleeing abroad. However, when it was later discovered that Princess Olga and the children remained at Beli Dvor, the perpetrators relaxed. For Paul, the first indication of any trouble was when his train was stopped at Viskovci at 4am, on 27 March, and his A.D.C. was informed over the telephone that, "There is some trouble in Belgrade". The line subsequently went dead and so the Prince and his party continued on to Zagreb.[161]

Unknown to Paul, at 11.30 pm the previous evening, General Mirković had mobilised his forces and instructed the seizing of Belgrade's airport, post office, police headquarters and the radio stations. Cvetković and Cincar-Marković were then arrested at their homes by special detachments and taken to the War Office. General Simović arrived there at 4am to be informed by Mirković, that the coup had been successful. Simović then summoned the leaders of all the political parties and, in their presence, prepared the text of the King's proclamation, which declared that Peter had assumed power from the Regency and had asked General Simović to form a government.[162] Major Knežević was subsequently entrusted with the task of venturing up to Dedinje to have the relevant documentation signed by King Peter. The latter action would legitimise Simović's position as Prime Minister. However, when Knežević arrived at Dedinje at 6am, General Kosić, the King's Governor (who up till now had known nothing of the events of the coup) refused to allow him entry.[163] The King was then awakened by his valet Radenko and subsequently received Kosić who informed his 'completely bewildered' master that a coup had taken place.[164] The young King then conferred with the Court Minister, Antić, who advised him to do nothing until he had spoken to the Prince Regent. A stand-off now ensued between the "rebels" outside the gate and the guards inside the palace compound.

Over at Beli Dvor, Olga and her family knew nothing of the coup. The Princess had been awoken 'by sounds of strange movements in the garden' and observed 'troops in large numbers standing about with guns.' On further enquiry she was informed, 'it was to protect us in case of trouble' as General Simović had instigated a coup d'état, proclaimed Peter as King and locked up the former government. Thereafter, Peter came over to lunch and would spend the rest of the day with his Aunt and her family.[165] Although the Princess then tried to 'sit quiet praying for the best', she must have felt unsettled when most of the regular A.D.C.'s were removed, along with Antić, 'although Peter begged to keep him...'[166] Prince Alexander clearly recalled listening to a radio broadcast featuring a young man pretending to be King Peter and declaring he had dismissed the Regency and assumed full regal powers.[167] Olga later informed Marina, 'the poor child [Peter] knew <u>nothing</u> of the proclamation he was supposed to have made nor of his soit-disant speech by radio.'[168] At no stage did she observe, as Winston Churchill would fancifully write, 'the young King...climbing down a rain-pipe' to 'escape from Regency tutelage'.[169]

The Regent, meanwhile, had arrived in Zagreb at 6am. With only a vague idea of recent happenings, Paul sent for the Deputy Prime Minister Vladko Maček who, having spoken to a Croat colleague in Belgrade, was able to give the Prince a clearer idea of the previous night's events. Paul sighed deeply and said, 'What's to be done?'[170] He subsequently went with Maček (and accompanied by an officer loyal to Mirković who acted as a "guard" over the Regent) to see Dr Subašić, the Croatian governor at his residence. There they were joined by General Marić, the Croatian military commander and three members of the Croat Peasant Party. Maček firmly opposed any attempt by the Regent to give ground to the revolutionaries[171] and as Olga subsequently informed Marina, 'begged him to stay with him assuring him of his loyalty and refusing to join the new gov[ernment] unless D[icky] was given full power.'[172] Maček also offered the Prince the use of a Croat-dominated division of the Royal Yugoslavian Army, in an attempt to resist the coup and provide some leverage in any negotiations with the rebels.[173] However, the exhausted Regent instead pleaded with the Croatian leader to join the new Simović government so as to avoid a civil war. On a more personal note, the Prince also pointed out that his wife and his children were currently in the hands of the rebels.[174]

Before returning to Belgrade, Paul made contact with the British Consul in Zagreb, T.C. Rapp and asked him 'to intervene with the present government and facilitate [his] departure' along with his family to Greece and thence to England.[175] Paul left Zagreb at noon in the company of Dr Subašić, and travelled by train back to Belgrade, where he was met at Zemun Station, in the early evening, by General Simović. They immediately drove off together to the War Ministry where the

Prince and his co-Regents signed documents abdicating their powers. Paul was apparently told bluntly 'you will have to abdicate immediately otherwise you and your family will all be shot.'[176] The Prince then travelled by car out to Beli Dvor where his very relieved wife and family were waiting to greet him. Shortly thereafter General Simović arrived and Paul went upstairs to the private apartments to pack for as Olga recalled, 'We were told it was best all should leave for Greece tonight with our three children, English nurse and two maids...'[177] A train had already been organised to transport them to Athens. However, neither Paul nor Olga was informed that Eden had already instructed Ronald Ian Campbell 'to facilitate Prince Paul's departure via Greece to Cairo. Not, repeat not, proposed [that] they should come to England.'[178]

While Peter 'begged'[179] his uncle to take him along with the family, the servants carried out trunks and loaded them into the palace cars. However, such was the rush that Olga left behind her photograph albums and the children's' diaries.[180] As the family departed, just after 11pm, the weeping King embraced his aunt who admitted to finding it 'heartrending to leave him alone'.[181] Waiting at the little station near Beli Dvor were an outwardly friendly Ronald Ian Campbell and Terence Shone (now back briefly in Belgrade). It was to be this two-facedness on the part of the British officials which angered Olga most about the whole episode, for she was keenly aware that the BBC were already broadcasting "fake" news bulletins indicating that her family had fled to Germany.[182] The Princess would have been even more indignant had she read the *New York Times* next day: This carried an article by the journalist Ray Brockby, in which he recalled telephoning the British Legation on the morning after the coup and asking "Who's there?" He received the jovial reply, "Bloody well everybody, we're having champagne. Come on."[183] In London, Henry Channon fretted over Paul's safety and rang Marina and Queen Marie to inform them of events.[184] Meanwhile King George VI telegraphed his good wishes to King Peter.[185]

Chapter 15 Political Prisoner

As she travelled through Thessaly en route to Athens on 28 March, Olga was feeling torn: Naturally, she was looking forward to seeing her mother and her homeland, but the Princess was also aware that the Yugoslav decision to sign the pact had not been well received in Athens. A telephone conversation, during a stopover at Larissa, with Princess Nicholas did little to reassure her; although 'relieved to hear her voice', Olga was stunned to discover that her mother seemed 'to credit the false rumours that P[aul] had gone to Germany, incredible.'[1] Arriving in Athens at 10am the following day, the Yugoslav royals were greeted at the station by King George and various family members. While the others proved convivial, the Princess noted that, 'Mummy [was] the only one to greet Paul very stiffly'. Nevertheless, Olga tried her best to smooth matters, and observed: 'Mummy, Paul and I retired to her salon to talk quietly and for him to explain his point'. However, the worst happened, '[Mummy] listened then turned on him terribly; implying *our* country could be sacrificed to save Greece!'[2] This diary entry is interesting for it shows that Olga now regarded Yugoslavia as 'her' country and that her primary loyalty no longer rested with the land of her birth. But how could it be otherwise, after her long years of devoted duty and sacrifice following King Alexander's death? Furthermore, the Princess came to the defence of her husband as she was 'proud' that he 'did what he knew was right which was to save his people from being slaughtered and the country from being destroyed by the Germans.'[3] Following the altercation with his mother-in-law, Paul was intent on leaving Athens, so others (including Crown Princess Frederika and Lilia Ralli) rushed over to Psychiko to act as peacemakers. Fortunately, these interventions appeared to be successful, Olga noting with relief, 'Thank God, for my sake, all is patched up'.[4] This was perhaps a rather optimistic assessment, for throughout the rest of the family's stay, Princess Nicholas studiously avoided the subject.[5]

However, it was not only Paul's mother-in-law who disapproved, as Olga acknowledged to Marina in a letter of 1 April: 'And here the feelings are hard against him considering him as having let them down!' Indeed, it was 'agony to know everyone [is] speaking of him like this and [yet] expressing loyalty to me-as though at a moment like this I wouldn't stick to him, having shared it together for the past tense weeks.'[6] The family were now 'advised' by King George not to go into Athens 'till the air cleared a bit.'[7] Fortunately, cousin Georgie had at least taken time to have a long talk with Paul and, according to Olga, proved 'very understanding and kind and more ready to listen to his point of view than the others...'[8] The King was also able to confirm that it had been the British and the SOE who had been behind the coup.[9] Ironically, Eden was currently in Athens for talks but declined Paul's offer to meet. This is unsurprising for Chips Channon had observed that at the Foreign Office in London, 'the feeling against the Regent is growing. He has done worse they say than Boris [of Bulgaria], Carol [of Romania] or Leopold [of Belgium]: He sold out England.'[10] This attitude would also soon be reflected by British officials at all levels of the Colonial and Dominion Offices. Interestingly, although the British King and Queen were saddened by the turn of events, the latter, in particular, remained loyal to the Prince and informed Lord Halifax 'with all his faults *I would trust him before any of these politicians'*.[11]

Meanwhile, the Princess' letter to her youngest sister provided her with a rare chance to unburden herself: 'My heart is too full and sore to put into words all I feel or to describe all we have suffered.' Olga admitted, 'I have aged 50 years' but observed that no one 'has suffered more than [Paul] through it all.' She stressed that 'this coup was done behind Dicky's back without warning' and warned that the new Yugoslav government was 'full of the worse scum'. Furthermore, Simović had acted 'only from personal ambition' and 'all they want is to have the boy [King Peter] in their power to do what they like [and] now they are attracting the very danger one was trying to keep out and I fear it looks like an attack from the Germ[ans] any moment.' The Princess remained deeply traumatised by the experience and acknowledged, 'I live in a dream and can't grasp all that's happened. I pray for Faith and courage.' She signed herself off as 'Yr. sad old Atinse.'[12]

Unknown to Olga, the Duke and Duchess of Kent had lunched with Churchill at Chequers on 30 March. Marina was placed between the American Ambassador and the Prime Minister and did her best to advance the cause of her beleaguered sister and brother-in-law. 'Of course, Prince Paul could not possibly come here', Churchill indicated at once, adding that it was being arranged to send him either to India or South America as a 'sort of semi-prisoner-of-state'.[13] Indeed, at the Foreign Office some impertinent bureaucrats advanced that, 'Any reasonable island should be good enough' [The Seychelles, Mauritius and Ceylon were all mentioned]. In a way, Paul and Olga's "connections", be they royal or otherwise, were working against them, as officials were at pains to treat the couple with 'rigour' in order to dispel any notion that they were receiving favourable treatment.[14] It perhaps did not help that Princess Olga-anxious about King Peter's wellbeing-made the mistake of twice trying to telephone him in Belgrade. On both occasions, she was given the brush-off by officials.[15] Furthermore, Paul sent a telegram to Maček in an attempt to encourage the vacillating Croats to stick with the new Serbian-dominated government for the sake of national unity.[16] Meanwhile, the new Yugoslav Foreign Minister, Momčilo Ninčić, had already asked Ronald Ian Campbell to arrange to have the Prince sent away from Athens, 'to prevent him intriguing with prominent politicians in Yugoslavia.'[17] The Princess remained blissfully unaware of Ninčić's action and was busily looking over several houses in Athens 'as we must rent one.'[18]

However, events soon took a catastrophic turn: On 6 April Germany declared war on both Yugoslavia and Greece. The Foreign Office in London was immediately enveloped in 'an atmosphere of great depression' as they realised that all their SOE machinations had been in vain.[19] The Luftwaffe swiftly launched an air attack on Yugoslavia from Romania and 17000[20] were killed over the next few days during "Operation Punishment". Olga now earnestly hoped that the Yugoslavs would now fight their corner[21] but she was subsequently astounded to learn (through the Greek Crown Prince) of a 'panic' in the Yugoslav ranks which resulted in 40,000 troops surrendering without even engaging in combat. The Princess observed angrily that this would allow German forces to advance virtually unchallenged on Salonika, 'What a disgrace!'[22] Perhaps they were taking their cue from King Peter and his government, whom a German radio station crowed had 'left the capital before the first bomb fell.'[23] Yugoslavia formally capitulated on 17 April.

In Greece, things were also growing difficult. The Princess noted four air raids over Athens on 6 April alone. On 9 April, German forces invaded Greece from Bulgaria and occupied Salonika. Olga mentions that the Greek royal family were now considering evacuating to Crete.[24] The following day, Crown Prince Paul informed Olga and Paul that the Greek government wanted the Yugoslavs to leave, as their safety could no longer be guaranteed. It was subsequently 'arranged' that they fly to Egypt.[25]

The little group boarded a RAF aircraft at Tatoi Aerodrome at 12.45pm on 11 April. The Princess somehow found time to pray over her father's grave beforehand and later confessed to Marina that, 'no words can describe the horror of leaving darling Mummy in these conditions...'[26] As the plane ascended into the sky, Olga wrote in her diary that, 'My heart broke to leave Greece-so beautiful from the air.'[27] Fortunately, the aircrew were 'charming' and when the family landed at Heliopolis, they were greeted by a familiar face, Peter Coats, a very intimate friend of Henry Channon and A.D.C. to General Wavell. Coats thought the Princess 'more beautiful than I had ever seen her'[28] although looks must have been deceptive for Olga felt 'in a sort of trance, hardly alive...'[29] Despite their ordeal, Prince Paul insisted on buying gifts for the RAF airmen.[30] This was a generous gesture for the family had left Belgrade with only 230,000 dinars (£920).[31]

Fortunately, Coats had brought two cars to transport the family and their luggage to their billet, a three-bedroom house outside Heliopolis, which belonged to a British officer captured in Libya. Terence Shone's wife was waiting to greet everyone at the door and the Princess was pleased to find that she had thoughtfully brought over some of her own towels and sheets. A local Greek-born grocer (who initially mistook Olga for Marina) subsequently called-by with a provision list from which the Princess was able to select a few items. Meanwhile, a group of British army sentries kept a watchful guard on the front lawn outside.[32]

Terence Shone called the following day and invited everyone over to his residence for lunch. The Prince took the chance to have a 'long talk' with Shone[33], and emphasised that he and Olga wanted to live 'quietly and unnoticed' somewhere; Kenya and South Africa were mentioned as possible refuges, although the Princess opined that she had hoped for Portugal or Switzerland.[34] But above all, what she truly craved, at this juncture, was her mother's approval and 'to be worthy of you...' Her thoughts were also with Greece and she prayed, 'May God in His great mercy spare our beloved land and all our sacred traditions...'[35]

The British Ambassador, Sir Miles Lampson, and his wife Jacqueline visited the royal couple for tea on 15 April and 'couldn't have been more amicable'.[36] Lampson was so shocked at their treatment that he fired off a telegram to Eden stating: 'I am rather appalled at humiliating conditions in which Prince Paul and Princess Olga are held here.' The Ambassador had also gained the firm impression of 'their detestation of the Axis and all its works,' and suggested that he might entertain them to lunch or dinner. Interestingly, the British diplomat also seemed to adopt a more compassionate approach towards Olga than her husband observing, 'Whatever the faults of Prince Paul (and they are manifest) *surely it is not right to ignore Princess Olga as a Greek princess and sister of the Duchess of Kent?*'[37] However, Eden's reply was uncompromising: 'Bad idea to entertain them or exceed original instructions.'[38] Needless to say neither Olga nor Paul saw the Lampsons again.

As it was Easter, the Greek Minister in Cairo made arrangements for an Orthodox priest to call at the house to take the Princess' confession, thus enabling her to receive Communion. There was a visit too from the Yugoslav Minister, who informed Paul that King Peter and his government had arrived in Alexandria en route to Palestine. Olga noted with derision that the Yugoslav exiles were apparently now blaming the

British 'for letting them down!'[39] Peter, meanwhile, sent them 'loving messages'.[40]

On the evening of 18 April, the Prince and Princess were officially informed in a 'polite letter' from Sir Miles Lampson that arrangements were being made for the family to travel by air to Kenya on 24 April. Olga initially seemed to be under the impression that she and Paul had some choice in the matter, for she informed Princess Nicholas that, '*Before consenting* to this we want to make sure of the kind of life down there and how we will be treated...'[41] In fact, Lampson had previously raised the possibility of a move to Kenya with the royal couple during his visit to Heliopolis. He had subsequently been in communication with the Kenyan Governor, Sir Henry Moore, and it is clear from the telegraphic traffic that the Princess' reaction to the Kenya suggestion had been lukewarm, at best: She was particularly 'preoccupied' over the suitability of educational facilities for the children and concerned too that she and Paul might be ostracised socially. [42]

Olga was temporarily uplifted by the arrival of Lilia Ralli on 21 April. She brought with her a heartfelt letter from Princess Nicholas, who indicated that she 'couldn't face another upheaval in her life' and had decided to remain in Athens. Olga's 'head and heart' were soon 'in a torment' over her mother's future, under the rule of the advancing Germans, particularly when she heard over the radio that the rest of the Greek royal family had left Athens on 23 April aboard two British cruisers. Furthermore, she was still trying to come to terms with her own recent experiences and confessed to Marina that, 'It seems impossible to grasp the rapidity of all that has happened and the tragedy and collapse of Yugoslavia-the loss of all we had, friends etc.'[43]

Despite the Princess' earlier misgivings, the family were soon informed that they were being sent to Naivasha, some 60 miles outside Nairobi. Although resigned to her fate, Olga firmly believed that, 'Enfin we are in God's hands and will be guided.'[44] The family departed Heliopolis on 25 April and were driven to the banks of the Nile and transferred to a waiting flying boat which flew them, in stages, to Kisumu, on the shores of Lake Victoria. On 27 April, just as German troops were entering Athens, the little group embarked the Governor of Kenya's train and spent a long day and night travelling eastwards to Naivasha. Sir Henry Moore had already been warned by his superiors in London that Prince Paul 'was not (repeat not) to be received at Government House'.[45]

The family's arrival at Naivasha on 28 April coincided with Paul's 48th birthday. Fortunately, the Prince had not lost his sense of humour. When he discovered that their Moorish-style "home", Oserian, had previously belonged to the recently-murdered Earl of Errol, Paul observed wryly, 'So they send me to the house of a murdered man on my birthday'.[46] The history of the house proved to be the least of their worries for Oserian was the complete antithesis of Beli Dvor: Not only had it been empty for three months but, as Olga noted with a sinking heart, it was 'dark and dirty, water filthy, no light-no wireless-garden a wilderness …'[47] The Prince and Princess were also peremptorily informed that a policeman, an Irishman called Swayne, had been assigned to them and would require to be accommodated in the house.

Almost immediately, there are signs of a deep inner strength coursing through Olga. While her husband sunk into 'the depths of gloom', she remained resolute and observed, 'We must not lose faith and courage.'[48] Next day, the determined Princess accompanied Paul to Nairobi to make representations to the Governor about the unsuitability of their accommodation. Sir Henry Moore duly telegraphed the Colonial Secretary, Lord Moyne, to say that Prince Paul 'does not wish to remain at Naivasha' but emphasised that the complaint was 'primarily' down to his wife who 'considers situation too remote from the shops, schools and doctors.' In addition, the couple indicated they would prefer a move to South Africa.[49] As she awaited developments, Olga spent a full morning with her two maids Milka and Urania beating the dirt from the mattresses and carpets.[50] The Colonial Office's curt response was that the family should 'put up with it' until alternative housing could be arranged at Limuru or Nairobi.[51] However, Sir Henry had already indicated to Lord Moyne that he was concerned about the latter option as 'there has already been adverse criticism…' over the royal couple's presence.[52] The Colonial Secretary replied that he was 'content' to leave it the Governor to decide whether the family should remain at Naivasha or not, but poured cold water on any move to South Africa.[53] In the interim, it had been arranged that the Princess would be able to write to Marina via the Governor's diplomatic bag.[54]

When she started to arrange her menus, Olga discovered that the cook could not speak English, so she had to rely on Mr Swayne or the head "boy" to translate. Undaunted, she quickly taught herself to make simple meals, such as scrambled eggs and sausages. The Princess also came across a little church further round the lake where the intermittent services held there proved 'such a comfort'.[55] Olga and Paul soon established a friendly rapport with a French aristocrat Count Roger de Perigny and his English-born wife Margaret who lived nearby at the imposing Kongoni Lodge. The couples would meet regularly to play tennis on the de Perigny's court and the Count and his wife subsequently introduced their royal neighbours to other families in the area, including a retired naval officer, Captain Rawson and his wife. The Princess also forged friendships with local farmers such as the Traffords and Marshalls, as well as with a Mrs Giselle Rocco, a mother-of-three, who ran her farm single-handedly, as her Italian husband Mario had recently been interred by the British. These individuals would form the core of Olga's intimate circle of Kenyan friends and her diary was soon filled with entries for lunch or "tea and tennis" parties. Occasionally, small dinner dances were held and it was at such an event that the Princess made the acquaintance of several South African army officers who were stationed at nearby Gilgil. However, when all else failed, the Prince and Princess would entertain themselves with a game of Lexicon after dinner.

Olga was delighted when Mr Swayne was transferred to other duties, for she had taken an almost instant dislike to the policeman.[56] The Irishman was immediately replaced by Major Sharpe, a portly, ruddy-faced, middle-aged government official who would act as the family's "minder". He informed the delighted Princess that the Governor had instructed him 'to hunt' for another house for the family[57]. Indeed, within days, the Prince and Princess were making a second trip to Nairobi, during which Paul was received in private by the Governor.[58] What the outcome of this meeting was is unclear but, the following day, Major Sharpe took Olga and Paul to inspect a house near the capital, although this was deemed 'just a bit small.'[59] Meanwhile, another residence (viewed during a later visit to the capital) was dismissed as 'not wildly attractive.'[60] The capricious Princess would soon come to regret not seizing this opportunity to move house. But, for the moment, Olga and Paul made do with regular stays at the Norfolk Hotel when in the capital. For reasons of security, the police were informed in advance of any visit and the family travelled under an 'assumed name' to avoid attracting undue attention.[61] It was in Nairobi that the Princess undertook most of the shopping (although the stores were expensive and lacked choice). When in town, Olga would invariably attend church services at St Andrews (the "Scots Kirk") and dine regularly at the Lobster Pot on Government Road.

Unlike Swayne, Major Sharpe initially seems to have found favour with the Princess who thought him 'cheerful'[62] and a 'nice, cultured man and pleasant for P[aul] to talk to...'[63] She and the boys subsequently made a visit to his home, some ninety miles distant from Naivasha, where Olga was taken both by the 'fascinating garden,' and the fact that 'Sharpie's' pet elephant, Dixie, would follow him around like a pet dog.[64] Since Major Sharpe lived so far from Naivasha, he was given the use of a small bedroom at Oserian where he usually spent half the week. To Olga's delight, Sharpie was soon 'putting order' among the "boys" (whom she found 'rather lazy') as well as organising the supplies and payment of the household bills from funds provided by Prince Paul.[65] Such practical help was indeed beyond measure and the Princess soon came to regret the Major's absences, noting that 'He helps so much to lighten the gloom.'[66] However, in addition to making himself popular and indispensable, Sharpe was in an unusually powerful position, for as Olga acknowledged to Marina, 'He is the only link we have with the outside world.'[67]

The Princess had by now established a routine of rising early to give Alexander and Nicholas lessons in French grammar. This was followed by gardening or a walk in the bush. The arrival of a new car proved particularly welcome as Olga was now able to make regular trips to the station at Naivasha, to collect the provisions she had pre-ordered from shops in Nairobi. On 11 June, the Princess celebrated her 38th birthday with little fuss, though Paul spoiled her with the gift of a Cartier brooch. That evening, at dinner, she 'silently drank [a toast] to M[ummy], sisters and absent friends-sad to have no word from them.'[68] Nevertheless, overall, Olga's attitude remained positive, 'One must be grateful for a roof and food compared to the misery of others.'[69]

On occasion, the Princess encountered pre-war friends: In mid-June, she enjoyed a gossipy lunch, at the de Perigny's, with Mrs Paula Allen, whose name had once been romantically linked with the Duke of Kent. Olga also received some news concerning Prince Amedeo: He had recently been placed under house arrest in Kenya by the British, following the surrender of Italian forces in East Africa. By chance, a few weeks later, while staying at the Norfolk Hotel, Prince Amadeo spotted his Yugoslav friends and sent Paul a note to say he would like to see them. Although, the Prince demurred, Olga had no such reservations and agreed to meet the Duke of Aosta 'outside'. She thought Amedeo 'looked drawn' and he admitted he was 'v[ery] lonely' and had 'been through hell...'[70]

As her confidence in domestic matters grew, the Princess started holding regular lunch parties. Since her keen political antennae had not deserted her, she made sure to invite those with influence. The guest list included the likes of Ferdinand Cavendish–Bentinck'[10] who, Olga noted, possessed 'power in the gov[ernment] of this colony and works with the governor'.[71] Yet, the Princess could still experience alarming moments of uncertainty and confided to Marina, 'I sometimes feel in a dream; that everything is somehow unreal, that we are not in Africa at all...such a curious detachment of the spirit from the body.'[72] Furthermore, the absence of news about her family in Europe was particularly troubling: 'The hardest' was the silence from her mother and sister Elisabeth,

---

[10] Ferdinand Cavendish-Bentinck, the future 8th Duke of Portland, Chairman of the Agricultural Production and Settlement Board for Kenya (1939–1945)

although, in mid-July, Olga finally received a letter from Princess Nicholas (dated 14 June) in which she stated she was well and carrying on with her charity work.[73]

Communications with Marina also proved erratic and the Princess soon began 'to fear' that her letters to the Duchess of Kent were either being censored or kept back from her by the Foreign Office.[74] Even when Marina's letters did arrive, Olga found herself having to respond to pointed questions surrounding the events of 27 March. These enquiries seemed to be in response to a recent article in *The Times* which alleged that when Paul left Belgrade for Brdo on the eve of the coup, he was actually intending to flee Yugoslavia. The Princess responded to these 'falsehoods' robustly by making the perfectly reasonable point that if her husband had been intent on absconding, why would he have left her and the children behind in Belgrade and taken only one suitcase with him? In addition, why would he have endured a fourteen-hour rail journey when he could so easily have taken a forty-minute 'air hop' to German-occupied Hungary? For good measure, Olga added, 'All his past life and all the records at yr. F[oreign] O[ffice] can show that he was working in the closest cooperation with Engl[and] during the whole of his regency.' Having warmed to her theme, she also emphasised to Marina that Paul's immediate reconciliatory post-coup actions in Zagreb had earned him the gratitude of Simović who, on the Prince's return to Belgrade, '*thanked him profusely for bringing the Croat [Ban of Croatia, Ivan Šubašić] back with him and for his patriotic action in reconciling both parts of the country.*' The Princess also noted with slight sarcasm that, 'We left Zemun Station with full honours at 11.30 that night seen off by Sim[ović], various other ministers, the Br[itish] Minister and Shone (who surely wouldn't have come had D[icky] been wanting to run away the night before to Germ[any]!!! *Sim[ović] again thanked D[icky] for his unselfishness and begged him to go on helping the gov[ernment] through his connections in England etc!!*[75] However, Olga's remarks must be read against the background of Paul's treatment at the War Ministry at the time of his abdication. Indeed, far from appearing grateful, Simović and his Government-in-Exile had spread the untruth that Prince Paul was intriguing to undermine the position of King Peter and his mother. The Yugoslav Foreign Minister informed a sceptical British Ambassador in Cairo, 'that it was for that reason the Yugoslav Prime Minister was so anxious to get King Peter to England [from Palestine] as soon as possible.'[76] The Slavs duly achieved this objective for, on 24 June, Peter flew to Poole Harbour by flying boat to be greeted by the Duke of Kent.

Whether as a result or not of these false allegations, on 23 June, Major Sharpe informed the Prince and Princess that he had been asked to attend a meeting with the Governor in Nairobi next day. Sharpie somewhat turned the psychological screw by telling Olga that 'he fears they wish us to have someone always near us (like a spy) which he has no time for'.[77] Following the meeting, Olga and Paul had a 'long talk with Sharpie, about our position here-he said *we* are looked upon [by the British government] as political prisoners...an awful shock to P[aul].' Rather than give the royal couple a chance to digest this information, the Major added self-servingly, 'that people complain of our frequent visits to town-not so much for me *but that P[aul] should not go without Sharpie,*' which Olga thought 'unfair'.[78] It is no wonder that the Prince became so 'v[ery] low' that he refused to go to either the de Perigny's or Rawson's for tennis, his wife making 'the excuse he wasn't well.'[79]

In addition to the aforementioned anxieties, the family were experiencing money worries. Olga informed Marina, in late June, that the Prince's monthly Yugoslav apanage payments of £500 had suddenly stopped and asked her sister if she could try and see 'the boy [Peter] alone' to 'remind him' of this obligation.[80] However, the young King was already sending out mixed messages, which seemed to vary according to his audience. On a visit to the Duke and Duchess of Kent, Prince George noted that Peter 'was full of talk and confidence' and appeared 'devoted' to Paul 'and realised everything you had done for him & the country-really very touching'.[81] Nevertheless, in a BBC radio broadcast to Yugoslavia on 2 June, Peter indicated that he disapproved of the actions of his Uncle Paul's government and in a clear broadside aimed at the former regent opined, 'my free-minded Serbs, Croats and Slovenes chose again to follow the truth: *Neither to bargain with nor submit to tyrants.*'[82]

In early July, Major Sharpe informed Olga that the Governor was currently in South Africa staying with his close friend, the Prime Minister, Field Marshal Jan Smuts, 'and would find out about our moving there.'[83] Unfortunately, Smuts took the view that there 'would be difficulty in complying with [the] security arrangements resulting from Prince Paul's position as a political prisoner...'[84] As it was now clear the family were likely to remain in Kenya, the formal procedures to be adopted regarding communications were finalised, in July, at Secretary of State level in both the Foreign Office and the Colonial Office. Princess Olga's letters (both to her and from her) were to be received at the Colonial Office and forwarded to a Mr Addis at the Foreign Office 'for the usual procedure' i.e. censoring. This included letters and parcels to and from Princess Marina.[85] Once cleared, the items were returned to the Colonial Office for forwarding either to the Princess in Kenya or (if from Olga) to the intended recipient in London. Furthermore, under the same agreement, all telegrams-including those from royalty-were required to be 'authorised for transmission'.[86] As time passed, Olga sometimes circumnavigated the system by sending letters to Marina via her friend Joan Ali Khan, the British-born wife of Prince Ali Khan, in Nairobi.[87]

As the weeks turned to months, the Princess sometimes found it a struggle to keep her children occupied. She made ice cream with young Nicky and generally tried to divert this sensitive and intelligent child. Fortunately, Alexander was a swarthy, outdoor type who enjoyed riding, shooting and driving. He had bonded well with Sharpe and sometimes accompanied him on excursions into the bush. Nevertheless, neither boy had friends of their own age with whom to play and the Princess was increasingly concerned about her sons' education-or the lack of it. It was eventually arranged that Nicholas would receive weekly Latin lessons from a master at the Prince of Wales School in Nairobi.

Meanwhile, on the international front, the Princess was growing increasingly furious at Britain and the United States' 'quite mad' backing of Stalin's Soviet Union[88]. She was particularly disturbed that 'They don't see the danger.' Olga's ire was compounded when she later learned that 'even the old Archb[ishop] of Canterb[ury] prays for a Soviet victory'.[89] To this Romanov descendent, the 'murderers and blasphemers'[90] of Soviet Russia remained the ultimate enemy: 'One can't contemplate but with horror a Soviet victory and all it would mean to the world we have known.'[91]

Paul was currently in agony from an attack of lumbago. Nor was he uplifted by more misleading articles in *The Times*. The first credited Simović and King Peter with 'the historical reversal of Yugoslav [foreign] policy;'[92] while the second claimed that Cvetković had only signed the Pact, against his better judgment, at the insistence of the Prince Regent, who had then departed Belgrade for Brdo *after* the coup, but was turned back and sent to Athens.[93] Fortunately, the Prince was cheered by the arrival of a letter, on 1 August, from the Duke of Kent; George informed Paul that he had been 'misjudged' and that 'it was obvious what you did was for the best'.[94]

Olga was still focused on finding a new home 'as this is impossible to get used to.'[95] However, a letter from Marina brought the unwelcome news that she had gained little headway in trying to discuss the family's financial situation with King Peter, as his omnipresent mother constantly interjected on behalf of her son.[96] Paul, meanwhile, wrote an illuminating response to the Duke of Kent in which he indicated that he and Olga were still reeling from being 'misjudged and treated overnight as enemies [of England].' Furthermore, *The Times'* misrepresentations had 'really upset us beyond words.' He continued, 'let me add that nothing can ever diminish our love for your dear country or change our feelings. We only live for the day when we can again see the white cliffs and you all again.' The Prince also acknowledged the effect of exile on his wife, 'It is hard to see O[lga]'s suffering ...' Although she was 'So brave and so efficient, doing things you wouldn't expect servants to do,' the Princess was invariably 'so tired' and plagued by a persistent, racking cough.[97] Providentially, word was received of some new accommodation; a six-bedroomed property, Preston House, located four miles further along the lake would become vacant in late August.

Despite the detailed arrangements which had been put in place for the handling of the family's mail, by mid-August Marina was growing concerned at not having received any mail from Olga for over six weeks. She decided to raise the matter with the relevant officials. The disruption was apparently due to a backlog of mail awaiting 'covert censorship'.[98] Indeed, the Colonial Secretary had previously informed Eden that the censorship of Olga's mail made him 'a little uneasy', and he wondered, 'Is it really necessary that Princess Olga's letters to her sister be censored?'[99] The Foreign Secretary was adamant the practice should continue and assigned a Mr Labouchère (and subsequently a Mr Peter Loxley) to personally check all correspondence between the sisters. "Normal" service seems to have been restored by 12 August, with Marina telegraphing Olga to say she had 'joyfully received' her letters of 19 and 24 June.[100]

To celebrate King Peter's eighteenth birthday, the British government organised a Service of Thanksgiving at St Paul's Cathedral, on 6 September. The day did not go unnoticed by Olga in Kenya for she observed that, 'Peter is eighteen today and officially of age, if only Pacey could have handed over to him in the way he hoped'.[101] However, the Yugoslav monarch had made no attempt to make contact with his Aunt and Uncle and a hardness was gradually emerging in the Princess' attitude towards him. She noted, 'his weakness of character is even more evident now, allowing himself to be so completely overruled by his ministers' opinions, as not to insist on being informed as to his uncle's whereabouts and means of living...And to think of all he owes him!'[102]

By the autumn, Alexander and Nicholas were settling into new schools. Quiss was boarding at the Francis Scott High School in Nakuru (which had an agricultural and technical focus) while Nicholas was enrolled at the Pembroke School at Gilgil. Elizabeth, meanwhile, was taught during the Kenya years by Miss Ede. Olga found that her daughter was 'not easy to manage as her mood changes easily-but [she is] fascinating and very witty at times...'[103] It helped that Elizabeth had a good friend in the Marshall's daughter Ann.

On 27 September, Olga and Paul finally moved into Preston House and the Princess observed enthusiastically, 'with the furniture, flowers, bright chintzes and decent light...it feels like a new era to be out of gloomy Oserian at last..'[104] However, Major Sharpe was still keeping a conveniently tight rein on proceedings and, to Olga's distress, had sacked 'our head boy John *whom we liked and could speak to*-said he was drunk and rude to him....'[105] Nonetheless, the Princess' domestic talents continued to grow apace: She knitted dishcloths, arranged the flowers and instructed the servants on how to serve the drinks.

Despite the move to Preston House, Paul was increasingly 'in the depths of gloom' and 'usually' remained in bed 'almost till lunch time...'[106] Matters had not been helped by a new press campaign against the Prince by an aggrieved London *Evening Standard* diarist. The latter had recently discovered that the Governor had deliberately held back five telegrams, sent by the journalist from London to the British United Press correspondent in Nairobi, requesting detailed information on Paul's life.[107] Like an excited wasp, this chronicler then took to the pages of his London paper decrying the Governor's actions and referring to the former Regent as the 'Quisling Prince' who lived in a 'comfortable' home looked after by 'a small staff', but whose presence in Nairobi was 'not appreciated'.[108] Unfortunately, the contents of these articles were repeated in the *Mombasa Times* and syndicated as far afield as Australia, under the headline "Prince Paul Has Easy Time on Kenya Estate".[109] Olga later learned from Alexander that he was being taunted and bullied at school as a result of the articles.[110]

In fact, the Prince was far from 'comfortable': While the Foreign Office had arranged that the British government should pay the rent for wherever the Prince was accommodated, this was so as to underline 'the fact that it is, in a sense, prison'.[111] Indeed, Lord Moyne subsequently informed the Duke of Kent that the British Government paid the rent as 'Prince Paul *and Princess Olga* were regarded as political prisoners...'[112] As for the rest of the family's expenses: Staff, food, schools, medical expenses, repairs, petrol-all these fell to be paid by the Prince. Certainly, on arriving in Kenya, Paul had immediately to draw £1000 from his capital at Coutts in London to pay for such outgoings.[113] It also did not help that Oserian and Preston House were large establishments with basic running costs (excluding rent) of £200 per month.[114] In addition, for tax purposes Paul was classed as a British resident and required to pay 15% of his income in tax.[115] Furthermore, despite Olga's earlier plea to Marina, Paul's apanage payments had still not been restored, although the Duke of Kent was now pursuing the matter as a matter of urgency[116] as well as liaising with Coutts bank for Paul's gold and dollar funds to be liquidated, so as to provide much-needed sterling funds.[117]

The Duke of Kent also proved a useful source of information about Queen Marie and warned Paul: 'I think the fat one and Simović have talked a lot and told a lot of lies and suggested you wanted the throne etc', although Prince George had apparently 'warned everyone not to believe a word she [Mignon] says. She really is a bitch....'[118] One can but wonder if she was behind King Peter's continued criticisms of his Uncle in public, which included barbed references to the 'unpopular' regency 'only one of whom exercised full influence in State affairs'.[119] Paul was rightly shocked by 'the ingratitude and downright nastiness from those for whom I slaved and worked.'[120]

As Christmas approached, Olga would have been touched if she known of the effort shown by friends and family in sending Christmas messages and presents out to the family in Kenya. Marina generously dispatched four Christmas parcels in late October (doubtless anticipating a delay) and also thoughtfully sent a greetings telegram on Christmas Eve to cheer the family. Chips Channon decided to send the Princess some books 'which I know she wants more than anything...'[121] Meanwhile, at Preston House, the family had erected a small 'makeshift' Christmas tree in the sitting room; while Paul rang a bell, on Christmas Eve, to signal that the children could come in from the garden to open their gifts.[122] This was followed by a joyous Christmas Day party at a neighbour's house. Yet, as the year drew to a close, a downcast Paul informed Prince George that, 'We have been abandoned by everyone.'[123]

With the dawn of another year, the Princess too was feeling the strain and admitted to her mother that 'this long separation is a torture' and prayed 'for patience to bear it...' Olga's chief desire for the New Year was a 'reunion' with all her loved ones and friends.[124] At the end of January, a form of plague raged through Naivasha, spread by fleas from rats that had arrived in a consignment of cotton wool balls from Uganda. The Princess was vaccinated, but experienced such a bad reaction that she spent four days in bed with a high fever. However, she seemed more concerned for Paul who, she informed Marina, was 'mentally starved' and 'a shadow of what he was and so broken in spirit.'[125] Duly alarmed, the Duke of Kent asked the Colonial Office if it would now be possible for the Prince and his family to be relocated to South Africa. The matter was referred to the Foreign Secretary who gave a negative response on the grounds that 'political objections ...cannot be overcome at present.'[126] Prince George immediately wrote to Paul to inform him of Eden's decision. Meanwhile, differences were already appearing amongst the Yugoslav Government-in-Exile and, on 12 January, King Peter appointed a former law professor, Slobodan Jovanović, as Prime Minister in place of Simović.

In early March, the Princess received 'a great shock' when she was informed of the death of her friend Amedeo of Aosta, from a combination of tuberculosis and malaria.[127] A concerned Olga had previously asked to pay him a visit, but it seems that she had to be content with sending violets.[128] The title now passed to her cousin Irene's husband, Aimone.

Meanwhile, Prince Paul asked Major Sharpe to speak to the Governor about his perilous financial circumstances and, more particularly, about reviewing his tax status.[129] The situation only served to increase Olga's feelings of disgust towards Queen Marie and King Peter; she complained to Princess Nicholas, 'we might not exist for them and not a penny has come ever since we left home from him!'[130] Indeed, after subsequently reading the February edition of *Life* magazine (in which Peter opined that, "U[ncle] Paul did a lousy job!"), she informed Marina, 'It certainly doesn't show him up in a nice light and anyone with any insight for character can't but sum him up as a spineless, ungrateful little pipsqueak!' Olga blamed Mignon whom, she observed, 'is showing her true spirit'.[131]

The Princess continued to make a concerted effort to adapt to her new life: She was now sufficiently competent in Swahili to communicate with the native staff (who called her 'Memsahib')[132] With petrol in short supply, she also took up cycling and confessed to Marina that she often wore trousers 'to save my dresses and for housework or gardening.'[133] Indeed, as the first anniversary of their leaving Yugoslavia passed, the Princess joked to her mother that 'the days of smart ensembles, hats, gloves seem far away...'[134]

In the spring, Olga was buoyed-up by the news that Eden had granted Lilia Ralli a visa to come to Kenya. Moreover, Paul had at last found an interest: He now regularly played bridge at the de Perigny's house and sometimes remained to dine there. Furthermore, by mid-April, the Duke of Kent was able to confirm that the Yugoslav civil list payments would soon resume.[135] However, there was a nerve-racking delay of several weeks before Paul's bank in Nairobi was able to confirm that the £6500 of arrears due had been received. Indeed, it had required the 'splendid' intervention and 'ceaseless energy' of Miss Fox to finally expedite the transfer.[136]

In mid-May, Olga received a telegram from her cousin Crown Prince Paul in South Africa informing her that Frederika had given birth to a daughter, Irene, on 11 May. Fortuitously, the Prime Minister of the Union, Field Marshal Smuts, had taken a keen interest in the Crown Prince and his family. At Preston House, the Princess listened-in to a radio broadcast by Winston Churchill which she subsequently dismissed as 'The usual fine oratory covering a lot of hypocrisy.' She 'specially' objected to his praise of the Soviet Union.[137] More upsetting, however, was a letter from Alexander in which he indicated that returning to school after Easter 'was like going back to prison.'[138] This could hardly have come as a surprise, as Olga and Paul were aware that both of their sons were regularly subjected to taunts about their father.[139] Although the Princess would have preferred for her eldest child to finish his schooling and obtain his Cambridge Leaving Certificate, she readily acknowledged it was his 'dream and ambition' to join the Royal Air Force. Olga was equally concerned that Nicholas was now 'beyond' the level of teaching at Pembroke School.[140]

On her return from a visit to Nairobi, the Princess was greeted by the troubling news that Elizabeth had swellings on her neck. The child and Miss Ede travelled to Nairobi to consult a throat doctor, Dr Boyle, who later assured Olga that his investigations had revealed nothing untoward.[141] In early June, Alexander attended a medical examination for entry into the RAF. He passed A1, which Paul observed was 'a great shock' to his mother![142] After securing the Yugoslav government's permission, the Duke of Kent had managed to secure an agreement, whereby Alexander would initially be taken on as RAF ground crew until he reached the age of eighteen. Thereafter, he would be able to undergo training as air crew.[143] The Princess commented to Foxie, 'My heart sinks to think of his training in the RAF but it's not fair to stop him doing something useful which he has set his heart on. My one prayer is that this ghastly war is over before he has any part in it.'[144]

Given the circumstances, it is hardly surprising that there continued to be tensions between Olga and Paul and the Prince confided to Prince George that they were both 'concealing from each other how we [really] feel.'[145] As a distraction, the Prince and Princess lunched at the Lobster Pot with Colonel Palewski, the Commander of the Free French Army in East Africa. It was a pleasant encounter and the General was subsequently invited to dine with the couple at Preston House.[146] Palewski, of course, was a man of influence and would soon be promoted to the post of De Gaulle's Directeur du Cabinet. He also proved most obliging and carried letters to London for Marina and Miss Fox.[147]

On 5 July, Olga was overjoyed to receive a telegram from the Duke of Kent to say that Marina had given birth to a son, Michael,[11] and that both were doing well. The following day, the Princess sent a congratulatory air graph to the happy parents in England, but her own celebrations were cut short by the news that Alexander required emergency surgery, in Nairobi, for the removal of his appendix. The Princess was clearly shocked by the suddenness of her son's illness and, when she subsequently received a batch of six letters from England, opined gratefully to Miss Fox: 'Never have letters from those I love been a greater blessing than now.'[148] However, this was as nothing compared to the events of 24 July, when Lilia Ralli 'suddenly seemed to drop from the sky' on Olga's lawn just in time for tea. For the Princess, the arrival of her old friend 'wiped out 15 months of separation and loneliness.' She

---

[11] Michael George Charles Franklin (1942-)

also enthused, 'Such a loyal faithful friend is rare!'[149] A few nights later, Olga and Lilia dined with Count de Perigny and five Free French airmen. Both ladies decided to wear evening dresses, 'as we felt the men would welcome a change from the women in uniform, they see all the time.'[150] The two friends were soon sharing the latest gossip from England, contained in a letter from Marina, concerning King Peter's engagement to 'Sandra' [Princess Alexandra of Greece] and 'how he bought a ring from [Mignon] to give her!'[151] King Peter had first met Alexandra-the daughter of the late King Alexander of Greece and Aspasia Manos-at an Allied Officers' Club tea party in the Grosvenor House Hotel in London in 1941.

British officials, meanwhile, continued with their policy of ostracising the Prince and Princess: When the Duke of Gloucester paid a visit to Kenya, Olga was informed by Major Sharpe that the Foreign Office in London had intervened to veto a possible meeting.[152] The Princess was, of course, unable to be present at her nephew Michael's christening at Windsor on 4 August, but she was at least able to help Alexander celebrate his 18th birthday, on 13 August. As part of the festivities, some Masai women gave a dancing display on the lawn. Olga reflected that her son was now 'virtually grown up though very young in character, [and] has a sweet, easy nature'.[153]

Chapter 16 Mercy Mission

On 26 August Olga's diary entry begins, 'A terrible tragedy crushed us today with the news that our darling Bunna [Prince George] crashed yesterday in a plane...' The Duke of Kent had been flying from Invergordon, in Scotland's Easter Ross, to Iceland on a 'special mission' for the RAF, when his Sunderland Flying Boat crashed into a low mountain, Eagle's Rock, just north of the village of Berriedale. The Duke's private secretary, equerry and valet were also killed. A tail gunner, Andrew Jack, was the only survivor and the crash was blamed on pilot error.[1] However, such details would hardly have registered with Olga and Paul, who were both 'heartbroken and miserable.'[2] The Princess lamented, 'My poor precious F'al, <u>what</u> I wouldn't give to be near her.' Olga's immediate concern was, 'How will she live and manage...?'[3] The following day, the grief and shock remained as raw as ever and the Princess admitted to having 'broke down' when thinking of 'little intimate details' of George's life with Marina. Olga found the only solution was to throw herself into several days of 'strenuous housework', and then retire to be bed exhausted.[4] By a cruel twist of fate, on 28 August, the Princess received a letter from Marina (dated a month earlier) in which she described, in detail, a new brooch Prince George had given her as a souvenir of Michael's birth. She had also enclosed some snaps of herself with her new-born baby and this only served to further torment her sister who bewailed, 'How I ache to see her.'[5]

Olga listened intently to a radio broadcast of the funeral from Windsor on 29 August. The arrival of a telegram from Marina, next day, 'so full of pathos and misery!' finally gave the Princess 'the courage' to write to her widowed sister and 'just let my heart speak.'[6] She also sent a telegram 'to tell her what she already knows, that my heart aches for her-and my love and prayers surround her.'[7]

In her wildest imaginings, Olga could not have foreseen what happened next: On 1 September, just as she was starting out on a walk, an official car drove up at Preston House and the Governor's Private Secretary emerged 'with a wire to me from Bertie asking me to come to F'al as he thinks she needs me for a short time...'[8] The telegram ended by making it clear the invitation was for her alone, 'So sorry Paul cannot come, but am sure you can bring a maid.'[9] The Princess thought that King George VI's invitation was 'like an answer to prayer.'[10] Nevertheless, she did not give an immediate reply to the waiting official and doubtless pondered the risk of undertaking such a long journey in wartime, particularly when she would have to leave behind an emotionally-wounded husband and young children. However, Paul 'was v[ery] unselfish... and told me to stay as long as At[inse][12] needs me though it means still greater loneliness for him...'[11] It was not until next day, after travelling to Nairobi, that Olga finally sent a reply to Bertie: 'Deeply grateful for your kind suggestion and touching thought. Accept with great pleasure...' She also requested that Lilia Ralli accompany her, rather than her 'useless' Greek maid.[12] The King cabled back that he was 'delighted' and he would now inform Marina of the 'welcome news'.[13] Telegrams were subsequently sent by the Colonial Office to the Governors of Kenya, Uganda, Nigeria, Sierra Leone and the Gambia instructing them to 'take all possible steps to facilitate [the Princess'] journey...' but emphasising that publicity should be avoided.[14] The Acting Governor [Moore was currently in London] and Olga agreed that she and Lilia would leave for Europe a week later, by the B.O.A.C. flying boat service from Port Bell, Uganda.[15] However, the Princess was careful to try and obtain clarification in advance, as to whether 'England' or Prince Paul would pay for the 'expenses of the trip.'[16] The matter was referred to Sir Alexander Hardinge, the King's Private Secretary for consideration. His response of 9 September was, however, only communicated to Kenya by the Colonial Office *after* the Princess was already en route to England: 'Regret there are no public funds in this country from which the journey of Princess Olga and Madame Ralli could be met. The charge must therefore presumably fall on Prince Paul, unless some other arrangement can be made within the family when Princess Olga arrives'.[17] This seems unfair, to say the least, given that the Princess was travelling at the request of the King to comfort her stricken sister.

In the interim, Olga rushed to the bank to take out her precious 'white jewels' for an unexpected airing in England followed by a trip to the doctor for a Yellow Fever inoculation.[18] However, the most difficult task she left till last: On 8 September, the Princess drove out to the aerodrome to bid Alexander farewell; he was en route to Bulawayo to commence his RAF training. Although she admitted the experience 'broke my heart',[19] Olga immediately telegraphed the King to say she intended to leave Kenya the following Thursday and added, pointedly, that 'Alexander has just left for Rhodesia where we trust he will distinguish himself in your service.'[20] This was doubtless a subtle reminder to Bertie as to where the true loyalty of her family lay.

---

[12] One of Olga's names for Marina, used frequently in private correspondence.

There was another emotional parting at Nsa railway station with a forlorn Paul and Nicholas as Olga and Lilia departed for Port Bell on 10 September. After travelling for twenty-four hours by train to the Ugandan capital, Entebbe, the duo overnighted at Government House as the guests of the Governor, Sir Charles Dunglass. The following afternoon, the Princess and Lilia departed Port Bell aboard a Junkers 55, reaching Lagos two days later (with overnight stops en route at Stanleyville and Doula). Next morning, they transferred to a four-engine Sunderland Flying Boat with a sleeping cabin, to fly through the night via Bathurst to Lisbon.

On the morning of 16 September, in the glare of a beautiful sunrise, Olga arrived in Europe after an absence of seventeen months. Paul's old friend, the diplomat Jock Balfour, was waiting to greet her and Lilia. Following a sightseeing tour of Lisbon, the ladies bathed and dined at the Balfour's flat, and the Princess lost no time in telling Jock about life in Kenya and of Paul's 'state of mind.'[21] Olga and Lilia then re-joined the seaplane for a night flight northward to Poole. On arrival in England, the Princess was greeted by Lord 'Sidney' Herbert, Marina's Comptroller and Private Secretary and a family friend Alfons ('Alik') Poklewski. The little group subsequently caught the train to London's Waterloo Station, where a car was waiting to convey Olga to Coppins. On arrival, she was greeted by Alik's wife Zoia (who had been Marina's constant companion since Prince George's death) and taken to Marina's sitting room. There then followed what the Princess describes as 'that moment of supreme emotion when we came face to face with each other and fell into each other's arms...'[22] Yet, Olga also found that 'Words between us are not needed. She knows how my heart beats with hers.'[23] Nevertheless, it all felt 'like a dream' owing to Prince George's absence and just as though 'he has flown away on a long journey...'[24] Olga's attention soon settled on little Michael: '[The] greatest blessing of all... that depends on her [Marina] so much and for whom she must live...'[25] His older siblings Edward and Alexandra were, meanwhile, being looked after by their nanny at Appleton House on the Sandringham Estate.

The day following her arrival, the King called on Olga (Queen Elizabeth remained at Balmoral, struck down with bronchitis). He proved to be 'full of heart' and the Princess seized the opportunity to speak of Paul 'and all he suffers from'[26] and 'stressing the isolation and patheticness of it all....' Olga was also astute enough to try and establish what the lie of the land was vis-à-vis King Peter and the Government-in-Exile: 'He [Bertie] said he [Peter] is badly advised, the Gov[ernment-in-Exile] all hating each other and that he [Bertie] doesn't even know whom to trust among them.'[27] Thereafter, the Princess drove the short distance to Windsor to lay flowers on the Duke of Kent's coffin. On her return, she took tea with Henry Channon who confirmed that 'Houdri [Queen Marie] continues to speak bad of us...[and] that the Yugoslav Gov[ernment-in-Exile] is hated by [the British] F[oreign] O[ffice] who alone is responsible for our treatment.'[28] Another visitor to Coppins, Nancy Astor, also 'quoted some unkind things Marie and the boy [Peter] say about us. Incredible.'[29] Queen Marie made no attempt to make contact, forcing Olga to conclude that 'she must hate my being here'.[30]

The King returned to Coppins, on 20 September, for Sunday tea. It proved a somewhat uncomfortable encounter as Bertie produced a list of Yugoslav government officials for Olga to peruse. He then asked her to indicate who the 'bad' ones were 'as he can't make them out!'[31] The Princess responded briskly 'that I preferred not to mix up in that question' but also had the presence of mind to make a copy of the list.[32] Olga had already decided to maintain a low profile and was keen 'not to give the impressions of trading on [the current visit] to further our situation.' She also preferred to wait until someone asked to call on her rather than seek them out.[33] She did not have long to wait: Her first caller was Group Captain Sir Louis Greig, from the Air Ministry, who came to discuss Alexander. Apparently, there was a fear that those in opposition to King Peter's Government-in-Exile 'might make use of' Quiss during his sojourn in Rhodesia.[34] His mother would have been horrified had she known that, so far, her son had spent his time 'doing nothing' other than attending 'dances and cinemas'.[35]

The Duke of Kent's death seems to have spurred Olga into a new interest in the Afterlife. She talked to Marina on the subject 'by the hour'[36] and when Lady Patricia Ramsay came to lunch, she engaged 'Patsy' (whose father the Duke of Connaught had died recently) in 'a long spiritual talk.'[37] The Princess also raised the topic with the Greek Orthodox Archbishop Germanos when he came to bless Michael, but was disappointed to find that he had nothing new to offer on the subject. Olga also confessed to her mother that the constant need to 'brace myself to face Atinse [Marina] bravely' was taking its toll; she had recently 'collapsed' with grief.[38]

When Alexandra and Edward moved from Sandringham to Windsor at the end of September, the Princess rushed over to take tea with them and encountered the King. He indicated that King Peter wanted to visit Marina and Olga at Coppins, in order to offer his condolences. This put the Princess in a slightly awkward position, for if she declined to meet Peter it might make her seem churlish. A date was subsequently set for 6 October.[39] In the interim, Olga had a chance to meet and congratulate his fiancée Alexandra and her mother, Aspasia, over tea at Coppins. She was also much cheered by a lunchtime visit from a 'v[ery] sympathetic'[40] Queen Mary and later encountered Mrs Eleanor Roosevelt who demonstrated 'great simplicity and dignity.'[41] Miss Fox would often come down for an overnight stay and was 'always the same poor sweet and touching beyond words.'[42]

On 4 October, Olga accompanied Marina to a Memorial Service for Prince George, at the Greek Church in Bayswater. Eventually, the day of King Peter's visit dawned and the Princess recalled in her diary, 'Peter came to l[unch] alone. [It was] rather an ordeal to see him again-we tried to put him at his ease, as he seemed pale.' His Aunt made sure to provide him with details of the family's life in Africa, as well as emphasising the precarious state of his Uncle's health. The young man asked her 'to give P[aul] his love...'[43] Olga also tactfully 'thanked [King Peter] for the monthly help,'[44] but made sure to point out that the payments were once again in arrears. After mumbling some 'vague' excuses, Peter 'promised it'll be alright.'[45]

Interestingly, as Olga's visit continued, there was a gradual mellowing in the attitude of officials, particularly within the Colonial Office. The Princess was astute enough not to overplay her hand, but she certainly had the ear of those of influence, including Paul's old Oxford friend Bobbety Cranborne, who had recently replaced Lord Moyne as Colonial Secretary. As early as 2 October, there were discussions about the Prince's 'status' between Cranborne and Sir Alexander Cadogan, the Permanent Under-Secretary at the Foreign Office.[46] Fortuitously, Sir Henry Moore, the Governor of Kenya, was still in London and admitted to the Colonial Office that the matter was causing him 'some embarrassment'. This prompted Cranborne to send Eden a Minute expressing his doubts over the Foreign Office's view that the Prince was a 'political prisoner'. Bobbety also believed that, with Paul currently in receipt of a Yugoslav government allowance (and his elder son serving in the RAF), 'To maintain the position that he is a dangerous enemy seems impossible, and it puts the authorities in Kenya in a situation of perpetual embarrassment.' Indeed, Cranborne expressed the hope that he could now 'give some guidance to the Governor as to his [Prince Paul's] status and in particular give him permission to visit him or to receive him at his office at Government House...'[47] However, Bobbety's hopes were soon to be dashed, for the following day, the government announced in the House of Commons that Prince Paul was not admitted to Kenya as a refugee, but that his status was that of a 'political prisoner, subject to surveillance'.[48]

Meanwhile, Olga received intriguing news from Alik Poklewski: One of King Peter's Government-in-Exile, the Slovenian Miha Krek, wanted to meet her 'in secret from the others.'[49] The meeting took place a week later at the Poklewski's cottage near Coppins, during which Krek informed the Princess that King Peter was 'wrongly having his head twisted' against Prince Paul by his Serbian-dominated London political entourage; the Foreign Minister Ninčić was proving to be 'the most revengeful'. Olga was also interested to learn that the Apanage money was being paid by the British Foreign Office as a lump sum ('en gros') to Peter 'to deal out' and 'all get', although some including 'the bitch' [Queen Marie] were opposed to Paul receiving any of the funds whatsoever.[50]

With Marina contemplating a return to public duties, the Princess thought she and Lilia might be able to return to Africa in early November.[51] However, as the date drew closer, Olga admitted to Princess Nicholas that she was 'dreadfully torn' at leaving her widowed sister but 'I keep thinking of D[icky]'s loneliness and depression down there and how he must miss me'. She added, 'I think that in a quiet way I have been able to help him and have found out much that was inexplicable up to now.' Above all, her stay in England had helped her to gain a sense of perspective: 'and confidence that all will blow over with time.'[52] But there was trouble ahead...

On 15 October, the Princess learned that the 'odious' Member of Parliament for St Marylebone, Captain Cunningham-Reid, had asked Anthony Eden 'two unpleasant questions' in the House of Commons the previous day. The first concerned the surveillance Paul was subject to as a political prisoner.[53] After the Foreign Secretary had given the relevant details about the police guard, Cunningham-Reid turned his attentions to Olga, demanding to know 'Can my Hon. Friend say whether the wife of Prince Paul is also a political prisoner, and, if not, why not?[54] Marina became so incensed on her sister's behalf that she immediately wrote (initially, without Olga's knowledge) to Churchill who assured her that Eden would make a statement in Parliament 'and not to worry.'[55] It subsequently transpired that someone in Kenya, who had a grudge against the Governor[13] had, out of revenge, contacted Cunningham-Reid and provided him with the necessary (mis)information with which to launch the attack.[56]

The timing of Cunningham-Reid's intervention was most unfortunate, as officials at the Foreign Office were also beginning to review their handling of Prince Paul. One, a Mr Rose was moved to minute, 'Personally I have always felt that our treatment of Prince Paul has been "petty and unworthy of us". For years he was our loyal friend, giving us valuable information and helping our cause as far as he could...'[57] However, any attempt by the Foreign Office to remove 'the

---

[13] To do with Sir Henry Moore's refusal to sanction the supply of a large quantity of petrol.

rather ineffective but humiliating restrictions' under which Paul was held would prove troublesome, as Cunningham-Reid had only recently received a government assurance that the Prince was being treated in exactly the same way as any other political prisoner.[58] Furthermore, the Captain's recent comments in Parliament had led to renewed press interest in Kenya regarding the former Regent, with reports from the British press being routinely carried by the *East African Standard* and the *Mombasa Times*.[59] In the circumstances, it is hardly surprising that British government officials remained reluctant to act. Meanwhile, having read through her husband's Kenyan correspondence with the late Duke of Kent, Olga's 'great anxiety' now was 'will he [Paul] be able to live through it [exile] and remain normal?'[60]

Soon thereafter, Paul sent a telegram to Coppins stating he was 'very anxious' about another arrears of Apanage money.[61] If anything, this latest contact combined with Cunningham-Reid's recent attacks, only served to make the Princess even more determined to achieve changes in her family's living conditions in Kenya. On 22 October, Olga lunched with Lord Cranborne and was keen to set the record straight: She impressed on Bobbety that Paul was 'paying the full scale of taxes' and that the civil list allowance from the Yugoslav government was, at best, sporadic. Furthermore, their 'personal resources' were much constrained as the greater part of the Prince's personal capital had been invested in dollar securities which remained frozen. Indeed, Olga was at pains to emphasise to Cranborne that Paul's income was 'simply not adequate to meet the expenditure involved' and skilfully added that, 'it would make a great difference if they could have a slightly smaller house nearer to Nairobi', as this would allow Nicholas to live at home and reduce the family's travelling expenses. Cranborne was sympathetic and minutes that, 'the present position as stated by Princess Olga is difficult to defend' and added, 'I certainly feel that he should be relieved from taxation' particularly given that 'he is technically a prisoner' whom the British government 'compel...to live in a house which involves heavy expense.'[62]

Surprisingly, during this lunch, Olga was a bit lukewarm in her comments about Sharpie and seemed intent on delicately planting seeds of doubt in Cranborne's mind as to the Major's suitability. She certainly succeeded in giving the impression that, 'he was clearly not a congenial companion, having nothing in common with them'; Bobbety now questioned if it might 'be worth considering whether he might be replaced by a more suitable person.'[63] The Princess' diplomatic attempts to get rid of Major Sharpe were, in part, because he was a 'spy'[64] but also reflected her distaste at discovering he had a 'reputation as a pansy [homosexual]'.[65]

In early November, Olga was informed by Lord Cranborne that there was 'no prospect' of her and Lilia 'making the whole [return] journey by air' to Kenya as the 'pressure on airspace is so terrific...'[66] Bobbety now proposed that Olga and Lilia should travel by sea to South Africa and fly from there up to Kenya. The Princess was understandably annoyed by this change and informed Mr Keenleyside, an Air Ministry official engaged to handle the details of her passage home, that 'a [proposed] sailing ...for Durban' was 'too soon for [her] convenience.'[67]

British officials would soon wish that they had been more amenable in assisting the Princess with her passage "home", for on 11 November (Armistice Day) Captain Cunningham-Reid launched an even more venomous attack on Olga in parliament. After summarising the surveillance provisions previously mentioned pertaining to Prince Paul in the debate of 14 October, he asked 'But what are such precautions worth when simultaneously the companion of this dangerous traitor, his wife, Princess Olga, *who incidentally has a dominating character*, is allowed to move about Kenya and this country as a rule unaccompanied, just as she wishes, in a position to see, hear or say anything she likes?' He continued 'I hope that this lady is more to be trusted than her husband. I hope her loyalties lie over here rather than in Kenya, or rather than with her sister, who is married to a German, Count Toerring'.[68]

In another foray, on 17 November, the Captain then sought to position the Princess as a Nazi by citing some flattering comments Hitler had made about her during the 1939 State Visit. He went on, '[She] hates the Bolsheviks, and-very naturally, for that reason alone-has been drawn towards the Nazis, for they also hate the Bolsheviks'. Cunningham-Reid indulged too in complete lies, stating *'The Princess seldom came to this country, but was constantly in Germany'* and was a 'persona grata within that very small inner Nazi circle that surrounds Hitler...'. However, the Captain was to sink even lower, saying: *'We have deliberately brought this sinister woman over to the British Isles, and have allowed her to all intents and purposes complete freedom. She has been in touch with officials in key war positions. Who knows that we may not by such an injudicious act have endangered the lives of countless soldiers, sailors, and airmen? What right have we to take a chance with the lives of our fighting men by giving these fantastic privileges to a dangerous Royal enemy?*[69]

Olga's diary makes no mention of these more sustained attacks on her character. However, Marina was certainly aware and deliberately hid the newspapers from her sister. Indeed, the Duchess' concern was such that she met with Churchill, on 12 November, and 'begged' him to ensure that Olga could return to Kenya by air. He claimed to know 'nothing' about a sea journey but thought that there was a distinct possibility the Princess and Lilia could fly back to Kenya on Field Marshal Smuts' plane the following week.[70] Although this was duly arranged, Olga's intended departure was delayed further as Lilia Ralli was taken ill with a 'bilious attack and fever.'[71]

The Princess used this hiatus to seek out the journalist Harold Nicolson and thank him for writing a more balanced article about the Prince[72] which would subsequently appear in the *East African Standard*. Furthermore, on 18 November, Olga was introduced to Field Marshal Smuts, when he called on Marina at Buckingham Palace. She was much taken with this 'sweet old man' who kindly offered to take a letter to Paul, as he was making a stopover in Kenya on his way south. Smuts was also able to inform Olga (who had been unsure of her eldest child's exact whereabouts) that Alexander was currently stationed at Lyttleton Camp, outside of Pretoria.[73]

However, a meeting over tea at Coppins, on 22 November, with Panagiotis Pipinelis, the former Greek Minister to the Soviet Union, was to prove much more unsettling. Pipinelis 'deplored' the Communist 'system and mode of life' and warned the Princess 'what a future danger they will be' with their 'astonishing, fanatic[al] patriotism...'[74] These words had a particular resonance with this direct descendant of the Russian Tsars. Equally unsettling, and a source of 'regret' for Olga, was the news that Colonel Oliver Stanley had replaced Cranborne as Colonial Secretary, 'as I had spoken so openly to the latter and was counting on his help'.[75]

Meanwhile, without Olga's supporting presence, Cunningham-Reid's attacks weighed heavily on Paul's mind and he went into a 'severe depression'.[76] The Prince now rose late, ate little and survived on a daily cup of hot chocolate brought in by Miss Ede.[77] Indeed, in late November, when the local physician, Dr Bunny, paid Paul a visit, what he found so disturbed him that he made a 'special' visit to Nairobi to meet the Governor[78] and expressed his fear that, 'there may be a rapid deterioration in his [Prince Paul's] personal condition if her [Princess Olga's] return is further delayed.'[79] This meeting left Moore 'in considerable anxiety'[80] and he telegraphed the Colonial Office, on 1 December, to inform them of the situation and also urging them to ascertain when Olga would return. The Governor further requested that the Princess be made aware of the seriousness of her husband's condition.[81] However, this information was held back by Marina, as both she and Zoia Poklewski felt this would spare Olga unnecessary anxiety about a situation over which she had no control.[82]

Fortunately, the contents of Sir Henry Moore's telegram were taken seriously in London and on 4 December, the new Colonial Secretary telegraphed the Governor in Nairobi asking him to '*Please inform Prince*

Paul that he may expect Princess Olga back very soon in good time for Christmas.'[83] The Princess, meanwhile, was informed of an anticipated departure date of 15 December. Olga duly wrote to King Peter to tell him of her imminent departure and asked to see him again.[84] She also found time to enjoy the delights of the annual Christmas pantomime at Windsor Castle, although she was miffed that Alexandra and Edward had only been given a 'short scene and were not seen enough.'[85]

On 11 December, the Princess was informed that her departure had been postponed until 20 December, due to the number of American troops requiring transportation to North Africa. Unfortunately, this meant that she would not be reunited with her husband in time for Christmas. This news only served to further aggravate the Prince's depression, especially as it coincided with the *Mombasa Times* publishing another negative article.[86] There was also now evidence that Paul was deliberately not eating.[87]

Olga and Marina lunched, on 12 December, with Henry Channon and Valentine Lawford, Eden's private secretary. The latter opined that the Foreign Minister was 'relaxing in his attitude towards P[aul] now.'[88] In the afternoon, Oliver Stanley called at Coppins to take tea with the Princess and 'promised his help'.[89] He subsequently reported the substance of their 'long talk' in a 'private and personal' minute to Eden. Olga was by now clearly well-versed in her approach to British officialdom and the Colonel noted that, 'the talk was very much on the same lines as the one with Bobbety [Cranborne].' The Princess emphasised that the 'main difficulty is the question of their house' which was 'much too big' and 'much too expensive'. However, somewhat unhelpfully, Stanley also informed Eden that, 'Although I think that this desire for a smaller house is genuine, *it is no doubt partly inspired by a hope that the smaller house will be nearer Nairobi and that there will be increased opportunities for visits there*' which might give rise to '*possible difficulties*'[90] presumably in terms of public comment.

Unfortunately, Captain Cunningham-Reid seems to have been under the impression that the Princess had already departed for Kenya and asked Eden in Parliament, on 16 December, why she had 'been allowed to leave this country during the war?'[91] The Foreign Secretary told him tartly 'Princess Olga is still in this country. She came for a special purpose, and when that purpose has been fulfilled, His Majesty's Government see no reason why she should not return to Kenya.'[92] The Captain on hearing this became even more loathsome and again sought to portray Olga as some sort of enemy agent who 'will be able to convey information to her quisling husband...'[93] It was now patently clear that the sooner the Princess left for Kenya the better.

A few days later, Olga received a Christmas card from Bertie and Elizabeth, enclosing a letter from the King to Paul to thank him for allowing the Princess 'to come over here to be with Marina in her great sorrow.'[94] The Princess was later invited to call on the King and Queen, at Windsor, on 20 December (the fortieth anniversary of Prince George's birth) and the royal couple both bid their friend 'a tender farewell'.[95] Sadly, she heard nothing further from King Peter.[96]

Shortly thereafter, the Princess' departure was postponed for a second time, and she was growing increasingly anxious about Paul and the children. As she listened to carol singers perform "Silent Night" in the entrance hall at Coppins, her thoughts turned to her beloved daughter in Kenya, 'How my Libiss [Elizabeth] would have loved it.'[97] However, there was also some positive news: That very day, Eden informed Colonel Stanley that he could 'see no objection' to Paul and his family being allowed to move to a smaller house.[98] The Colonial Secretary relayed this news to Olga by letter on Christmas Eve and also indicated that he had already instructed the Governor to facilitate such a move.[99] The Princess must have felt that all her Christmases had come at once when Sir Louis Greig then telephoned to say that her flight to Kenya was now re-arranged for 28 December.[100]

As Christmas day dawned, Olga put on a garment on loan from Molyneux to help little Alexandra celebrate her sixth birthday. The exiled King George of the Hellenes came to lunch and afterwards everyone listened to Bertie's traditional Christmas broadcast. On Boxing Day, there was some welcome news of Alexander, when Marina received a festive air graph greeting from her nephew. Gallingly, on 28 December, Greig informed the Princess, at the very last minute, that her departure had again been postponed until 30 December. Somehow, Olga coped stoically with this ever-changing drama, observing: 'One makes a constant effort to be cheerful and have a fresh store of courage,' but she was forced to admit it was 'rather a strain.'[101]

Meanwhile, in Kenya, despite his instructions to find the family a new home nearer to Nairobi, Sir Henry Moore seemed more focused on gathering information on Paul's current financial situation, in order to present a strong counter-case for the family to remain at Preston House. On 29 December, he telegraphed the Colonial Office stating he had 'obtained the following information privately from Sharpe,' [Thus confirming the latter's role as a spy]: The Prince's personal income was estimated at £3350 per annum, excluding the 'irregular' Yugoslav apanage payments (which were currently four months in arrears). The Governor noted that if all these monies were received this would result in an annual income of £9,350, while a 'revised estimate' of Paul's total annual expenditure was £4440. Sir Henry was also at pains to highlight the difficulties of finding a suitable residence and, given that the family apparently required accommodation for nine people, he 'did not see how [Prince Paul] could manage with a smaller house.' For good measure, Moore added, 'In view, however, of the state of public feeling here which is still SIMMERING, I could not advise this [move]'. The Governor was nevertheless wary of Olga and was anxious to ensure that, should there be any trouble on her return to Kenya, the Colonial Secretary would endorse Moore's view, 'that any house near Nairobi would be inadvisable both in their own and the public interest.'[102]

At Coppins, there was one final piece of pre-departure news: Sir Nevile Henderson died on 30 December. The Princess noted, with resignation, 'another old friend gone to a happier world.' Nevertheless, she and Marina now focused on remaining 'natural and cheerful and face the parting bravely-what else can one do. God will help us through.'[103] After another last-minute delay, Olga finally left Coppins, on 31 December, at 7.30 on a dark winter morning and observed, 'Agony kissing My F'al.'[104] Olga would later write to her sister that, 'I am so eternally grateful to God for the blessing of our time together...*it has strengthened me so much*.' She was also 'thankful if in a small way I was able to help you too to live on'.[105]

In London, the Colonial Secretary was already busy at work. He responded to Sir Henry Moore's telegram by stating that he understood the Governor's concern over 'the practical difficulties' of finding the Prince a 'more modest house.' Stanley was also at pains to point out that if the 'irregular' Yugoslav civil list funds failed to materialise, Paul's other income of £3350 would be insufficient to meet his current outgoings of £4440. He now firmly placed the onus on the beleaguered Governor to cooperate by 'securing a smaller house.' Moore was also given clear instructions that 'if the Princess raises the matter on her return, I suggest that you might cause her to be informed ......that you are bearing the matter in mind ...'[106] This was certainly not the response the Governor had been hoping for. Another route would need to be found.

Chapter 17 Despair and Hope

After departing Coppins, Olga and Lilia Ralli journeyed by road to Bristol, where they boarded an American flying boat which flew them over to Foynes, on the West Coast of neutral Eire. Unfortunately, a mixture of bad weather and wartime restrictions led to a series of delays en route (including a four-day stopover in Bathurst). They eventually landed in Nairobi, on the afternoon of 12 January, and were met by Major Sharpe who drove them straight to Preston House. Although the Major forewarned Olga that the Prince had taken to his bed shortly after Christmas and had not risen since, she was still shocked to find her 'v[ery] wasted and thin' husband waiting at the door to greet her, leaning on a stick and wearing a dressing gown.[1] She was also alarmed to discover that Nicholas had been 'terrified' to see his father 'in such a state.'[2] However, instead of being revitalised by his wife's return, the Prince remained in bed, eating little and smoking 'no end.'[3]

The whole matter over Paul got Olga thinking and she rightly concluded, 'The trouble is deeper and will take long to cure.'[4] The Princess shared her concerns with Marina, in a letter of 16 January, admitting that her husband was 'far worse than I feared' and adding, 'If this situation goes on much longer D[icky] will fade away'. Fearing for her husband's sanity and very existence, Olga now made a desperate and heartfelt plea to her sister: 'My one hope now my F'al is that you will be able to help in this matter...,'[5] for the canny Princess had rightly surmised that, 'From London I feel I have more support than from the gov[ernor] here...'[6]

In the meantime, Dr Bunny wrote up a detailed medical report for the attention of the Colonial Secretary on the state of Paul's health. He found that the Prince had become almost a 'recluse' and 'morbidly introspective.' Furthermore, on several occasions, Paul had informed his doctor that his family were 'suffering unnecessarily because of him' and 'that it would be better for them if he were "out of the way"'. Fortunately, since Olga's return there had been 'a slight improvement, though a very slow one' and Bunny no longer felt that the Prince might try to take his life. The doctor suggested 'that a statement [about Paul's status] would make the situation easier.'[7] However, by this stage, the Princess felt 'that a change of abode here [in Kenya] will not make any difference.'[8] She was now pushing for a move away from the Colony. The Governor now seemed to be moving towards a similar view and had called in a Dr Jex-Blake, who apparently had a 'very high standing in the medical world' to deliver an 'essential' second opinion on Paul's health.[9] Jex-Blake called at Preston House on 6 February to examine the Prince and subsequently discussed his findings with Dr Bunny, Major Sharpe and the Princess. The news he imparted, Olga noted, was 'enough to make one's head buzz,' but basically confirmed that Paul was suffering from 'acute mental depression...'[10] Most worryingly, the doctor believed that '*the development of insanity in the form of melancholia is definitely to be feared...*' for the Prince had developed a 'complete disgust with his life and indifference to its continuance.' Indeed, Paul still regarded his very existence as 'an embarrassment and even danger to Her Royal Highness and their children. *On this point, I was not able to shake him at all.*'[11] Jex-Blake informed the Princess that he would now write 'a strong report' for the attention of the Colonial Office and deliver it in person to the Governor for forwarding to London.[12] It is little wonder Olga confided to Marina, 'I am at my wits end...'[13]

In his subsequent correspondence with the Colonial Secretary, Sir Henry Moore, doubtless shaken by the contents of the doctors' reports, expressed the hope that, 'the earlier proposal that he [Prince Paul] should go to South Africa could be reconsidered, I believe that this would be the best solution.'[14] Moore was certainly pushing at open door where Oliver Stanley was concerned: The latter immediately wrote to Anthony Eden, acknowledging that while this was 'primarily a matter for the Foreign Office to handle', he found the doctors' reports to be 'most disturbing' and favoured 'getting him [Prince Paul] moved elsewhere where the local feeling might not be so strong and where greater freedom might be permitted to him.'[15] Winston Churchill (who had received a copy of Moore's recent correspondence) proved to be a stumbling block and informed Stanley, on 12 February, that 'I really do not see why we should worry about this man who did so much harm to his country and deprived it of its chances of striking a united blow for its liberties.'[16] However, in a master stroke, Eden and Stanley then joined forces to put intense pressure on their Prime Minister by signing a Joint Minute-prepared by Stanley and marked for Churchill's personal attention-pressing for the Prince's relocation. In the text, they noted neatly that, while agreeing with what the Prime Minister had minuted, 'as to the part Prince Paul has played in the destruction of Yugoslavia', nevertheless 'it would be extremely unfortunate if he became *permanently insane while in our custody...*' They then deftly pointed their Prime Minister in the direction where they wished the Prince to settle: 'If you agreed, we should like to ask the Dominion Secretary to approach Field Marshal Smuts to see if he would be prepared to accept Prince Paul in South Africa.' This, they posited, would avoid 'the greater risk of incidents with an unfriendly population' that a greater freedom of movement in Kenya Colony might attract.[17] This two-pronged attack seemed to do the trick and, doubtless in exasperation, on 20 February Churchill agreed to their request with the curt words 'Yes, certainly.'[18]

The British officials would undoubtedly be required to move with great speed, for Paul's clothes now hung on him 'like a scarecrow'[19] and Olga noted that he had recently consulted a lawyer, Dacre Shaw, about his will.[20] The Princess did, however, manage to enjoy a rare evening of escapism at a neighbour's house, playing backgammon, quaffing beer and conversing with a French pilot officer, Gabriel Prudhomme and his colleagues. She did not return home till gone 1.30 and 'crept quietly in.'[21] However, Olga was mostly focused on more pressing matters: Food was now subject to stringent controls and the bread ration had recently been halved. Furthermore, the Yugoslav apanage money was now five months in arrears[22] and Marina was delegated to speak to Bertie about it.[23]

By 25 February, Eden's Principal Private Secretary Oliver Harvey was busily liaising with his opposite number, Joseph Garner at the Dominion Office[14] regarding the Prince's possible move to South Africa.[24] A Secret telegram was sent by the Dominion Office to William Ormsby-Gore, the British High Commissioner to the Union of South Africa, on 1 March, asking him to 'raise' the 'question' of Paul and his family's relocating to South Africa with Smuts and, *'emphasising the very real danger that Prince Paul may become permanently insane if he remains where he is..'* The Field Marshal was to be offered the carrot that, 'We could slightly modify the conditions of the Prince's confinement if the Prime Minister thought this essential.'[25]

Meanwhile, following upon her receipt of Olga's letter of 16 January, with its despairing entreaty to come to Paul's assistance, Marina had requested a visit from the Colonial Secretary. Stanley was happy to oblige and drove down to Coppins on 27 February. On his arrival, the Duchess produced a typed extract from the aforementioned letter which gave emphasis to Paul's withered physical state and depression.[26] Stanley acknowledged that the Colonial Office were aware of the Prince's condition and that he personally had been involved in discussions with the Foreign Secretary. Indeed, he informed Marina 'for her own ear' that these deliberations 'did not exclude' the possibility of moving the Prince and his family elsewhere.[27] He also subsequently wrote to warn her to say nothing

---

[14] The British Government department responsible for handling relations with the 'autonomous communities' of the British Empire of which the Union of South Africa was one. In 1943, Clement Attlee was the Secretary of State.

to Olga of the 'possibilities' he and Eden were currently discussing as it would be 'dangerous to raise any hopes.'[28]

Fortuitously, down in South Africa, matters were moving quickly, for Smuts clearly remembered meeting Olga in London and noted that, '[She] made a most favourable impression and I think this is a proper case for hospitality or at least asylum on our part'. This positive response was duly communicated, on 4 March, to the Dominion Office by telegram, along with the observations that the Field Marshal had made it clear that the family would have to 'look after themselves' and would be subject to 'veiled' police surveillance.[29] Smuts also indicated that the family must live in Johannesburg and that responsibility for Prince Paul would rest with the British High Commission.[30] Pleading understaffing, Ormesby-Gore suggested a Doctor Tonking, who was on secondment from the Colonial Office and based at the British Trade Commissioner's Office in Johannesburg, as a new 'Keeper.'[31] Tonking possessed 'an admirable tact'[32] and 'considerable powers of persuasion'[33] and currently looked after the exiled ex-Shah of Persia.

On 16 March, while enjoying a stay in Nairobi, the Prince and Princess received a letter from the Governor, indicating that talks were ongoing with the South African Prime Minister about the possibility of the family being relocated to Johannesburg. However, Olga was not enthusiastic, 'For me the last place I'd choose' and adding, 'Not a word about the conditions.' Fortuitously, there was also an accompanying note from Smuts (which Paul was subsequently given sight of by Major Sharpe) which indicated that the family would only be subject to 'minimum restrictions.'[34] If the Princess hoped this development might cheer her husband, she was to be sorely disappointed for, by the following day, she noted that he was 'again in despair [as he is] sure nothing will improve and can't face going there under the same conditions as here.'[35] The despondent Princess later arranged to enjoy another escapist evening in the company of her 'v[ery] kind and friendly' companion, Gabriel Prudhomme. The duo dined at The Mascot and later took in 'a silly film.'[36]

Olga was clearly missing the wise counsel of Princess Nicholas and noted in her diary, 'How I long for her [Mummsie] is beyond describing.'[37] Yet, as the second anniversary of the family's departure from Yugoslavia approached, the Princess was also able to, 'Thank God it has taught me something and I can be grateful for the experience. I've gained in many ways.'[38] This is a fair assessment for, in often difficult and unfamiliar circumstances, she had learned to deal with people and situations alien to her status and social class. As a result, she had become a more rounded and stronger individual.

Shortly thereafter, Olga received a report from Marina of her meeting with Oliver Stanley: In keeping with the Colonial Secretary's wishes, the Duchess of Kent was deliberately guarded in her comments, leading her sister towards the (mistaken) view that the meeting had been 'v[ery] unsatisfactory'.[39] The Princess duly admonished Marina for her perceived shortcomings in a letter of 4 April: 'I am afraid my F'al you did not grasp the full gist of my letter [of 16 January] as, if anything it was an understatement...' With a move to Johannesburg now a distinct possibility, Olga churlishly informed her beleaguered sister that the doctors' reports had 'produced a denouement which my desperate appeal to you failed to produce...' Perhaps wanting to end on a more conciliatory note she finished, 'It upsets me to have to sadden you again with all this my own F'al in your already sad life *...but my life and his [Paul's] have been a daily agony since I left you...*'[40]

No sooner had this letter been despatched than, on 5 April, the Princess received another letter from Marina, dated 17 March. The Duchess of Kent was now aware that her sister had been informed of the possibility of a move south and 'strongly' advised her and Paul to undertake the move to Johannesburg, adding that Smuts was prepared to receive them privately.[41] A somewhat contrite Olga replied immediately, 'Your sweet letter...is so full of heart and understanding my precious F'al *that I feel a swine for writing in what may strike you as a hard tone yesterday*-nevertheless all I said is true and can be seen by other eyes than yours...'[42] Yet, unknown to the Princess, Marina was still stoically keeping up the pressure on Stanley to expediate the move or 'the consequences may be serious.'[43]

Lilia Ralli had recently decided to travel back to Egypt to care for her ailing father and, on 14 April, the Princess bid her friend an emotional farewell at Nairobi's aerodrome. That same day, the British High Commissioner in South Africa received a detailed response from the Dominion Office to an earlier query about expenses. Paul was to continue to pay for his everyday living costs, but the British High Commission would be responsible for paying the rent and rates of the Prince's residence 'on behalf of the United Kingdom government.' As a result, these outlays 'would be kept as low as is consistent with circumstances'.[44] Shortly thereafter, Olga had a meeting in Nairobi with Lady Moore (at the latter's request) and the duo enjoyed a 'long talk à deux about Smuts' proposal.'[45] The Governor's wife would subsequently inform the Princess that, 'she had written to Smuts after seeing me and he seems glad to welcome us and will muzzle the press'.[46]

However, most inconveniently, the results of a recent blood test revealed that Paul had malaria. This caused great consternation among the officials in London, who were currently trying to finalise arrangements for the move south. Indeed, King George VI arranged for a telegram to be sent to the Governor asking that, 'every possible medical assistance should be provided...' to the Prince.[47] On 25 April, Sir Henry Moore was able to report to his relieved superiors that Paul was suffering from a 'sub-tertian variety of Malaria' adding, 'His condition is not serious and he is not even confined to bed.'[48] Almost simultaneously, the Yugoslav Government-in-Exile decided to raise an objection with the Foreign Office over the South African move. Fortunately, this was quickly dismissed 'in view of [the] state of Prince Paul's health...'[49]

On Paul's 50th birthday, 28 April, Major Sharpe brought with him 'a very polite letter' from the Governor which 'officially' informed him that the family had permission to relocate to South Africa. Olga observed guardedly, 'so now the dye [sic] is cast. For Paul, of course it was pleasant news.'[50] The Prince responded that he and his family would like to leave by 28 May[51] but was 'particularly anxious' that Nicholas should remain for a period in Kenya to complete his schooling. The Governor proved sympathetic and foresaw 'no local objection' to this proposal.[52]

In early May, Olga and Nicholas travelled to Major Sharpe's home at Ndaragwa for a final visit. On her return to Preston House, Gabriel Prudhomme asked the family to make a similar visit to his home. However, the Princess noted that her husband was, 'against it for fear of offending Sh[arpie] as he and Pr[udhomme] are on bad terms [they had previously argued (over the Frenchman's friendship with Olga?) at a farmer's meeting].'[53] Olga was most disappointed: 'Such a pity as it might be such fun.'[54] However, she did manage a four-day outing to Diani Beach, near Mombasa, to bid farewell to Elizabeth and Miss Ede, who were currently enjoying an extended holiday there with Joan Ali Khan's family. Although the Princess enjoyed the rest, she was particularly upset when Elizabeth became 'weepy' as she took her leave.[55] Elizabeth and Miss Ede were to join the Prince and Princess in Johannesburg once they were more settled.

Back at Naivasha, Olga bid an emotional farewell 'to all our kind neighbours.'[56] She would have preferred to remain in Kenya and lamented that the only 'bright spot' in moving southwards was the chance of seeing Alexander.[57] Her only regret was that she had unburdened herself to Mrs Baird one evening and 'confidences' had been discussed.[58] By 8 June, the packing was completed and the Princess prayed 'for strength to make the best of it...'[59]

On 11 June, the Princess celebrated her 40th birthday at the Norfolk Hotel in Nairobi and observed, 'what a strange one being also the day of our departure from Kenya.'[60] She remained characteristically stoical and resolute: 'I'll try to make the best of new surroundings, new faces and a completely new life.'[61] That evening, Olga and Paul boarded a train to Kisumu, in the company of their escort, a Captain Holland, and a maid.

Chapter 18 South African Sojourn

The twelve-day journey to South Africa was long and convoluted: From Kisumu, the little group journeyed by steamer southwards down Lake Victoria to Mwanza where, on 14 June, they boarded the Governor of Tanganyika's private carriage for the long overland rail journey to Kigoma, on the shores of Lake Tanganyika. A boat journey to Albertville (where a 'loyal' Greek owner of a hotel refused to accept any payment for an overnight stay)[1] was followed by an exhausting 285-mile road journey to Kamina, Northern Rhodesia and then a five-day train journey southward to South Africa. On 24 June, the Prince and Princess reached Johannesburg and were greeted by Alexander (in RAF uniform) and a South African official who brought a 'charming message' from Field Marshal Smuts. Also present, were the Yugoslav consul and Dr Tonking, whom the Princess noted ominously was 'to look after us.' Feeling 'tired and bewildered,' the weary travellers were then whisked to a third-floor suite at the city's Langham Hotel to rest.[2]

As she ventured out next morning with Paul, Olga found the city to be 'noisy and material.' The couple subsequently joined Dr Tonking on a drive out to the leafy suburb of Houghton to inspect their four-bedroomed rented house at 42 Young Avenue. Next day, Smuts and his wife Ouma called on the couple at the Langham for tea and, although 'courteous', the Field Marshal was at pains to warn them to be wary of any involvement with the local Yugoslav community.[3] They heeded these wise words and duly declined an invitation to a Yugoslav charitable event, sending a donation instead.[4]

Within two weeks of their arrival, Paul and Olga had purchased a second-hand Ford car for a bargain £445 and employed a chauffeur called Israel. Unsurprisingly, the Princess was finding it hard 'to take up the threads of life again' and missed Kenya. However, she informed Foxie that the move was worthwhile as 'P[aul] is another person and began to revive as soon as we started [from Kenya].'[5] In early July, the Prince and Princess accompanied Alexander on a visit to Pretoria, as he wanted to introduce his parents to the Hugo family, who had been particularly kind to him. Although Olga thought the family 'very kind people' and 'devoted' to Alexander, she was not keen on the 'v[ery] bourgeois milieu', while Mrs Hugo was deemed 'a pushing snob.' The Princess thus felt it expedient to give her son 'a few words of warning' over his relationship with the daughter of the house, Yvonne.[6] She later 'begged' Paul to do likewise.[7] Unsurprisingly, the friendship soon fizzled out.

Olga continued to pine for news of her mother. Fortunately, on 6 July, she received two letters from Athens. In one, Princess Nicholas wrote that Countess Toerring had made a trip to Brdo and 'went...all over the house, crying, with the housekeeper! All in perfect order.'[8] A subsequent letter from Elisabeth (sent through Crown Princess Louise of Sweden) also happened to contain a recent photo of their mother. The Princess was taken aback, noting 'I had a shock to see how she had aged poor angel!'[9] It should be remembered that it had been two-and-a-half years since their last meeting.

On 13 July, Olga and Paul finally settled into their new home. As it was winter, the house proved 'icy'[10] and the Princess' luxurious Porthault bed sheets provided little warmth, so she was eventually forced to sleep under three blankets. Olga was also somewhat unsettled by the presence of the police guards who patrolled the grounds at night, for the area was notorious for burglaries. 'The monotony'[11] was occasionally broken by the presence of interesting (and influential) lunch guests, including Air Vice Marshal Matthew Frew. The latter was in charge of the South African Air Force's Directorate of Training and the Princess made sure to charm him while discussing Alexander's future career prospects. Another recipient of Olga's lunchtime charm was Cecil Syers, Britain's Deputy High Commissioner to the Union, who could prove useful to the family in any future dealings with the Dominion Office. Nonetheless, the Princess also comes across as cold and superior: A Major and Mrs Basson, took the trouble to host 'a huge tea' for the new royal arrivals in a private room at the Langham, but were peremptorily dismissed as 'Rather second rate.'[12] Nor, of course, did they happen to be particularly important or influential.

Following the Allied invasion of Sicily in July, Olga became focused on the fast-developing situation in Italy: Hearing of Mussolini's enforced resignation on 26 July she wondered, 'what will it lead to?[13] However, the Princess was also troubled to learn of another attack on Paul in the House of Commons by Captain Cunningham-Reid. Having heard of the Prince's recent move to South Africa, the MP was keen to know, 'Why has such favoured treatment been given to this foreign Royal quisling?'[14] Another MP, Mr Locker-Lampson, took exception to the question and, later that afternoon, he and Cunningham-Reid were observed exchanging physical blows in the Parliamentary precincts.[15] The matter was widely reported in the South African press and the Princess lamented that this 'new attack' was proving 'so upsetting for P[aul]'.[16] The Prince was doubtless moved by a message from Cardinal Maglione, whom they had met at the Vatican in 1939, enquiring after the couple's health. Olga was convinced this was as a result of Cunningham-Reid's recent outburst.[17]

In early August, Olga received news from London about King Peter's 'official' engagement to Princess Alexandra.[18] But this news was soon overshadowed by Cunningham-Reid asking the British Foreign Secretary, during a parliamentary debate, if Prince Paul's name 'has been, or is to be, given as a war criminal to the United Nations Tribunal for the trial of war criminals?' He also queried, 'Is my right Hon. Friend aware that millions of Yugoslavs consider that this man's treacherous collaboration with the Axis has been responsible for an untold amount of misery, humiliation and death...?'[19] A despairing Princess subsequently informed Marina that Paul had again fallen 'into the depths of gloom and despair' and was refusing to leave the house. She firmly believed that 'someone' had 'pushed' Cunningham-Reid to speak out again and wondered if it might be a member of Queen Marie's entourage.[20]

The Princess now wished to indulge in a little devious subterfuge: Knowing that there was no love lost between Mignon and her future daughter-in-law, and keen to have "inside" news from King Peter's camp, she asked Marina if she ever encountered 'Sandra' and wondered if 'perhaps it would be a good thing to revive her fondness for you'. She also pondered, 'if Zon [Zoia Poklewski] could worm something out of her mother [Princess Aspasia]!'[21] Olga was subsequently delighted to learn that neither Alexandra nor Aspasia were 'taken in' by 'the Houdri'. Nonetheless, ever-perceptive, she was also already questioning, 'if the girl [Alexandra] has enough strength of character to lead him [King Peter] the right way, only time will tell.'[22]

Meanwhile, the Princess' worst fear was that King Peter would eventually be forced to preside over a government of 'red leanings' [a reference to Josep Tito and his communist Partisan resistance fighters] as 'they will be capable of delivering D[icky] to Moscow!!...',[23] presumably for some sort of show trial. Olga's concern over the spread of Soviet influence was justified, as their communist militia were increasingly being called upon to fight Axis forces in the Balkans. The Princess also displayed remarkable foresight with regard to the Soviet Union's desire for territorial expansion: After reading about talks in Quebec between Churchill and Roosevelt[15] (and gleaning that Eden was about to visit Moscow to report on the proceedings) she agonised, 'If only the allies would realize the danger of drawing them [the Soviets] too much into the peace plan as they'll get a nasty shock over their ambitions.'[24]

The arrival of Elizabeth from Kenya, on 24 August, lifted Olga's spirits as it was a 'Joy to have my baby again.'[25] The Princess then decided it would be good to make a visit to Nicholas in Kenya, but Dr

---

[15] The First Quebec Conference 17-24 August 1943

Tonking informed her that this would not be possible 'as people here are beginning to feel the war restrictions and might criticise...'[26] Olga also had an illuminating encounter with an elderly neighbour who often sent her flowers. Calling by to thank her for this seemingly spontaneous gesture, the Princess was dumbfounded when the old lady let slip that she had received a letter from Mrs Smuts 'who asks her to be kind to us!'[27] An encounter with a Colonel and Mrs Craib would prove more auspicious: He was Superintendent of the Military Hospitals in the Union, while his wife was 'musical' and ran a 'pretty, tasteful house.'[28] The couple had two girls, one of whom, Pat, was around Elizabeth's age. Mrs Craib kindly provided the Princess with prospecti for suitable schools for her daughter and, on occasion, Olga and Paul would attend chamber music concerts at their home. The Prince and Princess also received an invitation to lunch from the Anglican Bishop of Pretoria, Wilfrid Parker and his wife Charlotte. However, despite these new social contacts, Olga remained resolutely indifferent towards South Africa. Indeed, when she heard that some acquaintances, the Garricks, were returning to England she bemoaned: 'How I envy them to leave this country!'[29]

In early October, the British High Commissioner, Lord Harlech, asked the Prince and Princess to Pretoria for the weekend. The duo also continued to widen their social circle in Johannesburg: In October, they were introduced to Lady Gertrude Albu who lived in great opulence at her Parktown mansion, Northwards. In addition to her eldest daughter Charlotte (the wife of the aforementioned Bishop Parker), Olga would also become particularly friendly with Gertrude's second-eldest child, Mrs Katherine Hay. Unfortunately, Lady Albu's son, Sir George Werner Albu, would cause a great deal of trouble for the royal couple in the future. There was news too of old friends: Mrs Sitter was currently living in Cape Town and had recently made a broadcast on the South African radio about Yugoslavia.[30]

The Princess would occasionally send letters through Prime Minister Smuts, who flew regularly to London on war business. However, this arrangement nearly came unstuck when Marina unwittingly acknowledged in a telegram *en clair* that 'she got my letter through Smuts!' This caused Olga to lament that 'the Br[itish] authorities are sure to know [of] it and won't like my sending letters otherwise than by their [diplomatic] bag-and we might get into trouble too...'[31] Fortunately, Elizabeth seemed to be settling down well and was now attending a Brownies group at the YWCA in Johannesburg. Olga found her daughter to be 'a fascinating companion-so like Nicky at this age-vitally alive and full of questions'.[32] In due course, the young princess was enrolled at St Andrew's School for Girls in the suburb of Senderwood.

As another year drew to a close, Olga was growing impatient with the war and the various alliances which made 'impossible to make head or tail as to who is on whose side.'[33] She certainly had a point for on 29 November, The Anti-Fascist Council for the National Liberation of Yugoslavia [AVNOJ] passed a resolution depriving the Government-in-Exile in London of its powers. In addition, King Peter and other members of his dynasty were forbidden to return to Yugoslavia until a referendum was held over the monarchy's future, at the end of the war. As if acting in tandem, at December's Tehran Conference, the United States and Britain (both keen to secure the continued cooperation of the Soviet Union in defeating Germany), agreed to officially recognise Tito's National Liberation Army as the main fighting force against the Germans in Yugoslavia.

Olga initial reaction to these latest developments was to take refuge in the past, but as she leafed through old family albums, she found that the images only filled her 'with sadness.'[34] The Princess now dabbled in spiritualism and recorded what she describes as the '1st spiritual circle of my life' during a pre-Christmas séance at the Albu residence. What information she garnered is unclear, but she certainly found the whole experience, 'deeply wonderful and convincing.'[35] On 15 December, Olga enjoyed her first reunion with a member of the Greek royal family, when she and Paul lunched with Crown Princess Frederika at Libertas, Smuts' official residence in Pretoria. She thought the Crown Princess 'grown and en beauté' and with 'so much to say after so long.'[36]

As she prepared a Christmas parcel for sending to Nicholas in Kenya, the Princess was pleased to learn that he was spending the Festive Season with her friends, the Bairds. However, she was also determined to have at least one son with her for the festivities and when Alexander announced he had not been granted leave, she immediately phoned Air Vice Marshal Frew who promised it would be arranged.[37] Quiss' presence would be particularly welcome for his mother admitted to feeling 'listless and low' with 'so much getting on my nerves that shouldn't.'[38] Worse still, was the 'awful' news that the 'upstart Tito' had the temerity to boast that 'Peter and his gov[ernment] don't count anymore...'[39] Olga was also struggling with the summery December weather and concluded that, 'It doesn't feel a bit like Christmas.'[40]

With the lease on Young Street due to expire, the Princess had already arranged, through Dr Tonking, for the British government to lease a much larger Elizabethan-style residence, Hathaway. The family moved house on New Year's Eve, with Olga questioning 'What does 1944 hold for us?'[41] In early February, the Princess made her first visit to Cape Town, to enjoy a five-week stay with her cousin Catherine. She travelled by rail under an assumed name and was instructed by the British High Commissioner to remain 'very quiet'. Nevertheless, Field Marshal Smuts and his family made her most welcome: She and Catherine usually spent Sundays in their company, either bathing in the sea or taking drives through the mountains for a picnic. Olga was amused that Smuts referred to all of the Greek royal family collectively as 'my children' and enthused to Marina that the Field Marshal 'couldn't be kinder to me...'[42]

Noel Coward happened to be on a goodwill tour of South Africa and the Princess attended his opening concert in Cape Town. "The Master" greeted her 'like an old friend' in his dressing room afterwards. However, earlier, there had been an awkward exchange with Frederika, who informed Olga that she 'just couldn't see anything in it [the performance], neither ... had Smuts.'[43] Yet, the Princess informed Paul that, on the whole, the Crown Princess had 'been sweet' and 'championed our cause with him [Smuts] several times.' Although Olga was equally absorbed in advancing her family's situation with the Field Marshal, her approach was subtler, as she explained to the Prince: 'At first I refrained from bothering him with our affairs, but gradually it has come out from his side.' However, she emphasised to her husband that, 'Whenever possible I do anything that can help you and I feel he is a true friend so please don't be sad and low.'[44] It would be fair to say that Olga's period in Cape Town represents a turning point in her family's fortunes, for having Smuts so firmly on their side could only prove beneficial.

On 20 March, King Peter finally married his fiancée Alexandra in a ceremony at the Yugoslav Legation in London. The newlyweds sent a telegram to Olga and Paul stating 'We are so happy to let you know we are getting married today, Monday. We are sure you will rejoice in our happiness.'[45] The King and Queen and Marina all attended the nuptials, although Queen Marie was a noticeable absentee. The Princess informed Foxie that she found Mignon's behaviour 'extraordinary', adding 'surely no one can have many illusions about her now!'[46] Nicholas arrived by air from Kenya on 25 March. His delighted mother had not seen him for nine months and observed that, 'He looks well and is a good half-head taller than one!'[47] Olga would often relax by riding out with her younger son (who enrolled at St John's School, Houghton Ridge) at the weekends.

Interestingly, the British Foreign Office were still taking a keen interest in the family: A Mr Sullivan of the British High Commission lunched with the Prince and Princess, in early April, and he subsequently informed John Greenway, Head of the Dominion Intelligence Department at the Foreign Office, that he found the couple to be 'fairly cheerful and well.' Sullivan also mentions that he had a meeting with their 'keeper,' Dr Tonking, prior to the lunch. The latter was clearly keeping a close eye on his "charges" and informed Sullivan that the Prince was 'nervous' about his financial position and, following upon recent developments in

Yugoslavia, now feared losing his monthly apanage payments. Tonking mentioned too that living costs were high in wartime Johannesburg and the family now faced the expense of another house move as the lease on Hathaway expired on 30 June. Indeed, the Prince was already selling some of his shareholdings through a local broker. Tonking's observations left Sullivan increasingly worried for the family's future and he confided to Greenway, 'I cannot think what is going to happen to them all...'[48]

In mid-May the Princess received a letter from her sister Elisabeth in Bavaria.[49] However, rather than bringing her comfort, Olga confessed to Foxie that such family correspondence only intensified 'the ache to seem them...'[50] Fortunately, Nicholas enlivened her days with his 'daily impressions' of his new school.[51] He faced considerable academic challenges, as in addition to learning Afrikaans, he had to embrace a totally different school syllabus geared towards the "Cape Matric" exams which he was due to sit in December 1945. His mother certainly believed he could cope with this task and admired his 'brilliant, enquiring brain'.[52] Elizabeth too was a conscientious pupil: The Princess described her to Kate Fox as 'a serious, practical, small person and very grown up for her age'.[53]

In the interim, King Peter bowed to a request from Churchill to dismiss his current Prime Minister, Božidar Purić. Olga followed developments as the young King subsequently appointed Ivan Šubašić as Prime Minister, with a directive to reach a settlement with Tito.[54] These negotiations resulted in the signing of the Treaty of Vis on 16 June[16] which removed Mihailović as War Minister and officially paved the way for the Partisans to be recognized as Yugoslavia's legitimate regular army. The Princess' nightmare scenario of Tito seizing power now took a step nearer. Nevertheless, the Prince and Princess must have felt a glimmer of hope for the future when they heard on the wireless of the Allied invasion of Europe on 6 June, D-Day. That evening they both listened to King George VI broadcast 'rather haltingly' to the Empire.[55] Yet, Olga also realised that her mother now faced increasing danger, as the Germans would fight tenaciously to maintain their grip over Greece. Stranded in South Africa, she lamented, 'It's awful to be so powerless to help.'[56]

Olga continued to face many challenges on the home front: On one occasion, Paul came into her room 'sobbing ...that he dreamed I was dead.'[57] Alexander was also somewhat perplexed by his father's behaviour and protested to his mother that Paul never talked to him. The Princess put this down to them being 'so unalike and tastes apart.'[58]

---

[16] Often referred to as the Tito–Šubašić Agreement.

Nevertheless, she was concerned about her eldest child's lifestyle and, 'fear the effect on him of the kind of people he meets.... as his judgement is poor. [I] Wish he could be among people of his own class.'[59] Fortunately, relations with the Smuts family remained cordial and Olga enjoyed lunching with them in Pretoria or taking tea at Doornkloof, their farm at Irene.

As the problem of finding a new residence grew ever more pressing: Prince Paul-probably at his wife's urging-mooted to staff at the British High Commission that his family might be allowed to relocate to Cape Town or the Natal Coast. However, British High Commission officials 'managed to steer him away from this'.[60] A new house, at a monthly rent of £100, was eventually found at the beginning of June, but came with the added complication that the owners were insisting on a long lease. Furthermore, Wierda House was situated in Sandton, some eight miles from central Johannesburg and thus inconvenient for Nicholas and Elizabeth's schools. Nevertheless, Olga tried to remain positive telling Marina, 'Enfin, one must make the best of it and we are lucky to have anywhere to go.'[61]

Most of the rest of her July diary entries deal with ailments in her own household: Elizabeth had a cold and tonsillitis; the Princess was suffering from headaches; Paul, meanwhile, was plagued with neuritis. Matters were not helped by servant worries: Olga's maid Urania was 'more than useless',[62] John the cook was rushed to hospital and Singh, the driver, often did not bother to turn up for work. Fortunately, the Princess found that undertaking endless mending proved a useful distraction.

By the end of August, Olga's concerns over Princess Nicholas's welfare intensified, for she was now convinced that as the German forces retreated northwards out of Greece, the Soviet forces, currently moving into Romania, would then 'pour down' into her homeland 'as they will need sea ports'.[63] Indeed, the thought of her Romanov Grand Duchess mother having to face the same Red Army forces who had murdered her family seemed to torment the Princess, who admitted to being 'sick with worry'.[64] To compound matters, on 12 September, King Peter, in keeping with the spirit of the Treaty of Vis, made a radio broadcast from London urging all Yugoslavs to join the National Liberation Army under the leadership of Marshal Tito. This force would join up with Soviet and Bulgarian armies to "liberate" Yugoslavia in the autumn.

The Princess was soon diverted by other happenings: While Elizabeth and her devoted nurse were holidaying at the Cape, Olga received a telegram to say that Miss Ede's oldest and 'favourite' brother had been killed in action in Italy. Naturally this proved to be 'an awful shock' for 'Nursie'.[65] A few weeks later, the Princess came to the aid of a local family, the Harwoods, when their nanny was suddenly taken ill. She unselfishly sent over Miss Ede to help out, a gesture which apparently left Mr Harwood (a widower), 'speechless with gratitude!'[66] Unfortunately, on 25 September, Paul was 'cornered' by a Yugoslav journalist from *Politika* who sought to question him about the Tripartite Pact. The Prince must have made some comment for Olga later noted that 'He is now worried lest the man repeats what he said.'[67] This latest episode seems to have almost tipped the Princess over the edge, for as she sat mending yet another pile of socks, she complained that she was 'sick of being housekeeper and a sort of nursery-maid!'[68]

Providentially, in early October, the family had a brief holiday in Pretoria at Libertas, courtesy of Smuts. Olga enthused to Marina, 'I must say its bliss to live again in space and luxury, with a huge bedroom and bath for each–reminds me of Beli Dvor days–*only then one took all this kind of thing too much for granted, as though it would last for ever.*'[69] The Field Marshal made time to talk to Paul and hopefully helped to raise his spirits after the recent encounter with the journalist.[70] Thereafter, the Princess learned that Sir Henry and Lady Moore were in Johannesburg en route to Ceylon (where Sir Henry had been appointed Governor-General). Her cousin Catherine had arranged to meet the Moores, whom she knew through Smuts, at the Langham Hotel to bid them farewell. Olga decided to accompany her and she explained her reasons to Marina, 'I made a point of it (never having clapped eyes on him) partly out of curiosity, partly to show it was beneath me to cherish any ill feelings. He asked me straight away about D[ickie]'s health... I was very sugary on purpose and wished him the best of luck in his future post–so that was that.'[71]

The British government was, meanwhile, turning its attention to the future 'welfare' of the Prince and Princess, as Dr Tonking was pressing for a return to his former Colonial Office duties in Mauritius, following the death of his other "charge", the ex-Shah of Iran. In early September, the Dominion Office sought guidance from the Foreign Office on how to proceed. The general view there was that Tonking's services could be dispensed with, for as Mr Dew, Head of the Southern Department, observed, 'we do not think that they [the Prince and Princess] can get themselves into much trouble at this stage of the war'.[72] The Foreign Office also seemed to adopt a compassionate approach to a request from Olga, that she and Paul–who had never been permitted to leave the high altitude of Johannesburg–be allowed to go down to Cape Town for three weeks.[73] However, it would be wrong to suppose that the Foreign Office was only acting out of kindness, for the Acting British High Commissioner had already reported to London that if Smuts was consulted on the matter, '[he] would almost certainly agree to their going to the Cape'. He also noted that if the visit was blocked, *'there will be an embarrassing argument with Princess Olga.'*[74]

The years of public humiliation and constantly fighting her family's corner, had undoubtedly transformed Olga into a wily and formidable operator. When Mr Jorgensen, the owner of the Young Avenue dwelling, sought to obtain 'further damages' over and above those already agreed with his letting agent, the pithy Princess informed Dr Tonking 'firmly' that she would 'not give way to blackmail'. She was quite prepared to call Jorgensen's bluff and, if necessary, give evidence against him in court.[75] After much deliberation, the Foreign Office in London decided to leave 'events to take their course' between the opposing parties.[76] However, things did not take the path that was anticipated: Mr Costar at the Dominion Office suddenly remembered that the tenants of the Young Avenue house had been the United Kingdom Government and not Prince Paul! Thus 'any legal liability must rest' with that department.[77]

In mid-October, Olga and Paul arrived in Cape Town and were greeted at the station by her Aunt Marie Bonaparte and cousin Eugenie. A few days later, news came through that the Greek Prime Minister Georgios Papandreou had returned to Athens, following a German withdrawal. The relieved Princess subsequently received a telegram from Marina to say 'Mummsie was well and happy now, thank God.'[78] Smuts was also able to reassure her that Elisabeth Toerring was currently in South Germany and being well treated.[79] Initially, Olga seemed in a carefree mood and, on several occasions, danced the night away with Paul at the Star Dust Night Club. However, her mood soon darkened when she heard that recently 'captured'[80] [since the Soviets were involved!] Belgrade lay 'in ruins' and this caused her to lament, 'how one longs to help those poor people.'[81] Her reaction was understandable, for both the Prince and Princess had sacrificed so much for Yugoslavia. Furthermore, Olga had not forgotten that, despite everything, she was still a Princess of Yugoslavia[17], with all its attendant obligations.

It was around this time, that the Princess heard rumours that Queen Marie was 'trying to push Tommy forward'[82] and that Mignon and Peter were not on speaking terms. Subsequently, King Peter contacted Paul, through Henry Channon, seeking his assistance in clarifying which jewels belonged to him (as opposed to his mother).[83] When King Peter and Queen Alexandra visited Marina at Coppins they had apparently displayed a 'hatred' towards Queen Marie, although Peter was apparently 'much better disposed' towards his Aunt and Uncle. The

---

[17] Olga's 'business card' stated she was Princess Paul of Yugoslavia, Princess of Greece and Denmark.

jewellery question must have been mentioned during the Coppins visit, for an unusually vengeful Olga later informed Marina, 'You might advise him [Peter] to threaten her [Queen Marie] that unless she gives up the emeralds at once, he will cut her monthly allowance by half!!' The Princess was also keen to press her sister into action again on her and Paul's behalf, observing 'as Mikros [Peter] seems so much better disposed towards us...it seems to me that now is the moment for him to say openly that we are members of the dynasty and no more outcasts.' However, this plea for Marina to nudge King Peter towards such an announcement was not Olga's only entreaty: She also implored her sister to help facilitate Alexander's relocation to England as, 'I should like him to mix with his own class again and be near you...'[84] In a subsequent letter, the Princess also required another 'great favour': Could Marina ask her Private Secretary, Lord Herbert, to make enquiries about the possibility of Nicholas 'going up' to Oxford (specifically Christ Church)-in the spring of 1946?[85]

Disobligingly, the ubiquitous Captain Cunningham-Reid addressed a Parliamentary Question to Eden on 6 December enquiring if 'Prince Paul of Yugoslavia is classed as a war criminal'. Eden replied briskly, 'No Sir.'[86] Such an infraction by the Captain would now cut little ice with Foreign Office officials who had already concluded that these attacks were 'his private vendetta against Prince Paul.'[87] Meanwhile, in Athens rioting broke out as communist partisans tried to seize control of the city. However, they were met with tough resistance from forces backed by the British military mission. Marina sent a reassuring telegram to South Africa to say that Princess Nicholas was unharmed, thus allowing Olga and her family to better enjoy their first Christmas together in three years.

1945 dawned with news of significant Allied advances throughout Europe, with Germany now under threat on all borders. On 3 January, the Princess received a letter from Ellen informing her of the recent death of her uncle, Prince Andrew, in Monte Carlo. However, Olga remained focused on the Soviet threat and, as communist forces advanced into Poland and East Prussia, she noted with distaste 'Only a miracle can stop these hordes now!'[88] In the interim, Paul continued to be pestered by journalists for comments on Yugoslav affairs, particularly his opinion of Tito who was appointed interim Prime Minister of Yugoslavia, on 7 March. He oversaw a provisional government which included members of the former Government-in-Exile who had recently returned to Belgrade from London. Although Olga was careful not to pass any public comment, she felt that King Peter had 'given in' to those seeking constitutional change by agreeing to the appointment of a Regency Council.[89] In fact, the young King had intended to issue a communiqué, on 11 January, rejecting the regency option, but Eden intervened personally to prevent this.[90] Faced with an impossible impasse, Peter eventually had little option but to agree.[91]

Unusually, it was the Princess who now admitted to suffering from 'mental depressions' as she learned of the 'Russian Hordes'[92] advancing ever closer to Berlin, while Munich was subjected to heavy bombing raids. However, the doctor attributed Olga's symptoms to 'the first signs of the change.'[93] Miss Ede was also increasingly a cause for concern: The Princess informed Marina that she 'can be very difficult at times and has a maddening way of nagging at the servants-several have already given notice because they can't stand her.' However, the problems with Nursie went deeper, 'She rather dominates Libiss and likes to have her entirely under her thumb and resents my authority which the child feels...' Apparently, when Elizabeth was alone with her mother, 'she couldn't be sweeter or easier but as soon as she gets under the other influence [of Miss Ede] its undone and she seems to slip away from me...' Matters were not helped by Nicholas' dislike of the nurse and 'sometimes he lets fly.' It was just as well that Alexander had become 'more matured and sensible ..always good tempered and unruffled-altogether a tuts and to me, something special.' Indeed, such was his close rapport with his mother that they would sometimes roll up the carpet, put on a record and dance together.[94] Nonetheless, the Princess later acknowledged that although Quiss showed her 'more tenderness', her other children 'all love me in their own individual ways.'[95] Unfortunately, the Prince and Princess were then the subject of complaint to the South African authorities by a Mr Waterson, concerning their monthly petrol allowance. Olga was upset by 'so much nastiness' which would ultimately lead to a substantial reduction in their ration. [96]

By mid-April, the American government was receiving reports from their Head of Intelligence in Belgrade, Lieutenant-Colonel Charles Thayer, that 'In foreign affairs, as in internal affairs, [Soviet] Russia is the lodestone governing Tito's policies.'[97] Perhaps, it is therefore unsurprising that the conclusion of hostilities in Europe, in early May, brought Olga little satisfaction. She noted in her diary, 'The war... is over after 5 years and 8 months. For what? One can't rejoice in a whole-hearted way knowing Russian power [has been] let loose over most of Europe.' She also cared deeply for the suffering of others: 'How can millions of starving people be fed? How [will they] ever rebuild the ruins.'[98] Despite her personal misgivings, the Princess dutifully attended an open-air Thanksgiving Service at the local Rosebank Church.

Olga was somewhat surprised to receive a letter from Princess Nicholas, in early June, indicating she had decided to fly to England to visit Marina. Indeed, it appeared that everyone seemed to be on the move, including Princess Eugenie, who had decided to leave Cape Town to join her parents in Europe. Given that Princess Catherine had lately moved up to Cairo, Olga would henceforth be the only member of the Greek Royal family left in the Union. Thereafter, the unseating of Churchill in the British general election, on 5 July, caused the Princess to hope that the new Labour government would 'be less cringing to R[ussia]' and display 'less hypocrisy'.[99] Anthony Eden was replaced as Foreign Minister by the socialist Ernest Bevin, and it was he who was now ultimately responsible for matters relating to Prince Paul and his family.

On 17 July, Olga received news that Queen Alexandra of Yugoslavia had given birth to a son, Alexander, in a suite at Claridge's. The British government had declared the room to be Yugoslav territory, to ensure that the Crown Prince was born on "home" ground. The Prince and Princess immediately sent a congratulatory telegram and Olga was overjoyed to see a picture of the baby in the *Illustrated London News*. However, she confided to Foxie, 'I just can't imagine Mikros as a father!'[100]

Just after the surrender of Japan, in mid-August, Olga entered the Norman Nursing Home for an operation on her thyroid gland. Apart from some post-operative queasiness, all went to plan and she was discharged on 1 September. Smuts sent her his 'heartfelt good wishes' for a full recovery and also relayed the welcome news that Crown Prince Paul and Frederika were due to visit Pretoria in early September.[101] Olga and Paul subsequently entertained the royal couple on several occasions at Weirda House and Smuts then hosted a farewell lunch for the duo at Libertas. However, what might have otherwise passed as a pleasant social occasion, soon took a darker turn when Frederika showed Olga, 'the most ghastly photographs taken in Athens of the massacres in Nov[ember] & Dec[ember] last year by the ELAS [Greek People's Liberation Army] maniacs-all told 60,000 harmless people were slaughtered in cold blood....' The effect on the Princess was salutary: 'I felt physically sick & speechless with horror.' However, Olga was equally convinced that atrocities were also occurring in Yugoslavia, for she informed Foxie, 'As to what Mr T[ito] does, *it's on a larger scale but even more unknown as he has no opposition or outside witnesses.*'[102]

In September, the latest Apanage payment failed to arrive,[103] a development which coincided with Doctor Dusan Nedeljković, the President of the Yugoslav War Crimes Commission, signing documentation, on 17 September, which branded Paul a war criminal and confiscated his assets.[104] She wondered if Queen Marie's finances had been similarly affected, 'and how she liked it!'[105] Mignon's response was to give a press interview in which she accused King Peter of depriving her of money. The Princess thought her behaviour was 'revolting beyond words.'[106] Faithful Miss Fox, meanwhile, consulted Sir Henry Channon over the money problem and by mid-November, a payment arrived which included any outstanding arrears.[107] In the interim, a 'very tired and ...very nervy' Miss Ede took a well-earned holiday.[108] During the latter's absence, the Princess informed Foxie, with some satisfaction, that Elizabeth had proved 'so sweet and tender' and 'doesn't seem to miss Nursie at all!'[109]

On the very day that elections were being held in Yugoslavia, 11 November, the Princess made a visit to Field Marshal Smuts and his wife at their farm in Irene. She only records enjoying a 'long talk...[about] world affairs'[110] but it seems highly likely that the election-and the ramifications for her family-would also have been discussed. Certainly, Olga was in despair when she learned, on 13 November, that the results were 'all in favour of Tito.'[111] Ever the realist, she must have realised that her family would not be returning to Beli Dvor. This fact was underlined when, on 29 November, the Constituent Assembly of Yugoslavia formally abolished the monarchy and declared the country a Socialist Federal Republic.

Thereafter, Peg of Hesse's brother Alexander Geddes came to tea and gave the Princess some welcome news of her Greek cousins in Germany. In addition, there was some unsettling news from both Marina and Miss Fox about the shocking treatment of Countess Toerring, at the hands of the occupying American forces. The Princess responded to Foxie, 'I am horrified and revolted about the way W[oolly] was treated and the way her private personal things were looted and spoilt-it's really unheard of on the part of the so-called "liberators" or restorers of order-[I] am very glad M[arina] complained to the Gov[ernmen]t!'[112] Olga was also concerned that there was still no word from Marina about Nicholas attending university in England. She therefore sought his headmaster's assistance in finding him a place at a local university (Witwatersrand), as he was due to leave school at Christmas.[113]

Out of the blue, a note arrived from Princess Nicholas, in December, proposing that she make a visit to South Africa. Olga's initial reaction was one of surprise, but as she reflected on it, she decided it was 'impossible' until the family were settled in a larger house. However, another major factor was that Ellen had asked her daughter to make an approach to Smuts to send his plane to Athens to fly her to Pretoria (as he had recently done for Crown Prince Paul and Frederika). Olga thought 'that's perhaps asking too much.'[114] Eventually, Princess Nicholas decided to remain in Greece to await developments there.

With Christmas approaching, and mindful of their reduced petrol ration, Olga took the bus into town for Christmas shopping. Sadly,

Alexander would not be present for the festivities, as he had just been posted to Ceylon. Money was again tight as no further payment had been received from King Peter. Nevertheless, the Princess was understanding and noted, 'Nor do I see how it can anymore as Mikros must be hard up himself.' However, her feelings towards Queen Marie remained decidedly glacial: Olga informed Marina that it would be 'amusing to know how Houdri will resign herself to living in lesser luxury as I don't imagine her appeals [for funds] to Tito will bear fruit and I can't feel sorry for her-que Dieu me pardonne.'[115]

As 1946 dawned, Olga enjoyed a holiday at a rented house in Rondebosch in the Cape. One Saturday, she joined Smuts and his family on a day excursion around the Cape Peninsula and marvelled at the Field Marshal's expert knowledge of the local fauna and flora. She later took tea with Mrs Smuts at her home, Groote Schuur, which was a great treat as Ouma possessed 'great character and knows her own mind and is too sweet.'[116]

On her return to Johannesburg, the Princess was delighted to learn that Nicholas had passed his school matric examinations 'brilliantly' and was now ready to start an Economics course at Witwatersrand University.[117] However, she had little time to reflect as she busied herself for yet another move from Weirda House to Atholl House. Unfortunately, in February, it was widely reported in the international press that Paul had been named as a 'Hitlerite' agent in a document prepared by the Yugoslavs for presentation at the International Tribunal at Nuremberg. The allegations, it was stated, were based on the testimony of Yugoslav quislings.[118] Thankfully, there was better news the following month, when Olga was able to speak by telephone to her sister Elisabeth for the first time in six years. She was currently enjoying her first post-war stay at Coppins. The Princess later recounted to Foxie, 'I can hardly tell you what a tremendous emotion it was, I had to bite my cheeks inside and pinch myself to stop my tears.'[119] Meanwhile, many of Olga's South African friends were now openly wondering 'why I don't just jump into a plane and fly to Coppins and see them'. She reflected 'Alas, it's not so easy much as I long to do it. I must just go on possessing my soul in patience till that blessed day comes.' Interestingly, one reason the journey north would have proved so difficult was because the Princess steadfastly refused to make use of her connections with Smuts, firmly believing that the limited aeroplane places available were needed 'for more vital reasons.'[120]

In April, Olga was uplifted by the result of the recent elections in Greece: When she learned that the mainly Monarchist national unity government, led by Konstantinos Tsaldaris, had secured 65% of the vote, her reaction was mainly one of relief that 'the com[munist] element is beaten...'[121] Meanwhile, Elizabeth, now aged 10, moved to a new school, Redhill, as it was more conveniently situated for Atholl House and the fees were half of those at St Andrews. The end of her time at St Andrews happened to coincide with the annual sports day and the child had hoped Prince Paul would attend to participate in the father's race. However, Olga was soon bemoaning to Foxie, 'but as you may guess he did not have the *courage* to come at all and face the crowds!'[122] She was clearly unimpressed. Yet the Prince had reason to be watchful, for he had recently been the subject of more 'poisonous articles' in the local *Sunday Times* newspaper. These were apparently penned by a communist friend of the pro-Tito Yugoslav consul in Cape Town. Olga became so infuriated by the attacks, that she sent a copy of an article to Smuts 'explaining who the author is.'[123] Fortunately, she seemed reassured by a subsequent declaration from the Field Marshal that 'we'd be safe as long as we stay under his protection.'[124]

Miss Ede then announced that she wanted to travel to England to visit her ailing mother. Olga viewed this as the ideal opportunity to dispense with the nurse's services, 'for Libiss' sake as the child has really outgrown her.'[125] However, Nursie later decided to postpone her departure.[126] Meanwhile, in London, the Foreign Secretary Ernest Bevin had decided that 'the future of Prince Paul and his family' be 'reconsidered'.[127] It was increasingly felt that the Prince could be released from his 'nominal' interment and thus absolve the British government of the burden of paying the rent on his residence.[128] The British High Commissioner, Sir Evelyn Baring, had already obtained an assurance from Smuts that the family would be allowed to remain in the Union if Paul's freedom was granted.[129] However, Michael Williams, Acting Head of the Foreign Office's Southern Department was at pains to minute that Paul would not be granted a United Kingdom visa and would be required to give an undertaking to refrain from any political activity.[130]

While Smuts concurred with the British proposals, he also caused eyebrows to be raised in Whitehall by informing Baring, 'emphatically... that he would resist any proposal to extradite Prince Paul for trial as a war criminal by a Yugoslav court, since he has no confidence in Yugoslav justice.'[131] The Field Marshal had a valid point for, in March, the Yugoslav government had steadfastly refused to hear exonerating evidence from United States military officers at the trial of Draža Mihailović. The royalist Chetnik leader was subsequently found guilty of high treason and war crimes, causing Olga to note with feeling that, 'Our hearts ache over the injustice.'[132] He was executed on 17 July.

On 18 May, Paul was informed by Sir Evelyn Baring of the decision to 'restore your full personal liberty' from 1 June.[133] However, Olga seemed more concerned about the forthcoming Greek plebiscite on the restoration of the monarchy. She had little faith in the current King, informing Foxie, 'Our dear G[eorgie] won't have the guts or the ability and [I] do wish he would pass on his rights to Palo whose heart and soul are with the country.'[134] A terrible gloom then descended over Atholl House when Miss Ede learned, in early June, that her mother had died. The Princess explained to Miss Fox that she 'did all in my power' to comfort the nurse as she 'collapsed in my arms'. Miss Ede's misery was compounded by the knowledge that she would soon be leaving the family's employ although, out of compassion, Olga informed Nursie, 'that there was no longer such a hurry.' Nevertheless, the Princess reflected privately that she had put up 'with much for the sake of peace.'[135]

As staples such as sugar and bread became increasingly scarce, Olga became a great supporter of the introduction of rationing in the Union and hoped it would stop 'the terrible hoarding and blackmarket.'[136] She was fortunate to have the services of a 'touching old Greek grocer' who never failed to provide her with the essentials. [137] Meanwhile, the Princess was also attempting to soothe the remorse of another old friend, Lilia Ralli. She was so ashamed at not having written to Olga during her South African sojourn, that her first letter contained 'endless apologies for nearly two whole pages!!!'[138] Mrs Ralli was due to visit Princess Nicholas in Athens so the Princess 'begged' her mother to reassure Lilia that she had 'forgiven her long ago knowing what a friend she is-and always will be.'[139]

Interestingly, King George VI was not informed of Prince Paul's 'release' until 8 July.[140] However, he lost no time in having his Private Secretary write to enquire if the Foreign Office would have any 'special reservations' with regard to a possible meeting between himself and Prince Paul during an upcoming visit to South Africa in early 1947.[141] Officials were unenthusiastic, and Bevin's Assistant Private Secretary, Mr (later Sir) Nicholas Henderson replied that, 'it seems to us preferable that such a meeting should be avoided, because it would be likely to give rise to unfavourable comment'. However, '*The same would not, we think apply to a meeting with Princess Paul, for which there are good family reasons*, but we suggest that any such meeting should be private...'[142] The matter was doubtless discussed by Field Marshal Smuts with the King and Queen during his visit to Balmoral on 14 September, for two weeks later, Olga wrote to Marina to say that Bertie and Elizabeth had been in touch and hoped to meet both the Prince and Princess during their forthcoming tour of the Union. This had left Paul feeling 'very consoled'.[143]

The Greek monarchy was restored in the plebiscite of 1 September, with 69% in favour of the King George II's return.[144] Despite her earlier misgivings about her cousin Georgie, Olga 'prayed for him to be guided to face all the awful problems before him' and also that 'his life be may be spared, because he is bound to be in constant danger'. The King's subsequent return to Athens, on 27 September, made the Princess particularly homesick and she hoped 'my turn is not far off'.[145] Thereafter, matters were not helped by Prince Paul being cast down again by a rumour of further trials in Belgrade, with his name apparently still appearing on a list of prospective offenders. Olga confided to Marina, 'Oh dear it's so hard at times to keep calm and confident and it's such a struggle against one's inner peace...*I wonder how much longer I can stand it and the longing to escape, on my own, grows ever more intense. If only D[ickie] could find some hobby however small, something to absorb his mind and not depend on me so much, it would make things easier...*' Nonetheless, the Princess immediately felt guilty about writing down these thoughts and added, 'My F'al I did not mean to blurt this out so crudely, it's just that at times it tends to get me down. *I simply live with the idea of going to Athens...*'[146] Troublingly, this was not just a passing phase, for three weeks later she informed Marina that, 'sometimes I feel so sick of doing my duty day after day...I know I am an ungrateful swine to say this but there it is!' Olga even posited that Marina might come to South Africa 'and then perhaps I might have gone back a bit with you! Amusant?' Even so, she was wise enough to realise, 'It's just a castle in the air and may lead to nothing.'[147] However, it is clear that the seeds of discontent and despair were growing apace.

The Princess' outbursts may also partly have been prompted by a recent visit from the British conductor Malcom Sargent, who was on a tour of South Africa. He had lunched with Olga and Paul at the Langham, despite having being warned by others not to see them 'as it might harm his visit here!'[148] Sargent subsequently visited them at Atholl House, during a rare Sunday off, and seemed remarkably chatty and most reluctant to leave. After riding out with Olga and Nicholas, he remained to lunch and tea and later joined the family for an informal dinner at the home of friends, the Forsyths. A few days later Olga attended one of his Johannesburg concerts.[149] These encounters were to be the beginning of a long and warm friendship and probably served to remind the exasperated Princess of what she was missing out on in Europe. Interestingly, Olga also seemed to be adopting an atypical laissez-faire approach to life, telling Foxie, 'In general, I believe more and more in each person's individuality and live and let live.'[150] One guest the Princess did not encourage was Major Sharpe. He had recently written to say he was coming to South Africa on holiday and asked to stay with the Prince and Princess. Olga immediately wrote back to say they did not have a guest room, but added tactfully that they would, of course, be glad to see him. The Prince, however, was 'sick with horror at the mere thought ...'[151]

The Princess' extended family were increasingly on her mind: Marina had lately forwarded one of Queen Mother Helen of Romania's letters, which Olga informed Foxie, was 'too pathetic for words'. Helen and her son King Michael had, more or less, been placed under house arrest by 'those dreadful [Communist] people.' On a happier note, Olga also deliberated on the developing romance between her cousin Philip and Princess Elizabeth [the future Queen Elizabeth II] and noted, 'I'd love to know the truth and feel there must be something in the air.' However, she was appalled when she learned that a friend of the Greek royal family, Mrs Foufounis, had asked Philip about it outright.[152]

When Olga learned, in October, that Alexander was to be demobbed at the end of the year, she expressed a 'dread' of him 'knocking about in S[outh] A[frican] society for months'[153] and decided to ask Marina if some work could be found for him in England.[154] The Princess then hoped to escape her troubles and fly to Athens in November before returning to spend Christmas at the Cape.[155] However, Field Marshal Smuts indicated to Princess Nicholas, during his subsequent visit to Athens in December, that Olga had been denied this opportunity at the insistence of the British government.[156] This must have proved a devastating blow.

Most unusually, the Princess was then caught off guard during a conversation with Alexander Geddes, at a pre-Christmas dinner party given by the mining magnate Harry Oppenheimer. She later informed Marina: 'He suddenly asked me if we would see B[ertie] and Eliz[abeth] when they come [on the upcoming Royal Tour]...I guilelessly replied that we hoped to and besides I know they hope to see us (a gaffe to add this I later realized). Anyway he proceeded to say that he thought it would be a great mistake... and dangerous in view of the press etc...that it would do them harm, that we had even much better arrange to go away, possibly back to Kenya!!' Olga 'was so taken aback with amazement that all I found to say was that we had no intention of asking to see them unless they wished it.' The Princess eventually managed to 'put an end to the conversation as he was talking loud enough for the other guests to overhear and [I] left feeling sick and upset.'[157]

Indeed, Olga's main concern was that Geddes had spoken with 'some authority' and as if he might have been 'voicing an official London opinion'. Eventually, it was arranged (through Harry Oppenheimer) for Geddes to take tea with the Princess at Atholl House. Olga saw him alone and 'He said he wished to apologise...adding that it had been entirely his own opinion *based on what certain people had told him here*...to this I said that it certainly looked as though he had been insinuating that we intended to do harm to B[ertie] and Eliz[abeth] by asking to see them whereas we would be guided by Pitus [Smuts] who was a great friend of ours...'[158] The Princess would later reveal to Marina that Geddes' 'informant' had been none other than Sir George Werner Albu[159] which doubtless explains why Olga had 'laid stress' to Geddes, during their Atholl House conversation, 'on how fond we are of both Mrs Charlotte Parker and Mrs Erroll Hay (sisters of Sir G[eorge] Albu) which seemed to surprise him.' The Princess stressed to Marina that the reason she wanted her to have knowledge of these conversations was because Geddes was a friend of Lord Louis Mountbatten and she felt that, 'he is quite capable of telling the story to him (to be repeated to B[ertie]) and thus giving a completely fake picture about us...'[160] In other words, she wished Marina to fight her corner in London.

Shortly thereafter, the family left Johannesburg to spend Christmas at the Cape. Olga was concerned that she had not heard from Smuts and complained of feeling 'washed out.' Meanwhile, Alexander (who was now officially on 'discharge leave') telephoned to say he would arrive by train in Cape Town on the afternoon of 30 December.[161] The international press had clearly been tipped-off about his leaving the RAF and were soon reporting that he 'hopes to be a businessman'.[162] Unfortunately, Marina's recent attempts to find work for him in England had proved fruitless.

Chapter 19 A Royal Meeting

The Princess began 1947 in the Cape at a 'nice supper party' attended by twenty guests at friends, the Dalrymple's.[1] Lady Moore (of Kenya days) and her daughter Deirdre were currently on a visit to Smuts and the Field Marshal broke his long silence to invite Olga and Paul to dine with them at Groote Schuur. Smuts greeted them warmly and handed the Princess a box filled with parcels from London and Athens, together with the poignant news, gleaned during his recent visit to Greece, 'that sweet Mummsie pines to see me![2] The Field Marshal continued to hold out the carrot that he would take Olga to Athens on his next trip to London. The Princess, however, was growing increasingly steely on this subject, and observed to Foxie, 'I'll remind him of that promise!'[3] But given his comments to Princess Nicholas, only a few weeks earlier, about the British government's position on the matter, could Smuts actually deliver? Certainly, a first step in the Princess' return to Europe was achieved, in February, when King George sent her a Greek passport.[4]

For the moment, the Prince and Princess concentrated on enjoying the Cape's busy social round: There was a delicious picnic with friends at Miller's Point, as well as a dinner for twelve at the Canada Restaurant hosted by the royal couple. However, on 28 January, Paul received a letter from an 'old friend' (who worked at the BBC in London) which repeated 'almost word for word' what Alexander Geddes had 'expounded' previously to Olga during his South African trip. Indeed, the Princess complained to Marina that Peg of Hesse's brother had 'spread [Sir George] Albu's opinions all over London giving the impression that he [Albu] spoke for South Africa!' As Olga had earlier predicted, this information eventually 'reached B[ertie's] ears as representing the general feeling in S[outh] Africa.' The fallout from all this would prove catastrophic, as on 29 January, Smuts sent for the Prince and Princess and 'told us that he had just had a letter from Bertie saying he thought it wiser <u>not</u> to see us…soit disant to protect our names from getting into the press [and] how sorry they were etc..'[5]

Olga recalled, 'It was all I could do to contain myself' and she informed the Field Marshal that she thought the King's decision was 'most unfair'. Furthermore, she felt that a meeting between themselves and the royal couple 'would have been a unique chance to disprove all the rumours still floating.' Unfortunately, the Princess then turned her guns on Marina, observing 'Very possibly B[ertie] acts on the advice given him and wishes to be careful *but forgive me my F'al if I say that I think if you had mentioned to him at once what Geddes said to me and where he got his information, B[ertie] would have seen it in its true light.*'[6] However, it later transpired that Marina had only been informed of the King and Queen's change of heart 'at the last minute before "they" left [England].'[7]

Olga and Paul left the Cape for Johannesburg the following day. A letter from Miss Fox informed the Princess that she had recently bumped into Queen Marie and her son Tommy at a saleroom and indicated that Mignon had spoken 'well' of Paul[8]. The Princess was unconvinced responding, 'I know of old how impossible it is to trust in her sincerity as she is incapable of loyalty.' Nevertheless, she was also pragmatic and added, 'God knows, we don't want to keep up this feud which is none of our making.'[9] Alexander, meanwhile, had secured a three-month trial undertaking inspection work for Pan-African Airways.

With the royal visit imminent, the Princess was continually fielding enquiries from friends as to when they were likely to meet the King and Queen. She informed Marina, 'We always reply we don't know and that it depends on them, if they have time etc...'[10] Olga currently seemed to find solace in the lectures given by Nicol Campbell, the head of the "School of Truth". She was principally inspired by the 'spiritual force'[11] of his message that Man is God in manifestation, not merely a forsaken individual fighting a losing battle against adverse situations and events.

On 17 February, *HMS Vanguard* docked in Cape Town and the Princess listened intently to the radio commentary of the royal family's arrival on her sitting room wireless. Later, she heard both the King's and Smuts' speeches at that evening's State Banquet in Cape Town's City Hall. Olga also learned that her cousin Catherine was to be married, in late April, to Major Richard Brandram, a British Royal Artillery officer. There was news too of her cousin Philip, whom the Princess noted had recently received British citizenship and was now simply known as Lieutenant Philip Mountbatten (this drew an exclamation mark in her diary entry).

Meanwhile, Miss Ede had left the family's employment to take up a new post. The parting had been particularly emotional for Elizabeth.[12] Unfortunately, within weeks, Nursie was taken ill with kidney stones and placed in a nursing home. Following her discharge, Olga kindly arranged for her to return to Atholl House to recuperate. Miss Ede now intended to sail home to England in mid-April. In the interim, the Princess interviewed the 'Scotch and cosy' Miss MacDonald as her replacement.[13] The latter had previously worked for Olga's friend Mrs Hay and would commence her duties in early May.

The Princess paid a visit to the Smuts family at Irene in mid-March but, frustratingly, nothing of consequence (including the royal visit) was discussed.[14] However, she soon discovered that the Field Marshal had put his foot down with royal officials, when they requested that the Yugoslav royals should leave town during the royal family's visit to Johannesburg.[15] On 1 April, Olga went out to a pavement near her home to catch a glimpse of the royal entourage as it drove-by en route to a Civic Reception. She thought the Queen was 'looking lovely and sweet', while the King looked 'very grim.'[16] That afternoon, Smuts arrived bearing a letter from the Queen stating that the Field Marshal would arrange a meeting between the British and Yugoslav royalties 'in some quiet place'.[17] Although, at the time, the Princess 'had no doubt' that a letter her sister Marina had written to the King 'may have helped matters',[18] Princess Nicholas subsequently informed Olga that Crown Princess Frederika had also intervened with her friend Smuts to help facilitate the reunion.[19]

However, no sooner had Olga read the contents of Queen Elizabeth's letter than she was 'shocked' to hear an announcement over the radio stating that her cousin King George of the Hellenes had died. This dreadful news coincided with the family bidding a final farewell to Miss Ede. Olga had to comfort the old nanny, who clung to her sobbing and asked pathetically, 'You will let me see her [Elizabeth] again, won't you?'[20] Years later, the Princess would inform her niece Helen that she thought that Miss Ede was 'left wing' and felt 'the nanny put the child [Elizabeth] against anything [such as] the aristocracy and maybe against her parents also.'[21]

In the meantime, final arrangements were made for the royal meeting which was to take place at the Smuts' farm at Irene on the afternoon of Sunday 6 April. Olga noted the Field Marshal would not be present as 'he has to go back to the Cape.'[22] Despite his absence, the reunion turned out to be 'very successful'[23]. After the Yugoslav royals had lunched with twenty-four members of the Smuts family the King, Queen and the Princesses Elizabeth and Margaret arrived at 3.30 prompt in a closed Daimler, accompanied by a large police escort, but 'no court.'[24] The British royals greeted Prince Paul and his family 'most lovingly' and everyone, including the 'whole Pitus clan' sat down to take tea.[25] Olga thought the King was 'drawn'[26] and 'twitchy',[27] while the Queen was 'as fresh and sweet as ever and the girls v[ery] nice and natural and well-groomed.'[28] The Princess informed Marina that Bertie 'only relaxed and laughed when the four of us were alone for 10 minutes in Pitus' study [after tea]...' During that brief interval, Olga mentioned to the Queen that Sir George Albu had played 'a sinister part' in trying to prevent their meeting[29] but Elizabeth 'did not seem to know anything about the G[eddes] intrigue...'[30] The Princess also took the chance to emphasise to the Queen 'about our future and how trying it is à la longue to live so far away from Europe and one's friends.' She then mentioned a possible move to Ireland 'which has often been mentioned to D[ickie] as an ideal place...' and the Queen 'seemed to think it a very good idea.' The reason the forward-thinking Princess mentioned a future move was because, as she later informed Marina, she was keenly aware, that, *'the '48 election is already being prepared here....[and] no one anticipates his [Smuts'] re-election [as Prime Minister]-with him no longer what he is, we should never get the same personal protection...'*[31] The British royalties duly took their leave at 5pm. Prince Paul's family attribute this meeting as having been of tremendous help to their father in terms of lifting his morale.[32]

Olga remained anxious about Alexander who was currently dating an English divorcee. She lunched with the couple at Dawson's Hotel and, surprisingly, deemed her son's beau 'quite nice.'[33] When he subsequently admitted to his mother that he was in love with the woman, she noted 'all I begged him was to go slow and decide nothing; *of course, we could not allow it.*'[34] Perhaps in an attempt to extricate him from this current romance, the Princess confided to Marina that the company who currently employed Alexander, 'engaged him for snobbish motives' and again emphasised that it would be better if he came to England 'and meet decent people, more his own class.'[35]

As a welcome diversion, Olga visited a local diamond factory, owned by an acquaintance Mr Kadinsky, where she was able to inspect the diamond necklace which was to be given to Princess Elizabeth as a 21st birthday gift.[36] She listened intently to the Princess' 21st birthday broadcast to the Empire from Cape Town, observing that it was delivered in 'a firm clear high voice.'[37] However, it seems that all Olga's recent worries were beginning to take their toll: A few days later, while playing a game of padder at the Hay's residence, she mentions 'awful palpitations; never before [experienced], had to lie down ...'[38] Although the attack would soon pass, it caused the Princess considerable distress.

By early May, as she listened on the radio to the return of the British royal family to London, Olga remained intent on sending Alexander to England. She now asked Marina to invite Quiss to join her in Scotland, in August, and emphasised that her eldest child badly needed 'so much understanding and help'.[39] Unusually, in Miss Ede's absence, Elizabeth too was proving difficult, being sometimes 'in a tiresome contrary mood'[40] as well as having 'fights' with both of her brothers.[41]

Meanwhile, the Princess' longing to visit Athens intensified when she learned that her sisters were due to undertake a two-week visit to Greece in June. Olga was determined to join them, but lamented that she had no visa. She wrote to Smuts both to inform him of her sisters' plans and 'asking his advice as to going myself.'[42] On 5 June, the Princess met with the Field Marshal in Pretoria and he informed her a flight was arranged for 9 June.[43] As she departed Atholl House for Athens on a crisp winter morning, Olga was distressed to find Elizabeth in tears. However, the pull of her mother and her homeland was now all-consuming and she was soon boarding a Dakota in Pretoria to whisk her to Greece. After overnight stops in Kenya, Khartoum and Cairo, she landed in Athens on 13 June.

Looking out of the aircraft window, the Princess was almost overcome with emotion when she suddenly espied Marina and Elisabeth waiting for her on the tarmac. Later, at Psychiko, 'Sweet mummsie' greeted her eldest child at the door. Olga was immediately struck by how 'v[ery] thin'[44] Ellen had become, but soon everyone was 'talking for hours'[45] about their different wartime experiences. After a late dinner, the Princess retired to bed exhausted, but happy to be reunited with 'my three Darlings'.[46] The sisters first excursion was to Tatoi, on 15 June, to visit the royal family's graves. They later visited the Bodossaki silk factory and Castella Yacht Club before attending a party in their honour at Diddie Serpieri's home. Sadly, Marina and Elisabeth had to leave on 22 June. After such a short but tender reunion, Olga admitted it was 'agony' to kiss her sisters' goodbye and watch them 'disappear into the blue...'[47]

The Princess' visit was originally intended to have been a short one. However, as she explained to Miss Fox, she had now 'given up' on this idea, as she wanted 'to have a quiet time with Mummy, see some friends & go sightseeing'. As if to justify her actions, she added, 'besides Paul urged me not to be in any hurry.'[48] Mother and daughter would talk late into the night or enjoy long walks in the Royal Gardens. Olga became acquainted too with Paul and Frederika's children Sophie, Constantine and Irene and took them on an excursion to a favourite beach at Kavouri, where she found the sea to be 'like liquid aquamarine'.[49] There was an emotional visit too with 89-year-old Sophie Baltazzi, Queen Olga's former Lady-in-Waiting, who 'was full of Amama's souvenirs.'[50] Memorably, on one particularly 'boiling' night, she dined with a group of friends by the sea at Phaleron, before going on to Vouliagmeni to bathe by moonlight into the early hours.[51]

On 4 July, Olga noted that her mother had received a letter from Marina with the news that Philip's engagement to Princess Elizabeth ('Lilibet') was to be announced on 10 July and 'he will be given the title Duke of Edinburgh!'[52] However, it was not all good news, for there was still ample evidence of the unsettled political situation in Greece: On 6 July, a huge explosion rocked the old Royal Stables which were currently being used as a military base. Thereafter, a communist plot to overthrow the government was unearthed and this led to 2000 arrests.[53]

The Princess' name day on 11 July-the first she had celebrated since leaving Europe in '41-saw the arrival of lots of friends at Psychiko bearing flowers and sweets. Nevertheless, the news that Alexander had failed to secure employment with the British Air Ministry and remained in South Africa, despite Marina's best efforts, upset Olga greatly.[54] She was now desperate to get him away from the clutches of his divorcee girlfriend, whom she labelled, 'that woman.'[55]

After a short visit to the islands of Petali and Sifnos in mid-September, the Princess wrote half-heartedly to Foxie, 'I suppose I shall have to think about returning to far away S[outh] Africa before long'.[56] However, for the moment, she contented herself by helping Frederika to choose outfits for the forthcoming royal wedding in London, from a selection brought from Paris by Jean Dessès. Olga's admiration for the young Queen continued apace and, after learning of Freddie's successful negotiations with US Senators to obtain aid for the poor, acknowledged, 'She has a great brain'.[57] However, the reality of the exacting challenges still facing the Greek royal family were brought home when Frederika telephoned from Salonika, at the end of September, to say that a bomb had been thrown from the crowd during a visit by King Paul to Edessa.[58]

By early October, Olga was actively making enquiries about a return to Johannesburg and told Marina 'It is *my duty* to get back to the family.'[59] As cholera was now stalking Athens, the Princess and her mother were required to have 'rather painful' inoculations.[60] Yet, there was no vaccine for the torment Olga felt over her cousin Helen's situation in Romania: Life under the Communist regime was 'rapidly getting worse' and, ominously, King Michael's personal pilot had recently been replaced. As both he and his mother were due to attend the forthcoming royal wedding, the Princess feared that instead of their plane heading for London, her relatives might instead be taken in 'another direction' (i.e. the Soviet Union).[61]

Around this time, Olga learned from Marina that Miss Fox was in the Private Ward at University College Hospital, London recovering from a slight stroke. The Princess wrote her Nurnie an upbeat letter, before going out to purchase an icon from Mount Athos as a wedding gift for her Mountbatten cousin. Although she was not attending the royal wedding, Olga informed Foxie that 'It touches me deeply that Philip would like me to be there as his godmother' but that even he had been forced to acknowledge 'how awkward it would be in the present circumstances.'[62] However, she was in good company, for none of Philip's three surviving sisters were invited as they were all married to Germans.

On 8 November, Frederika telephoned to say King Paul had contracted typhus. Princess Nicholas and Olga immediately rushed over to the Palace to find the Queen 'trembling and in tears of anxiety.'[63] Although Frederika was advised by doctors to attend the royal nuptials, the Princess observed that she 'has lost all her enjoyment in her clothes and her visit!'[64] Olga's presence must have proved a comfort to the distraught Queen as she prepared to depart for London, for the Princess would keep a close eye on the recovering, but enfeebled King, as well as helping to entertain the couple's children.

Smuts flew into Athens, on 15 November, en route to the royal wedding. He stayed overnight at the Royal Palace and indicated he would return in a few weeks to fly the Princess south.[65] Olga was certainly needed in Johannesburg as there were ongoing problems between Elizabeth and the new nanny, Miss MacDonald. The former, according to Paul's recollection, had adopted 'a hostile attitude to her Nursie (a very nice person) out of loyalty to Miss Ede.'[66] Furthermore, Alexander had lost his job as his aircraft firm had 'crashed.'[67] Fortunately, Nicholas was proving to be his 'old, sensible, self'.[68]

On the day of the royal wedding, 20 November, the Princess and her mother attended a reception at the British Embassy and listened to the ceremony on the wireless. Shortly thereafter, the Princess received the welcome news from Marina that Alexander was currently en route to England, where a resourceful English businessman friend of the family, Edward Beddington-Behrens (who was married to the Princess' kinswoman Princess Irina Obolensky) had found him 'a technical job.'[69]

At the beginning of December, Field Marshal Smuts arrived in Athens to transport Olga to South Africa. Movingly, on the morning of her departure, Princess Nicholas cut two roses from the garden for her daughter to take back with her to Johannesburg. These two devout ladies then said a 'little prayer' together in Ellen's bedroom before leaving for a family lunch at the Royal Palace. Later, at the airport, Princess Nicholas came briefly into the plane to bid Olga farewell. However, it proved 'agony to part' as at the last moment both mother and daughter lost their self-control and broke down in tears[70]. Nevertheless, as she prepared to face the travails of life in South Africa again, the Princess could draw on 'the happiness of my visit to Mummy and the strength she gives one will be something to draw fresh courage from and help me enormously to face the problems to come.'[71]

Olga landed at the aerodrome in Pretoria, in the late afternoon of 3 December, to find Nicholas waiting to drive her straight to Atholl House, where she was greeted at the door by Paul and Elizabeth. Predictably, she was already admitting to missing 'home and M[ummsie].'[72] It was not the most inspiring of homecomings: Paul complained to his wife that he was 'fed up with the monotony of this place'[73] while Nicholas feared he would 'stagnate' if he remained much longer in South Africa.[74] Sadly, Elizabeth had 'felt abandoned'[75] and now followed her mother around 'like a shadow'.[76] In addition, after six months in Europe, the Princess was feeling 'quite detached'[77] from local happenings and previously interesting dinner parties were now deemed 'rather heavy going'[78] while fellow guests were invariably 'noisy and vulgar.'[79] Olga turned to Nicol Campbell for guidance during this period and he advised that she 'must draw on my supply of strength and _not_ give in.'[80] Nonetheless, as she celebrated a quiet family Christmas, Olga's thoughts remained resolutely 'with my Mummsie and sisters.'[81] The year finished with the disturbing news that King Michael of Romania had abdicated. The Princess was filled with concern, both for him and for Sitta, and she wondered 'where will they go?'[82] As she listened to the New Year bells over the radio, signalling the dawn of 1948, she might just as well have been asking the same question of her own family.

It was at this juncture that the oft-mentioned idea that Prince Paul and his dependents might make their main residence in Ireland, suddenly gathered momentum. 'The Irish plan',[83] was originally the idea of Beddington-Behrens. He had previously-without Paul's knowledge-made approaches through the Irish High Commissioner in London, to ascertain if the Irish government would have any objections to the Prince and his family living in Eire. Indeed, just prior to Christmas, Beddington-Behrens had felt able to inform Paul that 'all is clear for you to go to Ireland.'[84] Smuts was informed of this development during a visit from the Prince and Princess on 6 January 1948. He immediately contacted a Mr Sedgwick at the British High Commission in Pretoria, to 'enquire whether the United Kingdom Government would have any objection to this course'.[85] However, in a letter to Miss Fox, Olga seemed distinctly cool about this proposal, 'I confess that apart from its being within an hour's flight from England _it is much too far away from Athens for my liking._' Apparently, she (and Paul) 'preferred' Switzerland, as it was 'more central and has good schools and I can reach Athens in 2 or 3 hours from there.'[86] Meanwhile, in London, Mr Price at the Commonwealth Relations Office (C.R.O.) [formerly the Dominion Office] had taken soundings from both the Foreign Office and the King. There was a positive response and Price subsequently instructed the British High Commissioner to notify the South African government that there was 'no [government] objection' to the Irish proposal.[87] Smuts duly informed Olga of this development by letter on 11 February.[88] Yet, the Princess still maintained to Miss Fox that the family's future plans remained 'vague' with 'either' Ireland or Switzerland being mooted as a future refuge.[89] In addition, there were subsequent entreaties from ex-King Carol of Romania and ex-King Umberto of Italy, for Paul and his family to join them in Portugal.[90] Fortunately, Olga had managed to obtain an extension on the lease of their current residence until the end of April, although she was increasingly focused on returning to Athens for the Orthodox Easter accompanied by Elizabeth.

Nevertheless, another bitter blow was about to befall the family as a result of an intervention by the British Foreign Secretary. During the earlier consultations between the C.R.O. and the Foreign Office, Ernest Bevin happened to be on a visit to the Isle of Wight and had been kept 'out of the loop' about the Irish plan by his officials. [91] However, when he later got wind of what had transpired, during a routine meeting with the Irish High Commissioner, Mr Dulanty, on 9 February,[92] Bevin was shocked and immediately put pressure on Lord Addison, the Secretary of State for Commonwealth Relations, either to reverse the decision or risk having it referred to the full cabinet.[93] Addison caved in[94] and on 2 March, arranged for the British High Commissioner in South Africa to inform Smuts 'urgently' of the British government's volte face[95]. It was left to the Field Marshal to write to Paul to explain that both the British and Irish governments were now actively discouraging him from 'nursing the idea of leaving S[outh] Africa' at all.[96] The Prince was naturally stunned and replied to Smuts on 6 March, 'I would like to know if I must now assume that I am to be considered a life prisoner...'[97] On the same date, Olga wrote to Kate Fox and, although she did not mention the Field Marshal's recent correspondence with Paul, she indicated that if the family were not able to return to live in Europe, they might obtain a loan to buy a house at the Cape.[98] The British government's reversal was a bitter blow to the Prince and Princess' future plans and during a meeting with Smuts on 26 March, Paul emphasised that his confinement in South Africa was 'affecting his health and state of mind.' However, the Field Marshal, who was about to call a General Election, informed the Prince that 'the British attitude appears to me [to be] dictated largely by solicitude in his own interest' and that he 'shared their doubts and hesitations.' The Prince then proposed that he and his family might move to Portugal. Although Smuts indicated he would make enquiries on his behalf, he also sought to dissuade Paul by warning him 'about the risks' he was 'running of being demanded by Jugoslavia to be handed over as a war criminal'.[99] For good measure, Sir Eric Machtig, Under-Secretary of State for Commonwealth Relations, personally intervened so as 'to defer' any soundings by South African officials with the Portuguese authorities.[100]

In the interim, Olga remained absorbed with her upcoming visit to Athens. By early April, she had arranged with a local department store to pack up and store the remainder of the family's belonging at the conclusion of Atholl House's lease on 30 April. Paul, who was already displaying signs of anxiety at his wife's forthcoming departure in the form of stomach spasms,[101] had decided to move to the lower altitude of the Cape to stay with friends and await developments. As Nicholas needed to remain in Johannesburg to complete his university studies, the Princess arranged for him to lodge with the Harwood family. On 23 April Olga and Elizabeth flew north to Athens. Paul was so 'low & miserable' that he simply could not bear to wave them off.[102]

Prince Alexander of Yugoslavia in RAF uniform, 1943

Memorial Service, Winhoring, 1956, L to R (front row) Princess Marina, Count Karl Theodor Toerring, Princess Olga, Hans-Veit Toerring, Helen Toerring. L to R (rear) Archduke Ferdinand of Austria, Princess Elizabeth, Princess Alexandra of Kent and Prince Michael of Kent.

Princess Olga in the 1950's by Cecil Beaton.

The wedding of Prince Alexander to Princess Barbara of Liechtenstein, Paris, 1973 L to R Prince Alexander, Princess Karoline of Liechtenstein, Princess Olga, Princess Barbara.

Princess Olga on holiday in Vaduz, 1977

Princess Olga's 80th birthday party, Thatched House Lodge, Richmond

Princess Olga with her grandsons L to R Dimitri, Dushan and Michel

Princess Olga attends a Memorial Service for King Alexander in Paris.

Chapter 20 Return to Europe

The Princess and her daughter arrived in Greece in good time for the Orthodox Easter. Olga was soon enthusing to Foxie: 'I simply can't believe that I am actually once more here and have spent a real Greek Easter after so many years! It's so lovely to have brought my Libiss and see her with Mummy who is getting to know her again-they are already great friends & seem to have a link between them.' Already present in Athens was Olga's cousin Sophie and her three eldest children, so this provided 'plenty of cousins' for Elizabeth to play with.[1] The visit coincided with the wedding, in Athens, of King Michael of Romania to Anne of Bourbon-Parma at the Royal Palace on 10 June. The marriage had proved somewhat controversial, as the Vatican refused to sanction the nuptials, as Michael followed the Eastern Orthodox faith. For the Princess, the event provided the ideal opportunity for a long-awaited reunion with Alexander and her many Greek cousins. She informed Miss Fox that their presence 'makes me feel several years younger in a funny way because I feel so happy in all the love that surrounds me.'[2]

But it was not all happiness: The Princess was concerned for the well-being of her recently-widowed cousin Irene, Duchess of Aosta. The latter related the harrowing story of her capture and internment by the Germans, along with her baby son Amedeo, following the Allied invasion of Italy. 'Tim' was eventually liberated from a Nazi concentration camp by French forces and spent some time in Switzerland before returning to her Florentian home, the Villa San Domenico. The experience had clearly told on Irene who appeared 'very thin and drawn'.[3]

The family celebrations continued apace, next day, as Olga celebrated her 45th birthday at Psychiko with a large family dinner party in her honour. However, the Princess informed Miss Fox that her greatest pleasure was watching Alexander and Elizabeth playing together in the sea 'and hear[ing] their happy laughter.'[4] There was word too of a rift between Tito and Stalin and, on 28 June, Yugoslavia was expelled from Cominform, the official forum of the international communist movement.

In Athens, the relatives were gradually dispersing and, on 10 July, Olga enjoyed a farewell tea at Psychiko with her cousins Sophie and Theodora. What she gleaned about conditions in post-war Germany caused her to note, 'I wish all the cousins could get out of there for the future of their children.'[5] By mid-September, the Princess was growing anxious about her own future and fretted to Marina that 'the knowledge that we have no fixed abode, not to say home is extremely unnerving to say the least!'[6] Fortunately, the family (apart from Nicholas who was completing his final year at Witwatersrand) were soon be reunited, as Paul had finally decided to settle, for the moment, in Switzerland. He flew out of Johannesburg on 12 October, arriving in Geneva three days later to be greeted by Alexander and Lilia Ralli. The trio were joined there, from Athens, by Olga and Elizabeth on 20 October, just in time to celebrate the Prince and Princess' Silver Wedding anniversary.

Initially, the couple established a temporary home at the Hotel des Bergues, on the shores of Lac Le Man. Henry Channon paid them a visit, in late November, and was surprised to find them living in 'three smallish rooms', which were in complete contrast to their 'vanished' and (now) 'Tito-occupied palaces' of Beli Dvor and Brdo.[7] After discussions with Paul, Chips remained 'absolutely convinced' that the Prince was innocent of any charge that he had damaged the Allied cause. Channon was also startled to learn that his friend still 'loved' the British.[8] Dragisa Cvetković also paid the family a visit; he had escaped from Belgrade, in September 1944, and was now settled in France. The ex-politician had a poor opinion of King Peter.[9] By this stage, Princess Nicholas was also becoming 'more conciliatory' in her attitude towards her son-in-law, after he had taken the trouble to send her a letter explaining the events of 1941 in detail.[10] The cash-strapped Prince, meanwhile, turned to his contacts in the art world (including Herr Böhler in Lucerne) to raise much-needed funds from the sale of his remaining works of art.[11] Indeed, in early December, the family felt it expedient to move to the Montreux Palace Hotel as it offered cheaper room rates.[12] However, even with this economy they were unable to afford to fly Nicholas back from Johannesburg for Christmas,[13] although Alexander joined them from England.

As 1949 dawned, Elizabeth was enrolled at St George's School, Clarens and Olga passed the time ironing her daughter's clothes or enjoying occasional lunches with Queen Ena of Spain at nearby Ouchy. On 21 January, Marina flew out to Switzerland to join Olga and their cousins Theodora and Sophie for a family reunion. As this was the first contact between Paul and Marina since Prince George's death, both were 'greatly émus...to meet again.'[14] However, this meeting drew a somewhat negative reaction from the press, who commented that 'the King [George VI] has no time for [Prince] Paul.'[15] It was perhaps fortunate that the newspapers did not pick up on the presence of Theodora and Sophie, who tactfully stayed at another hotel. These family visitors were just the tonic Olga needed and the foursome were soon descending a local mountain in luges 'crying with laughter.'[16] Nevertheless, all were disappointed that Elisabeth Toerring was currently too ill to join the party.[17]

When the others departed, Olga felt life was 'so empty' again.[18] Fortunately, Aunt Ena proved a wonderful source of gossip about the likes of the Duke and Duchess of Windsor, although her teatime visits invariably far-exceeded "the polite hour". The Princess also busied herself arranging for clothes, food and medicines to be sent to Greece, as contributions for a humanitarian aid fund set up by Queen Frederika.[19] She also came to the aid of Queen Anne of Romania, who was expecting her first child, helping her to assemble a suitable layette.[20] In March, Queen Marie broke her long silence and tactfully wrote to Paul that 'so much has happened during these last years that I am not going to attempt to say anything about them.'[21] Meantime, Olga was delighted to receive the news that Nicholas (who recently graduated with a first-class Bachelor of Arts degree in economics from Witwatersrand University) had been successful in securing a place at Christ Church and would commence his Oxford studies in the autumn.[22]

As the Easter school break approached, the Princess was keen to visit Paris to buy some much-needed clothes. During this sojourn, she paid a visit to Princess Eugenie at St Cloud and attended a preview of the new collection at Jean Dessès (at which she purchased an evening dress and a coat). On 15 April, Paul arrived in Paris and the couple enjoyed a private tour of the Palace of Versailles. A few days later, the Prince and Princess had their first post-war encounter with King Peter and wife Alexandra over tea at Lilia Ralli's home in Rue Scheffer. Olga found the couple to be 'v[ery] nice and affectionate'[23] and 'keen to know about the past; he rather full of himself but under her thumb. Both hate their mothers!'[24]

After returning briefly to Switzerland to see Elizabeth safely settled at school, Olga flew from Geneva to England for her first trip to Coppins since that sad wartime visit of 1942. Marina was waiting to greet her sister at RAF Northolt and there was also an emotional reunion with Michael, whom his Aunt observed 'marks the passage of time!'[25] Over the next week, the Princess was to be reunited with a plethora of royalties and friends: On the first day, the King and Queen came to lunch, followed at teatime by her cousin Philip and his new wife Elizabeth. Olga later lunched with Queen Mary and made a long-anticipated visit to Tsar Alexander III's daughter, Grand Duchess Xenia, at Wilderness House, Hampton Court. She and Marina also enjoyed a night out at the theatre in the company of the MP John ('Jack') Profumo (a brother-in-law of Harold Balfour)[18] and the Princess' recently-knighted friend from South Africa days, Sir Malcolm Sargent. After the performance, the sisters accompanied their companions to the "400" club for 'bacon, eggs and

---

[18] Profumo's name would one day be at the centre of one of the greatest British political scandals of the 20th century.

dancing.'[26] A few days later, Olga lunched alone with Sargent at his London flat and she would keep in contact with him during her upcoming visit to Greece. Indeed, it would be fair to say that the Princess was already falling under his spell, for she later confided to Princess Nicholas that, 'he made up to me ...but not in a heavy possessive way, yet rather tender and gentle, asking for nothing I was not prepared to give.'[27] On the eve of Olga's departure for Greece, the sisters brought Miss Fox down to Coppins for an overnight stay. Sadly, the ageing Foxie was 'full of complaints'[28] which was unfortunate as this was the last occasion she and Olga would meet.

On 6 May, the Princess flew to Athens. Most mornings, Ellen would join her daughter in her bedroom for a brief chat and then Olga would rise and potter in the garden or read. Mother and daughter sometimes ventured up to Tatoi for Sunday lunch with Paul and Frederika or entertained a steady stream of visitors at Psychiko, including the very deaf Princess Alice, who came to tea and 'talked long and v[ery] loud' such that 'we were worn out.'[29] Olga also made a determined effort to ensure her mother's house received a good spring clean; however, her high standards soon led to a confrontation with a 'lazy and rude' woman servant, Achillea, over the cleaning of the parquet flooring.[30]

The Princess also undertook some official duties: During a "Day of Mourning", she joined the King and Queen at the Cathedral for a service in remembrance of 28000 children 'abducted' by the communist rebels.[31] She later attended an event at the Academy of Athens, during which the King make an emotional appeal for funds to help the 700,000 homeless in Greece. It was during such occasions that Olga was at her most patriotic, noting proudly that 'no foreigners' were present.[32] It was not all duty: In addition to the usual steady stream of dinner and lunch invitations, the appearance of a group of French actors, in late May, further enlivened her social round. However, the most thrilling event, by far, was the arrival of Nicholas from South Africa, on 9 June, in good time for his mother's 46th birthday celebrations. The Princess was soon writing enthusiastically that 'everyone [was] charmed with Nicky's intelligent conversation and poise for his age'.[33]

Interestingly, it was during this visit that the Princess began to regard Frederika with caution, commenting on her 'strange nature.'[34] However, her reaction may have been, in part, due to the fact that the Queen had grown close to Princess Nicholas and, on one particular occasion, Olga seemed somewhat taken aback when 'Freddie' simply 'walked in suddenly' to her mother's house to partake of an impromptu supper and enjoy a long chat.[35] The Princess was also keen to avoid discussing politics with the Queen, preferring to limit their conversations to talk of love and marriage.[36] Olga currently favoured the 'brilliant' politician (and future Prime Minister) Spyros Markezinis, who was currently charged with encouraging Greece's economic recovery.[37]

A welcome guest passing through Athens was Field Marshal Smuts[19]. He arrived just in time to help Nicholas celebrate his 21st birthday on 29 June. That evening, Princess Nicholas organised a 'v[ery] gay party down by the sea' in her grandson's honour.[38] By coincidence, *HMS Vanguard*-the vessel which had transported the King and Queen to South Africa in 1947-arrived in Athens on a goodwill visit. The Princess was pleased to attend a cocktail party on board hosted by Rear-Admiral Robert Kirk Dickson, the Head of the British Naval Mission.

On 6 July, Nicholas left Athens to join his father in Paris, where the top floor of Lilia Ralli's house was currently being arranged as a make-shift pied-à-terre for the family. Meanwhile, Elizabeth was en route to England to spend her school holidays at Hove, in the company of her beloved Miss Ede. She would later join her brothers and the Toerring family for a large family reunion with the Kents at Coppins, in August. Although Olga received touching letters from everyone, the correspondence only served to remind her of all that she was missing. However, her attention was soon drawn towards the 'wonderful victories' being enjoyed by Greek government forces over communist guerrillas in the northern Gramos Mountain range.[39] This encounter marked the near-conclusion of the civil war and the Princess was full of admiration for General Papagos, the Commander-in-Chief, whom she described as 'such a splendid man and full of confidence, [and] is adored by the soldiers.'[40] She later attended a ceremony at the Royal Palace to mark his promotion to the rank of Field Marshal.

In September, Olga welcomed her siblings and Alexander to Athens. The three sisters took full advantage of this rare reunion, breakfasting together on Olga's balcony each morning and visiting Tatoi to admire a new herd of cows, recently flown in from Denmark to supplement their Apapa's original herd. There were outings too to Kifissia which remained 'exactly like in our childhood.'[41] However, the Princess found Alexander's presence something of an irritant as it proved 'difficult to talk' in his presence. [42]

In November, Olga was reunited with Elizabeth in Switzerland, after an absence of six months. She was keen to listen to all her daughter's news but was particularly perturbed to learn that she neither liked nor respected St George's new headmistress.[43] The Princess decided to visit the school, next day, to assess the situation for herself, and spoke to

---

[19] Smuts had been unseated as Prime Minister of South Africa in June 1948 by Dr Malan and his National Party.

various members of staff, including Elizabeth's form mistress and the school Matron. Olga seems to have been at her most formidable and 'was able to put a few matters straight which may help El[izabeth].'[44] Duly satisfied, the Princess boarded the train for Paris, where she now faced the challenge of finding a suitable home.

No sooner had Olga arrived in the French capital than she received the distressing news that Kate Fox had passed away peacefully in her sleep at the Iver Cottage Hospital. She flew over to London, on 21 November, to be met at the airport by Marina and Alexander who drove her straight to the hospital chapel to pay her final respects. The following day, Olga and Marina joined some of Miss Fox's relations at Croydon Crematorium for a 'sad little service...'[45] As Kate's bedridden sister Jessie was unable to attend, the sisters then drove over to her home at nearby Warlingham for tea. Miss Fox's death, while expected, still came as a bitter blow to the Princess, for Kate had been a constant presence throughout her life. Indeed, even during their long separations, the duo had remained the most faithful of correspondents. Long after her death (and those of her three charges), Foxie would remain something of a legend in the extended family.

On her return to Paris, Olga helped Paul to entertain Dragiša Cvetković and his wife to lunch at the Jockey Club. She was fascinated to learn that Mara Cvetković had only recently escaped from Yugoslavia by simply walking over the border into Italy. However, other encounters were not so welcome: While dining at the Méditerranée, she espied the Duke and Duchess of Windsor and adroitly fled upstairs to avoid an awkward encounter. After a pre-Christmas buying spree at Dessès and Molyneux in Paris, Olga returned to London where Marina had planned 'a v[ery] full week ahead.'[46] This included supper with the society photographer Cecil Beaton at the Savoy and tea with Queen Mary at Marlborough House. The sisters also lunched with the King and Queen and their daughter Margaret at Buckingham Palace. The British royals kindly asked if they could meet Alexander and Nicholas, so Olga brought them over for drinks the following day. The Princess was 'so glad that was done'[47] for she was aware that by receiving the young Princes, the King and Queen had sent out a strong signal of approval to London society. On Marina's birthday, 13 December, the sisters attended a charity ball and had such 'great fun'[48] that they did not retire till 4am!

The Princess returned to Paris to spend the Festive season with her family. On Christmas Day, everyone attended the morning service at the Greek Church before driving out to Duff and Diana Cooper's residence at Chantilly for an afternoon drinks reception. Unfortunately, the Salon was packed and Olga found the event 'completely bewildering'[49] and was 'much relieved' to leave. She also complained to Princess Nicholas that, in general, her own 'family atmosphere is not all peace and smoothness as you can imagine and I find it rather a strain at times.'[50] More precisely, Elizabeth was 'fierce in her affection for me and minds sharing me with her brothers.'[51] Furthermore, relations between Paul and Alexander remained 'as hopeless as ever', while the Princess was irritated over her (recently unemployed) eldest child's 'apathy and indifference about finding a[nother] job.' But, as she admitted to her mother, her dissatisfaction went much deeper: *'Quiss I always felt was closer to me and I had hopes in him and believed in him, as I often told him-but now I feel he is letting me down.'*[52]

As a new decade dawned, the family attended Princess Catherine ('Dolly') Radziwill's réveillon party. Olga seemed determined to make an entrance and wore a blue and pink satin dress by Dessès (although she joked to Princess Nicholas that it was her 'own creation' as she had insisted on altering both the original colour and length) accessorised by her favourite diamond crown brooch.[53] However, age seemed to be catching up with her, for after accompanying Elizabeth back to school at Clarens, the Princess was obliged to consult a Swiss specialist, Dr Bickel, about persistent gall bladder pains.[54]

The Prince and Princess had now established a daily Parisian routine which included lunching at Vatel's, followed by either an evening at the theatre or dinner with friends at the Ritz. These social occasions helped smooth Olga and Paul's reintegration into the upper echelons of French society. The couple also held a large drinks party, at Lilia Ralli's home, to thank the many friends who had entertained them since their return to the French capital. The Princess retrieved her best emeralds from Cartier in order to make a sparkling impression.[55] Meanwhile, despite her many years in Africa, Olga's sense of dynastic awareness remained as fierce as ever: She complained bitterly to Princess Nicholas that Grand Duke Andrei's morganatic wife, the Russian ballerina Mathilde Kschessinska, was 'openly' calling herself Grand Duchess Andrei which she found 'too disgusting'.[56]

In due course, an old acquaintance of Olga's parents', Madame Bousquet, called on the Princess at Rue Scheffer accompanied by a Mrs Carmel Snow, the Editor-in-Chief of *Harper's Bazaar* magazine. Olga later informed her mother that Mrs Snow had 'no idea' who she was but happened to mention that she was due to visit Greece on business and was 'madly keen' to meet both Queen Frederika and Princess Nicholas. On hearing this, the Princess immediately rose to the occasion and 'buttered her up and gave her a brief history of our family', including the fact that she was Princess Marina's sister!'[57] Interestingly, in addition to her mother, Olga also ensured that she informed her Athens friend, Mika Skouze, of Mrs Snow's Athens visit 'so that she can get hold of her before she falls into the wrong hands...'[58] Was the latter perhaps a reference to Queen Frederika?

Another person seeking Olga's assistance in providing introductions was Sir Malcolm Sargent, who was due to make a winter visit to Athens. The Princess was certainly keen that her mother should receive him, and wrote to her to say that 'I shall be so interested to hear your opinion of him my angel, please tell me!'[59] Princess Nicholas politely invited Sargent to tea but he clearly failed to impress and was crushingly dismissed as being overfamiliar and a snob.[60] Doubtless thrown by her mother's reaction, Olga's feelings toward the conductor appeared to wane and she reassured Princess Nicholas that, 'As for his "feeling" for me, such as it is, we meet too seldom for it to ripen into anything more than friendship. I know he is a coureur and always has a woman round [sic] the corner.'[61] Nevertheless, on his return Sargent wrote an effusive letter to Olga ('Madam-beloved Madam') to inform her that 'I have fallen completely for your lovely Greece' and adding that he was 'longing to see you again...'[62]

In early February, Olga and Paul ventured to Grasse to stay with Marie-Thérèse de Croisset and her family at the Villa Croisset. They then moved on to the nearby Château de Malbosc, the home of Olga's cousin Eugenie and her husband Raymundo ('Raymond'), Duke of Castel Duino. The latter hosted a large family lunch for his wife's 40th birthday, where fellow guests included King Michael of Romania, his wife Anne and her mother Princess Margaret of Denmark ('Meg'), a cousin of Prince Nicholas. However, the visit was not a complete success: Olga found the combination of Eugenie's loud voice and the squalk of her pet parrot during mealtimes somewhat tiresome;[63] while an excursion to Monte Carlo for lunch was ruined by the 'awful people' who frequented the Hotel de Paris.[64] Nevertheless, the Princess particularly approved of Eugenie's 'calm and patient' husband Raymond, who proved to be a thoughtful host and was 'full of little attentions'. She subsequently had long conversations with him on religion and spiritual guidance [65] and within weeks was informing her mother, 'I have a definite feeling, entre nous, that Raym[ond] has a tender feeling for me.... He is almost too attentive and empressé, even quotes me to her [Eugenie] and admires my clothes a bit too much in front of her... I can see it would not do to stay on too long.'[66]

Meanwhile, Alexander had found 'a job (of sorts)' with a company called Paris Shopping Advisons, which involved him matching customers to shops suitable for the items they wished to buy. He would then earn a commission on any subsequent purchases. However, rather than praise her son for finding new employment, his mother instead dismissed the post as not 'very dignified' and Quiss resigned at her insistence.[67]

Thereafter, the Princess informed her mother that she hoped to leave for Athens in May. But first, she required to undertake a delicate balancing act over what do with Elizabeth during her summer school holidays. The ensuing correspondence is a demonstration of Olga at her most manipulative: She expressed the hope that Elizabeth might come out to Greece in late July, in the company of her form mistress, Miss Ingleston, but cautioned Princess Nicholas that Paul-who was not due to visit Athens-must be handled carefully as he 'will mind not seeing her, though less [so] if he feels she is with me.'[68] However, Olga delayed broaching the subject with her husband directly preferring 'to let it come of itself gradually.' Meanwhile, the Princess primed her mother 'to say in your next letter, so I can read it to him, how much you would like to have Lib[iss] again, not having seen her for two years.' Olga also sought to influence Elizabeth by informing her that her grandmother would 'like her to come...' though she warned Princess Nicholas that 'if she protests ...he [Paul] will take her part and say I must not leave her for her holidays, which will make my stay with you much shorter'. She ended her letter with the tart-not to mention somewhat cold-observation that 'it would simplify my own plans so much more' if Paul had his own arrangements in hand.[69]

Nonetheless, another matter was currently proving even more pressing: Prompted by a 'rather cryptic'[70] letter from Aunt Moina, the Prince and Princess ventured for a week, in mid-March, to stay with Queen Mother Helen at the Villa Sparta, from where they made frequent visits to Pratolino. Moina was, by now, largely confined to a chair in her bedroom, but still wore make up and jewellery, including some 'enormous emerald poire earrings'. On one occasion, when Paul was absent, his Aunt asked Olga about her nephew's time in Kenya and 'wept...to hear of all his sufferings...'[71] Intriguingly, the aged scion used the visit to show the Prince a copy of her will.[72] This caused the Princess to inform Marina that, 'the visits are v[ery] necessary and promise a lot for the future.'[73]

On Olga's return to Paris, her convoluted scheme for the summer holidays appeared to be on the verge of unravelling, after she received a letter from Elizabeth indicating she wished to spend her summer holidays in the South of France. The Princess purposely kept the contents of this letter from Paul and, instead, read him an excerpt from a letter from Princess Nicholas containing the pre-arranged reference about wanting to see her granddaughter again. However, the Prince did not take the bait and merely commented that he 'doubted the child would want to come [to Athens].'[74] Olga thereafter adopted a petulant stance and decided not to attend her hostess Lilia's all-Greek cocktail party, on 24 March, noting that it was 'not given specially for me' and adding that it 'bored' her 'to plunge into that crowd so soon.'[75] Then, at Easter, the family took tea with King Peter and his wife in their luxurious suite at Paris' Plaza Hotel. The perceptive Princess was now convinced that there was 'something pathetic and pathologically wrong in the whole atmosphere [surrounding their marriage].'[76]

Olga and Elizabeth then enjoyed a post-Easter stay in England, during which the Princess helped Marina co-host a lunch at Coppins in honour of the departing South African High Commissioner, Leif Egeland and attended by Winston Churchill. Olga was placed next to Paul's old nemesis who proved 'vague at first, [but] talked more later'.[77] In fact, Marina had taken great care to ask her sister, in advance, if she had any objections to meeting the former Prime Minister. After talking it over with Paul, the Princess chose to adopt a magnanimous stance and informed her mother, 'What does it matter now after all! It's true he has written a lot of lies in his book about our story in '41 and has been attacked already but it interests me to meet him...'[78] Meanwhile, the unseasonable weather meant that the children were able to build a snowman at Coppins, which made for considerable merriment. Indeed, Olga's nephew Prince Edward has particularly fond memories of his Aunt during this period, 'She was always great fun...perhaps not quite as relaxed as my mother-slightly more formal in her manner.' Nevertheless, she possessed 'a wonderful sense of humour and the two sisters particularly ...together were non-stop laughing' and would switch into Greek if they wanted to discuss something privately. Edward was particularly impressed to learn that his Aunt Olga was able to speak some Russian.[79]

Despite the earlier reservations expressed to her mother, the Princess continued to see Sir Malcolm Sargent during this visit. Although others were usually present, Olga attended the theatre twice with him alone[80] and on one occasion they enjoyed a 'v[ery] cosy' supper together at his flat.[81] These encounters, she informed Princess Nicholas, had proved 'rather fun'. She was also able to report another satisfactory development: Marina 'would love to have [Elizabeth] for the summer holidays, thank God'.[82] So the path was now clear for another long Athens visit.

Olga and Paul dined with the Charles Mendls at their Versailles home, the Villa Trianon, at the beginning of May. A fellow guest was the wealthy entrepreneur and philanthropist Paul Louis Weiller, whom they had not seen since before the war. The Princess informed her mother that despite her 'personal dislike of the man' she 'had to make him des frais now' as he had recently offered Alexander a job as a hospital administrator. However, she 'would certainly have preferred' if the offer had come from somebody else. And the reason? Olga resented the fact that Weiller 'it seems, is completely white-washed from whatever dirty work he did during the war and received by everyone'. [83] This seems an unfair assessment given that Commandant Weiller was imprisoned by the Vichy government and was subsequently awarded the Medaille de la Résistance for his work with the Free French, following his escape from captivity.[84]

In late May, there was word from Elisabeth Toerring in Athens, that there had been a deterioration in their mother's health. Although Princess Nicholas had ongoing heart problems, she had recently given up smoking and was taking lots of rest. However, she had steadfastly ignored Queen Frederika's entreaties to consult a specialist.[85] It was therefore a somewhat apprehensive Olga who arrived in Athens, on 3 June, to find her mother in bed and looking drawn from constant angina attacks.[86] Ellen gradually improved and, on her eldest daughter's birthday, was able to rise from her bed to present her with the gift of an oil painting.[87] Paul, meanwhile, was staying at the French spa town of Vittel for a three-week "cure" interspersed with rounds of golf.

The Princess made a week-long visit to Mykonos, in early August, to stay with Diddie Serpieri and her family, accompanied by her good friend Mika Skouze and a police bodyguard. At that time, the island was totally unspoilt and devoid of cars and Olga was soon rising before dawn to drink coffee on the terrace, before venturing out with the local fishermen to catch huge eels or a stingray. After a siesta, she and the rest of the household would often enjoy an evening sail by *kaika* around the local islands. The Princess would return regularly to Mykonos over the next decade, usually in August, to be greeted by the same familiar beaming faces. As a souvenir of these visits, three models of the island's famous windmills, bearing the signatures of Olga, Diddie and Mika, sat atop the mantel piece of the Serpieri's sitting room.[88]

On the Princess' return to Athens in September, she was shocked to learn of the death of Field Marshal Smuts. She immediately telephoned Queen Frederika 'who had a special bond with him' to commiserate.[89] In subsequent years, Olga would often recall Smut's many kindnesses to her family.[90] As summer passed into autumn, Prince Philip arrived in Athens aboard his new command, the warship *HMS Magpie*. He paid a call on Princess Nicholas and her daughter, who thought him 'quite a tuts in his white uniform...'[91] All too soon, the Princess' visit was over and she flew to Geneva, on 27 October, for a reunion with Paul and Elizabeth. However, she was somewhat distracted by a telephone call from her sister Elisabeth, who was currently suffering from digestive troubles and nervous exhaustion. She wanted to consult her specialist in Lausanne, a Dr Rochat, so Olga decided she would remain behind in Switzerland to be with her. Although Countess Toerring was initially somewhat 'tired and drawn',[92] after a period of rest in a local clinic she appeared 'more relaxed' and planned to return to Bavaria to celebrate Christmas.[93] The Princess was briefly joined in Lausanne by Alexander, who informed his mother matter-of-factly that he was dating the Grand Duchess Charlotte of Luxembourg's eldest 'girl' Elisabeth.[94]

In mid-December, Paul telephoned his wife to say he had at last been able to lease an apartment on the Quai d'Orsay. However, when the Princess returned to Paris, she thought the accommodation 'filthy' and despaired that there was little with which to decorate the rooms, as the bulk of the family's possessions remained in storage in South Africa.[95] Nevertheless, she threw herself into decorating the place for Christmas and hired a new butler who had previously worked for the Duke and Duchess of Windsor. Unfortunately, he blotted his copy book by incorrectly referring to Wallis as 'Son Altesse Royale'.[96] There was news too of King Peter and Queen Alexandra: They were currently involved in a 'tragic' tug-of-war over the custody of their son Alexander.[97] Olga was therefore somewhat taken aback when they both arrived at the Quai d'Orsay on Christmas Eve, just as Paul was about to light the candles on the tree. The couple were now 'apparently on good terms' and remained for a full hour. However, it might have been better had they not visited, as Peter alarmed his Aunt by informing her that the Soviets were about to stage an uprising in Berlin and then intended to march right through Europe by the end of January![98] It is little wonder the Princess felt little compassion towards the 'shifty and nervous' ex-King. [99] Indeed, she later informed her mother that, 'his reputation here…is of the lowest. He places his confidence in crooks and mistrusts P[aul]!!'[100] Her opinion of Queen Alexandra was no better; she was deemed 'frankly mentally unbalanced and pitiful.'[101]

Paul was also unnerved by the European political situation (which Peter's comments can have done little to assuage) and decided to move Elizabeth to school in England as Switzerland 'if invaded would be like a mouse trap without a means of escape.'[102] Thanks to Marina's intervention, the school chosen, Tudor Hall, agreed to her niece starting after the Christmas break. Olga accompanied an apprehensive Elizabeth over to England on the boat train in mid-January and drove with her in Marina's car down to Banbury. The Princess later informed Princess Nicholas that Elizabeth 'sobbed when I kissed her goodbye saying it was like a prison with not a soul she knew.' For her part, Olga admitted that, 'It broke my heart to leave her like that' and, over the next few weeks, she would ring up the headmistress, Miss Inglis, on a daily basis to check on her daughter's progress.[103] The Princess and Marina were later joined at Coppins by their sister Elisabeth and were soon making the Countess 'cry with laughter with our nonsense and stupid jokes'.[104] Subsequently, Olga attended a matinée of a T.S Eliot play with Sir

Malcolm Sargent and she finally seemed to have found a measure of resolution as to the direction in which their friendship was moving. She informed her mother that, 'I discovered many new aspects in his nature I had not suspected and I think he will always be a true friend. I don't think that anything further would be satisfactory to me. He is too restless for one thing, so it's best to remain as we are. He has told me often that he loves me in a special way.' Nevertheless, she was certainly not averse to a new romantic opportunity and pondered, 'Shall I ever meet a really well-balanced normal man, au moral et au physique I wonder who could give me fully all I need? I certainly am not on the hunt for one, let come what must.'[105] Princess Elizabeth has observed that her parents had by now 'drifted apart as people do' and felt that a significant reason for this was that her father was 'terribly intelligent' and preferred more intellectual pursuits than his wife.[106] Olga, by contrast, increasingly 'only dreamed of Greece, her mother and sisters'.[107]

It is therefore unsurprising that Paul should find a special friend of his own and it was around this time that he formed a close friendship with Gabrielle Marie de Lambertye-Gerbéviller, the wife of Prince Armand of Arenberg. In 'Gaby' the Prince found a confidante who was 'attractive, interesting, smart and fun' as well as 'devoted to him.' The duo regularly visited art galleries and often travelled together on visits abroad. However, Princess Elizabeth is of the firm view that her mother had 'no idea' of this developing liaison[108] and regarded Gaby as a friend of the family.[109] She is often mentioned in the Princess' diaries as a guest at Rue Scheffer. However, Olga's niece Helen states that her Aunt talked of the relationship with her, but seemed content that Gaby was able to provide Paul with the sort of stimulating companionship he required,[110] which is understandable given that she herself spent so much of the year overseas.

Before leaving England on 13 February, the Princess accompanied Marina to tea with the King and Queen at Buckingham Palace. Bertie was 'full of jokes' remarking with a giggle, 'Good afternoon sisters, I can never tell you apart.'[111] There was further fun when the Duchess of Kent accompanied Olga back to Paris. During a mannequin parade at Dior, the Directrice placed the sisters on a sofa in the middle of the salon. The Princess later reported to her mother that they both 'nearly had fou rires [a fit of the giggles] looking at the expressions of some women in the crowd who obviously recognised Atinse [Marina] and tried to sweep a look at her while their eyes followed the dresses...'[112] Following Marina's departure, the Princess turned her attention to Alexander. She questioned him closely about 'his intentions' towards the Luxembourg Princess and indicated that 'it was high time he knew <u>what</u> he wanted, clearly, and let nothing stop him from getting it...' Alternatively, he could 'cut out marriage for a few years and fix on a job congenial to him…' The latter course seemed the more realistic option as Quiss admitted 'he was not in love enough to marry…'[113]

In early March, Olga once again tackled the tricky question of her annual summer visit to Athens: She admitted to her mother that, unlike the previous year, she could not 'abandon' Elizabeth and Paul 'again during the summer' and proposed a compromise of visiting Greece from May till early July. The Princess once again primed Ellen to send a letter mentioning this proposal as if it was her own idea.[114] This Olga read out to Paul and she was soon able to report to Athens that 'the question of my coming to you in May went off perfectly.'[115]

On 19 March, as the Princess prepared to travel to London, where Elizabeth was due to have surgery for the removal of her adenoids and tonsils, she experienced an attack of 'funny heart fluttering with rapid beats.'[116] Although Olga did not realise it, these heart palpitations would now become a regular occurrence throughout the rest of her life. Fortunately, Elizabeth's operation was a success, although on the day the surgery was performed, her anxious mother visited the nursing home on no less than three occasions. Nevertheless, the Princess still found time to have lunch alone with Sir Malcolm Sargent and, on 2 April, joined him, Marina and John Profumo to attend a stage adaptation of the melodrama "The Seventh Veil". This was again followed by supper and dancing into the small hours.[117] It was no wonder that her eyes 'ached' next day as she drove up to London to collect her daughter from the nursing home. [118]

Easter 1951 was spent with the de Croisset family at Grasse. As Marina and her eldest children were staying nearby at Malbosc with Eugenie and Raymond, Paul was able to enjoy a long-anticipated reunion with Edward and Alexandra, whom he had last seen in 1939![119] Olga, Paul and their daughter then travelled on to Florence for a stay with her cousin Helen at the Villa Sparta. They also took the opportunity to pay a visit to Aunt Moina.[120] Thereafter, Olga and Elizabeth accompanied Marina to events in London to celebrate the opening of the Festival of Britain and, for the first time since before the war, the Princess donned a tiara, to attend the Inaugural Concert with other members of the British royal family at the Festival Hall on 3 May.[121]

After a brief stopover in Paris to pack, Olga arrived in Athens on 13 May and was immediately thrown into a busy round of engagements which included a distinctly icy encounter, at a diplomatic reception, with the Communist Yugoslav Chef de Mission. The Princess informed Marina 'There was nothing for it but to swallow my feelings and not make an open demonstration…but my heart beat and I felt a bit sick. Fr[ederika] saw my effort and thanked me v[ery] sweetly after!'[122] However, this particular visit was overshadowed by a 'spirit of unrest.'[123]

Field Marshal Papagos resigned as Commander-in-Chief of the armed forces on 30 May, allegedly on health grounds. Despite Queen Frederika's assurances to Olga that Papagos had given 'no other explanation' for his action, the Princess firmly believed that her old war hero friend had simply allowed this to be said rather 'than admit P[alo] no longer trusts him...'[124] Papagos admitted as much when Princess Nicholas and Olga visited him at his home in Ekali on 2 June.[125] Thereafter, while the Princess made a brief trip to Corfu, her mother made a fruitless visit to Tatoi to try and advance Papagos' cause with the King and Queen. Olga concluded that it was 'tragic to see how misguided they are'[126] in believing that Papagos had been 'disloyal'[127] to the Crown particularly when 'the whole town'[128] of Athens was on the Field Marshal's side. However, the Princess' main concern was the toll this affair was taking on Princess Nicholas who was 'v[ery] tired from all this strain.'[129] Using her well-tuned political antennae, Olga opined to Marina that 'in the end Pap[agos] will be the only solution as the people still want him...' and wisely observed that 'It would add so much to his [King Paul's] prestige if he were to call Pap[agos] back rather than have him imposed on him.'[130]

Meanwhile, from Paris came the news that Paul had surrendered the lease on the Quai d'Orsay flat and that Alexander remained unemployed. Despite these concerns, Olga was in the mood for letting her hair down and came home 'with the dawn' from a delightful party at the Serpieri's,[131] while on another occasion she danced the night away till 3am at the Fantasia nightclub with a group of friends. There was also amusement of a different kind when the Princess and her mother became trapped in the lift in the Royal Palace and a footman had literally to lift them out.

In late July, Paul cabled to say that he taken out a short lease on the late Lady Mendl's Villa Trianon at Versailles. The Princess flew to Paris on 1 August and although she thought her new residence somewhat 'gloomy'[132], she was cheered by the news that Alexander had found a new post as a pilot with British European Airways, based in England. Shortly thereafter, the Duchess of Kent and her family arrived along with a 'mountain of valises' for a week's stay.[133] In mid-August, everyone moved on to Cap Ferrat to stay with the Duke of Arenberg at his 'sumptuous, palatial' villa.[134] The Riviera was awash with exiled royalty including the Count of Barcelona and King Farouk of Egypt, whom Olga espied gambling in the casino at Monte Carlo. Although she enjoyed the break, the sight of a hotel swimming pool full of 'awful naked people' somewhat dampened her pleasure.[135] Olga, Paul and Elizabeth then left Cap Ferrat for a stay with Aunt Marie Bonaparte and Uncle George at their St Tropez holiday home, Le Lys de Mer. However, the Princess was soon preoccupied by the Greek political situation and dismayed to learn that Field Marshal Papagos and his newly-formed Greek Rally party were unable to form a government, despite winning nearly 37% of the vote in the September elections. She criticised King Paul and Frederika, to Marina, for being 'prepared to trust those two traitors [Sofoklis Venizelos (son of Eleftherios) and Sofoklis' successor as Prime Minister, Nikolaos Plastiras] and suspect the one man [Papagos] who is loyal to them. It really makes me sick...'[136]

In mid-September, Olga accompanied Elizabeth back to England in advance of the start of a new school term. Paul had suggested that, as Marina was in Scotland, his wife and daughter might stay with Henry Channon. The Princess was firmly against this, citing her dislike of 'that pansy milieu.'[137] Instead, she arranged to stay at the Beddington-Behren's home outside Dorking. On Marina's return from Balmoral, Olga moved to Coppins where everyone was concerned about the health of King George VI who was to undergo surgery for the removal of his left lung on 23 September. The sisters ventured to Iver Church on the morning of the operation to pray for his safe recovery. Fortunately, the procedure seemed to go as well as could be expected and the Princesses took tea, the following week, with the Queen who was 'cheered' by their visit.[138]

On Olga's return to Paris, she and Paul found a townhouse to rent at 31 Rue Scheffer. The residence, situated almost directly opposite Lilia Ralli's home, was centrally-located and set over four floors, linked by a central stairwell. Unusually, it also came with a garage. On 20 November, Bertie and Elizabeth's daughter Margaret, arrived in Paris, accompanied by Marina, to attend a ball in aid of the Hertford British Hospital. Olga went out to Le Bourget to greet them and found that she was deliberately 'ignored' in the VIP lounge by the '[British] Embassy crowd'.[139] Furthermore, the Princess-with whom the Duchess of Kent was staying-was pointedly not included in the guest list for an official lunch in Princess Margaret's honour at the Elysée Palace. Nevertheless, a few days later, Olga and Paul were given an opportunity to entertain the young Princess when they hosted a private dinner in her honour at Maxim's.

The pre-Christmas period was busy socially: The Prince and Princess dined with Greta Garbo and Paul Louis Weiller at L'Escargot and attended a candlelight dinner at the Palais Lambert hosted by the American socialite Mona Williams. However, the occasion which Olga found the most poignant was organised by King Peter at the Plaza Hotel, on 13 December, to commemorate the Yugoslav Royal Family's Slava and during which an Orthodox priest said prayers 'for the suffering country.'[140] Following a family lunch with Eugenie and Raymond on Christmas Day at St Cloud, Olga boarded the Orient Express at the Gare de l'Est for a visit with her cousin Theodora and her husband Berthold at Schloss Salem. The Toerrings were fellow guests and the Princess thought her sister Elisabeth, who had undergone surgery for the removal of a tumour in Athens in the autumn, was 'so transformed and en beauté.'[141]

Although Olga missed the 1952 New Year celebrations in Paris, she, Paul and Elizabeth travelled by car to Brussels, in early January, for a stay with ex-King Leopold and his wife, the Princess de Réthy, at the Château de Laeken; Nicholas joined them from England. The Princess was sympathetic towards Leopold who 'could not be more charming and courteous' and had 'suffered so much.'[142] [20] Olga subsequently accompanied Elizabeth back to school in England where she was perturbed to find that Alexander had another 'new flame', a film actress and 'is sure he wants to marry this time'.[143] However, the Princess kept her cool and agreed to meet the couple at the Dorchester for lunch. Predictably, the girl was dismissed as 'rather boring bourgeois' and Olga undoubtedly hoped the romance would fizzle out.[144] Nevertheless, this mini crisis did not deter her from attending one of Sir Malcolm Sargent's concerts at the Royal Albert Hall and later dining with him and a group of friends.[145]

The Princess returned to Paris, on 24 January, to hold consultations with an interior designer in anticipation of the move to 31 Rue Scheffer. She then rushed back to London to be with Elizabeth, who was due to undergo surgery on an elbow at the London Clinic. On this occasion, Olga had accepted Henry Channon's kind offer of accommodation at 5 Belgrave Square and it was there, on 6 February, that Philip Hay, Marina's Private Secretary, informed her that King George VI had died peacefully in his sleep at Sandringham. The Princess was so shocked that when she imparted the tragic news to Chips, she lost her customary self-control and burst into tears.[146] Olga's thoughts were immediately with Bertie's widow, mother and elder daughter Elizabeth-the new Queen-who was currently en route from Kenya, where she had been undertaking a royal tour. However, this tragic event would have an unexpected consequence, for on 10 February, Philip Hay telephoned the Princess to inform her that both the new Queen and her widowed mother had extended an invitation to Paul to attend the late King's funeral at Windsor.[147] Olga found herself consumed with 'such emotion' as she greeted her husband at Heathrow Airport on 13 February, his first visit to England since 1939.[148] He was certainly made to feel welcome and, in the evening, joined Olga and Marina to dine with the new Queen and

---

[20] King Leopold had been placed under house arrest at Laeken in May 1940 following Belgium's occupation by Germany. He was later deported to Germany and then to Austria where he lived in fear of his life. His return to Belgium in 1950 provoked widespread protests and he abdicated in favour of his son, Baudouin, in July 1951.

Prince Philip at Clarence House. The following afternoon, the Prince and Princess drove over to Westminster Hall to view the late King's Lying-in-State and then dined at Henry Channon's home with King Peter and Queen Alexandra.

On 15 February, Olga and Paul drove the short distance from Coppins to Windsor to attend the royal funeral in St George's Chapel, where they were seated in the Quire. Most of the Yugoslav royal family-including Queen Marie-were in attendance, although the ever-observant Henry Channon noted that not one of them exchanged any form of greeting with the other. The presence nearby of Tito's official representative, General Peko Dapcević, can hardly have eased any tensions. Nevertheless, the Princess thought the funeral was 'magnificently done' and found it 'touching to see Eddie [her nephew, the Duke of Kent] in the cortège, so like his father...'[149] As Prince Paul was 'anxious' to pay his own homage to the late Prince George, he was permitted to make a private visit, on 26 February, to the Royal Vault to place some flowers by the late Duke's coffin.[150] He could now leave England safe in the knowledge that his place at the Court of St James was safely restored.

In mid-May, the Prince and Princess spent a few days in Florence, as the guests of Queen Mother Helen. They made several visits to Aunt Moina at Pratolino during which the Prince held business talks with his Aunt's advisors.[151] Thereafter, Olga departed for Greece for a two-month visit. Despite soaring temperatures, she quickly re-embraced her busy social life and made several sightseeing trips with friends to Patras, Olympia, Kastoria, Metéora and Mykonos. At Piraeus, she dined with Lord Mountbatten and his wife Edwina aboard his flagship *HMS Glasgow* and, in Athens, she paid a visit to the British Embassy where the recently-appointed Ambassador Charles Peake, who had previously served in Belgrade, informed her that Paul's Sèvres dinner service was still on display in the dining room at Beli Dvor. Sadly, Olga found her departure from Athens more trying than usual, as 'M[ummsie] is so broken at my going...'[152]

Olga, Paul and Elizabeth visited the Toerrings at their country estate at Jettenbach, in late August. It was during this visit that fifteen-year-old Helen Toerring began to appreciate her Aunt's qualities: She found her to be a 'complex' character who was invariably 'warm-hearted to anything [concerned with] family' as well as 'very loving and very nice with younger children'. She also admired the Princess' 'wonderful sense of humour' and recalls-almost with wonderment-how she 'could imitate everything-languages and noises and animals.' However, what Helen particularly remembers was the way her Aunt 'would concentrate on a child' and 'listen to you'.[153]

Thereafter, the Princess travelled to England to bid adieu to Marina and her nephew Edward as they set off from Heathrow on 27 September on an extensive, five-week official tour of the Far East. Olga stayed at the Dorchester, from where she entertained Marina's two younger children during their free time out of boarding school. The Princess was then invited by Queen Mary to join her on an afternoon sightseeing trip through London, in her impressive green Daimler, and listened politely as the doughty Dowager gave a running commentary on 'what she thought I didn't know'.[154] In the meantime, Nicholas was kept busy working at a London bank. Like Alexander, he had taken a keen interest in flying and had recently gained a commission in the Royal Air Force Volunteer Reserve. He would later go on to work for the Niarchos shipping company.

Meanwhile, in Paris, with his city centre residence suitably established at Rue Scheffer, Prince Paul was now able to embrace the Parisian life he adored. Chips Channon, on a visit, described his friend as 'the "Coq du village" and if no longer Regent of Yugoslavia, he is certainly Le Roi de Paris...'[155] His scintillating conversation was invariably peppered with a wonderful collection of historical anecdotes and also reflected the Prince's extensive knowledge of the arts. Such attributes, made him both a popular guest and a wonderful host. By contrast, Olga wrote to Marina that making her new home 'cosy' was a priority, for she intended to spend lots of time there 'and above all avoid all cocktail parties.'[156] The Princess' apparent anti-social stance in Paris-a complete contrast to her busy schedules in Athens and London-was partly because she never warmed to the French upper-class, nor did she much care for the culture or the food in France.[157] Furthermore, she had no real French friends and could be very shy with those she did not know. In these circumstances, Olga's niece Helen recalls, she would 'put on this air-she could be very grand.'[158] Therefore, the Princess' "refuge" increasingly became her first-floor sitting room, which she arranged for both comfort and convenience: A simple baize-covered card table was the perfect setting for a game of patience, while a comfy armchair opposite provided an ideal place to sit and read or solve crossword puzzles. However, there were still occasional outings; the first of these came in the form of a surprise invitation from the French President, Vincent Auriol. He asked the Prince and Princess to join him at a Gala Performance of Molière's "Tartuffe" at the Comédie Française. Olga needed little encouragement to slip into a new Dior evening dress for the occasion and noted in her diary, 'How times have changed!'[159]

In mid-November, the Princess was delighted to learn of Field Marshal Papagos' appointment as Greece's Prime Minister, with his Greek Rally party receiving 49% of the vote in recent elections. However, she was concerned about Queen Frederika's reaction and commented to Marina, 'I do pray that she will bring herself to cooperate in the general desire for a change in the country-I can't say more, you know what I mean...'[160] Olga's reticence was credible, for King Paul-who was heavily influenced by his wife-had earlier asked the Field Marshal not to stand as a candidate.[161]

As Christmas approached, the Princess helped her husband to entertain the American historian and writer, Jacob Hoptner, who had come to interview Paul about the 'truth' of the 1941 coup for his forthcoming PhD thesis.[162] Thereafter, she made a quick visit to England to celebrate Marina's birthday and to accompany Elizabeth (who had recently obtained her School Leaving Certificate) back to Paris. Christmas Day itself was celebrated at Paul Louis Weiller's Versailles home, where fellow guests included the British actor Sir Laurence Olivier and his wife Vivien Leigh.

As 1953 dawned, Olga and Paul had lunch with Winston Churchill's son Randolph at the Ritz. The latter asked the Prince if he would mind looking through Vladimir Dedijer's new authorised biography of Tito ("Tito Speaks") and make any 'corrections' he deemed necessary for inclusion in an upcoming review of the book by Randolph. Probably out of good manners, Paul agreed and Olga was moved to write, 'How strange are the turns of fortune.'[163] However, the Prince found Randolph's work to be such a 'mass of incorrect statements'[164] that he was delayed in joining his family for another new year stay with the Belgian royal family at Laeken.

On the family's return to Paris, Elizabeth was enrolled as a boarder at the Assumption Convent to study French. In February, the Princess enjoyed playing hostess to Marina and Elisabeth. The sisters played games of Canasta or enjoyed 'hilarious' dinners at the Relais and Châtaigner restaurants.[165] However, all were shocked to learn, on 25 February, of the untimely death of Princess Françoise of Orléans. Olga's thoughts were immediately with 'Fattie's' 14-year-old son Michael '[and] what his future will be.'[166] She and Paul subsequently attended the funeral at the Chapelle Royale de Dreux. Indeed, it seemed to be a time of distressing news, for when the Princess made an early Spring visit to England, she was informed that Queen Mary's heart was growing weak. Olga later visited her at Marlborough House and found her lying on a sofa and (mistakenly) convinced that she was on the road to recovery.[167] Another disturbing element to this visit was Tito's presence in London on a State Visit. The Princess was aghast to learn that he was currently staying at Alexander's birthplace, White Lodge, 'of all houses!'[168] Queen Mary died on 24 March and the Prince and Princess attended the funeral at Windsor on 31 March. In the evening, as if to further emphasise their return to the royal fold, they were among a privileged party of twenty-eight who dined at the Castle.[169] [21]

On 7 April, the family celebrated Elizabeth's 17th birthday with a lunch at the Jockey Club; Olga was moved to write, 'She is practically grown up now, it seems unbelievable.'[170] Paul turned 60 on 27 April, but his wife noted, with pleasure, that 'he certainly looks younger'.[171] Thereafter, the Princess helped Elizabeth to pack, prior to her departure to London for Queen Elizabeth II's Coronation on 2 June. As she and Paul were not attending, Olga listened-in regularly to radio broadcasts from London; these provided her with interesting details about the many distinguished guests. On Coronation Day itself, the couple watched the event on television at a friend's flat and though it 'v[ery] moving and fine.'[172]

The Princess celebrated her 50th birthday, on 11 June, and noted with disbelief, 'Doesn't seem possible and people kindly say I don't look it...' Paul was most generous, giving her gifts of a gold and diamond watch and two Dior dresses. She was also 'touched' to receive a telegram from Field Marshal Papagos.[173] Within days, Olga was back in Athens and enjoying lunch with Eleanor Roosevelt at Tatoi. Then, in late July, she entered the Red Cross Hospital in Athens to undergo surgery on her varicose veins. The Princess' convalescence was protracted and painful and, gallingly, just as she was beginning to recover, she fell and twisted her right ankle and was housebound for several weeks. However, once Olga had regained her mobility, she threw herself into a YWCA campaign to distribute clothes around Athens, to those who had been displaced as a result of recent earthquakes in the Ionian Islands. During her daily rounds, she was touched by the victims' gratitude and much-affected by accounts of the horrors they had experienced.[174]

On her return to Paris, the Princess was distressed to learn that King Peter's self-serving memoirs were about to be serialised in Britain's *Sunday Express* newspaper.[175] To exacerbate matters, in mid-October, Paul and Frederika arrived in Paris en route to the United States. The Queen was due to have dress fittings at Jean Dessès, at which Olga expected to be present. However, when the Princess telephoned Frederika at her hotel, 'she said their day was all planned and put me off...!'[176] Next day, during a family gathering at St Cloud, Olga discovered why the Queen had been so "off" the previous day: Frederika had discovered that Princess Nicholas planned to make an official visit to Salonika on 26 October, when the King and Queen would still be overseas. Frederika

---

[21] They fared better than Queen Mary's eldest son, the Duke of Windsor, who was not invited.

indicated that Ellen's actions 'looked wrong' and wanted the visit postponed. Indeed, she implied that Field Marshal Papagos was somehow manoeuvring the situation-and presumably Princess Nicholas-to his advantage, and 'wishing to shine in their absence'. A furious Olga later noted tersely in her diary 'A lot of trash.'[177] The Princess phoned the Greek royals' hotel next day in an attempt to speak to King Paul but his wife answered and gave Olga a 'long sermon on how hurt they feel about this lack of solidarity on M[ummsie's] part etc...' The Princess sought to defuse the situation by phoning her mother in Athens 'to beg her to put off going.'[178] Ellen duly reconsidered her position and subsequently wired the King and Queen to inform them that she would postpone the visit. Frederika then telephoned Olga to read her mother's telegram aloud to her. It is no wonder that the Princess 'felt sick and shattered all day'[179] and suffered from a splitting headache throughout the next. Nevertheless, she and Paul magnanimously welcomed Frederika and King Paul to their Rue Scheffer home for lunch on the day of their departure for the States. The Queen was apparently 'sick from nerves' and 'dreaded the journey into the unknown.'[180] This nervousness may, in part, have explained her unpleasant behaviour.

For Olga, matters had been further complicated by the fact that 'an army of pressmen'[181] were currently laying siege to Rue Scheffer, in order to observe the comings and goings of Marina and her daughter. They were currently in Paris as Alexandra was about to commence a French course at Mademoiselle Anita's finishing school. Eventually, Philip Hay had to be brought over from London to bring some order to the situation. These were hardly the ideal circumstances for the celebration of the Prince and Princess' 30th wedding anniversary on 22 October, but a family lunch was duly held at the Méditerranée restaurant, and Paul again spoiled Olga with the gift of a gold cigarette box, while she gave her husband a pair of sapphire cufflinks. Despite the bumpy start, the Princess enjoyed acting *in loco parentis* throughout her Kent niece's Parisian sojourn. She would later inform Marina that, 'I have grown to love her [Alexandra] as though she were my own child. In fact, I often catch myself talking about my daughters!'[182]

At Christmas, the Princess and her family joined the Kents at Coppins. Thereafter, the Prince and Princess accompanied Marina up to Sandringham as guests of the Queen Mother (the Queen and Prince Philip were currently on a Coronation tour of New Zealand). Olga, of course, enjoyed close family ties with Sandringham and during a tour of the rooms, she was intrigued to find the names of both of her parents etched into a window pane to commemorate a visit in 1905. On New Year's Eve, the party returned to Coppins, which was filled to capacity: Fourteen sat down to a sumptuous dinner, followed by 'champagne and hugs' as everyone heralded in the New Year of 1954.[183] Paul then journeyed north for a stay with Walter Buccleuch at Bowhill, while Olga joined Marina at a party at the Iver Old Folks Club, where the members' dubious attempts at amateur dramatics almost resulted in the royal guests dissolving into a fit of hysterics.[184]

However, the Princesses' mirth was to be short-lived for, on 17 January, the journalist John Gordon led a vitriolic attack in the *Sunday Express* against the 'quisling' Prince Paul and accused him of 'enjoying all the privileges that the protective Royal wrapping can give him.' Unfortunately, Marina was caught up in the cross-fire, having recently entertained her brother-in-law at Coppins. Gordon opined, 'I think she would be wise to persuade Paul to work out his penance else-where than in Britain.'[185] Olga must have been mortified, not only for her sister, but for Paul too. However, she realised that life had to go on and on her return to Paris, there was at least the welcome consolation of an evening with her husband at the Théâtre National de l'Opéra as guests of President René Coty.

Chapter 21 Tragedy upon Tragedy

The Princess returned to England to join both of her sisters at Coppins, in late February. The trio toured the Ideal Home Exhibition at Olympia, took tea at Royal Lodge with the Queen Mother and enjoyed a 'killing'[1] review at the Lyric Theatre. However, there was also a serious purpose to the visit, as the Princess had arranged an appointment with her gynaecologist, Mr Gilliat, who recommended that she should have surgery to tackle an ongoing 'woman's problem'.[2] The operation (a hysterectomy) was performed at the London Clinic on 14 March and left Olga in 'great pain'.[3] Indeed, she was required to remain in the Clinic until 3 April, as she required regular blood transfusions and Vitamin injections.

On the evening of 11 April, as she continued her recuperation at Coppins, the Princess enjoyed an early dinner and watched the popular television programme "What's My Line?" She later took a telephone call from her son Nicholas who indicated he would come to dinner the following Tuesday.[4] However, in the early hours of the next day, Nicholas was killed when his sports car skidded and overturned into a ditch at Ditton Corner, near Datchet. He drowned in only a few inches of water, as rescuers struggled in vain to lift the vehicle.[5] News of the crash was relayed by Philip Hay over the telephone, in the middle of the night, to Zoia and Alik Poklewski's son Vincent at the family's cottage at Coppins. He quickly dressed and rushed over to the main house, where he managed to rouse Marina who was 'deeply shocked' at the dreadful news, but soon composed herself.[6] At 8am, Marina entered Olga's bedroom to tell her 'that my precious Veezie was killed early this morning at 2am...' Her one solace was that 'He can't have felt any pain.' The Princess was gently informed that her son's body was currently resting at the Chapel at Slough Hospital and that Marina had already visited to pay her respects. The Duchess of Kent then had the unenviable task of breaking the news by telephone to Paul and Elizabeth in Paris. They both flew over to London in the afternoon. Olga somehow found the strength to phone Princess Nicholas to break the news in person. Meanwhile, 'masses'[7] of telegrams started to arrive. For the Princess, life would never be the same again and that evening she noted in her diary 'Oh! The morrow to face.'[8] Nevertheless, she drew particular strength from the arrival of Alexander who held his mother 'so gently in his arms' after flying over from the West Indies, where he was currently based.[9]

Nicholas' funeral was held at the Serbian Orthodox Church in London on 17 April. King Peter attended, and Olga drew great comfort from the singing of the choir and the many floral tributes. However, immediately thereafter, she fell into 'in a trance of pain'[10] but managed to select a hymn and a psalm for Nicholas' committal service at Iver church, on 20 April. Only close family and a few intimate friends attended, including his childhood playmates Tommy and Andy. It speaks volumes about Olga's character that in the midst of such suffering, she made time to return to the London Clinic to hand over gifts to the nurses who had cared for her during her recent surgery.[11]

The Princess and Marina flew from Northolt to Munich, on 25 April, for a stay with the Toerrings. They were joined there later by Paul. Olga was still struggling to sleep, despite taking a pill[12] and noted sadly that the arrival of 'touching' condolence letters simply 'made my heart bleed again'.[13] Regrettably, ongoing problems with a wisdom tooth necessitated her return to London for its removal at a nursing home in Queen's Gate. She returned to Paris on 20 May. However, when Lilia Ralli called on her next day 'full of society news', the Princess found she could hardly bear to listen.[14] Even so, she found the strength to attend a packed memorial service for Nicholas, in early June, at Paris' Serbian Orthodox Church. Thereafter, Olga focused on replying to the many letters of sympathy, including one from her spiritual mentor and guide Nicol Campbell. The latter's constant prayers and School of Truth publications helped to sustain her throughout this difficult period. However, the Princess reserved her greatest praise for Marina ('My precious little F'al') who had been 'My greatest standby and support and comfort beyond anything I can ever express', during 'those dark hours...'[15] In a particularly selfless gesture, Marina had recently given her grieving sister a diamond cross which had been her last gift from Prince George prior to his untimely death.

However, the fallout from this tragic event would be extensive and enduring, as close family and friends observed: Vincent Poklewski thought that the Prince and Princess were 'broken, broken' by Nicholas' death, but also observed that Olga kept her misery 'carefully en famille'.[16] The Duke of Kent found his Aunt and Uncle to be 'absolutely shattered' particularly as 'He [Nicholas] was, I think, very distinctly the favourite.'[17] The Princess would forever remember her son with tremendous affection, observing 'He gave us joy, pride and satisfaction during all his short life.'[18] She reflected too that 'A sorrow such as that abides with one for ever, but to believe in the After Life with proofs of its richness and continuity changes the pain into Faith in a reunion.'[19]

This was also a most difficult time for both Alexander and Elizabeth: The former felt that Nicholas' memory was 'idolised' and he felt 'sort of pushed away.'[20] It did not help that Alexander was not an intellectual and his airline pilot's career was not viewed with any particular enthusiasm by either of his parents. Meanwhile, Elizabeth observed that her mother now went into a 'cocoon' and became increasingly focused on her mother and sisters.[21] Given this apparent lack of maternal attention, it is perhaps understandable that she would go on to become 'a very difficult teenager' whom her mother found 'hard to handle.'[22]

Despite the tragedy, the Princess decided to make her usual summer trip to Athens. Elizabeth only accompanied her mother as far as Bavaria, as she was joining Alexander and her Toerring cousins aboard a "match making" cruise for the young royalty of Europe, from Naples to Greece, organised by Queen Frederika. At Winhöring, Countess Toerring showed Olga through the little church which had recently been rebuilt in the grounds and the duo later visited the shrine to the Miraculous Madonna at Altötting, where Elisabeth had found much solace during the war years. The Princess left Bavaria for Athens, on 24 July, and she was met at the airport by an emotional Princess Nicholas and a group of twenty concerned friends. Despite the welcome, Olga could not help but notice that her mother was failing: Her circulation was poor; she was prone to dizziness and found climbing the stairs particularly tiring. The still grieving Princess decided not to accompany Princess Nicholas to a banquet in honour of Emperor Haile Selassie of Ethiopia at the Royal Palace, although she subsequently met him at a private lunch. Thereafter, she departed Athens for her customary summer visit to Mykonos.

Up until now, the Princess had eschewed Frederika's royal cruise, but when the group's ship, the *Agamemnon*, called at Athens on 30 August, she decided to join the party on board for the final two days. Although, 'dazed with [the] noise',[23] Olga was doubtless pleased to observe that Alexander was on very friendly terms with Princess Maria Pia, the eldest daughter of Paul's friend, King Umberto of Italy and his wife Queen Marie-José. Indeed, as she prepared to disembark, the Princess noted in her diary, 'God granting a nice event may take place this month for Quiss at last.'[24] Yet, Olga was leaving nothing to chance and, aided by Alexander, whisked the Italian royals off on excursions to Thebes, Eleusis and the beach at Kavouri. By 7 September, she was able to inform Marina that Alexander 'has already spoken to Beppo [King Umberto]' about a possible engagement to 'Pia' although Umberto was 'keen for them not to rush into it before thoroughly knowing each other...' However, the enthusiastic Princess had no such qualms and decided to telephone Paul in Geneva, confiding to Marina, '[I] pray to God he will be pleased that at last the boy has fixed his choice on a girl of his class after all the previous unsuitable ones.'[25] Unsurprisingly, the Prince was happy to give Alexander and Pia his blessing.

Given that her son would soon have a wife to support, Olga now focused on finding him some well-paid employment. A few days later, she accompanied Alexander and Pia on a short visit to Stavros Niarchos' yacht *Creole*, which was anchored near Athens. The shipping magnate had previously employed Nicholas and it was now Alexander's turn to have a 'discussion' with the tycoon.[26] This must have been successful for the Prince was subsequently offered a position in the company's Paris office.[27] On 22 September, Olga left Athens with Elizabeth bound for Switzerland and the official announcement of the couple's engagement on 24 September (Maria Pia's 20th birthday) at Queen Marie-José's residence at Merlinge. Alexander gave his bride-to-be a cabochon emerald engagement ring which Paul had sourced in Florence. Thereafter, the exhausted Princess returned to Paris where she hosted a visit from her sister Elisabeth and niece Helen, who was about to start a residential French language course in the city. Somehow, she also found time to travel to London to spend some time with Alexander, who later drove his mother down to Iver for an emotional visit to Nicholas' grave.

In early November, Olga visited Christian Dior with Paul to decide on an outfit for the wedding which was to take place at Cascais in February. It had already been agreed that she and Marie-José would wear long dresses as this would be 'more dignified', although the Princess was decidedly sceptical when she learned that the Italian Queen had decided to wear an ensemble of blue Brussels lace.[28] Interestingly, although Olga was on good terms with Pia's mother, she came to regard her as 'not "my cup of tea" but can be nice-a complete outsider otherwise.'[29] Perhaps as a result of Nicholas' death, the Princess again sought comfort from spiritualism and made a pre-Christmas visit to a psychic who claimed to have 'second sight' and told her 'some amazing things.'[30] Alarmingly, a week later, Olga experienced 'a blackout' followed by an attack of 'awful quick palpitations.'[31] A doctor reassured her that it was probably due to a 'thyroid disturbance' and prescribed weekly hormone injections.[32] The Princess drew particular comfort from Elizabeth, throughout this trying time, finding her to be 'so like my Veeze [Nicholas] in many ways.'[33]

The family's first Christmas without Nicholas was understandably a muted affair: Lilia Ralli was the sole guest at 31 Rue Scheffer. Nevertheless, Olga and Paul both felt they had to remain 'brave' for their daughter's sake[34] and the trio made a trip to the cinema to view the film "White Christmas" starring Olga's friend Danny Kaye. Unfortunately, the year ended with further sad news: Count Toerring wrote to say that Elisabeth was suffering from an attack of arthritis and rheumatism and had been admitted to a clinic for 'a complete overhaul'.[35] However, on 11 January 1955, the Princess received the shocking news that her sister had died. As Countess Toerring's daughter Helen was currently studying in Paris, it fell to her Aunt to quietly break the news of her mother's death. Afterwards, Olga put on a 'brave face' as she accompanied her niece on the night train to Munich.[36] On 14 January, following a private funeral service, Princess Elisabeth was laid to rest beside the little church at Winhöring. Back in Paris, Olga continued to watch over her niece and informed Marina that 'I pray so much all the time for her [Elisabeth's] guidance and try to let her know that in a small way I watch over this child she loved and give her all the love and understanding she needs.'[37] Certainly, it would be no exaggeration to say that the Princess would come to regard Helen as almost a second daughter.

Meanwhile, with her son's marriage festivities looming, Olga had little option but to temporarily put her grief to one side. Alexander and Maria Pia's wedding was a true society occasion, with over one hundred royal guests (though interestingly not King Peter) from nine dynasties in attendance. The royal party were joined by several thousand loyal Italians who made the long journey to Cascais to see their exiled King's eldest child marry. At the reception at the Palacio Hotel afterwards, guests feasted on turkey, lobster, chicken and foie gras. Fortunately for Alexander, his mother thoroughly approved of her new daughter-in-law.

Immediately after the wedding, the Princess flew to Athens to spend a few weeks with her grieving mother. She worked through her own sorrow by keeping busy with the household chores, including cleaning out the cat's 'winter sanctum' where 'the filth, dust and stench were indescribable.'[38] In mid-March, Olga flew in King Paul's private Dakota airplane from Athens to Florence for a stay with Queen Mother Helen. Although she had forewarned Aunt Moina of her impending visit, a message was sent down from Pratolino to the Villa Sparta to say 'with much regret that she is ill in bed and can't see me!'[39]

Following a late Spring visit to Coppins, the Princess and her husband enjoyed something of a reconciliation with Queen Marie, who visited Rue Scheffer on several occasions. Mignon subsequently wrote from the National Hotel in Lucerne to thank her hosts 'for the wonderful meals' and opined that 'It was good being able to talk as in the old days; bless you both for being patient with me.'[40] Paul then had to rush off to Pratolino to visit his ailing Aunt Moina, who died on 21 July. Olga later joined him and was moved to find that the staff of the Villa Demidoff at Pratolino had gathered at the front door to formally greet her as the new Châtelaine. Almost immediately, she began to tackle 'millions of jobs', starting with the discarding of 'masses' of artificial flowers.[41] Outside in the extensive grounds, she stopped to admire the giant statue of Il

Colosso dell 'Appennino, before supervising the planting out and reorganisation of the somewhat neglected garden. The Prince and Princess would remain at Pratolino until early October and, despite the mammoth task still facing them, they readily admitted to having become fond of this 'heavenly place.'[42]

As 1956, dawned Olga and Elizabeth joined Marina and Alexandra on a visit to Winhöring to commemorate the anniversary of Countess Toerring's death. The Princess then flew on to Athens where she found her mother 'so lonely' and 'touchingly glad to see me.'[43] Despite the death of Field Marshal Papagos the previous October, Olga still took a keen interest in Greek politics. As she awaited the results of February's General Election, she and Princess Nicholas joined the King and Queen at Tatoi, to listen to regular election updates telephoned up from the Interior Ministry. Frederika, Olga noted, was 'off her head with nervous anticipation.'[44] Konstantinos Karamanlis' right-wing National Radical Union was eventually declared the winner. After attending the wedding of Diddie Serpieri's daughter, Savina, at Pyrgos at the end of March, the Princess travelled on to Bavaria for her niece Helen's wedding to Archduke Ferdinand 'Ferdl' Habsburg, at Seefeld on 10 April. The newlyweds would subsequently make their home in Paris.

The Prince and Princess arrived in Italy, in late April, to enjoy another prolonged stay at Pratolino. Although the house was swarming with workmen and devoid of hot water, Olga focused on rearranging Moina's former apartments for her own personal use. As it was the Orthodox Easter, Marina flew out to join her sister and, on one occasion, Olga sprained her ankle 'playing the fool' as they walked in the garden.[45] Elizabeth too was settling in and taking regular Italian lessons with a Signora Morozzi in Florence.

At the end of May, Olga's long-time Athens friend, Mika Skouze, died. This was a major blow for the Princess who noted that such a death 'create gaps which cannot be filled and leave us suddenly lonely in the midst of crowds.'[46] Fortunately, Frederika phoned to say that Princess Nicholas-who had relied heavily on Mika for help and companionship in her widowhood-was bearing up; she also kindly arranged to send King Paul's plane to Florence to transport Olga to Athens to be with her mother.[47] However, when the Princess arrived at Psychiko, on 5 June, she found Princess Nicholas so 'broken and desolate' at the loss of this most faithful of friends,[48] that she persuaded her mother to take a holiday in Italy; they arrived at Pratolino, on 22 June. This proved to be an 'emotional day' for Ellen, as she was finally reunited with Paul after an absence of 15 years.[49] The duo had much to discuss and sat up talking until well after midnight. Princess Nicholas particularly enjoyed taking regular walks in the garden, although Olga noticed she quickly became short of breath. Fortunately, the Prince was 'most tactful and considerate' towards his mother-in-law and kindly arranged for her to have a private tour of the Uffizi Gallery. Nevertheless, Olga was often on tenterhooks and observed to Marina that 'a certain amount of sarcasm and irony do pierce through at times... It only means that I have to keep the scales well-balanced both ways by the use of much tact.'[50]

When Paul departed for Geneva, Olga decided to accompany Princess Nicholas on another of Frederika's royal cruises (this time leaving from Venice) as far as Corfu, where she disembarked and inspected some renovations to Mon Repos. In early October, she flew over to London with Elizabeth to attend Prince Edward's 21st birthday celebrations at Coppins. Unfortunately, the Duchess of Kent had sprained her ankle while playing tennis, so the Princess was tasked with carefully navigating her sister through the guests in a wheelchair. Soon after, she assisted Marina with the move into her new "grace and favour" apartments at Kensington Palace. An early guest was Queen Louise of Sweden, who came to tea and was presented with a silver box by the sisters, as a memento of Elisabeth Toerring, but also as a thank you for acting as a neutral conduit for the sisters' wartime correspondence. Then, in late October, Olga was horrified to learn of the Soviet invasion of Hungary and, on Armistice Day, ventured to St Mary Abbot's Church on Kensington High Street, to say prayers for the Hungarian peoples' suffering.[51]

In Paris, the Princess was persuaded by Lilia Ralli to attend a Greek Charity Bazaar where she won a 'hideous' dress in a raffle.[52] Perhaps it was just as well that Paul Louis Weiller encouraged his royal friend to treat herself to something from Dior as his Christmas gift. However, Christmas was no longer something Olga looked forward to: She was prone to reminiscing about the past and felt 'weighed down with extra sorrow' as she remembered those loved ones who had 'gone ahead.'[53] Nevertheless, on Christmas Eve, she joined Paul and Elizabeth to dine at Alexander and Maria Pia's home at Versailles and admitted to enjoying 'the delicious food and champagne.'[54] With Elizabeth out at a New Year réveillon party, the Prince and Princess spent the beginning of 1957 listening to the midnight bells from a nearby church and saying prayers for the year ahead. Cruelly, a further heartbreak was just around the corner.

Princess Nicholas' health had continued to deteriorate and, in early March, she suffered a heart attack. On 14 March, Olga and Marina flew into Athens in an aircraft of The Queen's Flight and were at their mother's bedside when she passed away at her Psychiko home, later that day. Ellen was buried beside her husband at Tatoi and her death would leave another gaping void in the Princess' life. Indeed, her daughter

Elizabeth felt her mother was 'crushed' by this third family death in as many years.[55] Nonetheless, in early June, she attended the wedding of Prince Tomislav (Tommy) to Princess Margarita of Baden at Schloss Salem. Sadly, in November, Olga's Uncle, Prince George, died at his home in St Cloud and this news only added to the 'deep feeling of gloom and doom' currently permeating Rue Scheffer. [56]

Following her mother's death, Olga coped with her grief by adopting a fixed routine. She also increasingly relied on Diddie Serpieri for her Athens news and particularly enjoyed their long chats à deux at the Serpieri's apartment in Paris' Lancaster Hotel or over lunch at Rue Scheffer. However, the Princess could never fathom out why Diddie was 'always cold' and preferred to wear her fur coat during her visits.[57] On occasion, the two friends would be joined by Lilia Ralli for what Olga referred to as 'a hen party lunch' at the Relais restaurant.[58]

Chapter 22 Grandmother

As 1958 dawned, the Princess must have yearned for a break from the tragedies of the past, and the 21st birthday celebrations for her niece Alexandra at Kensington Palace, on 6 January, provided just the opportunity. Twenty guests (including the Queen and Prince Philip) sat down to dinner that evening. They were later joined by an eclectic group of Alexandra's friends for an evening of dancing to a live band. Olga enjoyed herself so much she did not retire till 3.30am. However, the Princess had another particularly pleasing reason for looking forward to a brighter future: Maria Pia was pregnant and the happy event was due to take place in June. From the outset, Olga intended to be a hands-on grandmother and she even accompanied Maria Pia and Alexander to a pre-natal x-ray appointment, during which she was delighted to learn that there was a very real possibility that Pia might be carrying twins.[1]

Thereafter, the Princess flew to Athens to begin the difficult process of dispersing the contents of her late mother's home. Although she was initially somewhat unnerved by 'the empty silent rooms',[2] she quickly developed 'plans of action' for the task ahead.[3] Marina and Hans-Veit later arrived to select some items and on the first anniversary of Princess Nicholas' death, the trio attended a short memorial service at Tatoi. Inevitably there were discussions with the lawyer regarding staff pensions and taxes. After her sister and nephew's departure, the Princess spent a further two weeks cleaning, counting linen and dealing with the contents of Ellen's wine cellar. On 10 April, she finally bid an emotional farewell to both her late mother's home and the faithful retainers. Olga admitted in her diary, 'I had to steel my heart to keep it from dissolving.'[4]

In Paris, the Princess enjoyed spending time with her daughter-in-law and she was particularly interested in the special breathing exercises that Pia was learning. The duo posed together for the Italian magazine *Tempi*, with Olga apparently instructing Maria Pia on how to knit! Thereafter, the Princess rushed over to London to interview prospective nurses and buy layette items in Harrods. She also enjoyed her first trip in a helicopter, flying from central London to Henley-on-Thames for lunch with Sir Richard Fairey, the aircraft manufacturer. Back at Rue Scheffer, Olga and Paul again entertained Queen Marie to lunch. She was in good form and chatted to her hosts about her new car and a forthcoming trip to Lucerne.[5] It was fortuitous that Mignon seems to have finally made her peace with the Prince and Princess, as shortly thereafter her health declined rapidly.

However, in May, there was evidence of growing civil unrest in Paris, with the army patrolling the streets. Olga grew so concerned that she instructed Elizabeth to remain in England. As the disturbances continued, Maria Pia travelled to Switzerland, accompanied by Olga and Alexander, to stay with Queen Marie-José at Merlinge, until the situation stabilised. A week later, the trio returned to Paris and, at 10pm on 18 June, Maria Pia gave birth to twin boys at the Belvedere Clinic. Alexander and Olga celebrated by drinking champagne and this proudest of Greek grandmothers wrote at the top of her daily diary entry 'Birth of my 2 grandsons!'[6] On 24 June, the babies were taken home to Versailles in Olga's car in the care of their doting grandmother and a nurse, while Pia and Alexander followed on behind in their vehicle. An English nanny, Miss Bingham, was waiting to receive the new arrivals in the nursery. On what would have been Nicholas' 30th birthday-29 June-the Royal Families of Yugoslavia, Italy and Orléans gathered at Versailles for the twins' christening: They were named Dimitri and Michel. For Olga, her grandsons were everything and she quickly got into the habit of picking them up in turn and carrying them around the room.[7]

The Princess then departed for Pratolino and, in late August, she hurried to the station in Florence to greet Maria Pia, Dimitri and Michel as they alighted from the train. As the twins were both grandsons of King Umberto of Italy, their presence attracted widespread media attention. Indeed, Olga observed proudly that 'crowds of people rushed to look at them with touching remarks.'[8] The Princess also extended a warm welcome to a group of Italian monarchists (from Pisa) who called at Pratolino with a gift of sweets for Pia.[9] The house was soon filled to bursting point with family guests, as well as a constant stream of day visitors, including Cecil Beaton. However, all this entertaining must have taken its toll, for in early October, Olga endured another attack 'of those awful quick heartbeats'.[10] An electro-cardiogram subsequently revealed that the Princess had a strong but irregular heartbeat. Shortly thereafter, the Prince and Princess were distressed to hear of the death of Sir Henry Channon. Despite her reservations about him, Olga would rightly remember Chips as 'such a faithful friend.'[11]

During the now customary Christmas Eve festivities at Versailles, the Princess was at pains to ensure that, this being her grandsons' first Christmas, the 'babies' were brought downstairs to admire the candles on the tree. [12] Then, as 1959 began, Elizabeth left for a skiing holiday in Gstaad and Olga's niece Helen gave birth to a daughter, Sophie, at the

Belvedere Clinic.[13][22] Sadly, within weeks, the Princess was beset by more unhappy news when she learned that Ileana of Romania's pregnant daughter Minola had been killed, along with her husband, in an air accident in Brazil. She immediately wrote to the grieving mother to commiserate and noted, 'Oh! how I ache for her knowing that agony. I can share every phase of her suffering.'[14]

In Gstaad, Elizabeth was making lots of friends among the jet set, to her mother's obvious disquiet. Apparently, 'no arguments to press her to return made any impression.'[15] Olga's over-protectiveness was doubtless exacerbated by the recent speculation in the international press, as to whether Maria Pia's younger sister Maria Gabriella and the Shah of Iran might marry. The Princess observed that 'poor' Queen Marie-José was seemingly 'in despair and ill' at all the gossip.[16] However, Elizabeth soon returned to Paris and later travelled with her mother to London to celebrate 'English' Easter with the Kent family. Marina and Alexandra had just returned from a demanding five-week official tour of South America and Olga was concerned that her sister was looking 'too thin and drawn in the face'.[17] Afterwards, the Princess made a spring visit to Pratolino, ostensibly to discuss improvements on the house. Here again death seemed to stalk her, for she was immediately greeted with the news that Moina's younger sister, Elena, had passed away. After telegraphing Paul, Olga arranged for the local Russian Orthodox priest to conduct the funeral, which she attended as the principal mourner, dressed in black mourning clothes borrowed from her cousin Helen.

In mid-June, the Prince and Princess returned to Pratolino for consultations with an interior decorator about fabrics for use in the Empire Room and dining room. Unfortunately, further 'innovations' were at standstill 'for want of funds.'[18] Olga was soon distracted by a special picture spread in Italy's *Oggi* magazine to celebrate the twins' first birthday. When she proudly showed the images to her servants, they were soon 'in fits' of delight.[19] Indeed, the Princess seemed quite keen to promote Michel and Dimitri's public image, so when they arrived at Pratolino the following month, she permitted three Italian press photographers to take pictures of them with their delighted grandmother for general publication. (For good measure, Olga would later feature one of the snaps on the front of her Christmas card). Such publicity could have interesting consequences: When the Princess subsequently took the twins to a Florentine shoe shop to buy sandals, a woman rushed in off the street simply to admire them.[20] Back in France, the Princess would continue to monitor her grandsons' progress during her weekly visits to

---

[22] Sophie was Helen and Ferdl's second child. The eldest, Elisabeth was born in 1957.

Versailles and was touched to find that the twins called out 'Amama' the moment they heard her voice.[21]

Nevertheless, there was also a downside to the family living together under one roof in Italy: Olga soon discovered that she was required to 'smooth over many corners of bitterness' during a talk with Elizabeth and Alexander, after tackling them about coming home late the previous evening. Give that they were both adults, this might be regarded as over-interference. However, it seems that the Princess had 'slept but little...'[22] whether due to worry or indignation is unclear. The combination of the intense heat and a lack of sleep contrived to provoke another attack of the 'quick heartbeats' and Alexander was required to carry his mother up to her bedroom.[23] Shortly thereafter, Quiss left for England on business and would again earn his mother's displeasure for not keeping in regular enough contact with his wife.[24] Elizabeth fared little better: When she visited some friends for the weekend, her mother disapproved simply on the grounds that the location was 'not the place I'd like her to go often as the guests are so mixed as a rule.'[25] Clearly, Olga would have preferred her daughter to mix with only the upper-echelons of society. The Pratolino season ended with the funeral of Paul's old friend Bernard Berenson, who died on 6 October at the grand age of eighty-four; he was buried in the grounds of his beloved Villa I Tatti.

After a brief break with her cousins Helen and Irene in Venice, the Princess and Elizabeth travelled to England to help Marina commemorate what would have been her silver wedding anniversary on 29 November. The day was spent quietly 'en famille'.[26] During her stay, Olga had a most interesting encounter over lunch at Kensington Palace with a 'shy and unassuming' King Hussein of Jordan, whom she admitted to finding 'v[ery] attractive'.[27]

With the dawn of the "swinging 60's", Olga attempted to embrace the mood, albeit briefly, by visiting a night club with Elizabeth. She then decided to expand her artistic horizons by enrolling in a drawing course run by the École ABC. Much of the rest of her time was spent helping to organise the sale of Princess Nicholas' Fabergé collection through Sotheby's in London. The experts, she enthused, 'were in fits over the quality and quantity of [the] objects' and 'sure of getting high prices!'[28] In February, Olga and Elizabeth set out on a skiing trip to St Anton in Austria. However, the Princess' holiday routine was soon interrupted by news of the engagement of Princess Margaret to the British society photographer Anthony Armstrong-Jones. Olga was amazed and observed, 'What a come-down after reaching the age of 30! It's incredible.'[29] Marina was similarly 'staggered'[30] at the news. The sisters had, meanwhile, arranged to visit Athens in mid-March. However, on the eve of their departure, the Princess learned, during a talk with

Elizabeth, that she had met someone during her recent skiing holiday.[31] Olga was unaware, however, that her daughter had accepted an invitation from this new friend, a handsome clothing manufacturer called Howard Oxenberg, to visit him in New York.[32] She was therefore surprised to receive a telephone call, in Athens, from Paul informing her that Elizabeth had suddenly rushed off to America, simply leaving a note stating that she had a return ticket and 'not to worry' as she would telegraph later.[33] The Prince now wanted his wife to return to Paris immediately, so Olga informed her Greek friends and relations that her husband had taken ill and that his doctor had requested she return home.[34] Although Elizabeth later sent a telegram announcing her safe arrival in New York, her mother observed, 'where, with whom we don't know..' Interestingly, the Princess' 'terror' was that the press would learn of her daughter's adventure, so the focus was now on 'how to hush it up'.[35] Not perhaps the typical reaction of most parents.

On 7 April (Elizabeth's 24th birthday) Olga-who was now aware of the identity of her daughter's romantic interest-learned from Paul that their daughter had telephoned Rue Scheffer, while she was out, to say that she was happy in New York. Olga, however, was more concerned that many people, particularly among the 'mostly millionaire' Greek community in Paris, knew all about the situation.[36] Her fear now was that the news would be 'spread in Athens.'[37] The following week, the Prince and Princess spent Easter with the Duchess of Kent and her family at Kensington Palace. On Easter Sunday, Olga and Paul accompanied Marina and Michael to tea at Windsor Castle. Princess Margaret and her new fiancé Anthony Armstrong-Jones were both present and 'seemed blissful.'[38] Given the current situation with Elizabeth, and bearing in mind Olga's earlier derogatory remarks about the betrothed couple, this must have proved a particularly bitter pill for her to swallow. The Princess later visited Iver churchyard, 'by my precious child's grave, gay with flowers and [I] thought what a help he would have been now in this drama with Eliz[abeth] but it was not to be.'[39]

On returning to Paris, Olga watched Princess Margaret's wedding on television at her niece Helen's house. Then, on 21 May, the Princess notes in her diary that Marina telephoned from London with the news that her daughter Alexandra had just received a letter from Elizabeth in which she informed her cousin 'that since a few days she has become Mrs Oxenberg...' Meanwhile, that evening, the newspaper, *France Soir,* carried the story accompanied by a picture of Elizabeth. The Princess reaction, as it had been throughout this period, remained somewhat atypical of a mother's concern: She speculated that 'now the press is going to hound us and we shall get letters of sympathy.' Even worse, 'what will they say in Greece?'[40] The next day, Elizabeth phoned from

New York to say she and Howard had married several weeks earlier. She had hoped that her parents would have been the first to know, as she had written to her mother on the same day as to Alexandra and was 'sorry for the slip of our hearing it by the press.'[41] Although Olga was now determined to 'try to dwell' on her daughter's happiness, she found that 'the shock hits me again and again...' and she was 'longing to go to Prat[olino] for a change and be busy.'[42] The Princess' disposition was hardly improved by the unwelcome news that the recent sale of Princess Nicholas' Fabergé items at Sotheby's had only realised £12,400 compared to the £40,000 anticipated.[43]

At Pratolino, Olga focused on organising the construction of a sand pit for the twins, who arrived with their nurse on 5 July. Although the house was filled to capacity as usual, the Princess found time to watch the Olympics on television from Rome and sent a congratulatory cable to Crown Prince Constantine on his winning a gold medal in a sailing event. However, autumnal Paris was soon to provide a 'rather drab contrast' to the delights of Tuscany[44] and Olga's mood darkened when she received the dreadful news that the Count and Countess of Paris' son Francois had been killed by insurgents in Algeria. Naturally, she commiserated with her royal friends, but also found that their loss 'brought all the pain [of Nicholas' death] back afresh.'[45] The Princess seemed unable to shake off this feeling of melancholy and, most unusually, she was 'odious and abrupt' to Marina over the telephone, for which she immediately wrote to apologise.[46]

The main pre-Christmas event was the arrival of Elizabeth and her new husband Howard Oxenberg in Paris. They both lunched at Rue Scheffer, on 11 December, and Olga's 'first impressions' of her new son-in-law were 'good'. Later at Versailles, she was particularly pleased to find that Howard immediately made friends with the twins.[47] In a letter to Marina she noted of the newlyweds, 'The one comfort is to see the complete harmony between them and how well he understands her.'[48] Indeed, over time, the Princess would admit to a grudging respect for her daughter's actions, noting 'what courage she showed in daring it.'[49]

A three-week New Year visit to London by Olga was not initially a success: Marina was suffering from a virulent attack of 'flu to which the Princess also succumbed. The sisters, therefore, spent much of their time either recovering in bed or taking tea together in their respective bedrooms. However, as their health improved, the duo ventured out to a local Kensington health store to stock up on porridge, yoghurt and cream cheese and subsequently sat 'muffled' against the cold in Kensington Gardens 'like two old slums!'[50] Otherwise, Olga and Marina were at their most content either rearranging the drawing room furniture or eating dinner from trays as they watched their favourite television programmes. They were also uplifted by a phone call from their niece Helen, on 8 February, to say she had given birth to a son, Maximilian ('Max').[51]

The Princess returned to Paris, in late February, to find Elizabeth and Howard installed in the comfort of the Ritz. Even more exciting was the confirmation by Olga's gynaecologist that her daughter was expecting, with the baby due in late September. However, a current worry was the state of Alexander's marriage. When Quiss admitted to his mother that he was 'not happy… in lots of small ways…', she tried to make him see things from his wife's viewpoint, but concluded, forlornly, 'Oh! dear it is depressing.'[52] Fortunately, the Princess found solace entertaining her niece Helen for lunch at Rue Scheffer. The latter recalls that over time her Aunt 'sort of took the place of my mother very much and [was] very understanding and sweet.'[53] Olga paid regular visits to Helen's home in the Paris suburb of Garches, where she particularly enjoyed watching the children say their evening prayers.[54]

A most welcome event for the Princess was the long-anticipated official announcement, on 9 March, of her nephew Edward's engagement to Miss Katherine Worsley, the daughter of Sir William Worsley, the Lord Lieutenant of the North Riding of Yorkshire. The courtship had been a protracted one, allegedly at the insistence of Marina, who wanted to be sure that 'Kate' and 'Ed' were well-matched for the royal life of obligation which awaited them. Olga hinted at the difficulties in a letter to Marina: 'Now the thing is settled *and all the past strain forgotten*'.[55] The wedding was scheduled to take at York Minister on 8 June but, by the end of March, the Princess had already ordered a blue ensemble from Marc Bohan at Dior. She was introduced to Katherine during her customary Easter visit to Kensington Palace and thought her, 'V[ery] sweet and fair and upright, not a real beauty, but has charm.'[56] However, when Edward informed Olga that 'I frighten Kate!!' Olga remained totally unfazed and observed that she was 'a member of [Katherine's] in-law family *she must get used to…*'[57]

In early May, the Prince and Princess made a brief visit to Pratolino and helped to entertain the Queen and Prince Philip, who were staying with Queen Mother Helen at the Villa Sparta, following the conclusion of their State Visit to Italy. Olga then returned to London, where she entered into the pre-wedding preparations at Kensington Palace with typical gusto. This included accompanying Marina to Coppins to inspect the wedding gifts, which were neatly laid out in the music room. It proved to be an emotional visit and caused the Princess to reflect that this familiar old house was already 'waiting for the new generation.'[58] On the morning of 7 June, Olga and Paul joined the Kents and their entourage for the train ride north to York for the wedding. On arrival, the little group attended a wedding rehearsal in the Minster before proceeding to Nawton Tower at Helmsley, to spend the night as guests of Lord and Lady Feversham. The following day, from her front row seat in the South Sacrarium the Princess watched intently as Edward and Katherine (henceforth Her Royal Highness, the Duchess of Kent) exchanged their vows before the Archbishop of York. Thereafter, she attended an afternoon reception at the bride's childhood home, the elegant 18th century Palladian mansion of Hovingham Hall. The festivities did not end there: On 10 June, Olga was present at her cousin Philip's 40th birthday celebrations at Windsor Castle. Next day, she celebrated her own birthday at Kensington Palace with a celebratory cake and many gifts. Such simple gestures, she admitted, 'touched me to floods of tears.'[59]

The Princess arrived at Pratolino on 21 June and quickly set to work hanging pictures in the newly-renovated dining room. However, her exertions were soon interrupted by a telephone call from Marina informing her of the death of Queen Marie at her home in London. Olga observed sympathetically, 'It's a happy release for her, only 61.'[60] She accompanied Paul to London to attend the two-hour funeral service at the Serbian Orthodox Church on 2 July, and later joined other family members, including King Peter, at the Royal Burial Ground at Frogmore for the interment.

On her return to Pratolino, Olga fretted over the political situation in Berlin, where Communist East Germany had commenced building the infamous Berlin Wall, in a determined attempt to halt the flow of people into the Allied sectors. Then, leaving the twins in their nurse's care, the Princess and Marina joined their cousins Margarita and Sophie for a two-week cruise down the West coast of Italy. It was not all plain sailing: At Positano, Olga stepped down into a deep hatch and gashed her left shin. A doctor had to be called to stitch it. [61]

On 20 September, the Princess flew into to New York to await the birth of Elizabeth's first child. She stayed with a friend of Elizabeth's, Atalanta Mercati Arlen. The following afternoon, she accompanied her daughter to an 11th floor room at Doctors Hospital where, in the early hours of 22 September, Elizabeth gave birth to a girl, Catherine. The Big Apple experience proved to be quite an eye-opener for this royal grandmother. To pass the time, she decided to take a brisk walk through Central Park, but was disappointed to find it 'full of squirrels and dirty, screaming children!'[62] When Olga later re-entered the hospital, she was taken aback to observe 'crowds' of visiting relatives gathered at the nursery viewing window, 'like a zoo!'[63] A few days later, the Princess ascended the Empire State Building and was captivated by the 'staggering view'. She then dined with Howard Oxenberg at the Hemisphere Club, on the top floor of the Time-Life Building, and noted warmly that her son-in-law 'has nice, honest opinions and ideas and really loves and admires [Elizabeth].'[64] Olga also took the opportunity to visit the United Nations headquarters, where she listened to President Kennedy give a speech on nuclear proliferation. She kept a wary eye on the Soviet delegation and noted they did not bother to applaud.[65]

On 1 October, Elizabeth and Catherine arrived home at Park Avenue. The Princess subsequently attended the Broadway opening of Noel Coward's musical "Sail Away" and was rewarded with a warm embrace from "The Master". A few weeks later, Catherine was christened by a Greek Orthodox priest in the drawing room of the Greek shipping magnate Basil Goulandris' Manhattan apartment. Olga gave her grandchild a heart-shaped turquoise and diamond brooch as a memento of the occasion.[66] The Princess then attended a Polish Ball, at which the 'twist' (which she described as 'the new crazy, sexy dance'[67]) was performed. This was followed by a weekend visit, by train, to snowy Washington as the guest of the philanthropists Mr and Mrs Robert Bliss. However, Olga did not forget the local Yugoslav community and paid a visit to New York's Saint Sava Serbian Orthodox Cathedral, where she quizzed a priest on the work being undertaken to alleviate the suffering of Slav refugees. As she took her leave of New York, in early December, the Princess expressed an appreciation for having 'met with so much affection and kindness'[68] and returned from the States 'refreshed and very enthusiastic ...'[69]

Back in Paris, the Princess was shocked to learn from King Umberto, over dinner at the Ritz, that his wife Marie-José and her mother Queen Elisabeth had recently visited the Soviet Union and "Red" China. Worse still, they had accepted gifts from their communist hosts. Thereafter, Olga and Paul attended King Paul's 60th birthday festivities in Athens. This was the Prince's first visit since 1941 and Palo touchingly journeyed out to the airport to greet him in person. The celebrations commenced with a Thanksgiving Service at the Cathedral, on 14 December, and this was followed by a State Ball at the Royal Palace, during which Olga conversed with 'heaps of friends' and only 'withdrew' at 2.30am![70]

Unfortunately, the Prince and Princess had then to make an unplanned detour to Pratolino as the house had been burgled. Olga was distressed to discover that many items of sentimental value were missing including a ruby and diamond icon. The whole experience, she complained, 'makes one sick'.[71] Christmas at Versailles was a rather subdued affair and the atmosphere was hardly helped by Queen Marie-José handing round 'masses' of photographs from her Soviet trip, causing Olga to observe testily, 'I hardly saw them and asked her no questions.'[72]

In the spring of 1962, the Princess returned to Athens for the wedding of Paul and Frederika's daughter Sophie to Prince Juan Carlos of Spain. It was also around this time that the Princess learned, to her delight, that Elizabeth was expecting another child. Subsequently, during a sunny summer's day at Pratolino, a letter arrived from King Peter addressed to his 'Dear Uncle Paul'. The Prince happened to be away taking a cure but Olga had been 'authorized' to open his mail and what she read infuriated her. Written on 6 August, from the luxurious Hotel Metropole in Monte Carlo, it read, 'I am very distressed to hear again that certain émigré circles are saying that you are doing all you can to eliminate me as King and my son Alexander as Crown Prince, and future King.' Unbelievably, Peter also accused Paul of wishing to 'replace' him and his descendants 'from the legal and constitutional line of succession.' The letter continued: 'I can hardly believe that these dreadful rumours can be true, it seems so very out of character with your honourable behaviour.' Why then was Peter even listening to such gossip? The King went on to make the most humiliating of requests: He asked his Uncle as 'a loyal member of my family' to write 'by return of post' a letter 'stating that you and your descendants are loyal to the Karageorgević dynasty and its direct line of succession....' He had the impertinence to sign his epistle, 'Love Peter.'[73]

Ever-conscious of the sacrifice Paul had made in Yugoslavia and intolerant of Peter's patent disrespect and lack of family loyalty, the Princess wrote a reply of blistering Imperial frankness: She observed that the content of the King's letter, 'shows how little you know or care about Uncle Paul's upright nature and loyalty to you always, to dare accuse him of wishing to take you or your son's place in the line of succession .... Luckily your brothers trust and respect him [Prince Paul] and would be indignant to hear you had written such a letter.' If Peter was already aghast at Olga's bluntness, he was in for a further shock: *'If you had been half as true & loyal to him as he has been to you, I can assure you that nothing would have made us happier.'* The Princess made it clear that her views were also shared by Marina and Queen Mother Helen who 'were horrified by the tone of your letter.' Her epistle was signed with a perfunctory 'Yrs. etc. A[unt] Olga'.[74] It would be fair to say that relations between Peter and his Aunt and Uncle would never recover from this most unfortunate episode.

In November, Olga was thrilled to learn of her niece Alexandra's engagement to Angus Ogilvy, an Eton and Oxford-educated financier, whose father David, the 12th Earl of Airlie, was Lord Chamberlain to Queen Elizabeth the Queen Mother. This news was quickly followed by the happy news, from New York, that Elizabeth had given birth to a second daughter, Christina, on 7 December. Although the Princess wished that she could have been present at the birth, she was pleased to learn that the delivery 'was quick and normal'[75] and was soon devouring letters from the proud mother full of 'adorable details' about the baby's features and Catherine's reaction to her new sister.[76]

The New Year of 1963 found Olga somewhat under the weather with 'flu. The twins, meanwhile, were off to Gstaad for a holiday under the supervision of their nanny, Silvia. The Princess reflected on their differing characters: Michel was 'so sensible'[77] and possessed of the same 'keen, intelligent look'[78] as his late Uncle Nicholas. By comparison, Dimitri was a handful and 'can't be trusted alone a second!'[79] As was her custom, Olga was also keen to dispense advice: When she learned that her friend Diddie Serpieri was 'not overjoyed' at her son Fernand's recent engagement to a Swedish girl, [80] she wrote to advise her 'not to cut him off, but accept it if it's his happiness.'[81] It seems that the Princess-perhaps drawing on her earlier experience with Elizabeth-had adopted a more laissez-faire approach towards marriage.

Meanwhile, a cable arrived from Paul and Frederika inviting the Prince and Princess to Athens in March to celebrate the centenary of King George I ascending the Hellenic throne. The Princess was surprisingly ambivalent '[I] am in 2 minds about it as I feel I ought to go...' the downside being 'the extra clothes and expense'.[82] In view of the upcoming centennial festivities, it was particularly prescient that the Princess also received news of the engagement of Greece's Crown Prince Constantine to King Frederick of Denmark's youngest daughter, Anne-Marie. Olga observed, 'so the link back between Greece and Denmark is forged by the 4th instead of the 3rd generation which might have been Rico and me!'[83] She immediately sent a letter of congratulations to Queen Ingrid and, for good measure, arranged for the Danish Crown Princess, Margrethe ('Daisy') to lunch at Rue Scheffer.

On 11 March, Maria Pia gave birth to another set of twins, a boy and a girl, Serge and Hélène. Princess Olga then left for Athens to attend the Centenary Celebrations. The various events culminated in a gathering of 600 Mayors from all over Greece, at the Archaeological Society Hall. Nevertheless, it would be the scent of wisteria which proved the most lasting memory of this particular visit for the Princess, as it evoked 'such childhood memories.'[84]

At the end of April, Olga flew to England for the upcoming nuptials of her niece Alexandra. Frederika was also attending the wedding and the Princess was furious to discover that the *Sunday Express* had printed 'a stinking, vitriolic article' about the Greek Queen.[85] Olga and Paul attended a pre-wedding Ball for two-thousand guests given by the Queen at Windsor Castle. The Princess greatly admired Alexandra's new turquoise and diamond tiara (a wedding gift from her fiancé), but her most charming compliment was reserved for her daughter, Elizabeth, whom she described as looking 'divine'.[86] On 24 April, Olga joined Marina and the rest of her family at Westminister Abbey for 'Puddy's' nuptials. The Princess' front row seat in the Sacrarium allowed her ample opportunity to observe her niece who 'looked like an angel with F'al's rayon tiara and Mummy's lace on her veil'.[87] After dinner, Olga and Marina sat down to watch the highlights on television at Kensington Palace.

A few days later, Paul celebrated his 70th birthday, a milestone his wife somehow felt 'does not seem possible'.[88] In the evening, the Prince and Princess joined Elizabeth and Howard at Wilton's for a celebratory dinner. However, the London visit was soon to take an unexpected turn: While attending Sunday morning service at St Mary Abbot's Church with Marina, something the preacher said struck a chord with Olga and she was 'overcome with pent up emotion...' about Dimitri and Michel's 'lack of education' (though why is unclear as they had a governess) and more understandably 'missing my Veeze.' But perhaps what rankled most was 'the fraud about the younger twins.' The latter is Olga's first written acknowledgment of her firmly-held belief that Serge and Hélène had not been fathered by Alexander, but rather by Prince Michel of Bourbon-Parma, Princess Margaret of Denmark's son. Fortunately, both Marina and their mutual friend Turia Campbell proved 'so understanding' and the episode 'passed to lie deep again.'[89] It is worth noting that Olga most certainly embraced 'the juniors' as her grandchildren, always taking a keen interest in their doings and travelling out to Versailles each week by car for a visit, usually accompanied by useful gifts.

On 11 June, it was Olga's turn to celebrate another landmark birthday, her 60th, at Rue Scheffer. She was thoroughly spoiled receiving many gifts (including an impressive black crocodile Dior handbag from Paul). Later there was tea with the two sets of 'adorable' twins, followed by a visit to the theatre to see a production of Oscar Wilde's "The Importance of Being Earnest".[90] Shortly thereafter, the Princess departed to Pratolino to prepare the house for another busy summer, but she was temporarily distracted by news, in the English press, concerning her friend John Profumo: He had recently resigned as Secretary of State for War after admitting that he had lied to Parliament about his relationship with Christine Keeler, a call-girl who was also involved (separately) with the Soviet naval attaché and spy, Yevgeny Ivanov. Far from being censorious, Olga sympathised with Profumo's predicament noting 'I do pity him.'[91] She also received a fourteen-page letter from Marina giving her details of King Paul and Queen Frederika's recent (and stormy) State Visit to London. The Princess had already been outraged to read in the press that the couple had been greeted by 'booing and hissing' during an outing to the Aldwych Theatre.[92]

At Pratolino, Olga was cheered by the arrival of Elizabeth, Howard and her two granddaughters in late June. She particularly admired the new-born Christina's 'brown eyes and kind, round face'[93] and was soon busily preparing the 'big room' for the infant's christening, which was conducted by a Russian Orthodox priest.[94] Yet, the Princess also remained besotted by her elder granddaughter, 'That angelic C[atherine]' and bought her gifts of a doll's pram and a children's tea set.[95] However, less pleasing was the presence of *Vogue* magazine personnel who were making use of the large salon for a photoshoot featuring Maria Pia 'in various models and wigs.' The upheaval caused her mother-in-law to complain of 'a very agitated day'.[96] Each evening, the Princess read a bedtime story to Michel and Dimitri. Sometimes, she also indulged them with a game of make-believe, during which the boys pretended the couch in their grandmother's bedroom was a boat which would transport them on thrilling journeys to exotic locations.[97] However, Olga was also prepared to be firm: When Dimitri pinched Michel 'viciously' on the arm, she did exactly the same to him.[98]

Another relative contemplating matrimony was Hans-Veit Toerring. In the autumn, he brought his bride-to-be, Princess Henriette zu Hohenlohe-Bartenstein, to meet his formidable Aunt at Rue Scheffer. Still oblivious to the effect her forceful personality had on newcomers, Olga observed briskly that 'Etty' was 'v[ery] shy with me at first but I soon put her at her ease.'[99] Then, on 22 October, the Prince and Princess were joined by Diddie and Lilia, to toast 40 years of marriage. Unfortunately, within days, Olga was 'upset beyond words' to hear of the death of her dear friend Marie-Thérèse de Croisset.[100] She later attended the funeral service at Paris' Saint-Pierre de Chaillot Church.

In England, Danny Kaye proved the ideal pick-me-up, when he called on Olga and Marina at 'K.P.'[23] for cocktails on a cold November evening, so 'full of life and new energy and funny of course.'[101] However, when the Princess later learned of the assassination of President Kennedy, she was aghast and noted, 'such a shock to hear and so sudden and brutal.'[102] Furthermore, a television report of Kenya's independence celebrations caused her to wonder how the country would survive 'with all these mau-maus let loose.'[103]

Sadly, the New Year brought a further series of travails: Olga had been aware for some time that her cousin King Paul had become increasingly frail, but his death at Tatoi on 6 March 1964, as a result of complications following an operation for stomach cancer, still came as a terrible shock. Stoical to the end, Palo had delayed having surgery until

---

[23] Royal shorthand for Kensington Palace.

after the Greek General Elections in mid-February.[104] Meanwhile, Paul was diagnosed with glaucoma and admitted to Jacob Hoptner that he was beginning to feel his age.[105] However, he accompanied Olga to the wedding of their nephew Hans-Veit, on 20 April, at Bartenstein. The Princess then suffered a heart attack which was sufficiently severe to worry her husband 'considerably'. Doubtless her condition was not improved by the news that their landlord at Rue Scheffer wished the couple to vacate the property as he intended to sell it. By July, Paul was 'busy looking for a flat unsuccessfully' while his wife rested in the summer heat at Pratolino.[106] Fortunately, by mid-September, Olga felt well enough to fly to Athens to attend the wedding of King Constantine and his bride Anne-Marie on 18 September.

The Prince and Princess welcomed in the New Year of 1965 at a champagne party at Kensington Palace. Later in the week, Olga and Marina flew tourist class to Paris where, to their consternation, they were seated alongside a noisy crowd of 'singing and chanting' rugby players.[107] On 24 January, Winston Churchill died. The Princess had more reason than most to feel bitter at his treatment of both her and Prince Paul, but her comments were both restrained and succinct: 'The old man died at 9am peacefully-he was a great historical figure specially for England, though in some countries such as ours he failed to grasp their problems during the war and let them drift into the red block...'[108] When she later watched the funeral service on television she was struck by 'the divine singing and such wonderful order.'[109] By contrast, Olga seemed to ruffle the feathers of her daughter-in-law when she dressed Dimitri and Michel all in grey to attend a children's party at the Count and Countess of Paris' home at Louveciennes.[110] Relations with Alexander were also somewhat tense: When he returned to Paris from a skiing trip to Val d'Isère and spent the night at his club in Paris, rather than travelling directly out to Versailles to be reunited with his wife, Olga was displeased.[111] Nevertheless, within weeks, all seemed forgotten as Olga and Paul entertained their son and Pia to a champagne lunch at Rue Scheffer to celebrate their tenth wedding anniversary.[112]

Marital frictions continued to persist in the Princess' marriage: She was somewhat irritated by her husband's more relaxed approach to disciplining the twins. When Olga learned that Dimitri had been rude to his teacher in class, she 'tried to reason with him'. However, rather than support his wife's efforts, she complained that 'P[aul] of course burst out laughing and spoilt the effect of his [Dimitri's] guilt.'[113] The Princess also remained increasingly worried about their financial situation: At Pratolina, despite the sale of some land, 'troubles' continued to mount and proved such a drain on their funds that she described the situation as one of 'slow ruination.'[114] This did not deter the Princess from responding to a 'desperate letter' from a friend with some timely financial help.[115]

Thereafter, Olga paid a visit to the Greek Orthodox Church in Paris to pray for her father, on the 27th anniversary of his death. Unfortunately, her attendance coincided with a memorial service to commemorate the first anniversary of the death of the former Greek Prime Minister Sofiklis Venizelos. She was therefore forced to endure a 'heated' speech of admiration by the Greek Ambassador, Mr Kalergis, during which he also praised Sofiklis' father Eleftherios for his 'great services to Greece.'[116] It is a measure of Olga's sense of duty that she still felt able to entertain the Ambassador to tea at Rue Scheffer only a few days later. Certainly, the news from Athens was hardly uplifting: The former Greek Prime Minister George Caramanlis entertained the Prince and Princess to lunch and, Olga noted, 'gave us a dismal picture of pol[itical] things in Greece, comm[unists] infiltrating into everything-the army is loyal so far but it can't last'.[117] Meanwhile, a letter from Diddie Serpieri was 'full of misery and forebodings worse than usual.'[118] To compound matters, when the Princess went to lunch with her cousin Eugenie at St Cloud, a fellow guest, Mrs Eleni Kazantzakis [24] 'ran down' Queen Frederika and said 'she had done Greece much harm...' Ever loyal, the two royal cousins both rushed to Freddie's defence.[119] Another Greek friend, Nelly Mikronlaki, informed Olga that many in Athens missed Princess Nicholas' wisdom.[120] The Princess was sufficiently unsettled to consider putting the Russian Home under the auspices of the Greek Red Cross 'so it can be protected and financed.'[121] Tellingly, she decided not to send a telegram to Frederika on her 48th birthday, 'as she never replies'.[122]

As the days lengthened, Olga flew over to London for a spring stay with Marina at Kensington Palace and demonstrated a rare modicum of sympathy towards the Windsors: The Duke had recently undergone eye surgery at the London Clinic and the Princess observed from press photographs that his wife Wallis, 'looks drawn and sad'.[123] Marina duly called on the couple at Claridge's and later informed her sister that Wallis had greeted her with a deep curtsey, before taking her to see the 'frail' Duke. The ageing duo had both been 'most friendly and seemed touched' by her visit.[124] The chance of a family rapprochement now seemed a distinct possibility for, during a visit by the sisters to the Queen Mother at Clarence House the following day, Queen Elizabeth asked Marina about her visit and saw 'the sense of a closer understanding and said

---

[24] Mrs Nikos Kazandzakis was the wife of the author of the book Zorba the Greek which was released as a film in early 1965

she'd visit them like a shot if they wanted to see her'. Olga responded diplomatically that 'it might be a good move.'[125]

At the end of March, Elizabeth made a visit to Paris. She and her mother shopped at Dior and took tea at Bagatelle in the Bois de Boulogne. When Olga later watched her daughter leave for a party at the fashion designer Jacqueline de Ribes' home, she thought her 'too lovely.'[126] In mid-April, the Prince and Princess again celebrated the Orthodox Easter in London. During this stay, Olga could not resist consulting a spiritualist, Mrs St. George, who informed the Princess that 'those who loved me' (including her parents and her paternal grandfather) had come through with some 'moving and true' messages.[127]

Back at Rue Scheffer, she and Paul welcomed their nephew Edward and his wife Katherine for a short visit. In addition to taking them out to Versailles, the young couple were royally entertained each evening at some of Paris' best restaurants. However, the pace seems to have been too much for Olga who had another of her "turns" and unobtrusively called in a nurse to administer a restorative injection. She then departed for Pratolino and was soon in deep discussion with Queen Mother Helen about her recent visit to Athens. Sitta, she observed, had 'felt so put aside and ignored by Fr[ederika]' while the palace was 'so changed, [the] staff unhappy.'[128] Thereafter, the twins and their younger siblings Serge and Hélène ('the juniors)' [129] arrived for their summer stay. Michel and Dimitri were now reaching the age when they were more aware of the reactions of others and when 'Dimi' wondered, during a visit to Florence, why the women in the street paid him so much attention, his grandmother informed him, 'it's because his mother is Italian.'[130]

Throughout the summer, the Princess experienced difficulties sleeping and a Dr Weber prescribed a new pill called Revonal to alleviate the problem.[131] Olga undoubtedly remained 'very anxious'[132] about the political situation in Greece and was dismayed to learn that Constantine had named his newly-born daughter Alexia and 'not Olga which is sure to have been popular, especially since poor Tino is on the verge of a pol[itical] clash.'[133] The latter is a reference to the resignation of Prime Minister Georgios Papandreou, following the King's refusal to appoint him to the additional post of Defence Minister. Constantine then asked Georgios Athanasiadis–Novas to form a government, but the latter was forced to resign, in early August, after the Greek parliament refused to ratify his appointment as Prime Minister.

In mid-October, Olga travelled to New York to visit Elizabeth and her family. She enjoyed the novelty of shopping for provisions in a supermarket and thought it 'amazing' that her daughter was able to cook a 'fast' lunch 'most efficiently' from a recipe book.[134] Catherine and Christina adored their grandmother and the Princess was touched by the way they would creep into her bedroom first thing.[135] However, it was not all sweetness and love: Olga felt that her son-in-law was 'too strict' with his daughters.[136] Thereafter, the Princess attended a memorial service on Long Island for her late cousin Xenia-the younger daughter of her father's sister Marie-who had died the previous month at her cottage at Glen Clove. Olga and Elizabeth then flew up to Boston to visit the Museum of Fine Arts and lunch with Paul's old friend, the Director, Perry Rathbone. On another occasion, a lift operator recognised Olga, and to her surprise and delight, addressed her in fluent Greek![137]

On her return to Europe, the Princess sympathised with the Rhodesian Prime Minister Ian Smith's attempts to maintain minority white rule in his country, through a Unilateral Declaration of Independence (UDI). She speculated that he was probably trying to avoid a 'reign of terror' similar to that recently experienced in the Belgian Congo.[138] Then, during her customary pre-Christmas visit to London, Olga suffered an attack of heart palpitations which were so severe that Marina felt compelled to call in her own doctor, who administered a steadying calcium shot. Despite this, the Princess slept little that night due to persistent pains in her chest and neck. She described this latest attack as 'the longest crisis.'[139]

Chapter 23 'So many problems'

As Olga had continued to feel 'lousy'[1], right into the New Year, a doctor in London ran a very thorough set of medical tests and informed her that she had a particularly bad case of bronchitis. He prescribed a course of powerful antibiotics. In spite of this troubling diagnosis, Olga attended the wedding, on 20 January, of Henry Herbert (a godson of the late Duke of Kent) at Holy Trinity Bromptom, followed by the reception at St James's Palace. This was probably foolhardy, as on her return to Paris, she complained of feeling totally exhausted.[2]

In the early Spring, the Princess entertained Howard Oxenberg's cousin Muriel Murphy to lunch at Rue Scheffer and noted cagily that, '[she] adores and admires Eliz[abeth]-sees Howard's qualities, *but also what divides them...*'[3] Then, two weeks later, Elizabeth telephoned her mother from London and informed her that she was over on a brief visit.[4] Although debilitated with sinusitis, Olga flew over to England for a talk with her daughter, who explained that she 'no longer can stand living in N[ew] Y[ork]'.[5] However, on her return to Paris, the Princess received some particularly good news: Olga and Paul's landlord at Rue Scheffer had obligingly offered to sell the house to the Prince, 'at a low price'.[6]

In early May, Queen Mother Helen suffered a slight stroke and Olga fell and sprained her ankle while paying her a visit. However, by early June, she had recovered sufficiently to open up Pratolino for the summer. As Olga and Paul were now contemplating selling the Villa Demidoff, in order to purchase a smaller property nearby, the Princess spent much of her time selecting items of silverware, which were later sold to a Russian dealer from Rome.[7] In addition, Olga sold a selection of porcelain through Sotheby's in London and was delighted when the items obtained good prices.[8]

Elizabeth, Catherine and Christina arrived at the Villa Demidoff for a visit in late June and the Princess learned that her daughter was thinking of settling with her children in London. The amicable unwinding of the Oxenberg's marriage must have been a source of concern to Olga, who had recently written to Howard to 'tell him he has been much in my thoughts and [I] shall always value his friendship.'[9] Unfortunately, when Mr Oxenberg subsequently telephoned Pratolino to make arrangements to visit his daughters, he mentioned the contents of his mother-in-law's letter to his unsuspecting wife. Elizabeth was, understandably, 'very hurt' by her mother's covert action, while Olga reasoned it was 'wrong of him [Oxenberg]' to have discussed the letter.[10]

A holiday on Elba with Marina helped Olga to overlook these family complications. She was further distracted by the news that Rico and Ingrid of Denmark's daughter Margrethe was engaged to marry a French diplomat, Count Henri de Laborde de Monpezat. Rather than be joyful, the Princess was disapproving and noted, 'How can the parents really like it?'[11] Olga's hypercritical mood continued following her return to Paris: When she and Paul took their son and the twins out for Sunday lunch, the Princess observed harshly that, 'He [Alexander] sees them little and has no camaraderie with them beyond severe remarks so they were both silent...'[12] Furthermore, Maria Pia was deemed to have indulged in 'rather cheap publicity' for appearing in an Italian publication 'showing off a mass of jewels and dresses...'[13] Elizabeth fared no better: When Olga paid a pre-Christmas visit to her new home in London, she dismissed it as 'rather drab and suburban and sad...'[14] But, in a sense, was it not Olga who was 'sad'?

Marina celebrated her 60th birthday on 13 December. The event was commemorated by a family outing to the theatre to see the West End comedy "There's a Girl in my Soup". Olga reflected that it was 'wonderful to see the two couples (Kent's and Ogilvy's) so united and happy.'[15] That her own childrens' marriages were now over, in all but name, was further underlined in an article by the syndicated newspaper columnist Suzy Knickerbocker who observed that 'Paris is alive with rumours that Maria Pia will divorce Alexander of Yugoslavia and marry yet another Prince.'[16] Such speculation, along with what the Princess now referred to as 'the tension around me'[17] continued to cast a cloud over the forthcoming Festive season, despite the fact that it would be the first time that Olga would celebrate Christmas surrounded by both of her children and all of her grandchildren.

The Princess celebrated the New Year of 1967 with her sister at Kensington Palace. She admitted to feeling her age and a visit to her London oculist, Mr Rycroft, established the existence of cataract in the left eye.[18] Shortly thereafter, the Princess was distressed to learn that her cousin Irene had been diagnosed with cancer and faced the disagreeable prospect of six weeks of gruelling radiotherapy treatment. Such painful news only served to make her more possessive of the twins: She and Paul regularly entertained Dimtri and Michel to lunch at a restaurant, Le Londres. However, when Alexander and Maria Pia once asked to come too, Olga complained that this 'ruined the joy of having them alone.'[19] She was also becoming increasingly reliant on Marina for advice and praised her 'sense and good judgement and nobility of soul...'[20] The

Princess' niece Helen and her family ('the Ferdls') were another constant source of solace, while for spiritual comfort, Olga now invariably eschewed the services at the Greek Orthodox Church, in favour of the more uplifting-and less political-surroundings of a nearby Roman Catholic Church.

Meanwhile, Alexander's marriage continued to unravel to his parents' obvious distress. In early March, Quiss called at Rue Scheffer to discuss the matter (separately) with his parents.[21] Despite these ongoing family problems, the Princess journeyed to Lausanne to comfort her cousin Irene and accompany her to a radiotherapy session. Touchingly, she gave 'Tim' a 'folding icon' which had once belonged to Princess Nicholas.[22] Thereafter, Olga flew to Athens for a spring break with the Serpieris, who were welcoming hosts and quickly brought her up to speed on the deteriorating political situation. King Constantine came to lunch and was 'full of chat' and 'amusing'.[23] A few days later, the Princess also partook of a vegetarian lunch with Frederika. However, there was an element of tension in the air, as Olga 'refused' the Dowager's Queen's suggestion that they have pre-lunch drinks at the Hilton, preferring to opt instead for the Intercontinental.[24] Prior to leaving Athens, Olga 'took every opportunity to quiz' King Constantine's new political adviser Bitsios and found him to be 'au courant of everything'.[25] Although she did not realise it, this would be the Princess' final visit to Greece.

Back in Paris, the Prince and Princess lunched with their son and learned that he had recently spoken to his mother-in-law Marie-José 'in front of Pia' about 'his wish to divorce.' Indeed, Alexander and his wife had already visited his lawyers. Olga mentions too that photographs of Maria Pia and Prince Michel of Bourbon-Parma taken together, which had featured in a recent edition of *Gente* magazine, proved 'the last straw' for Alexander. Certainly, the whole divorce saga was taking its toll on the Princess who admitted to being 'v[ery] nervously upset.'[26] An Easter sojourn in London was just the tonic Olga needed, and she was soon enjoying the company of her 'good and gentle' granddaughters.[27] However, on 21 April, the Princess received the 'upsetting news' that there had been a military coup d'état in Athens[28]. When she later learned that the Greek Embassy in London had been overrun by people protesting against the coup, she decided it would be safer for her and Marina to avoid attending the Easter services at the Greek Orthodox Church in Bayswater, in case of further trouble there.[29]

In early May, Olga made a visit to Aylesbury to consult a famous faith healer, George Chapman, about her ongoing sinus problems. Mr Chapman would ostensibly go into a state of trance, thus allowing the spirit of an ophthalmic surgeon, Dr William Lang, to "operate" through him to facilitate a medical solution. The Princess found this a positive experience and soon 'felt better...'[30] Interestingly, Chapman maintained that the purpose of his healing mission was to prove that there was life after death. Like the Princess, he had suffered the loss of a child.[31] In the interim, Count Toerring had suffered a stroke at Winhöring; he died, on 14 May, without regaining consciousness. Olga flew to Bavaria for the funeral, but as she watched her brother-in-law being laid to rest beside his wife, the Princess found herself pining for her late sister.[32] Fortunately, this sad event was followed by the heartening news that Queen Anne-Marie had given birth to a son (to be named Pavlos) which Olga felt was 'sure to strengthen' the monarchist cause in Greece. [33]

Meanwhile, the columnist Suzy Knickerbocker was now speculating that as soon as Alexander's divorce was finalised, he would marry a divorcee, Minouche Le Blan.[34] To add to Olga's discomfiture, on her arrival at Pratolino in late June, she discovered that the local newspapers were also carrying widespread coverage of her son's divorce. Even so, the Princess and her husband were also still keen to focus on the future and their 'very capable' Swiss lawyer Mr Lenz suggested that they should consider selling their Italian estate the following year.[35] The one positive was that the local authorities had now granted Prince Paul permission to sell-off individual lots of land, thus increasing the overall value of the estate.

However, for the moment, the house was soon fit to bursting: Catherine, Christina and their nanny, Eva arrived on 12 August, quickly followed by Alexander. The most notable absentees were Michel and Dimitri, who were currently with their grandfather in Portugal. The Princess originally discouraged their presence due to the 'snag' that they were originally to have been supervised at Pratolino by a male companion who was a Braganza cousin of Queen Marie-José. This placed the status-conscious Olga in a quandary: She felt it would be 'impossible' to have this social equal in the house 'to be treated like a tutor'.[36] King Umberto must have realised her quandary and telephoned to say that the twins would arrive on 24 August and their "minder" would stay in a local hotel 'and take them out *when we wish*.'[37] Fortunately, Marina arrived to lighten the mood, especially with 'the kids' who loved 'dancing round her.'[38] However, all too soon, Olga had to endure the 'wrench' of bidding all of her grandchildren goodbye.[39] The girls left with Elizabeth for the coast, while Maria Pia arrived to gather up the twins and drive them to a new boarding school in Gstaad. Unfortunately, rather than let matters rest, the Princess notes that she used this opportunity to have 'an open talk with Pia about her cheap articles [in *Gente* magazine]'.[40]

At the end of October, the Prince and Princess returned to Paris to discover that Alexander had moved into a flat in Montmartre. Olga, Paul and Lilia Ralli subsequently paid him a visit and found him 'calm and happy'. Perhaps out of tact, Alexander never spoke of his latest '"love"' [presumably Miss Le Blan] but his mother still wondered, 'How will it end?'[41] Nevertheless, she was pleased to learn that Alexander and Pia remained on friendly terms.[42] The Princess then made a late autumn trip to London, during which Marina asked her sister to join her for an audience with the Orthodox Patriarch Athinagoras at Lambeth Palace. It proved to be a very spiritual experience for Olga who 'felt deeply stirred and cried, not bitterly more like rain on a thirsty earth' as 'he gave me a long look into my soul.'[43] Interestingly, there was already a sign that Marina was not in the best of health for Olga mentions that her sister eschewed attending the annual Diplomatic Reception at Buckingham Palace 'as it means so much standing and she has often felt faint.'[44] This did not deter the sisters having 'a furore among the hats' at Fenwick's department store.[45] Thereafter, they attended 'a very moving and sincere' séance, using assumed names, with the medium and spiritualist Mrs Ena Twigg. During the one-and-a-half-hour consultation, the late Duke of Kent, Nicholas and their sister Elisabeth apparently 'came through', although only the medium could see and hear them.[46]

On 13 December, the Princess 'phoned Marina to wish her a happy 61st birthday. However, Olga was distracted by further news from Greece: In an attempt to reverse the April military coup, King Constantine had appealed to his people, via a short wave transmitter at Kavala (some 100 miles East of Thessaloniki), to revolt against the dictatorship.[47] Although the King had support among military units in the north of Greece, the attempted counter-coup ended in failure and, on 14 December, Constantine and his family were forced to flee the country and seek refuge in Italy. The Princess' sympathies lay with her King, and she noted, 'It's said that Tino acted too hastily but without the army what chance had he? *What an agonising day this has been, it made me feel quite ill-we know what exiles mean…*'[48] Olga later learned, through her cousin Helen, that their Greek royal relations were living at the Villa Polissena, a Hesse family residence in Rome. However, Sitta's attempts to visit had been met with indifference; Helen would subsequently inform the Princess that Frederika had been 'short' with her over the telephone 'and didn't seem keen to see her.'[49] Olga continued to follow events in Athens keenly and observed that the Colonels had specified that a condition for Constantine's return was that he 'must reign, not rule and no longer be head of the armed forces.' She wondered, '*Can he accept? He has the chance of saving the dynasty and the gov[ernment] can change in time-else its exile or a republic.*' Nonetheless, the astute Princess also opined that the decision did not rest solely with the King but also 'depends on how Fr[ederika] influences him.'[50] Certainly, Sitta would later report that Constantine's mother 'seems in control of everything.'[51] The events of the past year had certainly told on Olga and she informed her sister that she felt unable to come over to England to welcome in the New Year as usual. Marina understandably, 'sounded upset.'[52]

As 1968 dawned, a Greek friend Liza Averoff came to tea at Rue Scheffer and gave Olga 'her Athens impressions' including the information that the Royal Palace was 'sealed up, servants paid off, court dispersed'.[53] At the end of January, the Princess and Marina received the British Ambassador to Greece, Sir Michael Stewart, at Kensington Palace. He expressed the hope that 'Tino' would return as soon as possible. He also had some kind words about Frederika and opined that 'her courage and good works have been so much forgotten.'[54] Yet, even during such sad times, Olga and Marina had not lost their sense of fun: When the duo visited the Royal Academy to see an exhibition of drawings of 'some beauties', they were also greatly amused by the 'extraordinary human types in the visitors.'[55]

The Princess returned to Paris, on 10 February, to learn from Paul that Michel and Dimitri's academic prowess had fallen short of the expected standard. She immediately took matters in hand and phoned their headmistress, Madame Racine, who informed her that the boys could easily do better if they didn't 'waste their time in constant nonsense and silly jokes.' It was agreed that the headmistress would now send Olga a weekly update of their marks.[56] Michel, in particular, seems to have quickly pulled up his socks and was soon 'au tableau d'honneur.'[57] His grandmother immediately wrote to inform him 'that it was the nicest present he could give me.'[58] Nevertheless, she still could not resist pointing out errors in his grammar!

Chapter 24 'I am the only one left...'

As winter turned to spring, the Princess bemoaned her 'old wrinkled neck' and decided to have Princess Nicholas' pearls turned into a choker-style 'collar de chien' by Cartier to camouflage it.[1] With Easter approaching, the Princess focused on entertaining Michel and Dimitri during their school break. The trio would often enjoy post-prandial 'long talks' on subjects such as King's and regent's powers (which of course provided Olga with the ideal opportunity to discuss their grandfather's regency).[2] Michel recalls that it still rankled with his grandmother 'how unfair the English had been with him [Prince Paul] in Yugoslavia when he had always tried to help them...'[3]

The Prince and Princess then celebrated the Orthodox Easter at Kensington Palace. During this trip Olga was introduced, at a dinner party in honour of Peter Ustinov, to Elizabeth's 'young man Neil Balfour of 24-tall and attractive and v[ery] nice.'[4] The Princess also made another outing to Mr Chapman at Aylesbury. Chapman or rather "Dr Lang" would subsequently claim to have received a message from Nicholas 'to say how happy he is in the spirit world', which Olga found 'v[ery] moving and comforting.'[5] On 3 May, after a 'cosy' lunch with Alexandra at Thatched House Lodge, the sisters, accompanied by Marina's grandson James, drove out to Heathrow. After saying their farewells on the tarmac, Olga took her seat in the aircraft and watched as Marina and James 'went off hand in hand...'[6] This would be the last interaction the Princess would have with her younger sister.

On her return home, the Princess experienced a brief but painful heart 'flutter' and the doctor prescribed some new sedatives which unfortunately only served to make her feel 'low and drugged'.[7] However, she was distracted by students from the Sorbonne flying red flags and rioting in the street outside her home, resulting in a pithy response by armed police. Although alarmed, Olga went out as usual despite the absence of public transport. Eventually, Paul concluded that it might be best if they left for Pratolino and, on 23 May, following some 'violent'[8] fighting in the Boulevard St Germain, the Prince and Princess (carrying her jewels retrieved from Cartier) decided to motor to Belgium to stay with their friends, the Lignes, at Hainaut 'and then see how to proceed.'[9] The couple then caught a flight from Brussels to Geneva, from where they travelled by rail to Pratolino, for what was to be their final summer season at this summer retreat. Yet, trouble seemed to follow them: Early on 5 June, Maria Pia phoned from Paris to impart the 'ghastly' news that Robert Kennedy had been assassinated. [10] Shortly thereafter, Olga and Queen Mother Helen drove up to Rome to visit Frederika for the day. It was not a pleasant experience as the ex-queen 'talked without stopping' and was 'bitter and revengeful...'[11]

However, there was worse to follow: On 17 July, a phone call from Zoia Poklewski at Kensington Palace sent a shiver down the Princess' spine: Marina had been admitted to the National Hospital for Nervous Diseases, two days previously, for 'various tests' as her left leg had given way twice, causing her to stumble and fall. Zoia indicated that Princess Alexandra would phone in two days' time with an update. Olga's immediate reaction was one of confusion, 'I can't make it out exactly what is the cause and God give the Drs can treat it.' To add to her distress, the day the Princess received this disturbing news also happened to be the 50th anniversary of 'that ghastly tragedy at Ekaterinburg.'[12] Paul advised his wife to call up Philip Hay, who duly confirmed what Zoia had imparted and reassured Olga they would keep in touch.[13] A few nights later, Olga relates that Alexandra called to say her mother was being discharged from hospital, under the care of a nurse, as the leg was still not functioning properly. Apparently, Marina still intended to pay a visit to Pratolino.[14] However, what Alexandra did not tell her Aunt was that her beloved sister had been diagnosed with an inoperable brain tumour and there was no hope of recovery. The following evening, an unsuspecting Olga called Marina (who was also [mercifully] kept in the dark about the true nature of her illness) and established that she was about to commence a course of physiotherapy and seemed 'full of courage and confidence in accepting this trial'.[15] But why was the Princess, of all people, not told the truth at this stage? The Duke of Kent states that, 'My recollection is that we were rather keen to avoid anyone knowing what was wrong with my mother so I'm afraid we practised a certain amount of deceit in order to conceal what was the real problem.'[16] However, the arrival of the twins temporarily preoccupied the Princess: When Dimitri asked his grandmother why he could not have breakfast at 10 or 11am and lunch at 3pm, he was told matter-of-factly that, 'we are not a pension with the staff to do it.'[17]

On 9 August, Marina phoned to say her doctor had informed her that she could not travel to Pratolino for the foreseeable future. There is a sense that Olga now feared there was more to all this than met the eye, for that evening she wrote to Alexandra, *telling her to phone me anything she wants me to know.*[18] The Princess' mood was temporarily uplifted by the arrival of her daughter and granddaughters. The trio were accompanied by Elizabeth's new beau, Neil Balfour, who Olga noted was 'clever and wise beyond his years' and a good influence on her daughter.[19]

On 25 August, the 26th anniversary of Prince George's death, the Princess 'thought of my F'al so much' but noted there was 'no more news.'[20] However, the following afternoon, Alexandra telephoned her Aunt to inform her that 'my precious F'al had a slight stoke last night...' Although Marina had woken up in the morning, she 'spoke with a thickness' before falling into a coma at 9 am. Her niece now 'begged' her Aunt 'to come at once.' Angus Ogilvy kindly arranged the flight bookings from London, while Olga 'packed in a daze.' Fortunately, Elizabeth was on hand to accompany her shocked mother to England. Nonetheless, despite Alexander driving his mother and sister at speed to Milan, they missed their direct flight and had to take a later one via Paris. It was, therefore, 11.30 pm before they reached Kensington Palace. The Princess was alarmed by Marina's 'fluttery breathing' and a 'sweet' nurse agreed with her assessment that the end seemed near.[21] What Olga does not say in her diary is that she was 'outraged that she hadn't been informed until after her sister lost consciousness.'[22] The Duke of Kent admitted his aunt 'was quite upset.... but I took full responsibility and said you know "it was for your sake and for hers." It was a difficult time obviously.'[23]

Olga's diary entry of 27 August simply notes, 'My uniquely precious little F'al passed away in peace at 11.40am.' Marina suffered no pain and her distraught sister had risen at 4am to maintain a bedside vigil. It seems to have been left to the doctors to explain to the Princess that her sister had a brain tumour, adding that they had not expected the end so soon.[24] On the eve of the funeral, Olga placed an 'intimate card' in Marina's oak coffin before it was driven down to Windsor. Somehow this small gesture made her feel 'more at peace'.[25] On the day of the funeral, 30 August, the Princess (wearing her sister's black coat, organza hat and mourning veil, for she had no time to pack her own mournings) and Prince Paul travelled from Kensington Palace to Coppins in Marina's Rolls Royce. The Duke of Windsor joined them for a family lunch, 'like a ghost from the past'.[26] At 2pm, the immediate family motored over to St George's Chapel where Olga and Paul took their seats in the Quire. The moving service-conducted by the Dean of Windsor-appropriately included the Collect Hymn from the Burial Office of the Holy Orthodox Church, *Give Rest, O Christ, to Thy Servant with Thy Saints*. As the conclusion of the service, 'all the closest,' including King Constantine, travelled by car to the Royal Burial Ground at Frogmore, where Marina was laid to rest beside her beloved 'Bunna'. Interestingly, Prince George's mortal remains had only been moved to Frogmore, from the Royal Vault, the previous evening. After a brief reception at the Deanery, Olga and Paul returned to Kensington Palace.[27] The following morning, the Princess went over to Buckingham Palace to spend an hour with her Aunt, Princess Alice. 'Shish' proved particularly 'kind and understanding with all her memories of the past, F'al's birth etc. that only she can now remember.[28] Thereafter, Olga seemed in no hurry to leave Kensington Palace, as she settled down to write letters of thanks to friends and entertained various royalties, including Prince Tomislav, to tea. Nevertheless, her return to Pratolino was inevitable and on her final morning in London, 7 September, she 'collapsed in sobs' as Chin, Marina's dog, was led in for a final farewell. After a light lunch at Coppins, the Duke of Kent saw his Aunt off at Heathrow Airport.[29]

Relatives, including her daughter Elizabeth, felt Marina's death seemed 'the final blow' for the Princess and that she now 'really only lived for the moment that she could again be with her sisters and mother. Her life was crushed when they all died.'[30] Her niece Helen admits that for a long period thereafter, her Aunt just 'shut down'. Furthermore, with Marina's death, her strong links with the centre of British royal life diminished and 'she had loved the royal life.'[31] But there may have been more to her increasingly withdrawn behaviour: As Zoia's son, Vincent Poklewski, observed, although the Princess was 'interesting in conversation and could be gay and amusing, she fundamentally did not believe in troubling other people with her feelings'.[32] Furthermore, Olga would have been able to draw comfort from her firmly-held belief, 'that loving ties continue in the life to come *which is the one that really matters.*'[33]

In late September, Olga received a letter from her nephew Edward informing her that Marina's Memorial Service would take place in Westminster Abbey on 25 October. However, she inexplicably became confused over the date of the earlier 40-day Greek Orthodox Parastas (Memorial) Service at the Greek Orthodox Church in Bayswater (thinking it would be on 5 November, rather the correct date of 5 October) and she was unable to attend due to long-standing commitments to do with the sale of Pratolino. Fortunately, the official Memorial Service went as well as could be expected and the Princess listened intently as the Dean of Westminster, Dr Eric Abbott, praised Marina's grace, beauty, spontaneity, courage and 'unswerving service to this land of her adoption.'[34] Olga later travelled down to Frogmore with Prince Edward to inspect his parents' graves. This was followed by tea at Coppins, during which the Duke of Kent gave his Aunt some small mementoes belonging to his late mother. Intriguingly, on the final evening of this English visit, a Slovenian lady, Mrs Stankovic, called at Philip Hay's home to meet Olga and return a photo album that had been confiscated by the Germans at Brdo 25 years previously.[35]

In late November, the Princess received a letter from the Duke of Kent asking his Aunt to return all of his mother's letters to her, so they could be placed in the Royal Archives. (Philip Hay had already indicated this would be expected).[36] However, she was not to be rushed, 'I replied to Ed that I will *eventually* return the letters but they contain many intimate details that can never be published.' This request only served to remind her of how much she missed her sister, 'ringing each other up, our special noises and jokes, *the awful void* without her presence...'[37] Indeed, a few days later, Olga took a solitary walk through the wintry Tuileries Gardens in an attempt 'to recapture our childhood when we stayed with Gammy at the old [Hotel] Continental: Now no sisters to share it with anymore.'[38] Meanwhile, a friend, May Moncrieff, wrote to say that she had recently visited her medium, a Mrs Mackenzie, who had supposedly made contact with Marina. The latter apparently understood how much Olga missed her presence and sent her 'all her love.'[39] Whether such well-meaning offerings were helpful to the grieving Princess is highly questionable. Unsurprisingly, during the Christmas celebrations at Versailles, Olga's mind was elsewhere, 'I was calm inside, thought of Windsor, Frogmore, K.P. and knew F'al was close to each and all.'[40]

As another year unfolded, Paul spent much of January in bed with sciatica, while his wife ventured to Italy to search for a new villa and to go through lists of items at Pratolino with a Sotheby's Representative, Mr Dauphiné, for the upcoming sale of the villa's effects in April. On her return to Paris, Olga received 'a long sort of "dutiful" letter from Ed (obviously told by Ph[ilip] Hay that I [have] never heard from them in months) giving me their general news.' He also mentioned that his mother's legatees ('who?') had received 'their things.' His Aunt observed with irritation: 'I never saw the will and still no mention of giving a souvenir to P[aul] of all people who knew my F'al the longest...' She added, 'This hurts me so much.'[41] The Princess was also concerned about the health of her cousin Margarita, who enjoyed a week's stay at Rue Scheffer but 'smoked without stopping.'[42]

In late March, the Princess arrived at Clarence House for a stay with the Queen Mother and the duo enjoyed a 'très aimable' dinner.[43] She then met with Philip Hay to discuss some answers to questions sent by a Mrs Stella King who was writing a biography of Marina. Later, after reading the proofs, she would berate the talented authoress' 'trashy, common style.'[44] The Queen kindly invited Olga to lunch on 20 March; a fellow guest was Prince Charles whom she thought 'a charming, natural, manly youth with a deep voice.'[45] After a weekend visit to Lady Catherine Brandram at Marlow, the Princess returned to London to lunch with a friend, Alice Winn, and listen to a taped séance, with Mrs Twigg, during which Marina allegedly 'spoke through her.' However, on this occasion, Olga appears sceptical, observing that it was not her sister's style of speaking.[46] Still, memories of her late sister continued to surround her: During an overnight stay at Windsor Castle with Paul, for the Dedication of the recently completed King George VI Memorial Chapel, Olga was given a bedroom previously used by Marina and slept badly.[47]

In April, the Princess returned to Italy for the impending sale at Pratolino. She could not resist a last visit to her former home and wandered unrecognised through the rooms. When the four-day auction commenced, on 21 April, Mr Clark of Sotheby's would phone Olga each evening at the Villa Sparta with the daily total.[48] The sale would eventually raise $727,216.[49] Meanwhile, over at the Villa Sparta, there was a sudden deterioration in the atmosphere, following the arrival of Frederika and her daughter Irene. The former queen was also accompanied by a tiny poodle puppy, against the express wishes of her 'livid' hostess who 'made her feelings clear'. Frederika then became 'indignant' and took Olga to her room so as to 'let fly against Sitta'. The Princess was having none of it and told her firmly 'to control herself.'[50]

As her 66th birthday approached (the first since Marina's death), Olga noted forlornly 'I am the only one left of my family...'[51] Sadly, spiritualism continued to remain at the forefront of the Princess' thoughts and when she met up with May Moncrieff at the De La Pace Hotel in Florence for lunch, the duo enjoyed a long discussion on the subject.[52] Luckily, Olga was suddenly drawn back into the everyday world by the welcome news that Elizabeth and Neil Balfour were soon to marry. Indeed, on her return to Paris in late June, the Princess was touched to find a 'very moving' note from Neil 'asking for my blessing...'[53]

With Pratolino no longer available to them, the Prince and Princess spent part of the summer at the Park Hotel on Florence's Piazza Galileo, before moving, in mid-August, to Munich's Hotel Continental. From there, Olga made a day trip alone to Salzburg to view her niece Helen's new house. The Princess took the trouble to obtain the phone number of Frau Goering from a friend and arranged to visit her at her modest Munich flat. Hermann Goering's widow was now 72 and 'not well'[54] but seemed 'touched' to see Olga whom she kissed 'lovingly'. Over coffee 'Emmy' discussed 'bits of her life since '39' and introduced the Princess to her daughter Edda.[55] There was also an emotive reunion with one of her former employee's at Beli Dvor, Anitsa (who still lived in Belgrade). She informed Olga and Paul that while Beli Dvor had remained largely undisturbed during the German occupation, thereafter the Russians and 'partisan savages' had torn up the Savonnerie carpet to make garden mats. The Princess was also incensed to learn that 'their fat wives took my dresses and cut them to fit them'.[56]

In Paris, Alexander had purchased a new flat and Olga visited him for tea and 'a friendly chat.' She was careful to keep off the subject of his love life but came away with the heartfelt observation 'if only he and

P[aul] could be better friends!'[57] Indeed, Quiss was certainly 'unhappy' to have 'lost his father's respect and confidence...'[58] Thereafter, Olga and Paul flew to London to attend Elizabeth's wedding. However, the flight was delayed due to an altercation between an abusive, 'drugged' hippy and a fellow passenger sitting next to Olga.[59] On their arrival, the Prince and Princess lunched at Brown's Hotel with Neil's mother Lilian ('Big') with whom Olga immediately established an excellent rapport. On the wedding day (23 September), the Princess accompanied her daughter to René for the bride-to-be to have her hair coiffed prior to the ceremony at Chelsea Registry Office. This was followed by a splendid reception at Claridge's. The Balfours then departed for Madrid, where Neil was currently based. It seems to have been a time for weddings as Howard Oxenberg was also remarrying; Olga sent him a note offering her good wishes and reflected, 'He is often in my thoughts and I hope he is really happy.'[60]

As autumn turned to winter, the Princess received the sad news that her Aunt, Princess Alice, had died in London. She observed, 'She is really the last of the family gone and now we are the old generation.'[61] However, the Princess was unable to attend the funeral at Windsor as flights from Orly were cancelled due to fog. Nonetheless, Olga continued to remain focused on events in Greece: She gave tea to her friend Panagiotis Pipinelis, currently the Greek Foreign Minister, who stressed to his hostess that 'His one hope and object is Tino's return as soon as possible.'[62] Christmas shopping, meanwhile, had its hazards: On entering the Jansen boutique to buy a table for Alexander's flat, the Princess glimpsed the Duchess of Windsor. The latter remained an anathema to Olga, who evaded her whenever possible. A few weeks later, Wallis ('Votre Altesse to all the eager females') happened to be placed in an enclosed cubicle next to Olga's at Alexandre, the hairdresser. The American irritated the Princess by talking loudly in bad French, while eating grandiosely from her 'usual' large picnic hamper. By contrast, Olga made do with her usual coffee and a ham baguette.[63]

The Princess was concerned when, on Christmas Eve, a rather gaunt Lilia Ralli arrived with her Christmas parcels and explained she simply did not feel well enough to attend the festivities at Versailles. Although the Prince and Princess attended as usual, they were home by midnight to exchange their Christmas gifts à deux. The year (and decade) ended in relative misery with a faulty boiler, no hot water and Olga suffering from a nasty cold.

Chapter 25 Failing Health

As a new decade dawned, the Princess was weakened by several attacks of 'heart flutters', one of which occurred in mid-January, while Paul was in Switzerland. However, in March, she made a spring visit to the Villa Sparta. It was during this Italian stay that Paul called his wife from Geneva with the worrying news that his doctor had discovered that he had an abnormally high white blood cell count.[1] The Prince subsequently consulted a Professor Barnard in Paris, who confirmed that he had leukaemia, but added that it was not an aggressive or 'serious' type and gave him a course of vitamin B6 tablets.[2] Fortunately, the Prince and Princess were able to draw comfort from the news that Elizabeth was expecting a child in the summer. The couple also endeavoured to see Dimitri and Michel each Sunday, when they lunched together at the Trianon Palace Hotel. They were cheered too by visit from Cecil Parrot and his wife, in early April, during which the four friends talked 'non-stop' of their children, the past and King Peter's deteriorating health (he was suffering from cirrhosis of the liver).[3]

In late May, Olga flew over to London to be with Elizabeth for the birth. She arranged to stay with 'Auntie' Alice Athlone at Kensington Palace. This 87-year-old grandchild of Queen Victoria, who like Olga had lived for a period in South Africa[25], was soon imploring her guest to join her in endless games of scrabble and canasta. In many ways, the two Princess' were complete opposites: Princess Alice was an early riser and ate her breakfast fully-dressed in the long gallery of her home at 9am prompt. However, Olga preferred to breakfast at leisure in bed and this would soon prove her undoing: One morning, Paul telephoned early and his wife was forced to run down a long corridor in her dressing gown, to take the call in the private secretary's office.[4] An indefatigable Auntie also roped the Princess into weeding her garden and, on one occasion, Olga became so exhausted from her endeavours that she was forced to take a nap.[5]

On 6 June, Elizabeth gave birth to a son, Nicholas, at the Welbeck Street Clinic. Olga waited patiently outside the delivery room and was

---

[25] Alice's husband, Alexander, the Earl of Athlone (1874-1957) had been Governor-General of the Union of South Africa from 1924-1930. He was the youngest brother of Queen Mary.

rewarded by hearing the first cries of her new grandson. The Princess also called on Princess Margaret who had just returned from a visit to 'Titoland' and was happy to share her impressions of 'our dear Beli Dvor'.[6] Olga concluded her visit by attending the Queen Mother's 70th birthday party with Paul at Windsor Castle on 19 June. As the Prince and Princess had still failed to find a new summer home, they then spent several weeks at the Carlton Hotel in Lausanne prior to visiting various royal relations in Germany.

On 5 November, Paul and Olga received the sad news that King Peter had died in Los Angeles hospital from cardio-vascular complications following an attack of pneumonia. Prince Tomislav later informed them that the King's body was to be flown to London for a funeral service at the Serbian Church and then interred at Frogmore's Royal Burial Ground (by permission of the Queen). The Princess thought this was 'a great mistake' as this was private ground and 'no Yugoslav will be able to visit it.'[7] However, the funeral plans suddenly changed due to Peter's body remaining in the United States as result of 'intrigues'.[8] Instead, on 8 November, a Memorial Service was held at the Serbian Church in London, which the Prince and Princess both attended. King Peter was subsequently buried at the St Sava Monastery at Libertyville, Illinois in accordance with instructions left in his will.[9]

Just prior to Christmas, Olga experienced another 'heart flutter' and found that she was losing weight. A persistent cough troubled her into the New Year and she ventured out rarely. The Princess was also shaken by the news that Paul's recent blood tests had revealed an elevation in his white cell count.[10] Ironically, it was to be Olga's heart problems which caused the couple the most anxiety throughout the spring: After she had endured further 'flutters' in early March, the Princess entered a Geneva hospital for tests and a specialist concluded that her weight loss was due to the combination of a 'stimulated thyroid', a protein deficiency and a slight kidney infection.[11] Unfortunately, there was no firm conclusion on the cause of the heart palpitations.

On receiving the news that the Serpieris had bought a flat in Lausanne, Olga became increasingly keen to buy a house in Switzerland 'before we are too old to care.'[12] In the meantime, she contented herself with an early Spring sojourn with Helen at the Villa Sparta, and passed her time reading a copy of Frederika's soon-to-be published autobiography "A Measure of Understanding". The Princess concluded that 'Frederika's object is to make herself touching in the Greek peoples' eyes'.[13] A sceptical Olga noted too that 'the style is far richer than her normal' adding that 'one senses another pen arranging her phrases.'[14] Interestingly, the former queen had already asked Queen Mother Helen not to show certain parts of the book to the Princess as she was too "religious" to grasp her writing, a fact that Sitta unwisely shared with her cousin. Olga took her revenge, a few days later, during a lunch with Frederika in Rome, when she 'surprised' the budding authoress by displaying an adept ability to 'grasp her theory of the nuclear forces.' Furthermore, when the exiled ex-queen complained that most of the international press (and many Greeks) had been 'enchanted' by her memoirs, but that the British *Daily Telegraph* had not, the Princess informed her tartly that 'one mustn't expect all sugar.'[15]

Throughout this Italian interlude, Olga continued to suffer several attacks of heart palpitations. She became so frail, that Helen called in Dr Weber who gave his patient a 'cure' regime.[16] This was in addition to another British-made heart 'remedy' recently dispatched to the Princess by the Swiss heart specialist.[17] Yet, the 'flutters' continued apace as she moved on to Lausanne in mid-June and, at Sitta's urging, Olga consulted a local homeopath who gave her two prescriptions to take once Weber's 'cure' was finished. Which doctor was responsible for 'the sachets of 4 pills' she took before dinner that evening is unclear but they left her decidedly wobbly![18]

The Princess returned to London in July. On one particular occasion, she joined the Hays and her niece Alexandra on a visit to Alice Gloucester, who now lived in Marina's former apartments at Kensington Palace. The sight of these stalwarts of her late sister's life gathered together once more 'in that salon... finished me, in sobs...'[19] Clearly, memories of Marina could still evoke an outpouring of raw grief. Thereafter, Olga and Paul spent part of the summer at Rest Harrow, a house belonging to the Astor family in Sandwich, Kent. They were accompanied by Neil, Elizabeth, her children and the twins. Miss Ede, now aged 75, came for a visit and during a long talk, the Princess gleaned that the former nurse had endured a hard life and was now 'v[ery] believing, tolerant and gentle'.[20] However, a visit from Cecil Beaton was sadly overshadowed by the Princess suffering further 'flutter' attacks, culminating in treatment from a local doctor. Beaton would later write of the visit, 'It is sad to see Princess O[lga] in exile and she has never got accustomed to being treated as an ordinary citizen (one evening she got up from dinner and wanting us to stop our conversation, said "I'm standing", to which P[rince] P[aul] shot to his feet, bowed in an exaggerated way and said, "Oh, I beg your pardon, Madam"'.[21] If Beaton's account is accurate, was Paul simply making light of the situation or actually mocking his wife's regal behaviour?

In September, the Princess prepared for a visit from Frederika, who was spending a week at Paris' chic Raphael Hotel. To Olga's amazement, the former queen had asked Lilia Ralli to act as her Lady-in-Waiting and 'fix up parties for her!!'[22] The Prince and Princess arranged a special 'meatless and fishless' meal at Rue Scheffer for their vegetarian cousin, and although Frederika was cordial, 'there was no small talk', with the ex-queen preferring to discuss 'her brand of philosophy and religion' with Paul.[23] There was news too of a developing romance between King Peter's son, Crown Prince Alexander and Maria da Glória of Orléans-Braganza, a niece of Isabelle, Countess of Paris ('Bebelle'). 'Little' Alexander (who was currently serving with the British army in Northern Ireland) kindly sent his Uncle Paul a letter telling him of his new love, although the Princess was somewhat taken aback to learn that Maria da Glória's mother, Princess María, had written to the Countess of Paris 'asking for details about the boy whom none of them have heard of!'[24] As the couple's betrothal was imminent, Olga and Paul subsequently travelled to London and arranged with Cartier to have a diamond taken from a pair of Princess Nicholas' earrings and set into a ring for Alexander to give his fiancée. When informed of his Aunt and Uncle's largesse, the Crown Prince 'seemed overcome!'[25] The engagement would be formally announced to the press on 21 December.

Thereafter, Olga joined the Serpieris for a visit to a Parisian theatre to see the avant-garde revue, "Oh Calcutta". The cast appeared on stage mostly naked and the Princess was shocked by the 'indecent pornographic dialogues' but felt that this 'must surely wear out with time tho' it marks our epoch in an ugly way.'[26] Certainly, nowadays, even the sight of her beloved niece Helen wearing trousers was enough to draw some (rare) criticism: 'They don't suit her'.[27] Meanwhile, the Duke of Kent wrote to tell his Aunt that he was selling Coppins and moving to Anmer Hall, on the Sandringham estate. With so many changes, dwelling on the past must have seemed more reassuring and Olga spent the late autumn diligently reading through Princess Nicholas' diaries.[28]

As 1972 began, Olga was greatly concerned over what she regarded as the Soviet Union's increasing expansionist policies. She was convinced that the Maltese were trying to 'kick out' the British Navy from their bases on the island, which the Soviets would then 'pounce on.'[29] Furthermore, after reading a 'terrifying' article in the *Sunday Telegraph*, the Princess feared 'red influences' in England (where there was currently a miner's strike) and thought that the Queen was taking 'a risky chance' going off on an official tour of the Far East at such a difficult time.[30] She was anxious too about the health of her former fiancé, King Frederik of Denmark, who had recently suffered a heart attack and sent his wife Ingrid a telegram with best wishes for his recovery. However, when Rico died on 14 January, Olga admitted that it felt 'like another page of my youth torn out.'[31] She subsequently watched the funeral service from Roskilde on television.

In early February, Crown Prince Alexander brought his fiancée to dinner at Rue Scheffer. The Princess approved of Maria da Glória whom she found to be 'full of charm, brains and warmth,' and thought the couple 'madly in love'.[32]Alexander was 'trusting in' Paul and Olga 'to help and advise him' over the various complexities involved in a marriage between someone of the Orthodox faith and a Roman Catholic.[33] However, Olga was soon dismayed to read an article in the *Sunday Telegraph* which indicated that many Yugoslavs were 'indignant' over Crown Prince Alexander marrying a Roman Catholic 'without an orthodox ceremony before' and it even hinted that he might step down in favour of Prince Tomislav.[34] Olga was certainly on Alexander's side over his marriage[35] but she advised him to keep his own counsel for now.[36] Within days (and with the assistance of the Count of Paris), the Princess succeeded in persuading the bride-to-be's family to agree to an Orthodox marriage service being conducted prior to the Roman Catholic ceremony thus silencing the critics.[37]

On 28 May, the Duke of Windsor died. Although, the Prince and Princess were in London at the time (for a special engagement blessing service for Alexander and Maria da Glória at the Serbian Orthodox Church) neither of them attended the funeral at Windsor on 5 June. The couple returned to Paris in time to celebrate Olga's birthday over lunch with the twins at the Trianon Palace. There is evidence that the Princess had come to terms with Michel Bourbon-Parma's special place in Maria Pia and the twins' lives. On Dimitri and Michel's birthday, she had a very positive talk with 'Big Miche' and he subsequently sent her 'an enormous hortensia' with a card bearing a few kind words 'as I think he was touched by what I said to him' which had been 'on my mind for some time...'[38] By contrast, her relationship with Alexander was increasingly fraught: Olga noted that he had neither attended the twins' birthday celebrations nor sent a gift.[39]

The Prince and Princess travelled to Madrid, in late June, to stay with Frederika's daughter Sophie and Prince Juan Carlos at the Zarzuela Palace. Paul later had an audience with General Franco at the Pardo Palace, while his wife had a separate meeting with the Caudillo's wife, Carmen. Unfortunately, the ladies' conversation was rather stilted as the latter only spoke 'broken' French[40]. On 1 July, Olga and Paul flew to Seville to attend the Yugoslav royal wedding festivities at nearby Villamanrique de la Condesa. The Princess noted with feeling, 'How long we have toiled to make this day a success.'[41] The earlier Orthodox service, held in a courtyard off the village square, was deemed a 'great success' and, touchingly, Olga was given the honour of escorting the Crown Prince. Thereafter, she and Paul accompanied the couple and the bride's parents to the local village church for the Roman Catholic service.[42]

On the Princess' return to Paris, she was heartened to learn that the British Foreign Office were to allow access to previously unreleased documents (relating to Yugoslavia in 1941) and that after 31 long years 'justice is coming to light'.[43] Shortly thereafter, Marina's nephew Prince William of Gloucester was killed in an air accident. His mother Alice was naturally devastated and Olga immediately 'phoned to commiserate, but instead found that the grieving Duchess' 'pain haunts me...' as it brought back memories of her own anguish from eighteen years earlier.[44] The Princess also took a keen interest in the Queen and Prince Philip's State Visit to Belgrade. On her return, Lilibet provided Olga with interesting details of her stay at Beli Dvor over lunch at Buckingham Palace. These included some revealing observations on Tito's large appetite and table manners.[45] Paul then joined the Princess in London to attend the Queen and Prince Philip's Silver Wedding Service of Thanksgiving at Westminster Abbey on 20 November. He had some interesting news to impart: During his wife's absence, Alexander had brought a new 'girl', Princess Barbara of Liechtenstein, to lunch at Rue Scheffer. She 'was nice and quite pretty'[46] and there was the possibility that Quiss might remarry.

On her return to Paris, Olga immediately telephoned Alexander and invited him to tea. They initially discussed her son's wish to remarry. This latest development seems to have rattled the Princess who quickly turned the conversation round to the topic of her beloved twins 'and what a sad fact it is he shows them so little interest and affection.' When Alexander tried to put forward his viewpoint, there was not an ounce of understanding from his mother. Instead, she tactlessly informed her son that the twins now looked to Maria Pia's confidante, Michel of Bourbon-Parma, 'much more as a father'. Nevertheless, after having endured his mother's verbal onslaught, Alexander was finally able to obtain his parents' agreement to his remarriage.[47]

On 16 December, the Prince and Princess lunched with Frederika at a 'cheese restaurant' in Paris. Olga happened to mention the contents of a recent article in the *International Herald Tribune* which implied that King Constantine would return to Greece without any conditions. His mother replied that this was not true and immediately went off to telephone her son, causing the Princess to note 'We feel she dominates him still.' Privately, Olga was firmly of the opinion that Constantine 'ought to work with the Col[onel]s [of the ruling military junta].'[48]

As the year drew to a close, Alexander introduced 'his new flame'[49] to his mother, a prospect he subsequently admitted to find 'terrifying.'[50] Olga proved far from welcoming, eyeing Barbara up and down with a distinctly frosty stare and offering the impression that she had never heard of the Liechtenstein Princely Family.[51] It did not help that Quiss' intended was wearing trousers *'to meet me'*, an indication that the Princess regarded such attire as both disrespectful and decidedly lèse-majesté. Olga concluded that Barbara was 'pretty, self-possessed, [with] no sign of shyness and obviously [has] got him under her spell'.[52]The Princess therefore started the New Year of 1973 focused on finding out more 'details about *this Barbara*.'[53] This included consultations with a friend in Zurich[54] and also with Georgina ('Gina'), the wife of the Sovereign Prince of Liechtenstein. Both sources spoke well of Barbara, although Gina explained that her family had no great wealth. On hearing this, the Princess suddenly became concerned that 'maybe Barb[ara] had the wrong impression' of Alexander's own financial situation and was at pains to emphasise to Gina that her son only had a small flat and regular income from his employment at Cartier but no 'large fortune...'[55] Perhaps to her surprise, Olga later learned from the same source that Alexander's subsequent visit to the Principality had gone particularly well and everyone (including Barbara's parents, Prince Johannes of Liechtenstein and his wife Karoline) thought him 'charming'.[56] Certainly, the feeling was reciprocated and, on his return to Paris, Alexander informed his mother that his prospective in-laws were 'adorable'.[57]

On 7 February, Olga was annoyed to discover that Quiss' engagement was featured in the midday editions of *France Soir*. The Princess was concerned too that someone would inform Dimitri or Michel before she had the chance 'to prepare them'. However, Paul advised his wife against tackling Alexander directly over the matter.[58] Yet, even several weeks later, Olga was still struggling to embrace the situation: When Alexander and Barbara ('this time in a dress and hair piled high') came to tea, she made sure that only 'banalités' were discussed.[59] The Princess' angst was hardly helped by news of a plunging dollar which would eventually result in Paul and Olga's investment income being reduced by half.[60] To add to her perceived woes, during a subsequent visit to the Villa Sparta, Olga fell, twisted her ankle and chipped a bone on her foot. The doctor ordered her to rest for two weeks. However, even in Italy, there was no getting away from Alexander and Barbara's romance. Some friends, Jean and Bunny Boissevin came to lunch; they had recently met the couple and found Barbara, 'lovely and charming and him so in love!' The Princess' response was somewhat bizarre, 'I just said yes, but that I don't much relish having 2 daughters-in-law!'[61]

Thereafter, Cecil Parrott sought assistance from the Prince and Princess in connection with his forthcoming memoirs. Fortunately, 'a lot of questions were put right' during a 'long session' at Rue Scheffer, on17 April, and he left 'v[ery] pleased.'[62, 26] Paul and Olga then flew over to London, on the eve of the Prince's 80th birthday, to be present at a party in his honour at Clarence House, hosted by the Queen Mother. However,

---

[26] Cecil Parrot was now Professor of Central and South-Eastern European Studies at the University of Lancaster.

in general, Olga was falling out of love with London: She found Kensington High Street remarkably changed and particularly bemoaned the demise of her favourite Derry and Tom's department store, while the streets were deemed to be full of 'awful hippy people.'[63] The Princess happened to be still in the British capital, when she heard over the radio, on 1 June, that Greece had been declared a republic. Her thoughts immediately turned to King Constantine, '*My heart ached all day for him and all of us, the few of the family left without a country...*'[64] When the plebiscite required to ratify this major constitutional change subsequently confirmed that nearly 80% of the Greek people favoured a republic, Olga was 'stunned'.[65] However, she was not best pleased when the now ex-King Constantine went on to make a statement claiming 'that it's all a farce and he remains king just the same', observing that '*such words cannot help his cause.*'[66]

Meanwhile, at Rue Scheffer, a new butler Camille ('Cammy') arrived and the Princess took tea with Alexander, Barbara and her mother, Karoline. Olga seemed almost relieved to find the latter was 'a very nice person speaking good English and intelligent...'[67] The two mothers met alone the following afternoon for 'a talk' during which the Princess spoke to her 'v[ery] openly of Al's character etc.' Was she still hoping to derail the marriage? If this was her purpose, she had clearly failed for Karoline made it perfectly clear that her daughter and Alexander 'were made for each other'.[68] Olga now realised she had little choice but to 'face' the marriage but 'with no feeling it can last...'[69]

In late June, Olga made a trip to Denmark to stay with Princess Margaret of Denmark at her residence at Gentofte. She enthused, 'Here I am in the land of my ancestors at last...when I think I nearly came here in 1922 as a future Queen ..51 yrs ago!'[70] She walked through the beech woods (which reminded her of Russia) with her hostess to nearby Bernstorff, 'the old home of my gr[eat] gr[and] parents that Vuzzie and the others all loved.'[71] 'Meg' later provided the Princess with some 'fascinating' family correspondence and photo albums to look through. Although Queen Ingrid was away at her summer home at Gråsten, she kindly arranged for Olga to be given a private tour of the main state rooms of Fredensborg Palace.[72]

Olga and Paul spent the first part of August at Claridge's in London, from where they made regular visits to Elizabeth and Neil at Chelsea. The Princess deduced that Neil seemed 'more and more keen on politics.'[73] After a brief stay at the Carlton Hotel in Lausanne, the duo returned to Rue Scheffer to receive some news about Alexander's upcoming nuptials. Barbara's mother ('Princess Liechtenstein') had written to say that after several 'fruitless attempts' to obtain permission for a church wedding (Barbara was a Roman Catholic and, of course,

Alexander was a divorcé), it had been decided that the couple would marry at a civil ceremony, on 2 November, at the Mairie of Paris' 8th Arrondissement.[74] However, Olga continued to be unenthusiastic about the marriage and noted taciturnly that Princess Liechtenstein had dared to presume to address her by her Christian name, in her recent correspondence, although 'I had not asked her to'.[75]

The Princess entertained the Greek politician Spyros Markezinis and his wife to tea at Rue Scheffer, in late September. During the two-hour visit, Spyros 'unfolded' his plan to become Greek Prime Minister and organise fresh elections.[76] Shortly thereafter, the Princess was delighted to learn that he had been given a mandate to form a civilian government and observed, 'May God inspire him.'[77] However, it appears that ex-King Constantine did not approve of the new Prime Minister, causing his Aunt to note 'what a pity *and alas one knows who shaped that opinion for him*',[78] which can only have been a dig at Frederika. Unfortunately, the Princess seems to have discussed the matter with Queen Mother Helen for Paul would later warn his wife that 'he fears Sitta said too much [of Olga's feelings] to make Tino mistrust me...'[79]

In October, the Prince and Princess celebrated their Golden Wedding anniversary with a family party, hosted by Maria Pia, at Versailles. Olga was enchanted to receive a little gilt box from Paul which opened to reveal a miniature mechanical singing bird. However, on their actual wedding anniversary, the couple slipped unobtrusively into the Russian Orthodox Church to receive a thanksgiving blessing. After this celebration, the Princess' thoughts finally seemed to settle on Alexander's forthcoming nuptials. As a wedding gift, she decided to give her son a silver tea service which she had inherited from Miss Fox (and was originally a retirement gift from the three royal sisters to their beloved Nurnie). In addition, Paul gave his son amethyst cufflinks, while Barbara received Olga's diamond link bracelet and a gold cigarette case.[80] On the eve of the wedding, the Prince and Princess held a lunch party at Rue Scheffer for the visiting Liechtenstein contingent, with a menu which included 'the best' foie gras.[81] Following the civil ceremony at the Mairie next day, the wedding party drove off to a restaurant in the city's outskirts for a celebration lunch. Olga subsequently received a letter from Barbara thanking her for the gifts and 'full of tender feelings for Al. and us...'[82]

Even following her marriage, Barbara still experienced 'a difficult time'[83] from her mother-in-law. Olga's niece Helen ascribes this to her Aunt's shyness with outsiders or those she still deemed to be outsiders.[84] Even so, the Princess could undoubtedly be wounding, and once tactlessly informed her new daughter-in-law, "Oh I love Maria Pia so much".[85] Olga was then disconcerted to learn, from her ex-daughter-in-law, that

Alexander had telephoned to ask if Michel and Dimitri could join him and his new wife on a shoot 'and spend the night!!' She concluded, 'It's obvious that B[arbara] has started to plan ways of Al[exander] seeing more of his children' and added, 'as long as it does not mean drawing them away from their mother'. Indeed, Olga believed that 'a line must be drawn somewhere and he [Alexander] can't have it both ways.'[86] But perhaps it was the Princess who was trying 'to have it both ways', given that she had recently accused her son of showing little interest in his sons' upbringing. However, Barbara chose to remain positive and focused on building a better relationship between her husband and his parents. She regularly invited Olga and Paul to their home for Sunday lunch or afternoon tea and was pleased to find that they eventually became 'really close again.'[87]

During a subsequent pre-Christmas visit to Florence, the Princess received the news from Athens of another coup d'état, with Adamantios Androutsopoulos being appointed Prime Minister in place of her friend Spyros Markezinis, who had only himself taken on that role in October. Suddenly, her hopes of renewing her Greek diplomatic passport were dashed, although she later secured a French one through a contact at the Quai d'Orsay.[88] In addition, Olga received the disturbing news that her cousin Irene-now much weakened by ongoing treatment for throat cancer-was in hospital with bronchial pneumonia.

Christmas Eve was spent as usual at Versailles. Soon thereafter Crown Prince Alexander and his wife arrived to welcome in the New Year of 1974 at Rue Scheffer. Olga then ventured to London to see Elizabeth and Neil and her grandchildren. Otherwise, the Princess spent much of her time making a 'copy' of what she had written in her diary about the events surrounding the 1941 coup d'etat *from my own view point* for inclusion in Cecil Parrot's book.[89] However, the version which she supplied to the author was clearly a "revised" account, written with the benefit of hindsight and going into greater detail than the original diary entries. Olga had also been given the chance to read a rough draft of Cecil's book and was amazed at the British SOE's attempts 'to undermine and destroy P[aul]'s policy as Regent to a degree I never realized at the time.'[90]

Thankfully, as winter moved into spring, the Princess was at last warming to her new daughter-in-law Barbara noting, 'She [is] v[ery] tactful and nice, showing an interest in people of our family she has never heard of.' Olga particularly enjoyed the 'peacefully happy' family lunches at Alexander and Barbara's flat.[91] The Princess then decided to spend Holy Week in Florence and arrived just as her cousin Irene slipped into a coma. She died in the early hours of Easter Sunday. King Constantine travelled down from Rome for the funeral on 18th April. As Olga recounts it, over dinner the previous evening, the former sovereign had 'exposed his theory' on the 'chaos' prevailing in Greece, which to her displeasure he blamed on her friend Markezinis 'as usual' and the army.[92]

Olga celebrated her 71st birthday in Paris with lunch at her niece Helen's house. This event was followed by a summer visit to London, where she and the Balfours spent an idyllic midsummer day with the Ogilvys at Thatched House Lodge. However, no sooner had the Princess returned to Paris than she received a telephone call from the Duke of Kent informing her of the death of Zoia Poklewski. For Olga, this event marked the passing of 'the last link with the happy years and F'al in dear Coppins ...'[93] Sadly, Paul's health also continued to cast a long shadow: A recent x-ray had revealed 'a virus on the coating of his left lung' for which he was given a course of antibiotics.[94]

Meanwhile, in Greece, the military regime controlled by the hardliner Brigadier Demetrios Ioannidis crumbled over a growing crisis in Cyprus: A recent Greek-backed coup to unseat the island's legitimate Makarios government had provided Turkey with the ideal pretext for invading the north of the island on 22 July. Konstantinos Karamanlis was later invited to return to Athens, from his self-imposed exile in Paris, to form an interim national unity (civilian) government. Many of the Princess' friends in Athens thought that the time was now ripe for King Constantine to return. However, the politically astute Olga was far more cautious, 'Alas, I fear his return is a long way off as in 7 years the idea of monarchy has faded...'[95] Indeed, by September, following a conversation with Lilia Ralli (who had just returned from the Greek capital) she was even more pessimistic and opined, 'I don't see much hope for the monarchy.'[96]

Paul and Olga then moved on to the familiar environs of the Carlton in Lausanne. It was there that they learned that the Balfour's marriage had run its natural course and that Neil had moved out of the marital home.[97] Back in autumnal Paris, the Prince and Princess received the British historian Miss Phyllis Auty, who interviewed Paul for a book she was writing on his Regency.[98] However, the experience left him exhausted.[99] To add to his woes, rising inflation and staff costs were eating into the couple's already much-reduced income.[100]

A few months later, Olga learned of her daughter's new friendship with the Welsh actor, Richard Burton, and feared it would soon be all over the press.[101] Elizabeth subsequently brought 'Burton' to meet her parents at Rue Scheffer and they later lunched together at Pruniers. As she observed the nervous, chain-smoking actor, Olga acknowledged that he seemed 'clever and cultured'. Nevertheless, she thought him 'a hard type' and seemed disconcerted that her daughter was so 'adoring' of all that he said.[102] The following day, the Prince and Princess lunched again with the couple (this time at a hotel in the Rue des Beaux-Arts) at the conclusion of which Mr Burton 'took the plunge and told P[aul] he wished to marry our daughter!' Olga seemed taken aback by her husband's blithe response, "I hope you'll be very happy." When the actor then turned to the Princess, she opined unenthusiastically, 'She is old enough to know what she wants.'[103] However, in the taxi home, Olga finally let down her guard and 'cried all the way'.[104] Sleep evaded her that night as 'thoughts and worries went raging through' her mind; she also tormented herself over not remaining calm, in spite of having prayed to do so.[105] As with Alexander, she simply could not accept that Elizabeth was an adult with the freedom to make her own future decisions. Inevitably, Olga and Paul had several phone calls from the British and French press and when the Princess later watched Richard Burton on television announcing his marriage to "Princess Elizabeth of Yugoslavia", she observed cynically that this would provide 'better publicity than Mrs Balfour of course.'[106] Olga turned to her niece Helen for comfort and found 'her presence brought back my balance and logic as she too has so much of both of my precious sisters.'[107]

A couple of weeks later, Olga returned to London to stay with Alice Athlone at Kensington Palace and decided to visit Mrs Twigg for a 'quiet sitting'. The medium apparently 'saw and spoke to many of my dear ones' including her sisters and her recently-deceased cousin Irene.[108] The Princess must have gleaned some comfort from her 'sitting' for she slept better that evening.[109] She was further cheered by the news from Paris, that Paul had received a 'reassuring' result from his latest blood test.[110] Before she returned to France, Olga spoke by telephone to Howard Oxenberg who was staying at London's Berkeley Hotel. He had recently met Richard Burton and found him to be 'charming'. Howard also thought the actor would make Elizabeth happy, which was 'the chief thing'.[111] Indeed, as Christmas approached, the Princess gradually adopted a more sympathetic approach to her daughter's situation. However, Elizabeth and Mr Burton would never marry and eventually decided to go their own separate ways. As usual, Olga and Paul ventured to Maria Pia's Versailles home on Christmas Eve for 'the usual mad rush' of present giving.[112]

Olga flew over to London, in early February, to attend the wedding of Lady Catherine Brandram's son Richard. Meanwhile, in Paris, the Prince and Princess continued to see Alexander and Barbara regularly. Quiss clearly adored Barbara and told his father that she was 'the best wife a man can dream of'.[113] This happiness spilled over into Alexander's relationship with Prince Paul which, to Olga's delight, was now much closer.[114] To signal her pleasure at the success of her son's marriage, the Princess arranged for her friend, Father Oblensky, to conduct a short service of blessing for the couple at the Russian Orthodox Church.[115] Then, in late April, Olga joined her cousin Eugenie on a visit to Langenburg, to help their cousin Margarita celebrate her 70th birthday. While they were both touched to find the Greek flag flying from the castle ramparts in their honour, Olga became somewhat sniffy over the birthday girl's conspicuous smoking habit. Before departing, she gave everyone a lecture on 'the selfishness of people who smoke during meals...' However, her efforts were totally wasted on Margarita who 'calmly' continued to puff on regardless![116]

On returning home, the Princess hosted a large Sunday tea party to celebrate Paul's 82nd birthday. With so many friends and relatives in her age group now ailing, Olga took every opportunity to spread the 'faith' advocated by Nicol Campbell's "Path of Truth" to those in need, including Aunt Ena's daughter, the Infanta Beatriz.[117] However, when the latter's brother, Juan de Borbón, made a statement from his Portuguese home to the effect that he was the 'legitimate King' of Spain and calling for the ailing General Franco's retirement, the Princess deemed Don Juan's actions 'stupid and clumsy'[118] for she was aware that his son Juan Carlos had long been groomed to succeed the increasingly frail dictator as head of state.[119] [27]

In late July, Olga ventured to Gstaad with the senior twins for a stay in a rented chalet. Although she was soon bemoaning her teenage grandsons' untidiness, she adored their company and was happy that they were able to socialise freely with people of their own age. On occasion, the Princess talked to an 'understanding' Dimitri of Beli Dvor, Kenya and South Africa.[120] When Paul subsequently joined the trio, his wife would prepare him simple dinners of soup and scrambled eggs. Thereafter, the Prince and Princess moved to Lausanne, from where they made regular excursions to Geneva to sort out their financial affairs, as they were now officially domiciled in Switzerland for taxation purposes.[121]

In Paris, Olga was now obliged to take a taxi as the driver Fernand Bacca had retired.[122] He was not replaced. The Princess eventually made regular use of public transport, although she was 'like a little child' the first time she travelled by bus. Indeed, at this stage in her life, Olga's great-niece Sophie ('Sofinka') found her to be somewhat spoiled and 'never touched by the real world.'[123] She certainly continued to be aware of the 'large deficits'[124] in her and Paul's incomes and fretted that this might make it 'impossible' for them to carry on living at Rue Scheffer.[125]

---

[27] General Franco died on 20 November and Juan Carlos was proclaimed King of Spain two days later.

Nevertheless, the Princess maintained a keen sense of humour and was delighted to come across a children's book about a hamster called "Olga Polga".[126]

In mid-December, Olga had a surprise visit from her nephew Michael who brought 'a friend' to lunch. This turned out to be his future wife, Baroness Marie-Christine von Reibnitz. The Princess describes her as 'tall, Check [sic] and half Austrian, [with] long loose hair and quite pretty' and possessed of 'a very forceful and assured manner'. Nonetheless, she warmed to the Baroness and thought she displayed 'just the right influence' over her nephew.[127] As the year drew to a close, Olga was absorbed in reading a book, "Life in the World Unseen", which advocated that our actions in this life affect our future in the hereafter. This view, she concluded, 'simply confirms what I feel to be true.'[128]

Chapter 26 Alone

As a new year dawned, Elizabeth came over to Paris for a brief holiday at Rue Scheffer. Olga notes that she told her parents 'little about herself; more about the girls.'[1] The Princess was nevertheless determined to probe, although this proved counter-productive as Elizabeth eventually indicated that she was returning to London 'as she felt unwelcome and in the way.'[2] When the Princess subsequently browsed through her 1961 diaries, she fondly recalled her visit to New York for Catherine's birth and 'how lovely, affect[ionate] and natural Eliz[abeth] was with me..our jokes, my little gifts and now?'[3] Olga was equally inquisitive when news of the separation of Princess Margaret and Lord Snowdon broke while she was enjoying her spring stay at Claridge's: She telephoned the Queen over 'all this trouble' and was also on the verge of contacting Princess Margaret herself. However, Her Majesty wisely offered the 'advice' that she should instead write to her younger sister.[4]

On her return to Paris, Olga received the news that Alexander had left Cartier for a new position with Harry Winston, at a much-improved salary. She decided to entertain his new boss to lunch at Rue Scheffer and, keen to make a favourable impression, 'fished' out her pink diamond ring and emerald earrings for the occasion. These, she later noted with satisfaction, were 'greatly admired' by the executive.[5] However, she was not initially so enthusiastic over an invitation to attend, with Paul, the Queen's 50th birthday ball at Windsor Castle noting, 'of course we could not refuse but for me *it's an awful effort* to dress up and stay up late.'[6] Nevertheless, in the end, she again dressed to impress in a dark blue Dior mousseline evening dress accessorised with her best diamonds. It was certainly a busy time for such festivities, for the following month, the Princess travelled to Florence to attend Queen Mother Helen's 80th birthday celebrations at the home of her nephew, the Duke of Aosta. Although an ailing Paul subsequently joined his wife for a week's holiday at the Villa Sparta, on his return to Paris he felt 'too tired' to attend Hélène's confirmation at Versailles.[7] However, he and Olga were buoyed-up by a favourable review of Cecil Parrott's newly-published book "The Tightrope" in the Times Literary Supplement.[8] Shortly thereafter, the Princess attended the British Embassy's annual garden party (to celebrate the Sovereign's official birthday), and decided to have some fun at the expense of 'a Soviet fat woman who was smelling a pink rose....I don't know what urged me to ask her if she was French, guessing she was not-she looked nervous and walked off quickly-probably the Soviet Ambassadress.'[9]

On Olga's 73rd birthday, Paul gave his wife a bunch of Azaleas and some of her favourite Calèche perfume. The couple were joined at Rue Scheffer for a birthday lunch by Alexander, Barbara, her mother and Diddie Serpieri. A few days later, it was the twins' turn to celebrate their 18th birthday with a lunch at Versailles. However, behind the smiles, Prince Paul's strength continued to ebb amid the scorching temperatures and in mid-June, he received treatment for a streptococcal infection.[10] Disturbingly, the Prince's white corpuscle count continued to remain elevated.[11] Meanwhile, Olga was doing her best to assist her husband in 'sorting and classifying' his papers for forwarding to Columbia University, in New York, for inclusion in their archives.[12]

In July, the Prince's doctor requested a second opinion on his condition from Professor Jean Bernard, a renowned haematologist at the Institute of Leukaemia in Paris. Bernard examined the Prince on 20 July and prescribed a tonic, as he found his patient was 'too thin and tired.' Yet, Olga remained resolute, remarking, 'God is merciful and has all the healing power according to one's faith.'[13] The following month, Paul and Olga travelled to Lausanne for a holiday at the Carlton. Unfortunately, the journey only served to tire the Prince further and, at times, he could barely summon the energy to walk.[14] Queen Mother Helen was a fellow guest, although she too was failing and often suffered from 'turns' which triggered memory lapses.[15]

On their return to Paris in September, Olga realised that Paul was gradually slipping away from her. She wrote to Nicol Campbell begging for prayers to be said as 'so many miraculous cures have been thanked for through the Path'[16] and at times she even remained 'convinced of a complete recovery.'[17] However, the signs were increasingly unfavourable and, on 10 September, Paul was admitted to the American Hospital. After Olga and Alexander had endured a somewhat depressing meeting with Professor Bernard on 12 September, the Princess decided to phone Elizabeth, who arrived next morning from London. On 14 September, after maintaining an all-night vigil at her husband's bedside, the Princess returned briefly to Rue Scheffer to rest. However, she was roused, at 6.30pm, by an urgent summons from the hospital. Sadly, by the time she arrived, '<u>My Mincey had passed away peacefully...there are no words, just to thank God he never suffered and is happy...</u>'[18] Olga remained calm and composed a statement for the press.

Mourners soon began arriving in Paris for the funeral; these included all of the Princess' nieces and nephews, as well as the former Kings of Greece, Italy and Romania. Crown Prince Alexander of Yugoslavia flew over from his home in Brazil. On 17 September, in the presence of his wife and immediate family, Paul's coffin was transferred from the Chapel of the American Hospital to the Russian Orthodox Church, where it would remain until the funeral. Four former Royal Yugoslav Army officers provided a guard of honour.[19] The day of the funeral, 20 September, proved 'harrowing': Olga took a pill to calm her nerves before leaving for the church accompanied by her children. She was particularly moved by the presence of a large crowd of mourners, as well as by the 'masses' of wreaths carefully arranged on the steps of the church. As the Princess stepped inside to take her seat, her eyes were drawn to the cushion bearing her late husband's Garter regalia.[20] The presence of these symbols was particularly appropriate for, as the Duke of Kent recalls, the Prince 'of course thought of himself as an Englishman'...[21] At the conclusion of the service, the family accompanied the Prince's mortal remains to the Sainte-Geneviève-des-Bois Russian Cemetery, where they were temporarily placed in a 'caveau'.[22]

Fortunately, in the days immediately following her husbands' death, the Princess had the company of her grandson Michel, at Rue Scheffer. He was impressed that his grieving grandmother behaved 'with great courage and dignity and never complained.'[23] Olga found that 'sleep at night is merciful but the awakening is so desolate,' but she was comforted by her firmly-held belief that Paul and Nicholas 'are certainly reunited.'[24] Later, as she was packing up the Prince Paul's Garter Star, Ribbon and George for returning to the Queen through the British Embassy, the Princess received word from the Duke of Kent that there would be a service at St George's Chapel, in November, during which Paul's Garter banner would be 'laid up' on the Altar before being returned to the family.[25] There were also the inevitable financial matters to deal with and, initially, Olga did not even know how to write a cheque.[26] Although Paul had already set up trust funds for his wife and family, the Princess was still required to endure a meeting with her bankers to discuss taxation 'till my head nearly burst.'[27] Despite the kind ministrations of Barbara and her niece Helen, what Olga missed most was the 'daily companionship [and] exchange of thoughts' with her husband[28] and each evening as she passed Paul's bedroom she would murmur 'good night'.[29] A particular blow was the departure, on 7 October, of her Spanish maid Maria who 'hinted' that she had been 'badly treated and spoken to' by other staff members.[30] It seems that without the Captain at the helm, the household was quickly descending into disarray. The Princess now appeared to be 'lost'[31] and with no apparent desire to take on any responsibility.

Yet, friends and family continued to offer comfort: In late October, the Queen Mother made a visit to Paris on official business and asked

Olga to join her lunch party at the British Embassy. Queen Elizabeth made time to receive the Princess privately beforehand so they could reminisce about Paul.[32] In early November, there was a brief, but welcome visit from her niece Alexandra and her husband Angus Ogilvy. Meanwhile, Elizabeth suggested that they spend Christmas together, along with her children, in Switzerland and she subsequently arranged to rent a chalet in Gstaad.

The Princess then flew over to England and, on 23 November, drove down in Marina's 'dear old Rolls' from London to Windsor Castle for the 'lovely, moving' Garter memorial service which took place during Evensong.[33] However, Paul's death continued to take its toll and, next day, she forgot to join two friends for tea, venturing instead to visit her niece Helen at her London home.[34] Before leaving England, Olga met with the British historian Miss Phyllis Auty and it was arranged she would come to Paris, in early December, to consult the Princess' diaries. During the academic's visit, Olga also provided her visitor with 'a long account' of the family's Kenyan exile and the 'hostile attitude of Gr[eat] Br[itain]...', for she continued to hope that 'one day' Paul actions 'would be vindicated.'[35]

As this was the first Christmas following Paul's death, the Princess decided not to send Christmas cards; nor was she pleased to receive some bearing "merry" or "happy" greetings, noting 'some people have so little finesse.'[36] Nevertheless, she still wanted to look her best for the forthcoming Festive celebrations and dyed her hair using a rinse purchased from Helena Rubenstein.[37] Following Olga's arrival at Gstaad, she and Elizabeth joined Howard Oxenberg and his 'very sweet'[38] fourth wife Anne Hardwicke for lunch at the Bergrestaurant atop Mount Eggli. Otherwise, Elizabeth was kept busy cooking the turkey and trimmings for the Christmas Eve dinner, which was preceded by the usual opening of gifts. On Christmas morning, Olga walked to each local church in turn 'to say a prayer and light a candle'.[39] In late December, the Princess moved on to the Carlton in Lausanne, from where she made a visit to Queen Mother Helen and her family at Versoix. She was entranced when Sitta's daughter-in-law, Anne, showed a colour ciné film of her and King Michael's recent trip to Kenya, which included footage of Preston House. The Princess ended another traumatic year dining with her friends, the Mortons at their Lausanne apartment. However, despite the couple's best efforts, Olga admitted that 'My heart is heavy.'[40]

Of particular pleasure, in early February 1977, was the welcome news that Barbara was expecting a child. Thereafter, the Princess was due to meet officials at Morgan's Bank in Geneva, in an attempt to try and unravel Prince Paul's business affairs. The first meeting, on 14 February, lasted two hours and that evening Olga returned to Lausanne exhausted and suffered an attack of her heart palpitations.[41] Nevertheless, she gamely returned to Geneva next day and only then did she finally get things 'clear' in her mind.[42] Furthermore, the Princess also had the unenviable task of finding a suitable final resting place for Paul's mortal remains. Fortunately, kindly Irina Morton helped Olga contact officials at Lausanne's Bois-de-Vaux cemetery, where she chose a triple layer plot[43] for she intended to have Nicholas' mortal remains brought over from England and buried alongside those of his father.[44]

As the Princess gradually faced up to her new responsibilities, she 'started to live more again.' As she had done previously in Kenya and South Africa, Olga took over the running of the house and became adept at ordering the food and planning the menus for her thrice-weekly lunch parties with her niece Helen, although there was 'always a terrible fuss' if the latter asked to bring along a friend [45]. Indeed, there constantly seemed to be a 'complication' over the times and arrangements for any meal. Was Olga perhaps afraid of upsetting her maid Hélène, who one regular guest noted was more than capable of making it clear, by her facial expression, that things could be a bother?[46] Still, on the whole, the Princess became 'much more easy-going,'[47] although her diary entries also make it clear that she had once again found the confidence to tackle matters head-on, just as she was required to do in Kenya. Nevertheless, costs continued to weigh heavily on her mind and she soon arranged to sell a bronze and a clock at auction in Paris, as well as dispose of Paul's Mercedes motor car.[48]

In mid-April, Michael of Kent telephoned from the South of France to say he wished to bring his friend Marie-Christine for another visit. The trio lunched at the Relais and the young couple seemed 'relieved' to be able to speak to the Princess of how 'they long for a home and marriage.' Olga continued to warm to the Baroness, observing 'I like her, vivacious, forceful, obviously adores him'.[49] Touchingly, Marie-Christine later wrote to thank the Princess 'for letting [her] tell me all her troubles.'[50] Olga came to the conclusion that things would not be easy for the couple.[51] This was an understatement for not only was this Bohemian-born Baroness a Roman Catholic (meaning that any marriage between her and Michael would require the Prince to forfeit his place in the royal line of succession under the terms of the 1701 Act of Settlement)[28] but Marie-Christine was in the throes of divorcing her husband Tom Trowbridge (from whom she was estranged), as well as trying to have the marriage annulled by the Roman Catholic church.

---

[28] This provision has been subsequently repealed by the Succession to the Crown Act of 2013.

In late May, the Princess had 'a stupid fall in the street' and injured her right elbow, knee and thigh.[52] Then, one day, during a heart-to-heart, Barbara felt able to tell her mother-in-law that Alexander had 'minded being put aside by P[aul] for Nicky with whom Paul had more in common.. ' but tactfully acknowledged that his mother 'had often defended him.'[53] Olga was now also increasingly focused on welcoming a new grandchild into the world and she had already set aside a square solitaire diamond ring as a celebratory memento for the mother-to-be, while Alexander was to receive a set of his father's gold and sapphire cufflinks.[54]

In July, there was a brief visit from Elizabeth and her children (who were en route to Vittel for a holiday) during which Olga enjoyed the chance of bathing and putting little Nicholas to bed. She found her grandson to be 'affectionate, sensible and intelligent'[55] and seemed pleased he 'knows I love him and says so.'[56] The following month, Olga made her usual summer visit to Lausanne in the company of her cousin Helen. The cousins were joined for an overnight, at the Carlton, by Neil Balfour, who was currently undertaking research for a biography on Prince Paul. During an intensive session, the Princess did her best to answer his extensive list of questions about her late husband's life. Shortly thereafter, Paul and Nicholas' mortal remains arrived in Lausanne for interment. As she viewed the coffins, Olga felt, 'such an emotion and heart ache to stand by my two loved ones, father and son at last side by side.' Yet, she was also uplifted noting, 'How happy they are together now!'[57] On 30 August, Olga and Alexander (who arrived by train from Liechtenstein), attended the 'double funeral' which was conducted by a Greek Orthodox priest. As she departed the graveside, the Princess observed that 'a part of myself went into each grave...'[58]

Even at an emotional time like this, the family were forced to defend Prince Paul's reputation: Neil Balfour wrote to Alexander Macmillan, the scion of the well-known publishing family, to protest at an Epilogue which was attached to a recently re-issued edition of Rebecca West's "Black Lamb and Grey Falcon". This contained 'a repetition of all the war time propaganda which held out Prince Paul to be a treacherous quisling....' On behalf of Olga and the family, he asked for the removal of the Epilogue from the re-issued second edition and the inclusion of 'a carefully worded correction'.[59]

In early September, the Princess moved on to London, where she received an invitation to Sunday lunch with King Constantine and Queen Anne-Marie at their home in Hampstead. She thought the residence was 'nice and roomy' although 'not [decorated] in the best taste'.[60] Perhaps Olga should have recommended the services of the South African interior decorator Dudley Poplak, with whom she had struck up a firm friendship.

Poplak was not only a fellow devotee of Nicol Campbell but 'a highly spiritual soul' who recorded the 'voices of [spiritual] guides and people dead for over 500 years'.[61] The Princess subsequently visited his home in Eaton Square to listen to a selection and found the experience 'fascinating and deeply moving'.[62] Meanwhile, back in the land of the living, Elizabeth held a dinner party at her Chelsea home in her mother's honour, to which she invited a wide selection of Olga's friends.[63]

When the Princess arrived back at Rue Scheffer, on 25 September, she received the welcome news that Barbara had given birth to a boy in Vaduz at 3am that morning. He was named Dushan Paul.[64] The following week, she was driven by Alexander to Liechtenstein to visit her grandson: 'I took him in my arms for Q[uiss] to photograph' and found him 'very like he was.'[65] In the evening, Olga and Alexander dined at Vaduz Castle with the Sovereign Prince of Liechtenstein and his wife Gina. The Princess returned to Paris, on 12 October, to find many of the streets closed and a strong police presence in anticipation of a State Visit by Tito. As a distraction, she entertained her favourite great-niece Sophie to a viewing of Princess Nicholas' dresses and seemed touched that she showed such enthusiasm for 'that epoque'.[66] While Sophie did not much care for her great-aunt's 'dark, spooky' home, she certainly enjoyed an easy relationship with this 'jolly and sweet' grandmother figure. She particularly recalls the Princess' 'giggly sense of humour', as they sat together in the little sitting room at Rue Scheffer, sharing an intimate story or joke. Another vignette is of her great-aunt with sharpened eraser-pencil in hand, preparing to tackle 'her main morning passion', the *Herald Tribune* crossword.[67] (Indeed, no matter how inclement the weather, Olga went out each day to collect her newspapers from the kiosk in the nearby Rue de Passy). Sometimes the duo discussed history, with Sophie 'not [yet] realising she [Olga] was part of history.'[68]

As the autumn days lengthened, Lilia Ralli's health took a turn for the worse. She had contracted hepatitis following a blood transfusion and was further weakened by two angina attacks. The Princess faithfully ventured over to Lilia's flat most days and even arranged for a Red Cross nurse to sit with her dear old friend. When, on 26 November, Olga received the fateful news that 'my darling Zin' had passed away, she immediately took a taxi over to Lilia's flat to pay her own respects and to help greet the 'streams'[69] of anguished callers who called-by to reminisce over this most loyal and sociable of friends. On 30 November, the Princess attended Mrs Ralli's funeral in the Greek Orthodox Church and found the occasion to be 'a day of sadness and feeling of immense loss', although she drew comfort from the 'garden of flowers round her little coffin' that included her own floral tribute in the form of a cross in the Greek national colours. Despite having spent the day surrounded by family and friends, Olga now claimed to be 'alone on this life's plane' but 'feel surrounded and loved on the spiritual one.'[70] However, this did not deter the Princess from treating herself to a new dress from Franck for Dushan's christening at Alexander and Barbara's residence on 2 December. At the meal following the ceremony, and although 'choked with emotion', Olga rose to her feet and proposed a toast to the health of the parents and her grandson.[71] She continued to see a lot of the twins (who often stayed at Rue Scheffer overnight). However, this was not solely to enjoy their company, for the Princess realised that by 'Having the boys here I can follow them better.' But not everyone relished these visits: Her increasingly resentful maid Hélène made it clear that if Michel and Dimitri continued to stay regularly, she would have to leave due to the increased workload.[72]

As 1977 drew to a close, the Princess seemed in a positive mood and was looking to the future: She arranged for Paul's bedroom to be redecorated and accepted an invitation from the British Ambassador Nicholas Henderson to lunch at his residence on New Year's Eve. Furthermore, relations with both her children were harmonious and Olga confided that she felt 'calm and peaceful'[73] during the customary Christmas Eve celebrations at Maria Pia's home at Versailles.

In the spring, the Princess enjoyed a visit from her granddaughter Catherine and this was followed by a three-week sojourn in Lausanne and Florence with Queen Mother Helen. In May, Olga travelled on to London to stay with Aunt Alice at Kensington Palace, but was sad to find the ageing princess very bent and lame due to arthritis. The main purpose of Olga's visit was to convey Paul's Garter Banner to his old college, Christ Church, for display. She was accompanied there, on 27 May, by Elizabeth, Neil Balfour and his mother Lilian. The Princess also made time to dine with Prince Michael and Marie-Christine. The latter's first marriage had now been formally annulled by the Roman Catholic Church, and on 31 May, while Olga was still in London, it was announced that the couple had received the Queen's permission to marry.[74]

The Princess returned to Paris in time to celebrate her 75th birthday with her niece Helen at Garches, but observed that, '[I] don't feel it or really look it'.[75] On 30 June, she flew to Vienna with Alexander and Barbara to attend Michael's wedding. The trio were soon installed at the Schwarzenberg Palace Hotel (where Elizabeth joined them) and were later introduced to Marie-Christine's divorced parents, Baron Gunther von Reibnitz and Countess Marianne Rogala-Koczorowska. Despite Michael and Marie-Christine best efforts, for complex Canon Law and religious procedural considerations, it had not proved possible for the couple to marry in church. However, the obligatory Civil marriage ceremony took place that afternoon at the Rathaus (Town Hall), attended only by close family including Olga (who accompanied the bride and her mother by car to the ceremony). In the evening a banquet was held at the Schwarzenberg Palace, followed by dancing to Lehar's "Gold and Silver Waltz."[76] The Princess did not retire until 1a.m.[77]

The following morning, Olga joined the 'closest relations' in an oratory attached to Vienna's historical Schottenkirche, for a short Mass in English. However, she noted that there was no celebration or distribution of Holy Communion as anticipated, as this had been 'banned at the last minute, quite incredible'.[78] Michael and Marie-Christine had apparently only been informed of this latest blow during the wedding banquet, via a letter delivered from the Austrian Cardinal Franz Koenig.[79] It therefore now fell to Olga's old friend Father Charles Roux to bless the couple's wedding rings[80] and, in his sermon, denounce the 'bureaucracy' of 'authority gone mad' which had resulted in this predicament. The assembled group later joined the other wedding guests at the British Ambassador's Residence for a celebratory lunch.[81] Privately, the Princess was furious at this slight to her nephew, as was evidenced when she later wrote to the Prince of Wales to congratulate him 'on his moral courage'[82] for speaking out at the opening of the Fifth Salvation Army International Congress at Wembley, against 'religious intolerance' which he observed, 'can only bring needless distress to people'.[83]

Tellingly, Olga was now starting to suffer from slight lapses of memory, often mixing up the dates of entries in her diary and even admitting 'I can't remember what we did yesterday'.[84] Nevertheless, the Princess made her usual summer visit to Lausanne, but grumbled that her companion, Queen Mother Helen, tended to dwell 'too much on her grievances.'[85] She spent much of the time looking through correspondence to give Neil Balfour for his upcoming book and, on her return to Paris in September, proof-read several of the chapters.[86]

That autumn, the 'explosive' situation in Iran-where Islamic fundamentalism was on the rise and the Shah's position looked increasingly precarious-proved of particular concern to the Princess.[87] During an October visit to Langenburg, she was shocked to find her cousin Margarita 'changed and aged' and generally 'bad tempered and sharp all round'.[88] Olga must have been glad to move on to London to attend a Service of Blessing for Michael and Marie-Christine's marriage, performed by the Archbishop of Canterbury in the private chapel at Lambeth Palace. This was followed by an evening reception for the newlyweds at St James' Palace, during which the Princess was almost overcome with emotion as she spoke to many of Marina's former staff. During this London visit the Prince of Wales celebrated his 30th birthday and the Princess sent him a birthday card.

While in England, Olga continued with her quest to communicate with her deceased relatives: She attended several 'deeply moving' séances performed by a medium known to Dudley Poplak who claimed to have made contact with Nicholas, Paul, Princess Nicholas and 'the beloved sisters.' The whole experience provided the Princess with 'great peace.'[89] However, she was soon side-tracked when Alice Athlone-with whom she was once again staying-lost her balance and 'crashed' to the floor in her presence.[90] The nonagenarian Princess required to be hospitalised as she had severely injured her left shoulder. Auntie's kinswoman, Queen Juliana of the Netherlands, also happened to be on a visit to Kensington Palace. Olga liked the Dutch Queen's 'simple, friendly and direct' approach and the two enjoyed talking late into the evening.[91] However, Juliana was an early riser and when she knocked on Olga's bedroom door, next morning, to bid her farewell, the flustered occupant had still not dressed![92] Unusually, the Princess decided not to attend the Christmas Eve celebrations at Versailles and subsequently spent a 'solitary, quiet' Christmas Day. However, when her daughter-in-law Barbara telephoned from Vaduz with festive wishes, an unusually emotional Olga informed her that, 'I thanked God for her and what she is which I felt moved her as it moved me but it's the truth.'[93]

The Princess began this final year of the 1970's missing Lilia Ralli 'badly' for she now had 'no close friend to talk to.'[94] She wrote to Neil Balfour's mother Lilian to say that notwithstanding his forthcoming remarriage (to Serena Russell), she would 'continue to love him as before'.[95] Relations with Alexander continued to be particularly warm with his mother finding him 'v[ery] friendly and sensible'[96] during their regular lunches à deux. Yet, rather than focus on the present and the future, Olga could not resist her craving for the past: She again made contact with Dudley Poplak after seeing a 'light' in the dark and-at her request-he consulted his 'lady medium' who indicated this was for 'me to know they [the departed] were with me.'[97]

However, everyday events eventually drew the Princess back into the present: At the end of January, she was outraged to learn from her cousin Helen that Tatoi had been 'confiscated' by the Greek government and observed that, 'if no compensation is given it is pure theft.'[98] Thereafter, Olga was displeased to find that a *Sunday Telegraph* article commemorating Marshal Tito's thirty-five years in power featured a picture of the dictator and his 'fat wife' sitting in what was described as the garden of '"his"' residence at Brdo.[99] Then, Mara Cvetković's sister, who lived in Belgrade, came to lunch bringing with her a list of paintings made by Kashanian (the former curator of Prince Paul's museum), that included details of the pictures the family had left behind at Beli Dvor. The Princess' response was to observe tartly 'No question of giving any back of course.'[100] Otherwise, she continued to read (and correct) chapters of Paul's biography and took this process of 'careful revising'[101] very seriously indeed.

In early April, Olga received a quote (a 'huge sum')[102] from the decorators for cleaning the exterior stonework at Rue Scheffer which left her in despair. To finance the works, she decided to sell several items from her large silver collection, at a forthcoming Sotheby's sale in Zurich.[103] The Princess then travelled to London, in July, to attend the christening of Michael and Marie Christine's newly-born son, Frederick. She had been particularly keen for her grandson Michel-who was currently studying in London-to attend so that she could introduce him to the Queen.[104] However, this had not proved possible to arrange due to a limit on the number of those attending.[105] Nonetheless, having been thwarted in her attempts to have Michel presented to 'Lilibet', the determined Princess now focused her attentions on having her grandson invited to Clarence House to meet the Queen Mother. This was duly arranged and Queen Elizabeth was to prove a 'v[ery] sweet and warmly welcoming' hostess over lunch.[106]The Princess then moved on to Lausanne where she found her cousin Helen 'bent and crooked'.[107] Olga had no intention of allowing herself to deteriorate physically; she took a daily walk and followed a regular regime of isometric exercises. Both she and Sitta were shaken to learn of the murder, on 27 August, of Lord Mountbatten (whom Olga had recently met at the Kent christening) by the 'fanatic' IRA while on his annual holiday in County Sligo.[108] This event caused the Princess to fear for the safety of her cousin Philip and the Prince of Wales.

In mid-October, Olga returned to London to have some urgent dental work undertaken by her dentist, Mr Thompson. She paid an afternoon call on an increasingly fragile Alice Athlone at Kensington Palace. Auntie happened to complain that her devoted Canadian secretary, Miss Goldie, was a 'nuisance', but the Princess was having none of it, 'I sternly stopped that and defended her, adding that she was jolly lucky to be so well cared for...'[109] Later, in Paris, there was a brief blast from the past when Dimitri took his grandmother to the Grand Palais to view an exhibition of Russian icons and jewels from the Kremlin. As if by coincidence, Olga and her niece Helen happened to unearth one of Princess Nicholas' diaries, written in 1896, in which she described the Coronation of Tsar Nicholas II in Moscow. The Princess was subsequently invited to spend Christmas with her niece Helen, at her home near Salzburg. Olga enjoyed her Austrian sojourn, although again the emphasis remained on the past rather than the present: She lunched with a Count Moy (whose father had been the Austrian Ambassador to the Imperial Court at St Petersburg) and attended Sunday Mass at the

Cathedral in Salzburg. The highlight, however was a visit by car to 'dear Winhöring' where she visited Elisabeth and Toto's graves [110]. The Princess would continue to spend her Christmases in Austria for the foreseeable future.

Chapter 27 'Mental Drowning'

As the 1980's dawned, Olga initially continued to enjoy reasonably good physical health. In January 1981, the Princess came over to England for the funeral of her onetime hostess, Princess Alice, Countess of Athlone at Windsor. She still cut an impressive figure in her dark coat, black turban hat, and trademark bouton pearl earrings talking animatedly to the Queen. Soon thereafter, Olga received the news of the death of Frederika, in Madrid, from heart failure, while undergoing ophthalmic surgery. She did not attend the funeral at Tatoi on 13 February. However, in July, the Princess returned to England for a more joyous event: The wedding of the Prince of Wales to Lady Diana Spencer in St Paul's Cathedral. This provided her with the (now) rare chance to catch-up with most of her extended family.

Despite her advancing years, Olga continued to remember the birthdays of everyone in her large extended family and remained an enthusiastic correspondent, as evidenced by the neatly-arranged bundles of airmail letters in her sitting room at Rue Scheffer. Nevertheless, she was increasingly troubled by back pain and there were continuing signs of the confusion of old age: On one occasion, the Princess mislaid some translations of Prince Nicholas' plays; while in another instance, she forgot to take her jewels with her on holiday to Switzerland. Like many elderly ladies, Olga remained increasingly anxious about her living expenses, and believed she was 'living above my means...'[1] Indeed, the Princess even became convinced that she might soon have to sell Rue Scheffer.[2] To raise some funds, she sold a Maurice Atrillo painting at Sotheby's in London for £23000.[3]

Fortuitously, the Princess had made a new friend in Lausanne, the well-known, wealthy American socialite, Mrs Nesta Obermer. She now regularly spent long spells staying at Nesta's luxurious Swiss lakeside home, Villa Tourbillon, at Vaud, where she was given use of the spacious guest suite, as well as access to a team of staff who were happy to attend to her every whim. It is small wonder that she described Nesta as 'the most angelic hostess and delightful companion.'[4] This camaraderie was made all the easier by Mrs Obermer and Olga's mutual interest in music. Fortuitously, the socialite was a great friend of Yehudi Menuhin (who often came to stay) and the opera singer Dame Joan Sutherland, who lived nearby at Les Avants. On occasion, the Princess would accompany

Mrs Obermer to musical recitals at the Lausanne Academy of Music. There were house guests at Rue Scheffer too, including Nancy Leeds Wynkoop, the Woodstock-based daughter of Olga's late cousin Xenia. The duo discussed the case of Anna Anderson (who claimed to be the Grand Duchess Anastasia) and the Princess was fascinated to learn that Nancy 'quite believes in the identity of the "false" Anastasia as being the real one!'[5] Olga would later translate the memoirs of Nancy's maternal grandmother, Grand Duchess Marie Georgievna's memoirs from Greek into English.[6]

In May 1982, the Princess made a special journey to Versoix to attend Queen Mother Helen's 86th birthday party. Olga somewhat disapproved of her actress granddaughter Catherine taking the part of Lady Diana Spencer in the film, "The Royal Romance of Charles and Diana" (dismissed in her diaries as 'that film')[7]. She was, however, delighted to learn that the real-life Princess of Wales (as Lady Diana had become) had given birth to a son, William, and immediately sent the parents a telegram of congratulations.[8] Olga also enjoyed attending a cocktail party in honour of the Queen Mother given by their mutual friend Johnny Lucinge.[9] Of pleasure too, was a summer trip to Munich with her friend Mrs Obermer and the late Noel Coward's partner, Graham Payne, to attend a performance of the Rossini's opera "Cinderella". It was also around this time that the Princess was introduced to Britain's first female Prime Minister, Margaret Thatcher, at a lunch at Schloss Freudenberg, the Swiss lakeside home of Lady Eleanor Glover. Olga found the politician to be, 'very pleasant to talk to' and 'wise'.[10] Sometimes, it was left to the twins to cheer their grandmother up: On one occasion, Dimitri wrote a note to her on black paper using a gilt-type pen. This drew the repost, 'such a monkey!'[11]

As she prepared to travel to Salzburg for her great-niece Elisabeth's wedding in the autumn of 1982, the Princess admitted to feeling 'dead beat'.[12] Mental confusion continued to take its toll: She had been convinced that the wedding was on 21 October, but subsequently learned from Dimitri that the actual date was 9 October ('a great shock').[13] Nevertheless, she carefully selected an emerald cabochon brooch (which had originally been given by Grand Duchess Vladimir to Princess Nicholas) as a gift for the bride-to-be. Olga thoroughly enjoyed the wedding and remained at the reception at the Residenz Palace till 1 a.m.![14] The following month, the Princess travelled to Lausanne after learning from King Michael that his mother, Sitta was 'slowly sinking.'[15] Queen Mother Helen died on 28 November and the Princess noted forlornly, 'for her sake it's a happy release but oh! what it means to me...'[16] Alexander joined his mother in Lausanne for the funeral at the Greek Orthodox Church on 2 December. Olga was moved by the sight of hundreds of wreaths displayed throughout the building, but was, nevertheless, upset to find that none of Marina's children were in attendance nor was her cousin Philip (who was represented by the British Ambassador).[17] However, the Princess remained close to her Kent niece and nephews and when she reached her 80th birthday, in June 1983, Princess Alexandra threw a celebratory dinner party in her Aunt's honour at her Richmond home. The Duke of Kent recalls: 'She was in tremendous spirits-we had a wonderfully happy evening which I think she loved.'[18]

As the 1980's rolled on, so Olga became even more forgetful. Nevertheless, during these earlier stages of her mental decline, the Princess was largely able to screen the signs by keeping 'very much in control'.[19] In addition, as her great-niece Sophie points out, it would have been 'difficult' to pinpoint the onset of this deterioration 'due to her way of expressing herself for she had always been in the habit of "play acting" and saying if she spotted someone "Who is this person with that very strange look on her face coming into the room?", when she had known perfectly well who they were; so when the time came when she still asked the question (but no longer had the answer), it would not be so apparent.'[20] The Princess also now read less and less, but still loved 'dwelling on the past', particularly over her experiences at the Imperial Court in Russia. She would also sometimes let slip 'a little bit' of her thoughts on Queen Marie of Yugoslavia, particularly on her shortcomings where the education of her children was concerned. Interestingly, the Princess now rarely mentioned King Peter, nor did she want to reflect on wartime political events in Yugoslavia. However, she 'often' spoke about her wartime visit to Marina in 1942, and 'how terrible it was to arrive to a devastated sister ...'[21]

Although Olga still enjoyed her customary morning stroll to the Rue de Passy for fresh fruit and regularly took the number 22 bus to Marks and Spencer to indulge in their 'delicious, wide range',[22] she was increasingly concerned by the 'atmosphere of violence and strikes' in France[23] which she blamed on President Mitterrand's 'left regime.'[24] She also worried about 'arms escalations' and felt that 'the implications of a nuclear war are unthinkable.'[25] Meanwhile, her (unjustified) fears of penury continued to grow apace and had now reached the stage where she felt that she could no longer afford to heat her home.[26] In early 1984, Olga was dismayed to learn that Crown Prince Alexander and his wife had separated [they would divorce the following year]. In March, she attended a service in Westminster Abbey to commemorate the life of Noel Coward. During the proceedings, the Queen Mother unveiled a Memorial plaque to their mutual friend in Poet's Corner. Yet, much of the credit for the event must go to the Princess who, following a meeting with Graham Payne, had been inspired to write to the Dean about the creation of such a commemorative. She had backed this up with a similar letter to the Queen Mother.[27]

Unfortunately, around this time, Olga's friend Nesta (now in her nineties) was taken poorly following a fall and admitted to the Clinic Cécile in Lausanne. The Princess visited Mrs Obermer regularly, often walking up the steep hill from the Carlton Hotel to the clinic, which was no mean feat given that she had only recently been diagnosed with arthritis in the spine.[28] Nevertheless, with Sitta dead and Nesta confined to bed, it was often a solitary existence dining alone 'in my usual corner'[29] in the hotel's dining room. Fortunately, the Mortons continued to invite Olga regularly to lunch or dine with them, as did the Serpieris if they were in town. However, invariably the news they imparted that summer from Greece was '<u>too</u> sad for words...'[30] On her return to Paris, the Princess admitted to feeling 'so lost'[31] after mislaying her bag at the station. Such episodes alerted her to her mental shortcomings, although she still felt that 'I have time enough to sort my memory and get on with my book[29] *while I can make sense, but alas no one to keep my thoughts clear...*'[32] In early October, Mrs Obermer died peacefully at home. The Princess would later admit that the passing of this close friend and confidante left her feeling upset and 'mentally amputated'.[33] Nevertheless, Olga's sense of duty remained firmly intact and she soon stirred herself to attend events in Paris to mark the 50th anniversary of the death of King Alexander. Crown Prince Alexander and his four-year-old son Peter joined her, as did Prince Tomislav. The Princess was moved by the sizeable crowd at the King's imposing memorial in the Bois de Boulogne and later reflected that 'getting to know Sandro was a matter of tact, but I liked him a lot.'[34] Thereafter, Olga decided to sell some items of furniture through Sotheby's to further improve her cash-flow.[35] These would be included in the company's 'Bel Ameublement' sale held at Monaco's Winter Sporting, in June 1985.[36]

In the second half of the 1980's, as many old friends (including Diddie Serpieri) passed away, the Princess' diaries became increasingly uninformative, with days often left totally blank. Even she was acutely aware that there was 'nothing much to say'[37] with life now described as 'the usual monotony.'[38] Olga often went back to sleep after breakfast 'a thing I never did before'[39] and was sometimes forced to attend the American Hospital for treatment for arthritis.[40] Yet, certain events could still alleviate the tedium: When the Princess learned that her

---

[29] Mrs Obermer had recently urged Olga to write her autobiography. Although she had tentatively started to write down some recollections of her life, no book was ever completed or published.

granddaughter Christina was betrothed to marry the British artist Damian Elwes; she entertained the couple to lunch and thought them 'madly in love.'[41] On another occasion, the Countess of Paris called at Rue Scheffer to regale her hostess with details of her recent visit to Yugoslavia. This information seemed to strike a chord with the Princess who now 'wished I could go [back] there under another name.'[42]

In April 1986, Olga read of the death of the Duchess of Windsor at her home in the nearby Bois de Boulogne. She thought it 'unfair' that the Windsor's personal correspondence was to be published in the British press.[43] During this period, the Princess also saw an increasing amount of Neil Balfour and his wife Serena who invariably invited her to spend Easter and Christmas with them at their Yorkshire home, Studley Royal. Olga would accompany Serena on shopping trips to nearby Harrogate and was pleased to observe that 'we laugh a lot together'.[44] The Princess also sometimes holidayed with the Balfours in Biarritz in August. The downside of such visits was the inevitable return to Paris and isolation, although she tried to remain stoical, noting 'I must get used to my solitude and [not] ask or expect any pity.'[45] But was Olga really as lonely as she seemed to indicate? She certainly missed the twins who remained 'very precious'[46] but now lived in the United States (Michel in Palm Beach, Dimitri in New York). Nevertheless, she received regular visits from Alexander, Barbara and her grandson Dushan, as well as from Elizabeth when she was in Paris. She was also fussed over on a daily basis by her personal staff. Certainly, it did not help that the Princess often turned down invitations-including one to attend the Duke of Kent's 50th birthday party in London.[47]

By the end of the 1980's, Olga now often remembered 'nothing of where I went or [what I] did this day-rather alarming.'[48] The Princess compared this to 'mental drowning'[49] and tried to explain the experience to her niece Helen: 'She used to tell me sometimes-when she was still [living] in the house, "Something awful is happening. I do things and sometimes I think I am in front of a huge hole falling backwards-I don't know who is who and then it is normal again."'[50] This must have proved a disconcerting experience. Olga also now tired 'so easily'[51] that she was often abed by 10pm, even during the sunny evenings of late spring. Yet, the past remained firmly etched in her consciousness: When her maid Hélène returned from a holiday to Leningrad [as St Petersburg was then called] with an album of holiday snaps, this caused the Princess to remember 'vividly' the events of her childhood at Tsarskoe Selo and St Petersburg.[52]

In February 1987, Elizabeth married the Peruvian politician Manuel Ulloa Elías. The latter managed to arrange for his new wife to accompany him on a visit to Yugoslavia in May 1988. She was thus the first member of the Karageorgević dynasty to return home since 1941. During this visit, Elizabeth telephoned Olga from Belgrade 'amazingly clear and moving'[53] to inform her that she had been 'all over' Beli Dvor which was 'unchanged, clean and well-kept.'[54] The Princess subsequently received a 'long, fascinating' letter from her daughter describing the visit in detail.[55]

On 11 June 1988, Olga celebrated her 85th birthday at Rue Scheffer in the company of her cousin Sophie. Subsequently, a sore foot made walking increasingly difficult and the Princess began to pine for Elisabeth and Marina whom she missed 'so deeply'.[56] She also imagined, despite evidence to the contrary, that she had not been out of the house for three months.[57] As the year ended, so apparently did Olga's many decades of keeping a daily diary. This was perhaps fortuitous as what had once been detailed and illuminating entries had now been reduced to a few lines of confused banalities. Indeed, by the time of the death of her cousin Eugenie, in February 1989, Olga had largely withdrawn into a world of her own. It was now dangerous for her to leave the house unaccompanied, as she often became lost.[58] Eventually, for her own personal safety, the family decided to place her in a nursing home, just outside Paris, at Meudon, where she was 'beautifully looked after.'[59] She had a comfortable room (No. 223) with en suite bathroom and a nameplate on the door which bore the inscription "La Princesse de Yougoslavie." In the beginning, Olga would often ask the whereabouts of Prince Paul[60] and still recognised family members, including her niece Helen, although conversation was always limited to the past.[61] Sometimes, high-profile royal guests, such as the Prince of Wales, would call-by to pay their respects.[62] Her daughter-in-law, Barbara, recalls that even in her nineties 'she was still beautiful' with an elegant profile.[63]

By 1995 the Princess was totally unaware of where she was[64] and even failed to recognise close relatives. Olga eventually passed away on 16 October 1997, at the grand old age of 94. In a 'will' written in her 1943 diary she said she wished her heart to be buried at Tatoi, 'where I was born and where it belongs' with the rest of her remains to be buried at Brdo in the pine wood 'next to my husband.'[65] However, as already indicated, Olga had made other plans in the intervening years. The Princess' funeral service took place at the Greek Orthodox Cathedral in Paris on 23 October. In addition to family members, other mourners included various French royalties including the Countess of Paris and the Dowager Princess Napoléon. Noticeable absentees were the Duke of Kent (who was on an official tour of South Korea) and his sister Alexandra, who was undertaking engagements in the United States. The Queen Mother was also unable to attend but telephoned Alexander to offer her sympathy.[66] Although Olga was by now but a footnote in history, the French magazine *Point de Vue* covered the event extensively.[67]

Close family members then proceeded to Lausanne, where the Princess was buried in the Bois-de-Vaux cemetery, beside her beloved husband and Nicholas. Her coffin bore a simple brass plaque inscribed in French, "S.A.R. Olga Karageorgević Princesse de Yougoslavie 11.6.1903-16.10.1997".[68] And there seemed no reason to believe that the story would not end here.

However, during the Princess' mental decline, her daughter Elizabeth had secured access to previously unseen 'secret papers' from the British Foreign Office, which detailed the major role the Special Operations Executive (SOE) had played in relation to the 1941 coup. This included the names of Yugoslavs who had taken bribes from the British in their quest to overthrow the legitimate government.[69] Elizabeth subsequently arranged for these documents to be included as an addendum in an updated edition of Neil Balfour and Sally Balfour' biography of Prince Paul which was published in 1996.

In 2000, Elizabeth's citizenship was reinstated and she returned to live permanently in Serbia to continue with her quest to promote her family's memory, as well as correct the many falsehoods perpetuated against them during the Communist era. Subsequently, she worked alongside law Professor Oliver Antić, to seek Paul's official rehabilitation and to obtain a reversal, in the Serbian Supreme Court, of the Yugoslav State Commission's 1945 ruling that the Prince was a war criminal and enemy of the state. This milestone was finally achieved in December 2011. Doubtless fortified by this pleasing outcome, Elizabeth then sought the transfer of the mortal remains of her parents and her brother Nicholas from Lausanne to the Royal Mausoleum in the crypt of St George's Church at Topola. After extensive consultations with Swiss officials and the Serbian church and government, the Princess travelled to Switzerland on 26 September 2012 (where she was joined by Olga and Paul's grandchildren Michel, Nicholas and Catherine) to witness their exhumation and formally identify the remains.[70]

In early October, Elizabeth and her daughter Catherine stood at the Serbian border with Croatia, to greet the coffins and accompany them to Belgrade, where they were received at the Orthodox Cathedral by the Patriarch and a military guard of honour. A Memorial Service was held on 4 October and was attended by family members, the Serbian President Tomislav Nikolić, Prime Minister Ivica Dačić, government officials and members of the diplomatic corps. However, equally impressive was the steady stream of Serbians of all ages who filed past the coffins to pay their final respects to the former Prince Regent and his Consort.[71] Thereafter, the caskets were transported from Belgrade to Topola and, on 6 October, following a moving funeral service in the impressive Serbian-Byzantine domed church, Olga, Paul and Nicholas' mortal remains were finally laid to rest in the crypt with full State honours. This was a most fitting tribute to a couple who had sacrificed so much in order to serve Yugoslavia with such unwavering loyalty, following the untimely death of King Alexander.

In February, 2013, Princess Olga was rehabilitated by the Serbian Supreme Court. This paved the way for her son Alexander and daughter Elizabeth to make a successful claim for the return of a property in Belgrade, which had previously belonged to their mother, but had been seized by the communists after the Second World War. This villa-the former Montenegrin Embassy-has now been renamed the Villa Olga. If she were alive today, Olga would have been extremely proud of all that her daughter has achieved.

Notes on Sources

Abbreviations.

RA MKMD/OUT/FOX= Royal Archives: Miss Kate Fox's correspondence.
RA MKMD/PRIV/FORFF=Royal Archives: Letters from Princess Olga to Princess Marina.
CO=British Colonial Office Papers
FO=British Foreign Office papers
CAB=British War Cabinet papers
Columbia=Prince Paul's papers held at Columbia University, New York.
Princess Elizabeth Collection= correspondence provided by Princess Elizabeth of Yugoslavia.

Chapter 1 Setting the Scene.

1   Battiscombe, Georgina *Queen Alexandra* Constable and Company, London, 1969, p60
2   Broadberry Stephen and O'Rourke Kevin, *The Cambridge Economic History of Modern Europe: Volume 2, 1870 to the Present*, Cambridge University Press, pp 47-48
3   Christopher, Prince *Memoirs of HRH Prince Christopher of Greece,* Hurst and Blackett, London, 1938, p17
4   Quoted in King, Stella *Princess Marina: Her Life and Times* Casell, London, 1969, p8
5   Christopher, Prince op. cit., pp28-29
6   King, op.cit., p12
7   Christmas, Captain Walter *King George of Greece* McBride Nast and Company, New York, 1914, p148
8   Empress Frederick to Queen Victoria quoted in Duff, David *Alexandra Princess and Queen* Sphere Books Ltd., London, 1981 p162
9   Nicholas, Prince *My Fifty Years* Hutchinson and Co., London, 1926 p60
10 Princess Olga's diary 23 June 1973
11 King, op. cit., p14
12 King, op. cit., p16
13 Christopher, Prince op. cit., p32
14 The Broadford Courier 1 May 1896 accessed from Trove Australia www.trove.nla.gov.au 01 July 2012
15 Christopher, Prince op. cit., p71
16 Vassili, Count Paul *Behind the Veil at the Russian Court* Reprint Series, Forgotten Books, 2010, p125
17 Amalia Kussner Coudert The Century Magazine quoted in The Register (Adelaide) 24 November 1906 accessed from Trove Australia www.trove.nla.gov.au 25 June 2012
18 McLean, Roderick R. *Royalty and Diplomacy in Europe 1890-1914,* Cambridge University Press, 2007, p 22
19 Quoted in Zeepvat, Charlotte *From Cradle to Crown,* Sutton

Publishing Ltd, Stroud, 2006, p125

20 King, op. cit., p25

21 The Daily News (Perth) 19 December 1918 accessed from Trove Australia www.trove.nla.gov.au 29 June 2012

22 KR diary-7 August [1900]-St Petersburg quoted in Muylunas, Andrei and Mironenko, Sergei 'A Lifelong Passion-Nicholas and Alexandra Their Own Story', Weidenfeld and Nicolson, London, 1996, p199

23 The Western Mail 3 August 1901 accessed from Trove Australia www.trove.nla.gov.au 16 June 2012

24 The Argus Melbourne 5 May 1902 accessed from Trove Australia www.trove.nla.gov.au 16 June 2012

25 Beech, Arturo Dear Ellen... Eurohistory and Richmond House Books, 2011, p23,

26 Vickers, Hugo Alice Princess Andrew of Greece, Penguin Books, London, 2001 p68

27 Vickers op. cit., p69

28 Massie, Robert K, Nicholas and Alexandra Victor Gollancz, London, 1968, p61

Chapter 2-A Clannish Intimacy.

1 RA MKMD/OUT/FOX Invoices from M.E. Penson Juvenile Outfitter Mount Street London December 12 1902, March 20 and June 10 1903

2 King, Stella Ibid., pp32-33

3 Zeepvat, op.cit., p33

4 RA MKMD/OUT/FOX Princess Olga to Kate Fox 24 May 1946

5 Princess Olga's diary 24 May 1936

6 Baroness Helena von der Hoven serialised article in The Australian Women's Weekly 26 March 1938

7 Princess Olga 'Lest Memory Fails' Unpublished Memoirs, 1982, p3

8 RA MDKD/OUT/FOX Princess Olga to Kate Fox reminiscing over her 1908 diaries in letter dated 10 March 1946.

9 Zeepvat, op. cit., p71

10 Ellis, Jennifer The Duchess of Kent Odhams Press, London, 1952., p9

11 Nicholas, Prince op. cit., pp 200-202

12 Nicholas, Prince ibid., p206

13 KR [Grand Duke Konstantin Konstantinovich] diary 1 October 1905 [Old style] quoted in Muylunas and Mironenko, op. cit., p281

14 King, op. cit., p67

15 Bulow, Bernhard Prince von, Memoirs 1897-1903 Putnam, London, 1931, p168

16 RA MDKD/OUT/FOX Princess Nicholas to Kate Fox 14/27 November 1905

17 RA MDKD/OUT/FOX Princess Nicholas to Kate Fox 14/27 November 1905

18 Lest Memory Fails p4

19 Ibid.

20 Baroness Helena von der Hoven serialised article in The Australian Women's Weekly 26 March 1938

21 King op. cit., p36

22 Information provided by Prince Michel of Yugoslavia

23 King op. cit., p36

24 RA MDKD/OUT/FOX Princess Nicholas to Kate Fox 19/30 August 1908

25 King, op cit., p36

26 King, Ibid., p33

27 Nicholas, Prince op. cit., p197

28 Ellis, op.cit., p13

29 Bertin, Celia *Marie Bonaparte*, Harcourt, Brace, Jovanovich, New York, 1982, p 92

30 RA MDKD/OUT/FOX Princess Nicholas to Kate Fox 19 June 1913

31 RA MDKD/OUT/FOX Princess Nicholas to Kate Fox 27 November 1905

Chapter 3-The Russian Influence

1 Nicholas, Prince op. cit., p56

2 Lest Memory Fails p5

3 Ibid p6

4 Ibid p8

5 King, op. cit., p39

6 Ibid. p40

7 RA MDKD/OUT/FOX Princess Nicholas to Kate Fox 19 Oct/1 November 1907

8 Princess Olga to Princess Nicholas 27 July 1908 [Princess Elizabeth Collection.]

Chapter 4-Turbulent Times.

1 RA MDKD/OUT/FOX Princess Nicholas to Kate Fox 11/24 March 1909

2 RA MDKD/OUT/FOX Princess Nicholas to Kate Fox 11/24 March 1909

3 RA MDKD/OUT/FOX Princess Nicholas to Kate Fox 3/16 March 1909

4 RA MDKD/OUT/FOX Princess Nicholas to Kate Fox 11/24 March 1909

5 RA MDKD/OUT/FOX Princess Nicholas to Kate Fox 3/16 June 1909

6 Christopher, Prince op. cit., p112

7 Nicholas op. cit., pp 223-4

8 RA MDKD/OUT/FOX Princess Nicholas to Kate Fox 19 April/2 May 1910

9 RA MDKD/OUT/FOX Princess Victoria of Great Britain and Ireland to Kate Fox 5 July 1910

10 RA MDKD/OUT/FOX Princess Nicholas to Kate Fox 5/18 July 1910

11 RA MDKD/OUT/FOX Princess Nicholas to Kate Fox 18 June/1 July 1910

12 RA MDKD/OUT/FOX Princess Nicholas to Kate Fox 5/18 July 1910

13 Zeepvat, op. cit., p152

14 Norland Archive Kate Fox to Miss Sharman 14 April 1913 quoted in Zeepvat, Ibid., p150

15 RA MDKD/OUT/FOX Princess Nicholas to Kate Fox 30 August/12 September 1910

16 RA MDKD/OUT/FOX Princess Nicholas to Kate Fox 16/29 September 1911

17 RA MDKD/OUT/FOX Princess Nicholas to Kate Fox 15/28 October 1911

18 RA MDKD/OUT/FOX Princess Nicholas to Kate Fox 31 October/13 November 1911

19 Zeepvat, op. cit., p153

20 RA MDKD/OUT/FOX Princess Olga to Kate Fox 27 October/9 November 1912

21 Zeepvat, op. cit., p154

22 Ibid

23 RA MDKD/OUT/FOX Princess Nicholas to Kate Fox 23 January/ 5 February 1913

24 RA MDKD/OUT/FOX Princess Nicholas to Kate Fox 12/25 January 1913

25 RA MDKD/OUT/FOX Princess Nicholas to Kate Fox 17/30 January 1913

26 RA MDKD/OUT/FOX Princess Nicholas to Kate Fox 24 January/6 February 1913

27 RA MDKD/OUT/FOX Princess Olga to Kate Fox 27 September 1946

28 Grand Duchess Vladimir's words quoted in RA MDKD/OUT/FOX Princess Nicholas to Kate Fox 21 January/3 February 1913

29 RA MDKD/OUT/FOX Princess Nicholas to Kate Fox 16 February /1 March 1913.

30 RA MDKD/OUT/FOX Princess Nicholas to Kate Fox 24 January/6 February 1913

31 RA MDKD/OUT/FOX Princess Nicholas to Kate Fox 16 February /1 March 1913

32 Christopher, Prince op. cit., p 118

33 Lest Memory Fails p9

34 King, op. cit., p45

35 RA MDKD/OUT/FOX Princess Nicholas to Kate Fox 25 March/9 April 1913

36 RA MDKD/OUT/FOX Princess Nicholas to Kate Fox 8/21 April 1913

37 RA MDKD/OUT/FOX Princess Nicholas to Kate Fox 13/30 April 1913

38 Zeepvat, op. cit., p157

39 RA MDKD/OUT/FOX Princess Nicholas to Kate Fox 17/30 May 1913

40 Zeepvat, op. cit., p157

41 RA MDKD/OUT/FOX Princess Nicholas to Kate Fox 17/30 May 1913

42 RA MDKD/OUT/FOX Princess Nicholas to Kate Fox 25 July /7 August 1913

43 RA MDKD/OUT/FOX Princess Nicholas to Kate Fox 21 June 1913

44 Baroness Helena von der Hoven serialised article in The Australian Women's Weekly 26 March 1938

45 RA MDKD/OUT/FOX Princess Nicholas to Kate Fox 21 June 1913

46 RA MDKD/OUT/FOX Princess Nicholas to Kate Fox 18/31 August 1913

47 Olga's remarks quoted in letter RA MDKD/OUT/FOX Princess Nicholas to Kate Fox 24 September/7 October 1913

48 RA MDKD/OUT/FOX Princess Nicholas to Kate Fox 8/21 October 1913

49 RA MDKD/OUT/FOX Princess Nicholas to Kate Fox 10/23 December 1913

50 RA MDKD/OUT/FOX Princess Nicholas to Kate Fox 3/16 January 1914

51 RA MDKD/OUT/FOX Princess Nicholas to Kate Fox 11/24 May 1914

52 RA MDKD/OUT/FOX Princess Nicholas to Kate Fox 3/16-6/19 June 1914

Chapter 5-War and Revolution

1 Aronson, Theo Crowns in Conflict, Salem House Publishers, New Hampshire, 1986, p10

2 Lest Memory Fails 1982 p10

3 Nicholas, Prince op. cit., p256

4 Lest Memory Fails p12

5 RA MDKD/OUT/FOX Princess Nicholas to Kate Fox 2/15 September 1914

6 Lest Memory Fails p12

7 Lest Memory Fails p13

8 Lest Memory Fails p14

9 Lest Memory Fails p15

10 Lest Memory Fails p15

11 RA MDKD/OUT/FOX Princess Nicholas to Kate Fox 25 November/8 December 1914

12 RA MDKD/OUT/FOX Princess Nicholas to Kate Fox 11/24 October 1914

13 Aronson, op. cit., p93

14 Ellis, op.cit., p23

15 RA MDKD/OUT/FOX Princess Elisabeth to Kate Fox 17/30 June 1915

16 RA MDKD/OUT/FOX Princess Nicholas to Kate Fox 11/21 April 1915

17 RA MDKD/OUT/FOX Princess Nicholas to Kate Fox 6/19 August 1915

18 RA MDKD/OUT/FOX Princess Nicholas to Kate Fox 12/25 November 1915

19 RA MDKD/OUT/FOX Princess Nicholas to Kate Fox 6/19 August 1915

20 RA MDKD/OUT/FOX Princess Elisabeth to Kate Fox 26 November/8 December 1915

21 RA MDKD/OUT/FOX Princess Nicholas to Kate Fox 5/18 January 1916

22 RA MDKD/OUT/FOX Princess Nicholas to Kate Fox 1/14 March 1916

23 RA MDKD/OUT/FOX Princess Nicholas to Kate Fox 15/28 June 1916

24 RA MDKD/OUT/FOX Princess Nicholas to Kate Fox 7/20 December 1916

25 RA MDKD/OUT/FOX Princess Nicholas to Kate Fox 1/14 March 1916

26 Queen Marie of Romania to Lavinia Small 25 February 1928 quoted in Pakula, Hannah *The Last Romantic-A Biography of Queen Marie of Romania*

Weidenfeld and Nicolson, London, 1985, p367

27 RA MDKD/OUT/FOX Princess Nicholas to Kate Fox 1/14 March 1916

28 RA MDKD/OUT/FOX Princess Nicholas to Kate Fox 4/19 August 1916

29 RA MDKD/OUT/FOX Princess Nicholas to Kate Fox 7/20 December 1916

30 RA MDKD/OUT/FOX Princess Nicholas to Kate Fox 4 /17 November 1916

31 Greek Royal Family Website www.formerkingofgreece.org/en accessed 30 June 2012

32 Lest Memory Fails p16

33 Battiscombe, op. cit., p291

34 RA MDKD/OUT/FOX Princess Nicholas to Kate Fox 7/20 December 1916

35 RA MDKD/OUT/FOX Princess Nicholas to Kate Fox 7/20 December 1916

36 Warrnambool Standard 23 January 1917 accessed from Trove Australia www.trove.nla. gov.au 01 August 2012

37 King, op. cit., p60

38 The Register (Adelaide) 2 May 1917 accessed from Trove Australia www.trove.nla.gov.au 01 August 2012

39 Nicholas, Prince op. cit., p269

40 The Sydney Morning Herald 18 June 1917 accessed from Trove Australia www.trove. nla.gov.au 01 August 2012

41 United Service Cable in The Prahran Telegraph 23 June 1917 accessed from Trove Australia www.trove.nla.gov.au_01 August 2012

42 King, op. cit., p54

Chapter 6-Swiss Exile.

1 RA MKMD/OUT/FOX Princess Nicholas to Kate Fox November 26/9 December 1919

2 RA MKMD/OUT/FOX Princess Nicholas to Kate Fox 8/21 October 1917

3 RA MKMD/OUT/FOX Princess Nicholas to Kate Fox 3/16 November 1917

4 RA MKMD/OUT/FOX Princess Nicholas to Kate Fox 7/20 December 1917

5 RA MKMD/OUT/FOX Princess Nicholas to Kate Fox 7/20 December 1917

6 RA MKMD/OUT/FOX Princess Nicholas to Kate Fox 15/28 January 1918

7 RA MKMD/OUT/FOX Princess Nicholas to Kate Fox 16/29 June 1918

8 RA MKMD/OUT/FOX Princess Nicholas to Kate Fox 1/14 October 1918

9 Written response from Princess Elizabeth by e mail 2 June 2011.

10 RA MKMD/OUT/FOX Princess Nicholas to Kate Fox 20 July/2 August 1918

11 Nicholas, Prince op. cit., pp279-280

12 RA MKMD/OUT/FOX Princess Nicholas to Kate Fox 1/14 October 1918

13 RA MKMD/OUT/FOX Princess Olga to Kate Fox 18/31 January 1919

14 RA MKMD/OUT/FOX Princess Nicholas to Kate Fox 17/30 December 1918

15 RA MKMD/OUT/FOX Princess Nicholas to Kate Fox 23 February/8 March 1919

16 RA MKMD/OUT/FOX Princess Nicholas to Kate Fox 14/27 January 1919

17 RA MKMD/OUT/FOX Princess Marina to Kate Fox 2/15 April 1919

18 RA MKMD/OUT/FOX Princess Nicholas to Kate Fox 5/18 June 1919

19 RA MDKD/OUT/FOX Princess Nicholas to Kate Fox 9/22 July 1919

20 RA MKMD/OUT/FOX Princess Nicholas to Kate Fox 26 November /9 December 1919

21 RA MKMD/OUT/FOX Princess Marina to Kate Fox 1 January 1920

22 Western Argus 27 January 1920 accessed from Trove Australia www.trove.nla.gov.au 01 August 2012

23 Nicholas, Prince op. cit., p283

24 New York Times 29 December 1920 accessed from New York Times website www.nytimes.com 8 June 2015

25 Zeepvat, op. cit., p159.

26 Bonus, Wendy *The Faberge Connection: A memoir of the Bowe Family* iUniverse, Bloomington, 2010 pp108-9, 121

27 Lest Memory Fails p20

28 Lest Memory Fails p19

29 Lest Memory Fails p20

30 Ellis, op. cit., pp27-28

31 Lest Memory Fails pp 22-23

32 Field, Leslie *The Queen's Jewels* Weidenfeld and Nicholson, London, 1987, pp116-117

33 Christopher, op. cit., p154

34 RA MDKD/PRIV/FORRF Princess Olga to Princess Marina 7 November 1920

35 Van der Kiste, John *Kings of the Hellenes*, Sutton Publishing, Stroud, 1994. p128

36 Lest Memory Fails p17

37 RA MDKD/OUT/FOX Princess Olga to Kate Fox 21 January 1921

38 Ellis, op. cit., p29
39 Lest Memory Fails p37

Chapter 7-Bitter Lessons.

1 Lest Memory Fails pp 24-25
2 RA MDKD/OUT/FOX Princess Olga to Kate Fox 11 March 1922
3 Pencil draft of letter sent by Princess Nicholas to Queen Alexandrine of Denmark undated (Princess Elizabeth Collection).
4 Queen Alexandrine of Denmark to Princess Nicholas 1 May 1922 (Princess Elizabeth Collection).
5 Prince Nicholas to Princess Olga 19 July/1August 1922 (Princess Elizabeth Collection).
6 Prince Nicholas to Princess Olga 10/23 August 1922 (Princess Elizabeth Collection).
7 Pencil draft of letter sent by Princess Nicholas to Queen Alexandrine of Denmark undated.
8 Prince Nicholas to Princess Olga 10/23 August 1922 (Princess Elizabeth Collection).
9 RA MDKD/OUT/FOX Prince Nicholas to Kate Fox 20 August 1922
10 RA MDKD/OUT/FOX Princess Olga to Kate Fox 15/28 July 1922
11 RA MDKD/OUT/FOX Princess Olga to Kate Fox 27 July/9 August 1922
12 Princess Olga's diary 5 September 1922 quoted in Balfour, Neil and Mackay, Sally *Paul of Yugoslavia*, Canada Wide Magazines and Communications Ltd, 1996 p45
13 Princess Olga's diary 8 September 1922 quoted in Balfour and Mackay Ibid. pp 45-46
14 Princess Olga's diary 11 September 1922 quoted in Balfour and Mackay Ibid p 46
15 Lest Memory Fails p 26
16 Princess Olga's diary 11 September 1922 quoted in Balfour and Mackay op. cit., p 46
17 The Brisbane Courier accessed from Trove Australia www.trove. nla.gov.au accessed 12 August 2012
18 Conversation with Princess Alexander of Yugoslavia
19 Conversations with Princess Maria Pia of Bourbon-Savoy and Princess Alexander of Yugoslavia.
20 Princess Olga's diary 4 August 1977
21 Princess Olga to Princess Nicholas 12 April 1927 [Princess Elizabeth Collection]
22 Greek Royal Family website www.formerkingofgreece.org/en accessed 11 August 2012
23 The Australian Women's Weekly 16 April 1938 accessed from Trove Australia www.trove.nla. gov.au 10/08/2012
24 Olga's diary 3 October 1922 quoted in Balfour and Mackay op. cit., p47
25 Olga's diary 23 November 1922 quoted in Balfour and Mackay Ibid., p48
26 Olga's diary entry quoted in Balfour and Mackay Ibid., p49

Chapter 8-Betrothal and Marriage.

1 King, op. cit., p 90
2 Lest Memory Fails pp 26-27
3 Princess Olga's diary 1923 quoted in Balfour and Mackay op.cit., p51
4 Lest Memory Fails pp 26-27

5 Infante Alfonso, Duke of Galliera to Prince Paul 24 September 1968 Columbia Box 1

6 Princess Olga's diary Balfour and Mackay op. cit., p51

7 Princess Olga's diary 13 July 1923 quoted in Balfour and Mackay Ibid. p52

8 Princess Olga's diary 18 July 1923quoted in Balfour and Mackay Ibid. p53

9 Princess Olga's diary 20 July 1923 quoted in Balfour and Mackay Ibid. p53

10 Lest Memory Fails p27

11 Olga's diary 23 July 1923 quoted in Balfour and Mackay op. cit., p54

12 Lest Memory Fails p31

13 Lest Memory Fails p27

14 Olga's diary quoted in Balfour and Mackay op. cit., p54

15 Christopher, Prince op. cit., p156

16 Lest Memory Fails p27

17 Jankovic, Miodrag article "King Peter's Second Father" Novosti newspaper 21 December 2011, accessed through http://www.novosti.rs/dodatni_sadrzaj/clanci.119.html:358750-Kralj-Petar-drugi-otac 16 October 2013

18 Lest Memory Fails p28

19 Lest Memory Fails p34

20 http://thepeerage.com/p955.htm#i9545 accessed 27 November 2012

21 Lest Memory Fail p28

22 Interview with Princess Maria Pia of Savoy-Bourbon 10 June 2011

23 Jankovic op cit.,

24 Information provided by Judith Curthoys Archivist Christ Church Oxford by e mail 16/11/2012

25 Balfour and Mackay op. cit., p30

26 Balfour and Mackay Ibid. p32

27 Information contained in Oxford University's Roll of Service provided by Judith Curthoys Archivist Christ Church Oxford by e mail 16/11/2012

28 Balfour and Mackay Ibid pp 33-36 and Tucker & Roberts World War I ABC-CLIO, Santa Barbara, 2005, pp. 1075–6

29 Morning Bulletin 5 August 1939 accessed from Trove Australia www.trove.nla.gov.au 10 August 2012

30 Balfour and Mackay op. cit., p36

31 Balfour and Mackay Ibid. p38

32 For full background details see Sotirovic, Vladislav B. Creation of the Kingdom of Serbs, Croats and Slovenes, Vilnius University Press, 2007 pp72-104

33 Entry for Sir Henry Channon (1897–1958), Oxford Dictionary of National Biography, Oxford University Press, 2004; online edition, accessed 19 November 2012

34 Channon, Henry (1967). James, Robert Rhodes. Ed. Chips: The Diaries of Sir Henry Channon Weidenfeld and Nicolson, London, p29

35 Forbes, Grania My Darling Buffy-The Early Life of the Queen Mother Headline Richard Cohen Publishers London, 1999 p112

36 Shawcross, William Queen Elizabeth the Queen Mother: The Official Biography, Macmillan, London, 2009 p116

37 Information provided by Judith Curthoys Archivist Christ Church Oxford and also by the University Archives by e mails 16 November 2012

38 Forbes, op. cit., p184

39 Lest Memories Fail p32

40 Prince Nicholas to Queen Olga of Greece, 17/24 October 1923 [Princess Elizabeth Collection].

41 Princess Olga's diary entry October 1923 quoted in Balfour and Mackay op. cit., p 55

42 Princess Olga's diary 21 October 1923 quoted in Balfour and Mackay op. cit., p 55

43 Prince Nicholas to Queen Olga of Greece, 17/24 October 1923 [Princess Elizabeth Collection].

44 Prince Nicholas to Queen Olga of Greece, 17/24 October 1923 [Princess Elizabeth Collection].

45 Princess Olga's diary 22 October 1923 quoted in Balfour and Mackay op. cit., p 56

46 Prince Nicholas to Queen Olga of Greece, 17/24 October 1923 [Princess Elizabeth Collection].

47 Duchess of York to Lady Strathmore 26 October 1923 quoted in Shawcross op. cit., p200

48 Princess Olga's diary November 1923 quoted in Balfour and Mackay op. cit., p 57

Chapter 9 Belgrade, Bohinj and Beyond.

1 RA MDKD/PRIV/FORFF Princess Olga to Princess Marina 1 February 1924

2 Princess Olga's diary 27 January 1924 quoted in Balfour and Mackay op. cit., p58

3 Lest Memory Fails p35

4 Pakula, op. cit., p314

5 Parrot, Cecil The Tightrope Faber and Faber, London, 1975, pp18-20

6 Lest Memory Fails p35

7 Parrot, op. cit., p25

8 Lest Memory Fail p35

9 RA MDKD/PRIV/FORFF Princess Olga to Princess Nicholas 9 February 1924

10 Princess Olga's diary 1924 quoted in Balfour and Mackay op. cit., p59

11 RA MDKD/PRIV/FORFF Princess Olga to Princess Nicholas 9 February 1924

12 Ibid.

13 RA MDKD/PRIV/FORFF Princess Olga to Princess Marina 15 March 1924

14 Parrot, Ibid. p22

15 RA MDKD/PRIV/FORFF Princess Olga to Princess Nicholas 9 February 1924

16 RA MDKD/PRIV/FORFF Princess Olga to Princess Nicholas 9 February 1924

17 Lest Memory Fails p35

18 RA MDKD/PRIV/FORFF Princess Olga to Princess Nicholas 9 February 1924

19 Lest Memory Fails p36

20 Princess Olga's diary 20 April 1924 quoted in Balfour and Mackay op. cit., p58

21 Lest Memory Fails p36

22 Balfour and Mackay op. cit., p69

23 RA MDKD/OUT/FOX Princess Olga to Kate Fox 11 February 1928

24 RA MDKD/PRIV/FORFF Princess Olga to Princess Marina 25 October 1924

25 Lest Memory Fails p41

26 Balfour and Mackay op. cit., p65

27 Princess Olga's diary January 1925 quoted in Balfour and Mackay op. cit., p65

28 Princess Olga's diary 1925 quoted in Balfour and Mackay Ibid p66

29 Balfour and Mackay Ibid pp 66-67

30 Princess Olga's diary 1925 quoted in Balfour and Mackay Ibid p68

31 RA MDKD/OUT/FOX Princess Olga to Kate Fox 27 September 1925

32 RA MDKD/OUT/FOX Princess Olga to Kate Fox 27 September 1925

33 RA MDKD/OUT/FOX Princess Olga to Kate Fox 27 September 1925

34 Balfour and Mackay op. cit., p69

35 Balfour and Mackay op. cit., p68

36 Lest Memory Fails p41

37 Conversation with Prince Alexander of Yugoslavia April 2011

38 Lest Memory Fails p37

39 Pakula, op. cit., p324

40 Lest Memory Fails p41

41 RA MDKD/OUT/FOX Princess Olga to Kate Fox 15 January 1926

42 RA MDKD/OUT/FOX Princess Olga to Kate Fox 7 April 1926

43 RA MDKD/OUT/FOX Princess Olga to Kate Fox 24 April 1926

44 RA MDKD/OUT/FOX Princess Olga to Kate Fox 22 May 1926

45 RA MDKD/OUT/FOX Princess Olga to Kate Fox 1 June 1926

46 Princess Olga's diary 17 June 1926 quoted in Balfour and Mackay op. cit., p71

47 RA MDKD/OUT/FOX Princess Olga to Kate Fox 8 July 1926

48 RA MDKD/OUT/FOX Princess Olga to Kate Fox 1 September 1926

49 RA MDKD/OUT/FOX Princess Olga to Kate Fox 1 October 1926

50 RA MDKD/OUT/FOX Princess Olga to Kate Fox 4 November 1926

51 RA MDKD/OUT/FOX Princess Olga to Kate Fox 26 October 1926

52 RA MDKD/OUT/FOX Princess Olga to Kate Fox 4 November 1926

53 RA MDKD/OUT/FOX Princess Olga to Kate Fox December 10 1926

54 RA MDKD/OUT/FOX Princess Olga to Kate Fox 3 December1926

55 Chicago Daily Tribune 13 December, 1926 accessed from Google News www.news.google.com 20 December 2013

56 RA MDKD/OUT/FOX Princess Olga to Kate Fox 15 April 1927

57 Princess Olga to Princess Nicholas 12 April 1927 [Princess Elizabeth Collection.]

58 RA MDKD/OUT/FOX Princess Olga to Kate Fox 15 April 1927

59 RA MDKD/OUT/FOX Princess Olga to Kate Fox 29 April 1927

60 RA MDKD/OUT/FOX Princess Olga to Kate Fox 13 November 1927

61 Princess Olga to Princess Nicholas 12 April 1927 [Princess Elizabeth Collection].

62 RA MDKD/OUT/FOX Princess Olga to Kate Fox 29 April 1927

63 Princess Olga to Princess Nicholas 18 May 1927 [Princess Elizabeth Collection].

64 Princess Olga to Princess Nicholas 25 May 1927 [Princess Elizabeth Collection].

65 Princess Olga to Princess Nicholas 5 June 1927 [Princess Elizabeth Collection].

66 RA MDKD/OUT/FOX Princess Olga to Kate Fox 24 June 1927

67 RA MDKD/OUT/FOX Princess Olga to Kate Fox 11 July 1927

68 RA MDKD/OUT/FOX Princess Olga to Kate Fox 1 August 1927

69 RA MDKD/OUT/FOX Princess Olga to Kate Fox 1 August 1927

70 RA MDKD/OUT/FOX Princess Olga to Kate Fox 30 September 1927

71 RA MDKD/PRIV/FORFF
Princess Olga to Princess Marina
25 October 1927
72 Princess Olga to Princess
Nicholas 21 October 1927
[Princess Elizabeth Collection].
73 Princess Olga to Princess
Nicholas 6 November 1927
[Princess Elizabeth Collection].

Chapter 10-Finding One's Feet.

1 RA MDKD/OUT/FOX Princess
Olga to Kate Fox 13 November
1927
2 Princess Olga to Princess
Nicholas 16 November 1927
[Princess Elizabeth Collection.]
3 Princess Olga to Princess
Nicholas 31 December 1927
[Princess Elizabeth Collection.]
4 Princess Olga to Princess
Nicholas 16 November 1927
[Princess Elizabeth Collection.]
5 RA MDKD/OUT/FOX Princess
Olga to Kate Fox 14 January
1928 addendum 15 January 1928
6 RA MDKD/OUT/FOX Princess
Olga to Kate Fox 14 January
1928 addendum 16 January 1928
7 RA MDKD/PRIV/FORRF/
Princess Olga to Princess Marina
26 January 1928
8 RA MDKD/OUT/FOX Princess
Olga to Kate Fox 6 June 1928
9 RA MDKD/OUT/FOX Princess
Olga to Kate Fox 12 June 1928
10 RA MDKD/OUT/FOX Princess
Olga to Kate Fox 6 June 1928
11 Prince Paul to Mrs Berenson 4
May 1928 quoted in Balfour and
Mackay op. cit., p72
12 Lest Memory Fails p42
13 RA MDKD/OUT/FOX Princess
Olga to Kate Fox 20 July 1928
14 RA MDKD/OUT/FOX Princess
Olga to Kate Fox 30 July 1928
15 RA MDKD/OUT/FOX Princess
Olga to Kate Fox 27 August 1928
16 RA MDKD/OUT/FOX Princess
Olga to Kate Fox 8 September
1928
17 RA MDKD/OUT/FOX Princess
Olga to Kate Fox 16 February
1929
18 RA MDKD/OUT/FOX Princess
Olga to Kate Fox 4 April 1929
19 RA MDKD/PRIV/FORFF
Princess Olga to Princess Marina
7 June 1929
20 RA MDKD/OUT/FOX Princess
Olga to Kate Fox 17 August 1929
21 RA MDKD/OUT/FOX Princess
Olga to Kate Fox 24 September
1929
22 RA MDKD/OUT/FOX Princess
Olga to Kate Fox 17 August 1929
23 Stojadinović, Milan La
Yougoslavie Entre Les Deux
Guerres, Nouvelles Editions
Latines, Paris, 1979 p45
24 Stojadinović, Ibid. p241
25 Stojadinović, Ibid. p45
26 Duke of York to the Duchess of
York 8 January 1930 quoted in
Shawcross op. cit., p 313
27 RA MDKD/OUT/FOX Princess
Olga to Kate Fox 14 February
1930
28 RA MDKD/OUT/FOX Princess
Olga to Kate Fox 12 March 1930
29 RA MDKD/OUT/FOX Princess
Olga to Kate Fox 14 February
1930
30 RA MDKD/OUT/FOX Princess
Olga to Kate Fox 12 March 1930
31 RA MDKD/OUT/FOX Princess
Olga to Kate Fox 23 March 1930
32 RA MDKD/OUT/FOX Princess
Olga to Kate Fox 8 April 1930
33 RA MDKD/OUT/FOX Princess
Olga to Kate Fox 7 August 1930

34 Balfour and Mackay op. cit., p124
35 The New York Times 4 January 1931 accessed through New York Times website www.nytimes.com 21 October 2013
36 RA MDKD/OUT/FOX Princess Olga to Kate Fox 7 April 1931
37 Pakula, op. cit., pp 380-381
38 RA MDKD/OUT/FOX Princess Marina to Kate Fox 7 May 1931
39 Pakula, op. cit., p386
40 King Alexander to Prince Paul 13 May 1931 Columbia Box 1.
41 RA MDKD/OUT/FOX Princess Olga to Kate Fox 13 July 1931
42 RA MDKD/OUT/FOX Princess Olga to Kate Fox 11 October 1931
43 RA MDKD/OUT/FOX Princess Olga to Kate Fox 16 October 1931
44 RA MDKD/OUT/FOX Princess Olga to Kate Fox 19 October 1931
45 RA MDKD/OUT/FOX Princess Olga to Kate Fox 26 October 1931
46 RA MDKD/OUT/FOX Princess Olga to Kate Fox 22 October 1931
47 RA MDKD/OUT/FOX Princess Olga to Kate Fox 4 December 1931
48 RA MDKD/OUT/FOX Princess Olga to Kate Fox 17 December 1931
49 RA MDKD/PRIV/FORFF Princess Olga to Princess Marina 12 January 1932
50 RA MDKD/PRIV/FORFF Princess Olga to Princess Marina 30 January 1932
51 RA MDKD/OUT/FOX Princess Olga to Kate Fox 6 April 1932
52 I Tatti Prince Paul to Bernard Berenson 30 July 1932 quoted in Balfour and Mackay op. cit., p88
53 RA MDKD/PRIV/FORFF Princess Olga to Princess Marina 23 September 1932
54 RA MDKD/PRIV/FORFF Princess Olga to Princess Marina 2 October 1932
55 Princess Olga's diary 6 January 1933
56 RA MDKD/PRIV/FORFF Princess Olga to Princess Marina 14 December 1932
57 RA MDKD/PRIV/FORFF Princess Olga to Princess Marina 1 February 1932
58 Princess Olga's diary 5 February 1933
59 Princess Olga's diary 8 February 1933
60 Jelavich, Barbara, *History of the Balkans: Twentieth Century*, Cambridge University Press, 1983. p. 201
61 Princess Olga's diary 6 March 1933
62 Princess Olga's diary 23 February 1933
63 Princess Olga's diary 14 February 1933
64 Princess Olga's diary 18 March 1933
65 Princess Olga's diary 11 February 1933
66 Princess Olga's diary 15 February 1933
67 Princess Olga's diary 30 March 1933
68 Princess Olga's diary 7 March 1933
69 Princess Olga's diary 7 March 1933
70 Princess Olga's diary 15 March 1933
71 Princess Olga's diary 20 March 1933

72 Princess Olga's diary 11 June 1933

73 Princess Olga's diary 25 June 1933

74 Princess Olga's diary 27 June 1933

75 Princess Olga's diary 27 June 1933

76 Princess Olga's diary 28 June 1933

77 Princess Olga's diary 28 June 1933

78 Princess Olga's diary 30 June 1933

79 Princess Olga's diary 1 July 1933

80 Princess Olga's diary 2 July 1933

81 Princess Olga's diary 7 July 1933

82 Princess Olga's diary 30 July 1933

83 Princess Olga's diary 1 August 1933

Chapter 11 Two Weddings and a Funeral.

1 Princess Olga's diary 24 August 1933

2 Princess Olga's diary 9 September 1933

3 Balfour and Mackay op.cit., p87

4 Princess Olga's diary 10 September 1933

5 Princess Olga's diary 21 September 1933

6 King op.cit., p115

7 Princess Olga's diary 22 September 1933

8 Princess Olga's diary 11 October 1933

9 Princess Olga's diary 14 October 1933

10 Princess Olga's diary 21 October 1933

11 Princess Olga's diary 23 October 1933

12 Princess Olga's diary 3 November 1933

13 Princess Olga's diary 20 November 1933

14 RA MDKD/OUT/FOX Princess Olga to Kate Fox 4 December, 1933

15 RA MDKD/OUT/FOX Princess Olga to Kate Fox 6 December, 1933

16 RA MDKD/OUT/FOX Princess Olga to Kate Fox 23 November, 1933

17 Princess Olga's diary 29 December 1933

18 Princess Olga's diary 10 January 1934

19 Princess Olga's diary 23 January 1934

20 RA MDKD/PRIV/FORRF Princess Olga to Princess Marina 1 February 1934

21 RA MDKD/OUT/FOX Princess Olga to Kate Fox 5 February 1934

22 RA MDKD/OUT/FOX Miss Ethel Smith to Kate Fox 30 January, 1934

23 Princess Olga's diary 26 February 1934

24 Ristelhueber, René A History of the Balkan Peoples Twayne Publishers Woodbridge 1971 p302

25 The New York Times 10 October 1934 accessed from New York Times website www.nytimes.com 10 March 2013

26 Princess Olga's diary 3 March 1934

27 Princess Olga's diary 8 April 1934

28 Princess Olga's diary 1 May 1934

29 Princess Olga's diary 7 May 1934

30 Princess Olga's diary 8 May 1934

31 Princess Olga's diary 10 May 1934

32 Princess Olga's diary 12 May 1934

33 Princess Olga's diary 13 May 1934

34 Higham, Charles *Wallis The Secret Lives of the Duchess of Windsor*, Sidjwick and Jackson, London, 1988 p79

35 Princess Olga's diary 15 May 1934

36 Princess Olga's diary 16 May 1934

37 RA MDKD/OUT/FOX Princess Olga to Miss Fox 22 May 1934

38 Princess Olga's diary 16 May 1934

39 Princess Olga's diary 17 May 1934

40 Princess Olga's diary 23 June 1934

41 Princess Olga's diary 18 June 1934

42 RA MDKD/OUT/FOX Princess Olga to Kate Fox 14 September 1934

43 Princess Olga's diary 18 July 1934

44 RA MDKD/OUT/FOX Princess Olga to Kate Fox 7 September 1934

45 Princess Olga's diary 2 August 1934

46 Princess Olga's diary 5 August 1934

47 Christopher op.cit., p158

48 King, Stella op. cit., p117

49 Princess Olga's diary 21 August 1934

50 RA MDKD/OUT/FOX Princess Olga to Kate Fox 7 September 1934

51 RA MDKD/PRIV/FORFF Princess Olga to Princess Marina 26 September 1934

52 Princess Olga's diary 27 September 1934

53 Princess Olga's diary 28 September 1934

54 Princess Olga's diary 2 October 1934

55 Princess Olga's diary 4 October 1934

56 RA MDKD/PRIV/FORRF Princess Olga to Princess Marina 9 October 1934

57 Parrot, Cecil pp 39-40

58 Princess Olga in conversation with Balfour and Mackay for their book on Prince Paul.

59 Princess Olga's diary 8 October 1934

60 The Evening Independent October 9, 1934 accessed from Google News www.news.google.com 10 March 2013

61 Princess Olga's diary 9 October 1934

62 Princess Olga's diary 11 October 1934

63 Princess Olga's diary 11 October 1934

64 New York Times 10 October 1934 accessed from www.nytimes.com 10 March 2013

65 Parrot op.cit., p52

66 Undated Note Prince Paul to Princess Nicholas [Princess Elizabeth Collection].

67 RA MDKD/OUT/ FOX Princess Olga to Kate Fox 15 October 1934

68 Princess Olga's diary 13 October 1934

69 RA MDKD/OUT/ FOX Princess Olga to Kate Fox 15 October 1934

70 Pakula, op. cit., p401 and Parrot, op.cit., p60

71 Balfour and Mackay op. cit., p105

72 Notes made by Prince Paul 1945 Columbia Box 3

73 Prince Paul to Chips Channon 25 June 1945 Columbia Box 3

74 The Mercury Hobart 16 May 1938 accessed through Trove Australia www.trove.nla.gov.au 15 July 2013

75 Prince Philip of Hesse to the Prince Regent 13 January 1935 Columbia Box 2

76 Princess Olga's diary 29 October 1934

77 RA MDKD/OUT/ FOX Princess Olga to Kate Fox 3 November 1934

78 Princess Olga's diary 7 November 1934

79 Princess Olga's diary 10 November 1934

80 RA MDKD/OUT/ FOX Princess Olga to Kate Fox 16 November 1934

81 Herald-Journal November 13 1934 accessed from Google News www.news.google.com 08 March 2013

82 Princess Olga's diary 22 November 1934

83 Princess Olga's diary 24 November 1934

84 King, op.cit., p127

85 The Prince Regent to 'Jock' Balfour 3 November 1934 quoted in Balfour and Mackay op. cit., p104

Chapter 12-Queen in all but Name.

1 Princess Olga's diary 9 December 1934

2 Princess Olga's diary 15 December 1934

3 Princess Olga's diary 16 December 1934

4 Princess Olga's diary 23 December 1934

5 RA MDKD/OUT/ FOX Princess Olga to Kate Fox 20 December 1934

6 The Schenectady Gazette 19 December 1934 accessed from Google news www. news.google. com 31 March 2013

7 Princess Olga's diary 26 December 1934

8 Princess Olga's diary 30 December 1934

9 RA MDKD/OUT/ FOX Letters from Princess Olga to Kate Fox 11 December 1934

10 Princess Olga's diary 10 January 1935

11 Prince Philip of Hesse to the Prince Regent 13 January 1935 Columbia Box 2

12 RA MDKD/OUT/ FOX Letter from Princess Olga to Kate Fox 22 January 1935

13 Princess Olga's diary 9 February 1935

14 The Montreal Gazette 21 February 1935 accessed from Google news www. news.google. com 31 March 2013

15 Princess Olga's diary 6 March 1935

16 Princess Olga's diary 3 March 1935

17 Princess Olga's diary 20 March 1935

18 Princess Olga's diary 17 March 1935

19 Princess Olga's diary 10 March 1935

20 Princess Olga's diary 23 May 1935

21 Princess Olga's diary 14 May 1935

22 Princess Olga's diary 6 June 1935

23 Princess Olga's diary 7 June 1935

24 Princess Olga's diary 19 June 1935

25 Princess Olga's diary 2 July 1935

26 Balfour and Mackay op.cit., p111

27 Princess Olga's diary 21 June 1935

28 Princess Olga's diary 5 July 1935
29 Princess Olga's diary 13 July 1935
30 King George of the Hellenes to the Prince Regent 20 August 1935 Columbia Box 2
31 Princess Olga's diary 12 August 1935
32 Stojadinović, op.cit., p252
33 RA MDKD/OUT/ FOX Princess Olga to Kate Fox 24 August 1935
34 Princess Olga's diary 19 September 1935
35 RA MDKD/OUT/ FOX Princess Olga to Kate Fox 12 September 1935
36 Princess Olga's diary 28 September 1935
37 Van Creveld, Martin *Hitler's Strategy 1940-1941 The Balkan Clue,* Cambridge University Press, 1973 p5
38 Prince Paul to Chips Channon 1945 Columbia Box 3
39 Princess Olga's diary 14 October 1935
40 Princess Olga's diary 21 October 1935
41 Princess Olga's diary 31 October 1935
42 Princess Olga's diary 25 October 1935
43 Princess Olga's diary 10 November 1935
44 Princess Olga's diary 23 November 1935
45 Princess Olga's diary 30 November 1935
46 Princess Olga's diary 5 December 1935
47 Princess Olga's diary 3 December 1935
48 Princess Olga's diary 14 December 1935
49 Rothwell, Victor *Anthony Eden: A Political Biography,*
    Manchester University Press, 1992 p57
50 Princess Olga's diary 22 December 1935
51 Princess Olga's diary 1 January 1936
52 Princess Olga diary 19 January 1936
53 Princess Olga diary 21 January 1936
54 Princess Olga's diary 5 February 1936
55 Princess Olga's diary 1 March 1936
56 Stojadinović, op.cit., p87
57 Princess Olga's diary 16 March 1936
58 Princess Olga's diary 1 April 1936
59 Princess Olga's diary 7 April 1936
60 Princess Olga's diary 17 April 1936
61 RA MDKD/OUT/ FOX Princess Olga to Kate Fox 14 May 1936
62 Stojadinović to Prince Paul quoted in Balfour and Mackay op. cit., p131
63 Princess Olga's diary 5 June 1936
64 Princess Olga's diary 26 June 1936
65 Princess Olga's diary 1 July 1936
66 Princess Olga's diary 27 June 1936
67 Princess Olga's diary 1 July 1936
68 Princess Olga's diary 9 July 1936
69 Princess Olga's diary 3 August 1936
70 Princess Olga's diary 9 August 1936
71 Balfour and Mackay op.cit., p128
72 Princess Olga's diary 10 August 1936
73 Princess Olga diary 13 September 1936

74   RA MDKD/OUT/ FOX Princess Olga to Kate Fox 17 September 1936

75   RA MDKD/OUT/ FOX Princess Olga to Kate Fox 1 August 1936

76   RA MDKD/OUT/ FOX Princess Olga to Kate Fox 23 October 1936

77   Princess Olga's diary 2 November 1936

78   RA MDKD/OUT/ FOX Princess Olga to Kate Fox 23 October 1936

79   Maček, Vladko *In the Struggle for Freedom,* R Speller and Sons, New York 1957 p178

80   Princess Olga's diary 8 November 1936

81   The Chicago Daily Tribune November 14 1936 accessed from http://pqasb.pqarchiver.com/chicagotribune 02 April 2013

82   Princess Olga's diary 13 November 1936

83   Princess Olga's diary 15 November 1936

84   Chips: The Dairies of Sir Henry Channon, entry for 17 November 1936, p104

85   Prince Paul's diary 17 November 1936 Columbia Box 5

86   Princess Olga's diary 19 November 1936

87   Chips: The Dairies of Sir Henry Channon, entry for 19 November 1936 p106

88   Chips: The Dairies of Sir Henry Channon, entry for 3 December 1936 p116 and Princess Olga's diary 19 November 1936

89   Princess Olga's diary 19 November 1936

90   Princess Olga's diary 22 November 1936

91   The Times 3 December 1936

92   Chips: The Dairies of Sir Henry Channon, entry for 3 December 1936 p114

93   Chips: The Dairies of Sir Henry Channon, entry for 3 December 1936 p116

94   Princess Olga's diary 4 December 1936

95   Princess Olga's diary 5 December 1936

96   Princess Olga's diary 6 December 1936

97   Princess Olga's diary 7 December 1936

98   Princess Olga's diary 8 December 1936

99   Princess Olga's diary 11 December 1936

100   Duke of Kent to Prince Paul 16 December 1936 quoted in Balfour and Mackay op.cit., p137

101   Princess Olga's diary 25 December 1936

102   Queen Mary to Prince Paul 16 December 1936 Columbia Box 3

103   Prince Edward to Prince Paul 18 March 1937 Columbia Box 2.

104   Prince Edward to Prince Paul Box 18 March 1937 Columbia Box 2.

105   Princess Olga's diary 12 January 1937

106   Princess Olga's diary 27 February 1937

107   Princess Olga's diary 25 February 1937

108   Princess Olga's diary 25 March 1937

109   RA MDKD/OUT/ FOX Princess Olga to Kate Fox 10 April 1937

110   Princess Olga's diary 27 April 1937

111   Princess Olga's diary 4 May 1937

112   Princess Olga's diary 6 May 1937

113   Princess Olga's diary 10 May 1937

114   Princess Olga's diary 12 May 1937

115   FO 371/21196 Urgent Telegram 15 May 1937 Sir Eric Phipps

[British Ambassador Paris] to Foreign Office

116 Princess Olga's diary 25 May 1937

117 Princess Olga's diary 27 May 1937

118 Princess Olga's diary 3 June 1937

119 RA MDKD/PRIV/FORRF Princess Olga to Princess Marina 9 June 1937

120 RA MDKD/OUT/FOX Princess Olga to Kate Fox 5 June 1937

121 RA MDKD/PRIV/FORFF Princess Olga to Princess Marina 9 July 1937

122 Princess Olga's diary 15 July 1937

123 Princess Olga's diary 14 June 1937

124 Princess Olga's diary 13 July 1937

125 Princess Olga's diary 24 July 1937

126 Princess Olga's diary 24 July 1937

127 Princess Olga's diary 29 July 1937

128 Princess Olga's diary 28 July 1937

129 Princess Olga' diary 1 August 1937

130 Princess Olga' diary 2 August 1937

131 Princess Olga' diary 15 August 1937

132 Chips: The Dairies of Sir Henry Channon, entry for 27 August 1937, p170

133 Princess Olga' diary 14 August 1937

134 FO371/21197 Conversation between Prince Paul and Terence Shone First Secretary British Legation Belgrade

135 Princess Olga's diary 9 September 1937

136 Lampe, John R. *Yugoslavia as History: Twice There Was a Country*, Cambridge University Press, 2000 p179

137 Princess Olga's diary 10 September 1937

138 Princess Olga's diary 2 November 1937

139 Princess Olga's diary 12 November 1937

140 Princess Olga's diary 16 November 1937

141 Princess Olga's diary 17 November 1937

142 Princess Olga's diary 17 November 1937

143 Princess Olga's diary 24 November 1937

144 Princess Olga's diary 26 November 1937

145 Princess Olga's diary 10 December 1937

146 Princess Olga's diary 15 December 1937

147 Princess Olga's diary 11 December 1937

148 Princess Olga's diary 26 December 1937

149 Princess Olga's diary 6 January 1938

150 Princess Olga's diary 7 January 1938

151 Princess Olga's diary 8 January 1938

152 Princess Olga's diary 7 January 1938

153 Princess Olga's diary 8 January 1938

154 Princess Olga's diary 9 January 1938

155 Princess Olga's diary 27 January 1938

156 Princess Olga's diary 30 January 1938

157 Princess Olga's diary 31 January 1938

158 RA MDKD/PRIV/FORFF
Princess Olga to Princess Marina
3 February 1938

159 Princess Olga's diary 8 February
1938

160 RA MDKD/OUT/FOX Princess
Marina to Kate Fox 11 February
1938

161 Princess Olga's diary 24 February
1938

162 RA MDKD/OUT/FOX Princess
Olga to Kate Fox 1 March 1938

163 RA MDKD/OUT/FOX Princess
Olga to Kate Fox 1 March 1938

164 Princess Olga's diary 4 March
1938

165 Princess Olga's diary 2 March
1938

166 Princess Olga's diary 11 March
1938

167 Princess Olga's diary 14 March
1938

168 Princess Olga's diary 12 March
1938

169 Lewiston Evening Journal March
19, 1938 accessed through
Google News www.news.google.
com 08 April 2013

170 Princess Olga's diary 4 April
1938

171 Princess Olga's diary 5 April
1938

172 RA MDKD/OUT/FOX Princess
Olga to Kate Fox 8 May 1938

173 Princess Olga's diary 22 May
1938

174 RA MDKD/OUT/FOX Princess
Olga to Kate Fox 5 June 1938

175 RA MDKD/OUT/FOX Princess
Olga to Kate Fox 8 June 1938

176 Princess Olga's diary 21 June
1938

177 Princess Olga's diary 26 June
1938

178 Princess Olga's diary 18 July
1938

179 RA MDKD/OUT/FOX Princess
Marina to Kate Fox 30 July 1938

180 King Carol of Romania to Prince
Paul 24 August 1938 Columbia
Box 1.

181 RA MDKD/PRIV/FORFF
Princess Olga to Princess Marina
9 August 1938

182 RA MDKD/OUT/FOX Princess
Olga to Kate Fox 28 August 1938

183 Details on www.skepticism.org
accessed 14 January 2015

184 Princess Olga's diary 13
September 1938

185 Princess Olga's diary 15
September 1938

186 Princess Olga's diary 21
September 1938

187 Princess Olga's diary 22
September 1938

188 Princess Olga's diary 24
September 1938

189 Princess Olga's diary 26
September 1938

190 Princess Olga's diary 27
September 1938

191 Princess Olga's diary 30
September 1938

192 Princess Olga's diary 4 October
1938

193 Princess Olga's diary 26 October
1938

194 Princess Olga's diary 3 November
1938

195 Cohen, Philip Serbia's Secret War,
Texas A&M University Press,
1996 p18

196 Princess Olga's diary 17
November 1938

197 Princess Olga's diary 9 November
1938

198 Lampe, op.cit., p186

199 Chips: The Diaries of Sir Henry
Channon, entry for 6 December
1938 p223

200 Princess Olga's diary 28 November 1938

201 The Montreal Gazette 7 December 1938 accessed from Google News www.news.google.com 11 April 2013

202 Princess Olga's diary 6 December 1938

203 The New York Times 11 December 1938 accessed from New York Times website www.select.nytimes.com 22 October 2013

204 Princess Olga's diary 11 December 1938

205 Princess Olga's diary 19 December 1938

206 Princess Olga's diary 24 December 1938

207 Princess Olga's diary 31 December 1938

Chapter 13-Troubled Times

1 Balfour and Mackay op.cit., p163

2 van Creveld, op.cit., pp 6-7

3 RA MDKD/OUT/ FOX Princess Olga to Kate Fox 13 March 1939

4 Cecil Parrot to the Prince Regent 18 February 1939 Columbia Box 10

5 Peter, King A King's Heritage, Putnam, New York, 1954, p32

6 RA MDKD/PRIV/FORFF Princess Olga to Princess Marina 29 March 1939

7 RA MDKD/OUT/ FOX Princess Olga to Kate Fox 13 March 1939

8 RA MDKD/PRIV/FORFF Princess Olga to Princess Marina 29 March 1939

9 Balfour and Mackay op. cit., p168

10 RA MDKD/PRIV/FORRF/ Princess Olga to Princess Marina 11 April 1939

11 RA MDKD/PRIV/FORRF/ Princess Olga to Princess Marina 11 April 1939 attached 'List of Things of Value'.

12 RA MDKD/OUT/ FOX Princess Olga to Kate Fox 8 May 1939

13 Duke of Kent to the Prince Regent 24 April 1939 Columbia Box 2

14 RA MDKD/OUT/ FOX Princess Olga to Kate Fox 8 May 1939

15 van Creveld, op. cit., p7

16 RA MDKD/PRIV/FORFF Princess Olga to Princess Marina 11 May 1939

17 The Glasgow Herald 9 May, 1939 accessed from Google News www.news.google.com 16 January 2013

18 Balfour and Mackay op.cit., p173

19 The Catholic Herald 19 May 1939 accessed from www.archive.catholicherald.co.uk 31 October 2013

20 RA MDKD/OUT/FOX Princess Olga to Kate Fox 26 May 1939

21 Goering's testimony at the Nuremberg Tribunal, Day 82 accessed from http://gooring.tripod.com/goo28.html 12 April 2013

22 The Advertiser Adelaide 3 June 1939 accessed from Trove Australia www.trove.nla.gov.au 12 April 2013

23 RA MDKD/PRIV/FORRF Princess Olga to Princess Marina 3 June 1939

24 Balfour and Mackay op.cit., p176

25 Princess Olga to an American Envoy in Belgrade quoted in Irving, David The War Path 2003 p362 accessed on-line from http://www.fpp.co.uk/books/WarPh/WarPath.pdf 14 April 2013

26 Ibid p361

27 Interview with Archuchess Sophie of Austria, Princess of Windisch-Graetz 21 May 2015

28 Diary entry of Infante Alfonso, Duke of Galliera quoted by him in a letter to Prince Paul 29 December 1954 Columbia Box 1

29 Irving, op.cit., p361

30 Written response by Princess Elizabeth of Yugoslavia to the author by e mail 2 June 2011.

31 Princess Olga's recollections quoted in Balfour and Mackay op.cit., pp176-7

32 Conversation with Princess Alexander of Yugoslavia

33 The New York Times 6 July 1939 accessed from New York Times site www.select.nytimes.com 14 April 2013

34 Irving, op.cit., p361

35 RA MDKD/OUT/FOX Princess Olga to Kate Fox 18 June 1939

36 RA MDKD/OUT/FOX Princess Olga to Kate Fox 18 June 1939

37 Sir Nevile Henderson to the Prince Regent 27 July 1939 Columbia Box 6

38 Foreign Relations of the United States Diplomatic Papers, Government Printing Office, Washington 1957 pp 287-288 Joseph Kennedy to the Secretary of State 20 July 1939 quoted in Balfour and Mackay op.cit., p180

39 Chips: The Diaries of Sir Henry Channon, entry for 2 August 1939 pp254-5

40 Morning Bulletin 5 August 1939 accessed from Trove Australia www.trove.nla.gov.au 19 November 2012

41 Ramet, Sabrina The Three Yugoslavias: State-Building and Legitimation, 1918-2005, Indiana University Press, 2006 p106

42 RA MDKD/PRIV/FORFF Princess Olga to Princess Marina 4 September 1939

43 RA MDKD/PRIV/FORFF Princess Olga to Princess Marina 18 September 1939

44 RA MDKD/PRIV/FORFF Princess Olga to Princess Marina 4 September 1939

45 RA MDKD/PRIV/FORFF Princess Olga to Princess Marina 25 September 1939

46 RA MDKD/PRIV/FORFF Princess Olga to Princess Marina 11 September 1939

47 RA MDKD/OUT/FOX Princess Olga to Kate Fox 23 September 1939

48 RA MDKD/OUT/FOX Princess Olga to Kate Fox 9 October 1939

49 Sir Nevile Henderson to Prince Paul 22 September 1939 Columbia Box 6

50 RA MDKD/PRIV/FORFF Princess Olga to Princess Marina 16 October 1939

51 Queen Elizabeth to Prince Paul, 2 October 1939 Columbia Box 2

52 Duke of Kent to Prince Paul 25 October 1939 Columbia Box 2

53 RA MDKD/PRIV/FORFF Princess Olga to Princess Marina 16 October 1939

54 RA MDKD/OUT/FOX Princess Olga to Kate Fox 30 October 1939

55 RA MDKD/OUT/FOX Princess Olga to Kate Fox 30 October 1939

56 RA MDKD/OUT/FOX Princess Olga to Kate Fox 25 November 1939

57 RA MDKD/PRIV/FORFF Princess Olga to Princess Marina 13 November 1939

58 RA MDKD/PRIV/FORFF
Princess Olga to Princess Marina
4 December 1939

59 RA MDKD/PRIV/FORFF
Princess Olga to Princess Marina
29 November 1939

60 RA MDKD/PRIV/FORFF
Princess Olga to Princess Marina
29 November 1939

61 RA MDKD/PRIV/FORFF
Princess Olga to Princess Marina
20 November 1939

62 RA MDKD/OUT/FOX Princess
Olga to Kate Fox 1 January 1940

63 RA MDKD/PRIV/FORFF
Princess Olga to Princess Marina
18 December 1939

64 RA MDKD/PRIV/FORFF
Princess Olga to Princess Marina
19 January 1940

65 RA MDKD/PRIV/FORFF
Princess Olga to Princess Marina
1 January 1940

66 RA MDKD/PRIV/FORFF
Princess Olga to Princess Marina
1 January 1940

67 Duke of Kent to the Prince
Regent 12 January 1940
Columbia Box 2.

68 Brugere, Raymond, *Veni
Vidi Vichy* Calmann-Levy,
Varves, France 1944 pp
195-196

69 The New York Times 28 January
1940 accessed from New York
Times site www.select.nytimes.
com 17 April 2013

70 Anthony Eden to the Prince
Regent 8 February 1940
Columbia Box 2.

71 RA MDKD/OUT/FOX Princess
Olga to Kate Fox 20 January
1940

72 FO 371/25029 Ronald Ian
Campbell [British Minister
Belgrade] to Lord Halifax 25
January 1940

73 RA MDKD/PRIV/FORFF
Princess Olga to Princess Marina
22 January 1940

74 RA MDKD/OUT/FOX Princess
Olga to Kate Fox 11 March
1940

75 RA MDKD/OUT/FOX Princess
Olga to Kate Fox 20 March 1940

76 RA MDKD/PRIV/FORFF
Princess Olga to Princess Marina
8 February 1940

77 Princess Olga to Princess
Nicholas 13 March 1940
[Princess Elizabeth Collection].

78 Chips: The Diaries of Sir Henry
Channon, entry for 24 March
1940 p292

79 Chips: The Diaries of Sir Henry
Channon, entry for 25 March
1940 p292

80 The Duke of Kent to the Prince
Regent 2 April 1940 Columbia
Box 2

81 Chips: The Diaries of Sir Henry
Channon, entry for 29 March
1940 p292

82 Queen Marie of Yugoslavia to the
Prince Regent 8 April 1940
Columbia Box 3

83 Queen Marie of Yugoslavia
to the Prince Regent 30
April 1940 Columbia
Box 3

84 Princess Olga to Princess
Nicholas 14 April 1940 [Princess
Elizabeth Collection]

85 Princess Olga to Princess
Nicholas 14 April 1940 [Princess
Elizabeth Collection]

86 Balfour and Mackay op.cit.,
p195

87 Princess Olga to Princess
Nicholas 14 April 1940 [Princess
Elizabeth Collection].

88 Duke of Kent to the Prince
Regent 2 April 1940 Columbia
Box 2

89 Prince Paul to Princess Olga 15 April 1940 [Princess Elizabeth Collection].

90 Queen Marie of Yugoslavia to the Prince Regent 30 April 1940 Columbia Box 3

91 Princess Olga to Princess Nicholas 5 May 1940 [Princess Elizabeth Collection]

92 Prince Paul to Princess Olga 21 April 1940 quoted in Balfour and Mackay op.cit., p196

93 Princess Olga to Princess Nicholas 5 May 1940 [Princess Elizabeth Collection].

94 Princess Olga to Princess Nicholas 11 May 1940 [Princess Elizabeth Collection]

95 RA MDKD/OUT/FOX Letter marked Wednesday evening from Princess Olga to Miss Fox

96 Balfour and Mackay op. cit., p198

97 RA MDKD/OUT/FOX Princess Olga to Kate Fox 4 June 1940

98 The Calgary Herald 11 June 1940 accessed through Google News www.news.google.com 15 April 2013

99 Princess Olga's diary 4 October 1940 quoted in Balfour and Mackay op.cit., p200

Chapter 14-Yugoslavia in Crisis

1 King George VI to Prince Paul 3 July 1940 Columbia Box 1

2 Wheeler-Bennett, John *King George VI His Life and Reign*, Macmillan, London, 1958, p492

3 Duke of Kent to the Prince Regent 17 July 1940 Columbia Box 2

4 RA MDKD/OUT/FOX Princess Olga to Kate Fox 6 July 1940

5 Princess Olga to Princess Nicholas 16 July 1940 [Princess Elizabeth private collection]

6 Ileana, Princess *'I Live Again'*, Ladies' Home Journal, January 1952 accessed from www.tkinter. smig.net 15 July 2013

7 Onslow, Sue *Britain and the Belgrade Coup of 27 March 1941 Revisited* eJournal of International March 2005 p17 accessed on 15 July 2013 from www.researchgate.net/ publication/30522529_

8 Onslow Ibid. pp 29 and 38

9 Princess Olga's diary 4 September 1940

10 RA MDKD/OUT/FOX Princess Olga to Kate Fox 9 September 1940

11 Royal Romances *"King Carol and Magda Lupescu"* Marshall Cavendish ,1990, Vol. 32 p39

12 Balfour and Mackay op. cit., p206

13 Article 3 of the Tripartite Pact accessed from World War 2 database http://ww2db.com on 5 March 2016

14 van Creveld, op cit., p20

15 Princess Olga's diary 18 November 1940 Columbia Box 4

16 Princess Olga's diary 7 November 1940 Columbia Box 4

17 RA MDKD/OUT/FOX Princess Olga to Kate Fox 12 November 1940

18 King George VI to Prince Paul 14 November 1940 Columbia Box 1

19 CAB 65/10/13 UK War Cabinet Memorandum 21 November 1941 accessed from www. ukwarcabinet.org.uk 5 March 2016

20 FO371/25031 Telegram from Ronald Ian Campbell to Foreign Office 23 November 1940

21 CAB 66/13/41 UK War Cabinet Report of the Chief of Staff Committee 24 November 1940 accessed from www.ukwarcabinet.org.uk 5 March 2016

22 FO371/20351 Foreign Office to Belgrade 24 November 1940

23 van Creveld, op. cit., p78

24 van Creveld, Ibid. p64

25 van Creveld, Ibid. p65

26 van Creveld, Ibid. p65

27 Balfour and Mackay op. cit., p211

28 Hitler and Cincar Markovic conversation 28.11.40 Documents on German Foreign Policy [DGFP], Series D, Volume XI, Document No. 417 HM Stationery Office, London, 1956

29 Princess Olga's diary 5 December 1940 Columbia Box 4

30 von Heeren to German Foreign Ministry 7 December 1940 quoted in van Creveld, op.cit., p124

31 RA MDKD/OUT/FOX Princess Olga to Kate Fox 23 December 1940

32 RA MDKD/PRIV/FORFF Princess Olga to Princess Marina 23 December 1940

33 Onslow op. cit., p36

34 Ribbentrop to von Heeren 21.12.1941 DGFP, D, XI No.549

35 van Creveld, op. cit., p180

36 van Creveld, Ibid. p124

37 van Creveld, Ibid. p126

38 Princess Olga's diary 24 December 1940 Columbia Box 4

39 RA MDKD/OUT/FOX Princess Olga to Kate Fox 23 December 1940

40 Duke of Kent to Prince Regent 14 December 1940 Columbia University Box 2.

41 RA MDKD/PRIV/FORFF Princess Olga to Princess Marina 23 December 1940

42 Princess Olga's diary 1 January 1941

43 Balfour and Mackay op. cit., pp 215-216

44 Princess Olga's diary 7 January 1941

45 Princess Olga's diary 10 January 1941

46 Prince Regent to the King of the Hellenes quoted by Princess Elizabeth in You tube interview with Mira Adanja Polak uploaded 22 December 2011

47 Princess Olga's diary 12 January 1941

48 Chips: The Diaries of Sir Henry Channon entry for 12 January 1941 p348

49 D'Este, Carlo Warlord: A Life of Churchill at War 1874-1945, Allen Lane, London, 2009 p584

50 Chips: The Diaries of Sir Henry Channon, entry for 12 January 1941 p348

51 CAB/65/21/2 UK War Cabinet Secret Annexe Minute 2 14 January 1941 accessed from www.ukwarcabinet.org.uk 9 March 2016

52 Chips: The Diaries of Sir Henry Channon, entry for 16 January 1941 p348

53 Prime Minister to Foreign Secretary 14 January 1941 quoted in Churchill, Winston S., The Grand Alliance (The Second World War Volume III) Mariner Books (an imprint of Houghton Mifflin), Boston, 1986 p 140

54 Chips: The Diaries of Sir Henry Channon, entry for 16 January 1941 p349

55 Princess Olga's diary 17 January 1941

56 RA MDKD/OUT/FOX Princess Olga to Kate Fox 18 January 1941

57 Chips: The Diaries of Sir Henry Channon entry for 19 January 1941 p349

58 Princess Olga's diary 19 January 1941

59 Chips: The Diaries of Sir Henry Channon entry for 20 January 1941 p350

60 CAB/65/21/3 UK War Cabinet Confidental Annexe Minute 2 20 January 1941 accessed from www.ukwarcabinet.org.uk 9 March 2016

61 CAB 65/57/ UK War Cabinet Minute 28 January 1941 accessed fromwww.ukwarcabinet.org.uk 9 March 2016

62 van Creveld op.cit., p13

63 Hoptner, Jacob B. Yugoslavia in Crisis Columbia University Press, New York, 1962 pp 204-5

64 Princess Olga's diary 29 January 1941.

65 Princess Olga's diary 6 February 1941

66 Princess Olga's diary 12 February 1941

67 RA MDKD/OUT/FOX Princess Olga to Kate Fox 12 February 1941

68 Princess Olga's diary 6 February 1941

69 Princess Olga to Princess Nicholas 11 February 1941 [Princess Elizabeth Collection].

70 RA MDKD/OUT/FOX Princess Olga to Kate Fox 12 February 1941

71 FO954/33B Churchill to Eden 12 February 1941

72 Ribbentrop-Cvetković conversation 14.2.1941 DGFP, D, XII, No.47

73 Ribbentrop-Cvetković conversation 14.2.1941 DGFP, D, XII, No.48

74 Princess Olga's diary 14 February 1941

75 Princess Olga's diary 17 February 1941

76 Princess Olga's diary 11 February 1941

77 Princess Olga's diary 18 February 1941

78 Princess Olga's diary 19 February 1941

79 Princess Olga's diary 21 February 1941

80 van Creveld, op. cit., p127

81 FO954/33B Report on the Mission of the Secretary of State for Foreign Affairs to the Eastern Mediterranean February-April: First Discussions with the Greek Government February 22 1941

82 FO954/33B Report on the Mission of the Secretary of State for Foreign Affairs to the Eastern Mediterranean February-April: Attitude of Yugoslavia February 22-27 1941

83 Princess Olga's diary 26 February 1941

84 Princess Olga's diary 28 February 1941

85 Hugh Dalton to the Prime Minister 28 March 1941 quoted in Balfour and Mackay op. cit., pp310-11

86 Kosta Petrov Interview with Princess Elizabeth of Yugoslavia uploaded 21 January 2012 http://www.youtube.com/watch?v=fKywWOFuvIo

87 Private Typed Memorandum Undated Prince Paul to Princess Nicholas [Princess Elizabeth private collection].

88 Princess Olga's diary 2 March 1941

89 Princess Olga's diary 3 March 1941

90 German Foreign Ministry to von Heeren 7.3.1941 DGFP, D, XII No.130

91 Private Typed Memorandum Undated Prince Paul to Princess Nicholas [Princess Elizabeth Collection].

92 German Foreign Ministry to von Heeren 7.3.1941 DGFP, D, XII No.130

93 Prince Paul to Jacob Hoptner 21 October 1971 Columbia Box 3

94 Princess Olga's diary 4 March 1941

95 RA MDKD/OUT/FOX Princess Olga to Kate Fox 4 March 1941

96 FO954/33B Report on the Mission of the Secretary of State for Foreign Affairs to the Eastern Mediterranean February-April 1941 Attitude of Yugoslavia February March 3-9 1941

97 Anthony Eden to the Prince Regent 3 March 1941 Columbia Box 2

98 Princess Olga's diary 5 March1941

99 Balfour and Mackay op. cit., p227

100 Princess Olga's diary 6 March 1941

101 Balfour and Mackay op. cit., p228

102 Extracts of Report by Terence Glanville 27 September 1941 quoted in Balfour and Mackay op. cit., p316

103 Private Typed Memorandum Undated Prince Paul to Princess Nicholas [Princess Elizabeth Collection].

104 Princess Olga's diary 6 March 1941

105 von Heeren to German Foreign Ministry 7.3.1941 DGFP, D, XII No.131

106 Princess Olga's diary 7 March 1941

107 Princess Olga's diary 7 March 1941

108 FO954/33B Report on the Mission of the Secretary of State for Foreign Affairs to the Eastern Mediterranean February-April 1941 Attitude of Yugoslavia February March 3-9 March 1941

109 Princess Olga's diary 8 March 1941.

110 Princess Olga to Princess Nicholas 10-15 March 1941, written over 5 days [Princess Elizabeth collection]

111 van Creveld, op. cit., p128

112 Princess Olga's diary 9 March 1941

113 von Heeren to German Foreign Ministry 10.3.1941 DGFP, D, XII No.145; von Heeren to German Foreign Ministry 11.3.1941 DGFP, D, XII No.149

114 Princess Olga to Princess Nicholas 10-15 March 1941 [Princess Elizabeth Collection]

115 Private Typed Memorandum Undated Prince Paul to Princess Nicholas [Princess Elizabeth Collection].

116 Princess Olga's diary 11 March 1941

117 von Heeren to German Foreign Ministry 11.3.1941 DGFP, D, XII No.151

118 von Heeren to German Foreign Ministry 12.3.1941 DGFP, D, XII No.156

119 von Heeren to German Foreign Ministry 14.3.1941 DGFP, D, XII No.165

120 Princess Olga's diary 15 March 1941

121 Private Typed Memorandum Undated Prince Paul to Princess

Nicholas [Princess Elizabeth Collection].

122 Churchill to Roosevelt, 10.3.41, Foreign Relations of the United States Diplomatic Papers, Government Printing Office, Washington 1957, 1941, Europe Vol. II 951-2

123 Princess Olga's diary 14 March 1941

124 Princess Olga to Princess Nicholas 10-15 March 1941 [Princess Elizabeth Collection]

125 Princess Olga's diary 15 March 1941

126 RA MDKD/PRIV/FORFF Princess Olga to Princess Marina 15 March 1941

127 Private Typed Memorandum Undated Prince Paul to Princess Nicholas [Princess Elizabeth Collection]

128 FO954/33B Annex 17 Anthony Eden to Prince Regent 18 March 1941

129 FO954/33B Report on the Mission of the Secretary of State for Foreign Affairs to the Eastern Mediterranean February-April 1941 Further approaches to the Yugoslav Government March 9-24 1941

130 Hoptner, op. cit., p226

131 Princess Olga's diary 18 March 1941

132 FO954/33B Report on the Mission of the Secretary of State for Foreign Affairs to the Eastern Mediterranean February-April 1941 Further approaches to the Yugoslav Government March 9-24 1941

133 Balfour and Mackay op. cit., p237

134 Onslow, op. cit., p51

135 The Sydney Morning Herald 22 March, 1941 accessed from www. news.google.com 23 March 2016

136 FO371/30231 R2937/G, Philip Nichols file note, 24 March 1941 quoted in Onslow, op. cit., p45

137 New York Times editorial quoted in The Courier Mail 22 March 1941 accessed from Trove Australia www.trove.nla.gov.au 20 April 2013

138 Princess Olga's diary 20 March 1941

139 The New York Times 21 March 1941 accessed from New York Times website www.select. nytimes.com 20 April 2013

140 FO954/33B Report on the Mission of the Secretary of State for Foreign Affairs to the Eastern Mediterranean February-April 1941 Further approaches to the Yugoslav Government March 9-24 1941

141 Princess Olga's diary 21 March 1941

142 Princess Olga's diary 22 March 1941

143 FO371/30206 Report from Terence Shone sent by Ronald Ian Campbell to Anthony Eden 23 March 1941

144 FO954/33B Report on the Mission of the Secretary of State for Foreign Affairs to the Eastern Mediterranean February-April 1941 Further approaches to the Yugoslav Government March 9-24 1941

145 King George VI to the Prince Regent 23 March 1941 Columbia Box 2

146 Princess Olga's diary 23 March 1941

147 Balfour and Mackay op. cit., p239

148 Report by Terence Glanville 27 September 1941 quoted in Balfour and Mackay op.cit., p317

149 Princess Olga's diary 23 March 1941
150 van Creveld, op. cit., 1973 p138
151 Princess Olga's diary 24 March 1941
152 FO954/33B Report on the Mission of the Secretary of State for Foreign Affairs to the Eastern Mediterranean February-April 1941 Further approaches to the Yugoslav Government March 9-24 1941
153 Report on the Coup d'état by Masterson 27 March 1941 quoted in Balfour and Mackay op.cit., p314
154 Note from Ribbentrop to Cvetkovic 25 March 1941 quoted in Balfour and Mackay Ibid. pp338-339
155 Princess Olga's diary 25 March 1941
156 Chips: The Diary of Sir Henry Channon Diary entry for 26 March 1941 p362
157 Princess Olga's diary 26 March 1941
158 Associated Press report in Pittsburgh Post-Gazette 27 March, 1941 accessed from www.news.google.com 21 April 2013
159 Princess Olga's diary 26 March 1941
160 Peter, King op. cit., p61
161 Prince Paul to Jacob Hoptner 27 October 1960 Columbia Box 3
162 Report on the coup by Ilija Trifunović 27 March 1941 quoted in Balfour and Mackay op.cit., p314
163 Balfour and Mackay Ibid. p246
164 Peter, King op. cit., pp68-69
165 Princess Olga's diary 27 March 1941 version quoted in Parrot, op. cit., p107
166 RA MDKD/PRIV/FORFF Princess Olga to Princess Marina 1 April 1941
167 Interview with Prince Alexander of Yugoslavia April 2011
168 RA MDKD/PRIV/FORFF Princess Olga to Princess Marina 1 April 1941
169 Churchill Volume III op. cit., p143
170 Recollection of Dr Maček in Hoptner, op. cit., p260
171 van Creveld, op. cit., p143
172 RA MDKD/PRIV/FORFF Princess Olga to Princess Marina 1 April 1941
173 van Creveld, op. cit., p143
174 Balfour and Mackay op. cit., p246
175 FO371/30255 Telegram 14 from HM Consul-General Zagreb to Foreign Office 27.3.41
176 Interview with Princess Elizabeth of Yugoslavia You Tube uploaded 17 January 2012 http://www.youtube.com/watch?v=XcRYifAeycg
177 Princess Olga's diary 27 March 1941 version quoted in Parrot, op. cit., p108
178 FO371/30255 Telegram from Anthony Eden to Ronald Ian Campbell 27 March 1941
179 Prince Paul to Jacob Hoptner October 1973 Columbia Box 3
180 RA MDKD/OUT/FOX Princess Olga to Kate Fox 24 April 1946
181 Princess Olga's diary 27 March 1941
182 Princess Olga's diary 27 March 1941 version quoted in Parrot, op. cit., p108
183 The New York Times 28 March 1941 accessed through New York Times website www.select.nytimes.com 22 April 2013

184 Chips: The Diaries of Sir Henry
Channon Diary, entry 27 March
1941 p362

185 The Advertiser Adelaide 28
March 1941 accessed from Trove
Australia www.trove.nla.gov.au
22 April 2013

Chapter 15-Political Prisoner.

1 Princess Olga's diary 28 March
1941

2 Princess Olga's diary 29 March
1941

3 Written response by Princess
Elizabeth by e mail 2 June 2011
to the author.

4 Princess Olga's diary 29 March
1941

5 Princess Olga's diary 4 April
1941

6 RA MDKD/PRIV/FORFF
Princess Olga to Princess Marina
1 April 1941

7 Princess Olga's diary 30 March
1941

8 RA MDKD/ PRIV/FORFF
Princess Olga to Princess Marina
1 April 1941

9 Written response by Princess
Elizabeth by e mail 2 June 2011
to the author.

10 Chips: The Diary of Sir Henry
Channon, entry 29 March 1941
p363

11 Queen Elizabeth to Lord Halifax
23 April 1941 quoted in
Shawcross op.cit., p536

12 RA MDKD/ PRIV/FORFF
Princess Olga to Princess Marina
1 April 1941

13 Chips: The Diaries of Sir Henry
Channon, entry for 30 March
1941 p363

14 FO371/30255 Foreign Office
Minute 28 March 1941

15 Princess Olga's diary 31 March
and 1 April 1941

16 van Creveld, op.cit., p143

17 FO371/59538 Foreign Office
Minute by M.S. Williams 27
March 1946

18 Princess Olga's diary 2 April
1941

19 Chips: The Diaries of Sir Henry
Channon Diary entry 7 April
1941 p365

20 D'Este op.cit., p585

21 Princess Olga's diary 1 and 4
April 1941

22 Princess Olga's diary 8 April
1941

23 Lewiston Morning Tribune 7
April, 1941 accessed from Google
News www.news.google.com 24
April 2013

24 Princess Olga's diary 9 April
1941

25 Princess Olga's diary 10 April
1941

26 RA MDKD/PRIV/FORFF
Princess Olga to Princess Marina
13 April 1941

27 Princess Olga's diary 11 April
1941

28 RA MDKD/OUT/FOX Princess
Marina to Kate Fox 28 April
1941 (this letter also encloses a
copy of an earlier letter sent by
Peter Coats to Henry Channon).

29 RA MDKD/PRIV/FORFF
Princess Olga to Princess Marina
13 April 1941

30 RA MDKD/OUT/FOX Princess
Marina to Kate Fox 28 April
1941 (this letter also encloses a
copy of an earlier letter sent by
Peter Coats to Henry Channon).

31 Prince Paul to the Duke of Kent
18 August 1941 Columbia Box 3

32 Princess Olga to Princess
Nicholas 13 April 1941 [Princess
Elizabeth Collection].

33 Princess Olga to Princess Nicholas 18 April 1941 [Princess Elizabeth Collection]

34 RA MDKD/PRIV/FORFF Princess Olga to Princess Marina 13 April [addendum written 15 April 1941]

35 Princess Olga to Princess Nicholas 13 April 1941 [Princess Elizabeth Collection].

36 RA MDKD/PRIV/FORFF Princess Olga to Princess Marina 13 April [addendum written 15 April 1941]

37 FO371/30255 Sir Miles Lampson to Foreign Office 16 April 1941

38 FO371/30255 Telegram from Foreign Office to Sir Miles Lampson 17 April 1941

39 Princess Olga's diary 18 April 1941

40 Princess Olga to Princess Nicholas 18 April 1941 [Princess Elizabeth Collection]

41 Princess Olga to Princess Nicholas 18 April 1941 [Princess Elizabeth Collection]

42 FO371/30255 Sir Miles Lampson to Foreign Office 16 April 1941

43 RA MDKD/PRIV/FORFF Princess Olga to Princess Marina 24 April 1941

44 RA MDKD/PRIV/FORFF Princess Olga to Princess Marina 24 April 1941

45 FO371/30255 Minute by P[ierson] Dixon to Sir Henry Moore 19 April 1941

46 Miss Ede interview from 1977 quoted in Balfour and Mackay op.cit., p266

47 Princess Olga's diary 28 April 1941

48 Princess Olga's diary 28 April 1941

49 CO967/140 Telegram Sir Henry Moore to Lord Moyne 30 April 1941

50 Princess Olga's diary 30 April 1941

51 Princess Olga's diary 1 May 1941

52 CO967/140 Telegram Sir Henry Moore to Lord Moyne 30 April 1941

53 CO967/140 Telegram Lord Moyne to Sir Henry Moore 2 May 1941

54 Princess Olga's diary 3 May 1941

55 Princess Olga's diary 4 May 1941

56 Princess Olga's diary 30 April 1941

57 Princess Olga's diary 6 May 1941

58 Princess Olga's diary 8 May 1941

59 Princess Olga's diary 9 May 1941

60 Princess Olga's diary 31 May 1941

61 RA MDKD/PRIV/FORFF Princess Olga to Princess Marina 19 June 1941 [addendum 23 June 1941]

62 Princess Olga's diary 1 June 1941

63 Princess Olga's diary 7 May 1941

64 Princess Olga's diary 11 May 1941

65 Princess Olga's diary 21 May 1941

66 Princess Olga's diary 18 July 1941

67 RA MDKD/PRIV/FORFF Princess Olga to Princess Marina 19 June 1941 [addendum 23 June 1941]

68 Princess Olga's diary 11 June 1941

69 Princess Olga's diary Memoranda 31 May 1941

70 Princess Olga' s diary 4 July 1941

71 Princess Olga's diary 28 July 1941

72 RA MDKD/PRIV/FORFF Princess Olga to Princess Marina 19 June 1941

73 CO967/140 Telegram from Princess Olga to Princess Marina 14 July 1941

74 Princess Olga's diary 30 June
    1941
75 RA MDKD/PRIV/FORFF
    Princess Olga to Princess Marina
    19 June 1941 [addendum 23 June
    1941]
76 FO 954/33B Sir Miles Lampson
    to Foreign Office 31 May 1941
77 Princess Olga's diary 23 June
    1941
78 Princess Olga's diary 25 June
    1941
79 Princess Olga's diary 26 June
    1941
80 RA MDKD/PRIV/FORFF
    Princess Olga to Princess Marina
    19 June 1941 [addendum 23 June
    1941]
81 Duke of Kent to Prince Paul 1
    July 1941 Columbia Box 2
82 Speech quoted in Peter, King op.
    cit., p91
83 Princess Olga's diary 2 July 1941
84 CO967/142 Comments in a Draft
    Domion Office Telegram
    (prepared by the Foreign Office
    25 February 1943) for British
    High Commissioner Union of
    South Africa
85 CO967/140 Covering Letters
    from Miss Malleson, Colonial
    Office to Mr Addis, Foreign
    Office-various dates.
86 Copy of telegram from
    the Duke of Kent to Prince Paul
    24/10/1941 marked
    in ink 'Authorised for
    Transmission' M Ruth Malleson
    24/X/1941
87 Princess Olga's diary 25 July
    1941
88 Princess Olga's diary 13 July
    1941
89 Princess Olga's diary 10 August
    1941
90 Princess Olga's diary 12 October
    1941
91 Princess Olga's diary 21
    September 1941
92 The Times 4 July 1941 accessed
    from Google News www.news.
    google.com 24 April 2013
93 The Times 15 July 1941 accessed
    from Google News www.news.
    google.com 24 April 2013
94 Duke of Kent to Prince Paul 1
    July 1941 Columbia Box 2.
95 Princess Olga's diary 1 August
    1941
96 Princess Olga's diary 13 August
    1941
97 Prince Paul to the Duke of Kent
    18 August 1941 Columbia
    Box 3
98 CO967/140 Minute Eastwood,
    Colonial Office to Labouchere,
    Foreign Office 1 September 1941
99 CO967/140 Minute from Walter
    [Lord Moyne] to Anthony Eden 8
    July 1941
100 CO167/140 Telegram Duchess of
    Kent to Princess Olga 12 August
    1941
101 Princess Olga's diary 6 September
    1941
102 Princess Olga's diary 1 January
    1942 'Review of the past year'.
103 Princess Olga's diary 17 October
    1941
104 Princess Olga's diary 27
    September 1941
105 Princess Olga's diary 28
    September 1941
106 Princess Olga's diary 28 October
    1941
107 CO967/140 Most Secret
    Telegram Governor Kenya to
    Secretary of State for the Colonies
    16 July 1941
108 Comments of the London
    Evening Standard diarist (of 26
    September) quoted in The Argus
    (Melbourne) 3 October 1941
    accessed from Trove Australia

www.trove.nla.gov.au 26 April 2013

109 The Argus (Melbourne) 3 October 1941 accessed from Trove Australia www.trove.nla.gov.au 26 April 2013

110 Conversation with Prince Alexander April 2011

111 FO371/30255

112 CO967/141 Lord Moyne to the Duke of Kent 14 January 1942

113 CO967/140 Telegram Governor Kenya to Secretary of State for the Colonies 30 April 1941

114 Prince Paul to the Duke of Kent 21 November 1941 Columbia Box 3

115 Prince Paul to the Duke of Kent 18 August 1941 Columbia Box 3

116 CO967/140 Telegram Duke of Kent to Prince Paul 24 October 1941

117 Duke of Kent to Prince Paul 5 November 1941 Columbia Box 2

118 Duke of Kent to Prince Paul 5 November 1941 Columbia Box 2

119 King Peter's speech at a luncheon for the National Defence Public Interest Committee quoted in Peter, King op. cit., p104

120 Prince Paul to the Duke of Kent 16 November 1941 Columbia Box 3

121 CO967/140 Henry Channon to Eastwood, Colonial Office 22 September 1941

122 Princess Olga's diary 24 December 1941

123 Prince Paul to the Duke of Kent 28 December 1941 Columbia Box 3

124 Princess Olga to Princess Nicholas 5 January 1942 [Princess Elizabeth Collection]

125 RA MDKD/PRIV/FORRF Princess Olga to Princess Marina 30 January 1942

126 CO967/141 Lord Moyne to the Duke of Kent 19 February 1942

127 Princess Olga to Princess Nicholas 9 March 1942 [Princess Elizabeth Collection]

128 Princess Olga to Princess Nicholas 25 March 1950 [Princess Elizabeth Collection]

129 Prince Paul to the Duke of Kent 2 March 1942 Columbia Box 3

130 RA MDKD/PRIV/FORRF Princess Olga to Princess Nicholas 9 March 1942

131 RA MDKD/PRIV/FORRF Princess Olga to Princess Marina 14 April 1942

132 RA MDKD/OUT/FOX Princess Olga's to Kate Fox 30 May 1942

133 RA MDKD/PRIV/FORRF Princess Olga to Princess Marina 9 March 1942

134 Princess Olga to Princess Nicholas 30 March 1942 [Princess Elizabeth Collection]

135 CO967/141 Telegram Duke of Kent to Prince Paul 12 April 1942

136 RA MDKD/OUT/FOX Princess Olga to Kate Fox 30 May 1942

137 Princess Olga's diary 10 May 1942

138 RA MDKD/PRIV/FORRF Princess Olga to Princess Marina 19 May 1942

139 Prince Paul to the Duke of Kent 8 April 1942 Columbia Box 3

140 RA MDKD/PRIV/FORRF Princess Olga to Princess Marina 19 May 1942

141 Princess Olga's diary 6 June 1942

142 Prince Paul to the Duke of Kent 15 June 1942 Columbia Box 3

143 Duke of Kent to Prince Paul 25 March and 5 July 1942 Columbia Box 2

144 RA MDKD/OUT/FOX Princess Olga to Kate Fox 14 July 1942

145 Prince Paul to the Duke of Kent 15 June 1942 Columbia Box 3

146 Princess Olga's diary 6 July 1942

147 Princess Olga's diary 15 July 1942

148 RA MDKD/OUT/FOX Princess Olga to Kate Fox 14 July 1942

149 Princess Olga's diary 24 July 1942

150 Princess Olga's diary 26 July 1942

151 Princess Olga's diary 28 July 1942

152 Princess Olga's diary 15 August 1942

153 Princess Olga' s diary 13 August 1942

Chapter 16-Mercy Mission

1 Spartacus Educational http://www.spartacus.schoolnet.co.uk/2WWkentD.htm accessed 27 April 2013

2 RA MDKD/OUT/FOX Prince Alexander to Kate Fox 26 August 1942

3 Princess Olga's diary 26 August 1942

4 Princess Olga's diary 27 August 1942

5 Princess Olga's diary 28 August 1942

6 Princess Olga's diary 30 August 1942

7 Princess Olga's diary 31 August 1942

8 Princess Olga's diary 1 September 1942

9 CO967/141 Telegram King George VI to Princess Olga 31 August 1942

10 Princess Olga's diary 1 September 1942

11 Princess Olga to Princess Nicholas 5 October 1942 [Princess Elizabeth Collection]

12 CO967/141 Telegram Princess Olga to King George VI 2 September 1942

13 CO967/141 Telegram King George VI to Governor Kenya 4 September 1942

14 CO967/141 Telegram Thornley, Colonial Office to the Colonial Governors 4 September 1942

15 CO967/141Cypher Telegram Acting Governor Kenya to Colonial Office 5 September 1942

16 CO967/141Telegram Acting Governor Kenya to Colonial Office 7 September 1942

17 CO 967/141 Most Secret and Personal Telegram Thornley, Colonial Office to Acting Governor, Kenya 11 September 1942

18 Princess Olga's diary 5 September 1942

19 Princess Olga's diary 8 September 1942

20 CO967/141 Telegram Princess Olga to King George V1 8 September 1942

21 Princess Olga's diary 16 September 1942

22 Princess Olga to Princess Nicholas 5 October 1942 [Princess Elizabeth Collection]

23 Princess Olga's diary 18 September 1942

24 Princess Olga to Princess Nicholas 5 October 1942 [Princess Elizabeth Collection]

25 Princess Olga's diary 18 September 1942

26 Princess Olga's diary 18 September 1942

27 Princess Olga to Prince Paul 25 September 1942 quoted in Balfour and Mackay op.cit.,. p284

28 Princess Olga's diary 19 September 1942

29 Princess Olga's diary 28 September 1942

30 Princess Olga to Princess Nicholas 5 October 1942 [Princess Elizabeth Collection]

31 Princess Olga's diary 20 September 1942

32 Princess Olga to Prince Paul 25 September 1942 Balfour and Mackay op cit., p284

33 Princess Olga to Princess Nicholas 5 October 1942 [Princess Elizabeth Collection]

34 Princess Olga's diary 21 September 1942

35 Prince Alexander to Prince Paul 26 October 1942 [Arrrived Naivasha 28 November 1942] Columbia Box 2

36 Princess Olga to Princess Nicholas 5 October 1942 [Princess Elizabeth Collection]

37 Princess Olga's diary 24 September 1942

38 Princess Olga to Princess Nicholas 5 October 1942 [Princess Elizabeth Collection]

39 Princess Olga's diary 29 September 1942

40 Princess Olga's diary 2 October 1942

41 Princess Olga's diary 31 October 1942

42 Princess Olga to Princess Nicholas 20 November 1942 [Princess Elizabeth Collection]

43 Princess Olga's diary 6 October 1942

44 Princess Olga to Princess Nicholas 24 October 1942 [Princess Elizabeth Collection]

45 Princess Olga's diary 6 October 1942

46 CO967/141 Thornley, Colonial Office to Governor of Kenya 3 October 1942

47 CO967/141Minute Lord Cranborne to Anthony Eden 7 October 1942

48 Cairn Post 10 October 1942 accessed from Trove Australia www trove.nla.gov au 02 October 2013

49 Princess Olga's diary 9 October 1942

50 Princess Olga's diary 14 October 1942

51 Princess Olga to Princess Nicholas 5 October 1942 [Princess Elizabeth Collection]

52 Princess Olga to Princess Nicholas 24 October 1942 [Princess Elizabeth Collection]

53 Princess Olga's diary 15 October 1942

54 Question by Captain Cunningham-Reid to the Secretary of State for Foreign Affairs House of Commons Debate 14 October 1942 accessed through www.theyworkforyou. com/debates/ 30 December 2013

55 Princess Olga's diary 15 October 1942

56 CO967/142 Typed Extract from a letter from Princess Olga to Princess Marina January 1943

57 FO371/33448 Minute 16 October 1942

58 FO371/33448 Minute 19 October 1942

59 CO967/142 Report of 27 January 1943 from Dr Bunny to the Secretary of State for the Colonies

60 Princess Olga to Princess Nicholas 24 October 1942 [Princess Elizabeth Collection]

61 Princess Olga's diary 17 October 1942

62 CO967/141 Minute by Lord Cranborne 22 October 1942

63 CO967/141 Minute by Lord Cranborne 22 October 1942

64 Written response from Princess Elizabeth by e mail 2 June 2011 to the author.

65 RA MDKD/PRIV/FORRF Princess Olga to Princess Marina 26 September 1946

66 CO967/141 Lord Cranborne to Princess Olga 4 November 1942

67 CO967/141 Keenleyside, Air Ministry to Thornley, Colonial Office 12 November 1942

68 Comments by Captain Cunningham-Reid in Debate in House of Commons 11 November 1942 accessed through www.theyworkforyou.com/ debates/ 30 December 2013

69 Comments by Captain Cunningham-Reid, Orders of the Day in House of Commons 17 November 1942 accessed through www.theyworkforyou.com/ debates/ 30 December 2013

70 Princess Olga's diary 12 November 1942

71 Princess Olga's diary 15 November 1942

72 Princess Olga's diary 17 November 1942

73 Princess Olga's diary 18 November 1942

74 Princess Olga's diary 22 November 1942

75 Princess Olga's diary 22 November 1942

76 CO967/141 Telegram Governor Kenya to the Secretary of State for the Colonies 1 December 1942

77 Balfour and Mackay op.cit., p286

78 CO967/142 Governor Kenya to the Secretary of State for the Colonies 10 February 1943

79 CO967/141 Telegram Governor Kenya to the Secretary of State for the Colonies 1 December 1942

80 CO967/142 Governor Kenya to the Secretary of State for the Colonies 10 February 1943

81 CO967/141 Telegram Governor Kenya to the Secretary of State for the Colonies 1 December 1942

82 RA MDKD/PRIV/FORFF Princess Olga to Princess Marina 16 January 1943

83 CO967/141 Telegram Secretary of State for the Colonies to Governor Kenya 4 December 1942

84 Princess Olga's diary 9 December 1942

85 Princess Olga's diary 11 December 1942

86 CO967/142 Governor Kenya to the Secretary of State for the Colonies 10 February 1943

87 CO967/142 Report of 27 January 1943 Dr Bunny to the Secretary of State for the Colonies

88 Princess Olga's diary 12 December 1942

89 Princess Olga's diary 12 December 1942

90 CO967/141 Minute Colonel Oliver Stanley to Anthony Eden 16 December 1942

91 Question by Captain Cunningham-Reid to the Secretary of State for Foreign Affairs House of Commons Debate 16 December 1942 accessed from www. theyworkforyou.com/debates/ 30 December 2013

92 Response by the Secretary of State for Foreign Affairs to Captain Cunningham-Reid House of Commons Debate 16 December 1942 accessed from www.theyworkforyou.com/ debates/ 30 December 2013

93 Response by Captain
    Cunningham-Reid to the
    Secretary of State for Foreign
    Affairs House of Commons
    Debate 16 December 1942
    accessed from http://www.
    theyworkforyou.com/debates/ 30
    December 2013
94 King George VI to Prince
    Paul 19 December 1942
    Columbia Papers
95 Princess Olga's diary 20
    December 1942
96 Princess Olga's diary 21
    December 1942
97 Princess Olga's diary 23
    December 1942
98 CO961/141 Anthony Eden to
    Colonel Oliver Stanley 22
    December 1942
99 CO967/141 Colonel Oliver
    Stanley to Princess Olga 24
    December 1942
100 Princess Olga's diary 24
    December 1942
101 Princess Olga's diary 28
    December 1942
102 CO967/141 Telegram Governor
    Kenya to Secretary of State for
    the Colonies 29 December 1942
103 Princess Olga's diary 30
    December 1942
104 Princess Olga's diary 31
    December 1942
105 RA MDKD/PRIV/FORFF
    Princess Olga to Princess Marina
    16 January 1943
106 CO967/142 Telegram Secretary
    of State for the Colonies to
    Governor Kenya 1 January 1943

Chapter 17-Despair and Hope.

1   Princess Olga's diary 12 January
    1943
2   Princess Olga's diary 14 January
    1943
3   Princess Olga's diary 13 January
    1943
4   Princess Olga's diary 14 January
    1943
5   RA MDKD/PRIV/FORFF
    Princess Olga to Princess Marina
    16 January 1943
6   Princess Olga's diary 14 January
    1943
7   CO967/142 Dr Bunny to the
    Secretary of State for the Colonies
    27 January 1943
8   CO967/142 Extract from a letter
    of 16 January 1943 from Princess
    Olga to Princess Marina
9   CO967/142 Governor Kenya to
    Secretary of State for the Colonies
    10 February 1943
10 Princess Olga's diary 6 February
    1943
11 CO967/142 Report by Dr
    Jex-Blake to the Secretary of State
    for the Colonies 9 February 1943
12 Princess Olga's diary 6 February
    1943
13 RA MDKD/PRIV/FORFF
    Princess Olga to Princess Marina
    6 February 1943
14 CO967/142 Telegram from
    Governor Kenya to Secretary of
    State for the Colonies 9 February
    1943
15 CO967/142 Colonel Stanley
    to Anthony Eden 10 February
    1943
16 CO967/142 Prime Minster's
    Personal Minute 12 February
    1943
17 CO967/142 Joint Minute from
    Colonel Oliver Stanley and
    Anthony Eden to Prime Minister
    Winston Churchill 19 February
    1943
18 CO967/142 Copy of Minute by
    the Prime Minister to the
    Secretary of State for the Colonies
    20 February 1943

[19] RA MDKD/PRIV/FORFF Princess Olga to Princess Marina 15 February 1943

[20] Princess Olga's diary 15 February 1943

[21] Princess Olga's diary 28 February 1943

[22] Princess Olga's diary 18 February 1943

[23] Princess Olga's diary 18 February 1943

[24] CO967/142 Harvey, Foreign Office to Garner, Dominion Office 25 February 1943

[25] CO967/142 copy of Telegram Dominion Office to the British High Commissioner Union of South Africa 1 March 1943

[26] CO967/142 Extract from a letter of 16 January 1943 from Princess Olga to Princess Marina

[27] CO967/142 Minute by Secretary of State for the Colonies 1 March 1943

[28] CO967/142 Colonel Stanley to Princess Marina 1 March 1943

[29] CO967/142 Telegram no 325 from British High Commissioner Union of South Africa to Dominion Office 4 March 1943

[30] CO967/142 Telegram no 324 from British High Commissioner Union of South Africa to Dominion Office 4 March 1943

[31] FO371/44368 Syers, Office of the British High Commissioner to Costar Dominion Office 2 August 1944

[32] CO967/142 Telegram no 324 from British High Commissioner Union of South Africa to Dominion Office 4 March 1943

[33] FO371/44368 Sullivan, Office of the British High Commissioner to Greenway, Foreign Office 15 April 1944

[34] Princess Olga's diary 16 March 1943

[35] Princess Olga's diary 17 March 1943

[36] Princess Olga's diary 18 March 1943

[37] Princess Olga's diary 24 March 1943

[38] Princess Olga's diary 27 March 1943

[39] Princess Olga's diary 30 March 1943

[40] RA MDKD/PRIV/FORFF Princess Olga to Princess Marina 4 April 1943

[41] Princess Olga's diary 5 April 1943

[42] RA MDKD/PRIV/FORFF Princess Olga to Princess Marina 5 April 1943

[43] CO967/142 Duchess of Kent to Colonel Oliver Stanley 5 April 1943

[44] CO967/142 Telegram no. 539 Dominion Office to British High Commissioner Union of South Africa 14 April 1943.

[45] Princess Olga's diary 19 April 1943

[46] Princess Olga's diary 18 May 1943

[47] CO967/142 Telegram Secretary of State for the Colonies to Governor Kenya 23 April 1943

[48] CO967/142 Telegram from Governor Kenya to Secretary of State for the Colonies 25 April 1943

[49] CO967/142 Telegram no 576 from Under-Secretary of State for Dominion Affairs to British High Commissioner Union of South Africa 23 April 1943

[50] Princess Olga's diary 28 April 1943

[51] Princess Olga's diary 30 April

[52] CO967/142 Telegram from Governor Kenya to Secretary of

State for the Colonies 2 May
1943

53 Princess Olga's diary 9 May 1943
54 Princess Olga's diary 9 May 1943
55 Princess Olga's diary 22 May
1943
56 RA MDKD/PRIV/FORFF
Princess Olga to Princess Marina
8 May 1943
57 Princess Olga's diary 26 May
1943
58 RA MDKD/PRIV/FORRF
Princess Olga to Princess Marina
14 July 1943
59 Princess Olga's diary 8 June 1943
60 Princess Olga's diary 11 June
1943
61 RA MDKD/PRIV/FORFF
Princess Olga to Princess Marina
11 June 1943

Chapter 18-South African Sojourn

1 Princess Olga's diary 18 June
1943
2 Princess Olga's diary 24 June
1943
3 Princess Olga's diary 27 June
1943
4 Princess Olga's diary 30 June
1943
5 RA MDKD/OUT/FOX Princess
Olga to Kate Fox 1 July 1943
6 Princess Olga's diary 4 July 1943
7 Princess Olga's diary 11 July
1943
8 Princess Olga's diary 6 July 1943
9 Princess Olga's diary 6 August
1943
10 Princess Olga's diary 13 July
1943
11 Princess Olga's diary 18 July
1943
12 Princess Olga's diary 24 July
1943

13 Princess Olga's diary 26 July
1943
14 Comments of Captain
Cunningham-Reid in House of
Commons Debate 28 July 1943
accessed from www.
theyworkforyou.com/ 30
December 2013
15 The Worker, Brisbane 16 August
1943 accessed from Trove
Australia www.trove.nla.gov.au
02 October 2013
16 Princess Olga's diary 29 July 1943
17 Princess Olga's diary 3 August
1943
18 Princess Olga's diary 1 August
1943
19 Comments by Captain
Cunningham-Reid House of
Commons Debate 4 August 1943
accessed from www.
theyworkforyou.com/ 30
December 2013
20 RA MDKD/PRIV/FORRF
Princess Olga to Princess Marina
11 August 1943
21 RA MDKD/PRIV/FORRF
Princess Olga to Princess Marina
11 August 1943
22 RA MDKD/OUT/FOX Princess
Olga to Kate Fox 29 October
1943
23 RA MDKD/PRIV/FORRF
Princess Olga to Princess Marina
11 August 1943
24 Princess Olga's diary 19 August
1943
25 Princess Olga's diary 24 August
1943
26 Princess Olga's diary 31 August
1943
27 Princess Olga's diary 29 August
1943
28 Princess Olga's diary 29
September 1943
29 Princess Olga's diary 28
September 1943

30 Princess Olga's diary 20 October 1943

31 Princess Olga's diary 13 October 1943

32 Princess Olga's diary 8 October 1943

33 RA MDKD/OUT/FOX Princess Olga to Kate Fox 29 October 1943

34 Princess Olga's diary 14 December 1943

35 Princess Olga's diary 1 December 1943

36 Princess Olga's diary 15 December 1943

37 Princess Olga's diary 20 December 1943

38 Princess Olga's diary 19 December 1943

39 Princess Olga's diary 23 December 1943

40 Princess Olga's diary 25 December 1943

41 Princess Olga's diary 31 December 1943

42 RA MDKD/PRIV/FORRF Princess Olga to Princess Marina 7 February 1944

43 RA MDKD/PRIV/FORRF Princess Olga to Princess Marina 25 February 1944

44 Princess Olga to Prince Paul 1 March 1944 Columbia Box 3

45 Telegram from King Peter and Queen Alexandra 22 March 1944 Columbia Box 4

46 RA MDKD/OUT/FOX Princess Olga to Kate Fox 18 April 1944

47 RA MDKD/OUT/FOX Princess Olga to Kate Fox 31 March 1944

48 FO 371/44368 Sullivan Office of the British High Commissioner to Greenway, Foreign Office 15 April 1944

49 RA MDKD/OUT/FOX Princess Olga to Kate Fox 17 May 1944

50 RA MDKD/OUT/FOX Princess Olga to Kate Fox 1 June 1944

51 RA MDKD/OUT/FOX Princess Olga to Kate Fox 17 May 1944

52 Princess Olga's diary 29 June 1944

53 RA MDKD/OUT/FOX Princess Olga to Kate Fox 1 June 1944

54 Thorpe, D.R *Supermac: The Life of Harold* Macmillan Chatto and Windus 2010 p197

55 Princess Olga's diary 6 June 1944

56 RA MDKD/OUT/FOX Princess Olga to Kate Fox 9 June 1944

57 Princess Olga's diary 7 July 1944

58 Princess Olga's diary 10 July 1944

59 Princess Olga's diary 16 July 1944

60 FO371/443368 Secret Telegram no.1044 Acting British High Commissioner to Dominion Office 23 September 1944

61 RA MDKD/PRIV/FORRF Princess Olga to Princess Marina 1 June 1944

62 Princess Olga's diary 4 August 1944

63 Princess Olga's diary 24 August 1944

64 Princess Olga's diary 17 September 1944

65 RA MDKD/OUT/FOX Princess Olga to Kate Fox 31 August 1944

66 Princess Olga's diary 21 September 1944

67 RA MDKD/OUT/FOX Princess Olga to Kate Fox 25 September 1944

68 Princess Olga's diary 28 September 1944

69 RA MDKD/PRIV/FORRF Princess Olga to Princess Marina 8 October 1944

70 Princess Olga's diary 9 October 1944

71 RA MDKD/PRIV/FORRF
Princess Olga to Princess Marina
8 October 1944

77 ΓO/371/44368 Dew, Foreign
Office to Miss Staples Dominion
Offfice 4 October 1944

73 FO371/44368 Minute by Reed,
Foreign Office 26 September
1944

74 FO371/443368 Secret Telegram
no.1044 Acting British High
Commissioner to Dominion
Office 23 September 1944

75 FO371/44368 Syers, Office of the
British High Commissioner to
Costar Dominion Office 2 August
1944

76 FO371/44368 Laskey, on behalf
of Reed, Foreign
Office to Miss Staples, Dominion
Office 18
October 1944

77 FO371/44368 Costar, Dominions
Office to Acting British High
Commissioner to the Union of
South Africa 1 November 1944

78 Princess Olga's diary 27 October
1944

79 RA MDKD/OUT/FOX Princess
Olga to Kate Fox 5 November
1944

80 Princess Olga's diary 21 October
1944

81 Princess Olga's diary 6 November
1944

82 RA MDKD/PRIV/FORRF
Princess Olga to Princess Marina
2 September 1944

83 RA MDKD/PRIV/FORRF
Princess Olga to Princess Marina
8 October 1944

84 RA MDKD/PRIV/FORRF
Princess Olga to Princess Marina
24 November 1944

85 RA MDKD/PRIV/FORRF
Princess Olga to Princess Marina
20 January 1945

86 House of Commons Debate of 6
December 1944 accessed from
www.theyworkforyou.com/
debates/ 30 December 2013

87 FO371/443368 Foreign Office
Minute by (initials
indistinguishable) 30 November
1944

88 Princess Olga diary 28 January
1945

89 Princess Olga diary 30 January
1945

90 Memorandum for the President
11 January 1945 found at CIA
Library: www.cia.gov/library/
center-for-the-study-of-
intelligence/kent-csi/vol9no2/
html/v09i2a07p_0001.htm

91 The Evening Independent 24
January 1945 accessed from
Google News www.news.google.
com 09 June 2013

92 Princess Olga's diary 24 February
1945

93 RA MDKD/PRIV/FORRF
Princess Olga to Princess Marina
31 March 1945

94 RA MDKD/PRIV/FORRF
Princess Olga to Princess Marina
9 March 1945

95 RA MDKD/OUT/FOX Princess
Olga to Kate Fox 24 April 1946

96 Princess Olga's diary 17 March
1945

97 Memorandum for the President
15 April 1945 CIA Library
op. cit.,

98 Princess Olga diary 8 May 1945

99 Princess Olga diary 26 July 1945

100 RA MDKD/OUT/FOX Princess
Olga to Miss Fox 18 January
1946

101 Field Marshal Smuts to Prince
Paul 29 August 1945 Columbia
Box 4

102 RA MDKD/OUT/FOX Princess
Olga to Kate Fox 9 October 1945

103 Princess Olga's diary 12 September 1945

104 Jankovic, Miodrag Article entitled 'Criminal Code 3028' Novosti Newspaper Belgrade 20 December 2011 accessed through http://www.novosti.rs/dodatni_sadrzaj/clanci.119.html:358569-Zlocinac-pod-brojem-3028 on 16 December 2013

105 RA MDKD/OUT/FOX Princess Olga to Kate Fox 16 October 1945

106 RA MDKD/OUT/FOX Princess Olga to Kate Fox 9 November 1945

107 RA MDKD/OUT/FOX Princess Olga to Miss Fox 15 November 1945

108 RA MDKD/OUT/FOX Princess Olga to Kate Fox 16 October 1945

109 RA MDKD/OUT/FOX Princess Olga to Kate Fox 9 November 1945

110 Princess Olga diary 11 November 1945

111 Princess Olga diary 13 November 1945

112 RA MDKD/OUT/FOX Princess Olga to Miss Fox 7 December 1945

113 RA MDKD/PRIV/FORRF Princess Olga to Princess Marina 8 December 1945

114 RA MDKD/PRIV/FORRF Princess Olga to Princess Marina 8 December 1945 (addendum 12 December).

115 RA MDKD/PRIV/FORRF Princess Olga to Princess Marina 8 December 1945

116 RA MDKD/OUT/FOX Princess Olga to Kate Fox 27 January 1946

117 RA MDKD/OUT/FOX Princess Olga to Kate Fox 10 March 1946

118 The Canberra Times 11 February 1946 accessed from Trove Australia www.trove.nla.gov.au 11 May 2016

119 RA MDKD/OUT/FOX Princess Olga to Kate Fox 5 March 1946

120 RA MDKD/OUT/FOX Princess Olga to Kate Fox 10 March 1946

121 RA MDKD/OUT/FOX Princess Olga to Kate Fox 6 April 1946

122 RA MDKD/OUT/FOX Princess Olga to Kate Fox 6 April 1946

123 RA MDKD/OUT/FOX Princess Olga to Kate Fox 6 April 1946

124 RA MDKD/OUT/FOX Princess Olga to Kate Fox 24 April 1946

125 RA MDKD/OUT/FOX Princess Olga to Kate Fox 6 April 1946

126 RA MDKD/OUT/FOX Princess Olga to Kate Fox 27 April 1946

127 FO371/59538 Minute by J.R. Colville, Foreign Office 13 March 1946

128 FO371/59538 Minute by M.S. Williams, Foreign Office 27 March 1946

129 FO371/59538 Telegram no 69 British High Commissioner to Dominion Office 4 February 1946

130 FO371/59538 Minute by M.S. Williams, Foreign Office 25 March 1946

131 FO371/59538 Telegram 223 British High Commissioner to Dominion Office 23 April 1946

132 RA MDKD/OUT/FOX Princess Olga to Kate Fox 9 June 1946

133 FO371/59538 Sir Edward Baring to Prince Paul 18 May 1946

134 RA MDKD/OUT/FOX Princess Olga to Kate Fox 24 May 1946

135 RA MDKD/OUT/FOX Princess Olga to Kate Fox 9 June 1946

136 RA MDKD/OUT/FOX Princess Olga to Kate Fox 23 June 1946

137 RA MDKD/OUT/FOX Princess Olga to Kate Fox 24 May 1946

138 RA MDKD/OUT/FOX Princess Olga to Kate Fox 26 June 1946

139 RA MDKD/OUT/FOX Princess Olga to Kate Fox 23 July 1946

140 FO371/59538. J.N Henderson, Foreign Office to Sir Alan Lascelles (Private Secretary to King George VI) 8 July 1946

141 FO371/59538 Sir Alan Lascelles to J.N Henderson, Foreign Office 9 July 1946

142 FO 371/59538 J.N. Henderson, Foreign Office to Sir Alan Lascelles 23 July 1946

143 RA MDKD/PRIV/FORRF Princess Olga to Princess Marina 26 September 1946

144 Van der Kiste, op.cit., p172

145 RA MDKD/OUT/FOX Princess Olga to Kate Fox 27 September 1946

146 RA MDKD/PRIV/FORRF Princess Olga to Princess Marina 26 September 1946

147 RA MDKD/PRIV/FORRF Princess Olga to Princess Marina 17 October 1946

148 RA MDKD/PRIV/FORRF Princess Olga to Princess Marina 11 September 1946

149 RA MDKD/PRIV/FORRF Princess Olga to Princess Marina 11 September 1946

150 RA MDKD/OUT/FOX Princess Olga to Kate Fox 27 September 1946

151 RA MDKD/PRIV/FORRF Princess Olga to Princess Marina 26 September 1946

152 RA MDKD/OUT/FOX Princess Olga to Kate Fox 27 September 1946

153 RA MDKD/OUT/FOX Princess Olga to Kate Fox 3 October 1946

154 RA MDKD/OUT/FOX Princess Olga to Kate Fox 22 October 1946

155 RA MDKD/OUT/FOX Princess Olga to Kate Fox 22 October 1946

156 RA MDKD/OUT/FOX Princess Nicholas to Kate Fox 16 December 1946

157 RA MDKD/PRIV/FORRF Princess Olga to Princess Marina 3 December 1946

158 RA MDKD/PRIV/FORRF Princess Olga to Princess Marina 3 December 1946

159 RA MDKD/PRIV/FORRF Princess Olga to Princess Marina 6 February 1947

160 RA MDKD/PRIV/FORRF Princess Olga to Princess Marina 3 December 1946

161 RA MDKD/OUT/FOX Princess Olga to Kate Fox December 27 1946

162 The Argus 1 January 1947 accessed fromTrove Australia www.trove.nla.gov.au 3 August 2013

Chapter 19-A Royal Meeting

1 Princess Olga's diary 1 January 1947

2 Princess Olga's diary 8 January 1947

3 RA MDKD/OUT/FOX Princess Olga to Kate Fox 9 January 1947

4 RA MDKD/PRIV/FORRF Princess Olga to Princess Marina 6 February 1947

5 RA MDKD/PRIV/FORRF Princess Olga to Princess Marina 6 February 1947

6 RA MDKD/PRIV/FORRF Princess Olga to Princess Marina 6 February 1947

7 RA MDKD/OUT/FOX Princess Nicholas to Kate Fox 22 March 1947

8 RA MDKD/OUT/FOX Princess Olga to Kate Fox 27 December 1946

9 RA MDKD/OUT/FOX Princess Olga to Kate Fox 15 February 1947

10 RA MDKD/PRIV/FORRF Princess Olga to Princess Marina 6 February 1947

11 Princess Olga's diary 17 February 1947

12 RA MDKD/OUT/FOX Princess Olga to Kate Fox 6 March 1947

13 Princess Olga's diary 20 March 1947

14 RA MDKD/OUT/FOX Princess Olga to Kate Fox 19 March 1947

15 RA MDKD/OUT/FOX Princess Nicholas to Kate Fox 22 March 1947

16 Princess Olga's diary 1 April 1947

17 Letter from Queen Elizabeth to Princess Olga 28 March 1947 viewed at www.forum. alexanderpalace.org/ 01 April 2013

18 RA MDKD/OUT/FOX Princess Olga to Kate Fox 5 April 1947

19 Princess Olga's diary 2 May 1947

20 RA MDKD/OUT/FOX Princess Olga to Kate Fox 3 April 1947

21 Interview with Archduchess Helen of Austria May 2011

22 RA MDKD/OUT/FOX Princess Olga to Kate Fox 5 April 1947

23 RA MDKD/OUT/FOX Princess Olga to Kate Fox 8 April 1947

24 RA MDKD/PRIV/FORRF Princess Olga to Princess Marina 10 April 1947

25 RA MDKD/OUT/FOX Princess Olga to Kate Fox 8 April 1947

26 Princess Olga's diary 6 April 1947

27 RA MDKD/PRIV/FORRF Princess Olga to Princess Marina 10 April 1947

28 RA MDKD/OUT/FOX Princess Olga to Kate Fox 8 April 1947

29 RA MDKD/PRIV/FORRF Princess Olga to Princess Marina 19 April 1947

30 RA MDKD/PRIV/FORRF Princess Olga to Princess Marina 10 April 1947

31 RA MDKD/PRIV/FORRF Princess Olga to Princess Marina 13 April 1947

32 Interview with Prince Alexander of Yugoslavia April 2011

33 Princess Olga's diary 24 February 1947

34 Princess Olga's diary 8 April 1947

35 RA MDKD/PRIV/FORRF Princess Olga to Princess Marina 13 April 1947

36 Princess Olga's diary 13 April 1947

37 Princess Olga's diary 21 April 1947

38 Princess Olga's diary 27 April 1947

39 RA MDKD/PRIV/FORRF Princess Olga to Princess Marina 11 May 1947

40 Princess Olga's diary 14 May 1947

41 Princess Olga's diary 18 May 1947

42 Princess Olga's diary 26 May 1947

43 Princess Olga's diary 5 June 1947

44 Princess Olga's diary 13 June 1947

45 RA MDKD/OUT/FOX Princess Olga to Kate Fox 21 June 1947

46 RA MDKD/OUT/FOX Princess Olga to Kate Fox 21 June 1947

47 Princess Olga's diary 22 June 1947

48 RA MDKD/OUT/FOX Princess Olga to Kate Fox 21 June 1947

49 Princess Olga's diary 22 August 1947

50 Princess Olga's diary 30 July 1947

51 Princess Olga's diary 1 August 1947

52 Princess Olga's diary 4 July 1947

53 Princess Olga's diary 9 July 1947

54 RA MDKD/OUT/FOX Princess Olga to Kate Fox 13 September 1947

55 RA MDKD/PRIV/FORRF Princess Olga to Princess Marina 15 September 1947

56 RA MDKD/OUT/FOX Princess Olga to Kate Fox 13 September 1947

57 Princess Olga's diary 25 September 1947

58 Princess Olga's diary 30 September 1947

59 RA MDKD/PRIV/FORFF Princess Olga to Princess Marina 22 October 1947

60 Princess Olga's diary 24 October 1947

61 RA MDKD/PRIV/FORFF Princess Olga to Princess Marina 7 November 1947

62 RA MDKD/OUT/FOX Princess Olga to Kate Fox 5 November 1947

63 Princess Olga's diary 8 November 1947

64 Princess Olga's diary 11 November 1947

65 Princess Olga's diary 15 November 1947

66 RA MDKD/OUT/FOX Prince Paul to Kate Fox 21 October 1947

67 Princess Olga's diary 1 November 1947

68 RA MDKD/OUT/FOX Prince Paul to Kate Fox 21 October 1947

69 Princess Olga's diary 28 November 1947

70 Princess Olga's diary 2 December 1947

71 RA MDKD/OUT/FOX Princess Olga to Kate Fox 13 September 1947

72 Princess Olga's diary 3 December 1947

73 Princess Olga's diary 8 December 1947

74 RA MDKD/OUT/FOX Prince Nicholas ('Nicky') to Kate Fox 2 January 1948

75 Telephone interview with Princess Elizabeth of Yugoslavia 24 April 2011

76 RA MDKD/OUT/FOX Prince Nicholas to Kate Fox 2 January 1948

77 Princess Olga's diary 5 December 1947

78 Princess Olga's diary 13 December 1947

79 Princess Olga's diary 14 December 1947

80 Princess Olga's diary 9 December 1947

81 Princess Olga's diary 24 December 1947

82 Princess Olga's diary 31 December 1947

83 RA MDKD/OUT/FOX Princess Olga to Kate Fox 11 January 1948

84 Major Beddington-Behrens to Prince Paul 16 December 1947 Columbia Box 6

85 FO371/72606 Notes of Field Marshall Smuts' meeting with Prince Paul are contained in a memo written by R Sedgwick of the British High Commission in Pretoria on 7 January 1948 and

accompany a letter from the same author to Sir Eric Machtig [Private Secretary to Permanent Under-Secretary of State] at the Commonwealth Relations Office London.

86 RA MDKD/OUT/FOX Princess Olga to Kate Fox 11 January 1948

87 FO371/72606 Telegram no 53 Common Relations Office to British High Commissioner 5 February 1948

88 Field Marshal Smuts to Princess Olga 11 February 1948 Columbia Box 4

89 RA MDKD/OUT/FOX Princess Olga to Kate Fox 18 February 1948

90 King Carol of Romania to Prince Paul 27 February 1948 Columbia Box 1

91 FO371/72606 Foreign Office Minute 14 February 1948

92 FO371/72606 Foreign Office Minute 10 February 1948

93 FO371/72606 Minute from the Secretary of State for Foreign Affairs to the Secretary of State for Commonwealth Relations 26 February 1948

94 FO371/72606 Minute from the Secretary of State for Commonwealth Relations to the Secretary of State for Foreign Affairs 27 February 1948

95 FO371/72606 Telegram 91 Commonwealth Relations Office to British High Commissioner 2 March 1948

96 Field Marshal Smuts to Prince Paul 3 March 1948 Columbia Box 4

97 Prince Paul to Field Marshal Smuts 6 March 1948 Columbia Box 4

98 RA MDKD/OUT/FOX Princess Olga to Kate Fox 6 March 1948

99 FO371/72606 Field Marshal Smuts to British High Commissioner 30 March 1948

100 FO371/72606 Sir Eric Machtig C.R.O. to Sir Orme Sargent Foreign Office 6 May 1948

101 RA MDKD/OUT/FOX Princess Olga to Kate Fox 20 April 1948

102 RA MDKD/OUT/FOX Princess Olga to Kate Fox 4 May 1948

Chapter 20-Return to Europe

1 RA MDKD/OUT/FOX Princess Olga to Kate Fox 4 May 1948

2 RA MDKD/OUT/FOX Princess Olga to Kate Fox 14 June 1948

3 RA MDKD/OUT/FOX Princess Olga to Kate Fox 14 June 1948

4 RA MDKD/OUT/FOX Princess Olga to Kate Fox 14 June 1948

5 RA MDKD/OUT/FOX Princess Olga to Kate Fox 11 July 1948

6 RA MDKD/PRIV/FORRF Princess Olga to Princess Marina 14 September 1948

7 Chips: The Diaries of Sir Henry Channon, entry for 24 November 1948 p526

8 Chips: The Diaries of Sir Henry Channon, entry for 30 November 1948 p527

9 Princess Olga's diary October 1948 excerpts provided by Princess Elizabeth by email 13 March 2015.

10 Princess Elizabeth to the author by e mail 2 June 2011.

11 Balfour and Mackay op.cit., p299

12 RA MDKD/PRIV/FORRF Princess Olga to Princess Marina 30 November 1948

13 Princess Olga's diary October 1948 excerpts provided by

Princess Elizabeth by email 13
March 2015.

14 Princess Olga's diary 21 January
1949

15 The Mercury Hobart 22 January
1949 accessed from www.news.
google.com 12 March 2013

16 Princess Olga's diary 23 January
1949

17 Princess Olga's diary 25 January
1949

18 Princess Olga's diary 5 February
1949

19 Princess Olga's diary 11 February
1949

20 RA MDKD/PRIV/FORRF
Princess Olga to Princess Marina
1 March 1949

21 Queen Marie of Yugoslavia to
Prince Paul 14 March 1949
Columbia Box 3

22 Princess Olga's diary 17 March
1949

23 Princess Olga's diary 21 April
1949

24 Princess Olga's diary 22 April
1949

25 Princess Olga's diary 30 April
1949

26 Princess Olga's diary 2 May 1949

27 Princess Olga to Princess
Nicholas 29 January 1950
[Princess Elizabeth Collection].

28 Princess Olga's diary 5 May
1949

29 Princess Olga's diary 19 May
1949

30 Princess Olga's diary 17 August
1949

31 Princess Olga's diary 29 May
1949

32 Princess Olga's diary 14
September 1949

33 Princess Olga's diary 17 June
1949

34 Princess Olga's diary 26 June
1949

35 Princess Olga's diary 22 August
1949

36 Princess Olga's diary 24 August
1949

37 Princess Olga's diary 27 July
1949

38 Princess Olga's diary 29 June
1949

39 Princess Olga's diary 15 August
1949

40 Princess Olga's diary 20 July
1949

41 Princess Olga's diary 17 October
1949

42 Princess Olga's diary 6 October
1949

43 Princess Olga's diary 13
November 1949

44 Princess Olga's diary 14
November 1949

45 Princess Olga's diary 22
November 1949

46 Princess Olga's diary 6 December
1949

47 Princess Olga's diary 9 December
1949

48 Princess Olga's diary 13
December 1949

49 Princess Olga's diary 25
December 1949

50 Princess Olga to Princess
Nicholas 1 January
1950 [Princess Elizabeth
Collection]

51 RA MDKD/PRIV/FORFF
Princess Olga to Princess Marina
5 January 1950

52 Princess Olga to Princess
Nicholas 8 January 1950
[Princess Elizabeth Collection]

53 Princess Olga to Princess
Nicholas 1 January 1950
[Princess Elizabeth Collection]

54 Princess Olga's diary 12 January
1950.

55 Princess Olga's diary 25 January
1950

56 Princess Olga to Princess Nicholas 30 January 1950 [Princess Elizabeth Collection].

57 Princess Olga to Princess Nicholas 29 January 1950 [Princess Elizabeth Collection].

58 Princess Olga to Princess Nicholas 29 January 1950 [Princess Elizabeth Collection].

59 Princess Olga to Princess Nicholas 29 January 1950 [Princess Elizabeth Collection].

60 Princess Olga to Princess Nicholas 14 February 1950 [Princess Elizabeth Collection].

61 Princess Olga to Princess Nicholas 28 February 1950 [Princess Elizabeth Collection].

62 Sir Malcolm Sargent to Princess Olga 21 March 1950 [Princess Elizabeth Collection].

63 Princess Olga to Princess Nicholas 14 February 1950 [Princess Elizabeth Collection].

64 RA MDKD/PRIV/FORFF Princess Olga to Princess Marina 20 February 1950

65 Princess Olga to Princess Nicholas 14 February 1950 [Princess Elizabeth Collection].

66 Princess Olga to Princess Nicholas 28 February 1950 [Princess Elizabeth Collection]

67 Princess Olga to Princess Nicholas 9 March 1950 [Princess Elizabeth Collection].

68 Princess Olga to Princess Nicholas 28 February 1950 [Princess Elizabeth Collection]

69 Princess Olga to Princess Nicholas 9 March 1950 [Princess Elizabeth Collection].

70 Princess Olga to Princess Nicholas 9 March 1950 [Princess Elizabeth Collection].

71 Princess Olga to Princess Nicholas 14 March 1950 [Princess Elizabeth Collection].

72 Princess Olga to Princess Nicholas 21 March 1950 [Princess Elizabeth Collection]

73 RA MDKD/PRIV/FORFF Princess Olga to Princess Marina 27 March 1950

74 Princess Olga to Princess Nicholas 25 March 1950 [Princess Elizabeth Collection].

75 Princess Olga to Princess Nicholas 31 March 1950 [Princess Elizabeth Collection].

76 Princess Olga to Princess Nicholas 8 April 1950 [Princess Elizabeth Collection]

77 Princess Olga's diary 17 April 1950

78 Princess Olga to Princess Nicholas 31 March 1950 [Princess Elizabeth Collection]

79 Interview with the Duke of Kent May 2011

80 Princess Olga to Princess Nicholas 23 April 1950 [Princess Elizabeth Collection]

81 Princess Olga's diary 21 April 1950

82 Princess Olga to Princess Nicholas 23 April 1950 [Princess Elizabeth Collection]

83 Princess Olga to Princess Nicholas 9 May 1950 [Princess Elizabeth Collection]

84 Commandant Paul Louis Weiller's Obituary in The Independent, 11 December 1993 accessed from www.independent.co.uk 11 April 2017

85 RA MDKD/PRIV/FORFF Princess Olga to Princess Marina 13 May 1950

86 Princess Olga's diary 3 June 1950

87 Princess Olga's diary 11 June 1950

88 E mail from Savina Serpieri 7 July 2015
89 Princess Olga's diary 12 September 1950
90 Interview with Princess Barbara of Yugoslavia April 2011
91 Princess Olga's diary 18 September 1950
92 Princess Olga's diary 7 November 1950
93 Princess Olga's diary 8 December 1950
94 Princess Olga to Princess Nicholas 20 November 1950 [Princess Elizabeth Collection.]
95 Princess Olga's diary 17 December 1950
96 Princess Olga to Princess Nicholas 26 December 1950 [Princess Elizabeth Collection
97 Princess Olga's diary 19 December 1950
98 Princess Olga's diary 24 December 1950
99 Princess Olga's diary 5 January 1951
100 Princess Olga to Princess Nicholas 8 January 1951 [Princess Elizabeth Collection]
101 Princess Olga's diary 13 November 1951
102 Princess Olga to Princess Nicholas 26 December 1950 [Princess Elizabeth Collection]
103 Princess Olga to Princess Nicholas 22 January 1951 [Princess Elizabeth Collection.]
104 Princess Olga to Princess Nicholas 6 February 1951 [Princess Elizabeth Collection.]
105 Princess Olga to Princess Nicholas 6 February 1951 [Princess Elizabeth Collection.]
106 Conversation with Princess Elizabeth 23 October 2015
107 E mail from Princess Elizabeth to the author 11 July 2016
108 Conversation with Princess Elizabeth 23 October 2015
109 E mail from Princess Elizabeth to the author 11 July 2016
110 Telephone Conversation with Archduchess Helen of Austria July 2016
111 Princess Olga's diary 12 February 1951
112 Princess Olga to Princess Nicholas 19 February 1951 [Princess Elizabeth Collection.]
113 Princess Olga to Princess Nicholas 4 March 1951 [Princess Elizabeth Collection.]
114 Princess Olga to Princess Nicholas 4 March 1951 [Princess Elizabeth Collection.]
115 Princess Olga to Princess Nicholas 16 March 1951 [Princess Elizabeth Collection.]
116 Princess Olga's diary 19 March 1951
117 Princess Olga's diary 2 April 1951
118 Princess Olga's diary 3 April 1951
119 Princess Olga's diary 14 April 1951
120 Princess Olga to Princess Nicholas 22 April 1951 [Princess Elizabeth Collection.]
121 Princess Olga's diary 3 May 1951
122 RA MDKD/PRIV/FORFF Princess Olga to Princess Marina 19 May 1951
123 Princess Olga's diary 2 June 1951
124 Princess Olga's diary 30 May 1951
125 Princess Olga's diary 2 June 1951
126 Princess Olga's diary 5 June 1951
127 Princess Olga's diary 8 June 1951
128 Princess Olga's diary 7 June 1951
129 Princess Olga's diary 8 June 1951

130 RA MDKD/PRIV/FORFF
Princess Olga to Princess Marina
5 July 1951

131 Princess Olga's diary 20 June
1951

132 Princess Olga to Princess
Nicholas 2 August 1951 [Princess
Elizabeth private collection].

133 Princess Olga's diary 7 August
1951

134 Princess Olga's diary 17 August
1951

135 Princess Olga's diary 22 August
1951

136 RA MDKD/PRIV/FORFF
Princess Olga to Princess Marina
13 September 1951

137 RA MDKD/PRIV/FORFF
Princess Olga to Princess Marina
13 September 1951

138 Princess Olga's diary 3 October
1951

139 Princess Olga's diary 20
November 1951

140 Princess Olga's diary 13
December 1951

141 Princess Olga's diary 26
December 1951

142 Princess Olga's diary 7 January
1952

143 Princess Olga's diary 18 January
1952

144 Princess Olga's diary 19 January
1952

145 Princess Olga's diary 19 January
1952

146 Chips: The Diaries of Sir Henry
Channon entry for 6 February
1952. p563

147 Princess Olga's diary 10 February
1952

148 Princess Olga's diary 12 February
1952

149 Princess Olga's diary 15 February
1952

150 Princess Olga's diary 26 February
1952

151 RA MDKD/PRIV/FORFF
Princess Olga to Princess Marina
17 May 1952

152 Princess Olga's diary 19 August
1952

153 Interview with Archduchess
Helen of Austria May 2011

154 RA MDKD/PRIV/FORFF
Princess Olga to Princess Marina
3 October 1952

155 Chips: The Diaries of Sir Henry
Channon entry for 22 May 1951
p559

156 RA MDKD/PRIV/FORFF
Princess Olga to Princess Marina
17 October 1952

157 Interview with Archduchess
Helen of Austria May 2011

158 Ibid.

159 Princess Olga's diary 3 November
1952

160 RA MDKD/PRIV/FORFF
Princess Olga to Princess Marina
24 November 1952

161 Dimitrakis Panagiotis *Greece and
the English: British Diplomacy
and the Kings of Greece* I.B
Tauris Ltd London 2009 pp
73-74

162 Princess Olga's diary 4 December
1952

163 Princess Olga's diary 4 January
1953

164 Letter from Prince Paul to Jacob
Hoptner 21 January 1953
Columbia Box 3

165 Princess Olga's diary 21 February
1953

166 Princess Olga's diary 25 February
1953

167 Princess Olga's diary 14 March
1953

168 Princess Olga's diary 15 March
1953

169 Princess Olga's diary 31 March
1953

170 Princess Olga's diary 7 April 1953
171 Princess Olga's diary 27 April 1953
172 Princess Olga's diary 2 June 1953
173 Princess Olga's diary 11 June 1953
174 RA MDKD/PRIV/FORFF Princess Olga to Princess Marina 16 September 1953
175 Princess Olga's diary 6 October 1953
176 Princess Olga's diary 17 October 1953
177 Princess Olga's diary 18 October 1953
178 Princess Olga's diary 19 October 1953
179 Princess Olga's diary 19 October 1953
180 Princess Olga's diary 23 October 1953
181 Princess Olga's diary 24 October 1953
182 RA MDKD/PRIV/FORFF Princess Olga to Princess Marina 11 November 1953
183 Princess Olga's diary 31 December 1953
184 Princess Olga's diary 9 January 1954
185 John Gordon article in The Sunday Express 17 January 1954 accessed on 29 October 2012 from Google News www.news.google.com

Chapter 21-Tragedy upon Tragedy

1 Princess Olga's diary 2 March 1954
2 Princess Olga's diary 1 March 1954
3 Princess Olga's diary 14 March 1954
4 Princess Olga's diary 11 April 1954
5 Sunday Times (Perth) 2 May 1954 accessed through Trove Australia www.trove.nla.gov.au on 29 October 2012
6 Telephone Interview with Vincent Poklewski Koziell 16 June 2011
7 Princess Olga's diary 12 April 1954
8 Princess Olga's diary 12 April 1954
9 Princess Olga's diary 15 April 1954
10 Princess Olga's diary 17 April 1954
11 Princess Olga's diary 23 April 1954
12 Princess Olga's diary 27 April 1954
13 Princess Olga's diary 30 April 1954
14 Princess Olga's diary 25 May 1954
15 RA MDKD/PRIV/FORFF Princess Olga to Princess Marina 27 May 1954
16 Telephone Interview with Vincent Poklewski Koziell 16 June 2011
17 Interview with the Duke of Kent May 2011
18 Lest Memory Fails p42
19 Lest Memory Fails p43
20 Interview with Princess Alexander of Yugoslavia 8 April 2011
21 Interview with Princess Elizabeth of Yugoslavia 15 November 2013
22 Telephone interview with Princess Elizabeth of Yugoslavia 24 April 2011
23 Princess Olga's diary 30 August 1954
24 Princess Olga's Notes page preceding diary entry 1 September 1954

25 RA MDKD/PRIV/FORFF
    Princess Olga to Princess Marina
    7 September 1954
26 Princess Olga's diary 9 September
    1954
27 Australian Women's Weekly 2
    March 1955 accessed through
    Trove Australia http://trove.nla.
    gov.au/ndp/del/article/51596846
    26 October 2012
28 RA MDKD/PRIV/FORFF
    Princesss Olga to Princesses
    Elisabeth and Marina 14
    November 1954
29 Princess Olga's diary 20 October
    1977
30 Princess Olga's diary 25
    November 1954
31 Princess Olga's diary 3 December
    1954
32 Princess Olga's diary 9 December
    1954
33 Princess Olga's diary 11
    December 1954
34 Princess Olga's diary 24
    December 1954
35 Princess Olga's diary 29
    December 1954
36 Conversation with Archduchess
    Helen of Austria 18 May 2015
37 RA MDKD/PRIV/FORFF
    Princess Olga to Princess Marina
    4 April 1955
38 RA MDKD/PRIV/FORFF
    Princess Olga to Princess Marina
    4 April 1955
39 RA MDKD/PRIV/FORFF
    Princess Olga to Princess Marina
    16 March 1955
40 Queen Marie of Yugoslavia to
    Prince Paul 29 May 1955
    Columbia Box 2
41 RA MDKD/PRIV/FORFF
    Princess Olga to Princess Marina
    25 July 1955
42 Prince Paul to Jacob Hoptner 3
    October 1955 Columbia Box 3

43 Princess Olga's diary 22 January
    1956
44 Princess Olga's diary 19 February
    1956
45 Princess Olga's diary 6 May 1956
46 Princess Olga's diary 31 May 1956
47 Princess Olga's diary 1 June 1956
48 Princess Olga's diary 5 June 1956
49 Princess Olga's diary 22 June
    1956
50 RA MDKD/PRIV/FORFF
    Princess Olga to Princess Marina
    8 July 1956
51 Princess Olga's diary 11
    November 1956
52 Princess Olga's diary 9 December
    1956
53 Princess Olga's diary 23
    December 1956
54 Princess Olga's diary 24
    December 1956
55 Princess Elizabeth of Yugoslavia
    by e mail to the author 2 June
    2011
56 A Royal Quest Intelligent Life
    Magazine March/April 2013
    accessed from https://www.
    economist.com/1843/2013/03/13/
    a-royal-quest 13 April 2013
57 Princess Olga's diary 11
    December 1979
58 Princess Olga's diary 11
    November 1966

Chapter 22-Grandmother

1   Princess Olga's diary 15 February
    1958
2   Princess Olga's diary 9 March
    1958
3   Princess Olga's diary 10 March
    1958
4   Princess Olga's diary 10 April
    1958
5   Princess Olga's diary 20 May
    1958

6 Princess Olga's diary 18 June 1958

7 Princess Olga's diary 27 June 1958

8 Princess Olga's diary 21 August 1958

9 Princess Olga's diary7 September 1958

10 Princess Olga's diary 6 October 1958

11 Princess Olga's diary 8 October 1958

12 Princess Olga's diary 24 December 1958

13 Princess Olga's diary 19 January 1959

14 Princess Olga's diary 16 January 1959

15 Princess Olga's diary 27 January 1959

16 Princess Olga's diary 14 February 1959

17 Princess Olga's diary 26 March 1959

18 RA MDKD/PRIV/FORFF Princess Olga to Princess Marina 2 July 1960

19 Princess Olga's diary 21 June 1959

20 Princess Olga's diary 20 August 1959

21 Princess Olga's diary 14 February 1960

22 Princess Olga's diary 25 August 1959

23 Princess Olga's diary 25 August 1959

24 Princess Olga's diary 12 September 1959

25 Princess Olga's diary 25 September 1959

26 Princess Olga's diary 29 November 1959

27 Princess Olga's diary 8 December 1959

28 Princess Olga's diary 22 January 1960

29 Princess Olga's diary 27 February 1960

30 Princess Olga's diary 1 March 1960

31 Princess Olga's diary 11 March 1960

32 Williams, Emma op.cit.,

33 Princess Olga's diary 14 March 1960

34 Princess Olga's diary 14 March 1960

35 Princess Olga's diary 15 March 1960

36 Princess Olga's diary 7 April 1960

37 Princess Olga's diary 10 April 1960

38 Princess Olga's diary 17 April 1960

39 Princess Olga's diary 1 May 1960

40 Princess Olga's diary 21 May 1960

41 Princess Olga's diary 22 May 1960

42 Princess Olga's diary 23 May 1960

43 Princess Olga's diary 20 June 1960

44 Princess Olga's diary 4 October 1960

45 Princess Olga's diary 15 October 1960

46 RA MDKD/PRIV/FORRF Princess Olga to Princess Marina 28 October 1960

47 Princess Olga's diary 11 December 1960

48 RA MDKD/PRIV/FORRF Princess Olga to Princess Marina 12 December 1960

49 Princess Olga's diary 2 May 1961

50 Princess Olga's diary 7 February 1961

51 Princess Olga's diary 8 February 1961

52 Princess Olga's diary 1 March 1961

53 Interview with Archduchess Helen of Austria May 2011

54 Princess Olga's diary 7 March 1961

55 RA MDKD/PRIV/FORRF Princess Olga to Princess Marina 8 March 1961

56 Princess Olga's diary 30 March 1961

57 Princess Olga's diary 31 March 1961

58 Princess Olga's diary 4 June 1961

59 Princess Olga's diary 11 June 1961

60 Princess Olga's diary 22 June 1961

61 Princess Olga's diary 24 August 1961

62 Princess Olga's diary 22 September 1961

63 Princess Olga's diary 23 September 1961

64 Princess Olga's diary 24 September 1961

65 Princess Olga's diary 25 September 1961

66 Princess Olga's diary 18 October 1961

67 Princess Olga's diary 18 November 1961

68 Princess Olga's diary 1 December 1961

69 Prince Paul to Jacob Hoptner 9 January 1962 Columbia Box 3

70 Princess Olga's diary 14 December 1961

71 Princess Olga's diary 17 December 1961

72 Princess Olga's diary 24 December 1961

73 King Peter to Prince Paul 6 August 1962 Columbia Box 4

74 Princess Olga to King Peter 12 August 1962 Columbia Box 4

75 Princess Olga's diary 1 January 1963

76 Princess Olga's diary 14 January 1963

77 Princess Olga's diary 29 January 1963

78 Princess Olga's diary 5 March 1963

79 Princess Olga's diary 29 January 1963

80 Princess Olga's diary 10 January 1963

81 Princess Olga's diary 11 January 1963

82 Princess Olga's diary 22 January 1963

83 Princess Olga's diary 23 January 1963

84 Princess Olga's diary 30 March 1963

85 Princess Olga's diary 21 April 1963

86 Princess Olga's diary 22 April 1963

87 Princess Olga's diary 24 April 1963

88 Princess Olga's diary 27 April 1963

89 Princess Olga's diary 5 May 1963

90 Princess Olga's diary 11 June 1963

91 Princess Olga's diary 8 June 1963

92 Princess Olga's diary 11 July 1963

93 Princess Olga's diary 27 June 1963

94 Princess Olga's diary 27 July 1963

95 Princess Olga's diary 27 June 1963

96 Princess Olga's diary 17 July 1963

97 E mail 3 May 2011 from Prince Michel of Yugoslavia to the author

98 Princess Olga's diary 20 August 1963

99 Princess Olga's diary 19 October 1963

100 Princess Olga's diary 25 October 1963

101 Princess Olga's diary 13 November 1963

102 Princess Olga's diary 22 November 1963

103 Princess Olga's diary 11 December 1963

104 Greek Royal Family website article in Greek (translated into English) on the life of King Paul accessed from www. greekroyalfamily.gr 20 October 2013

105 Prince Paul to Jacob Hoptner 28 March 1964 Columbia Box 3

106 Prince Paul to Jacob Hoptner 5 July 1964 Columbia Box 3

107 Princess Olga's diary 8 January 1965

108 Princess Olga's diary 24 January 1965

109 Princess Olga's diary 29 January 1965

110 Princess Olga's diary 26 January 1965

111 Princess Olga's diary 27 January 1965

112 Princess Olga's diary 12 February 1965

113 Princess Olga's diary 28 February 1965

114 Princess Olga's diary 11 February 1965

115 Princess Olga's diary 9 February 1965

116 Princess Olga's diary 7 February 1965

117 Princess Olga's diary 23 February 1965

118 Princess Olga's diary 1 March 1965

119 Princess Olga's diary 5 March 1965

120 Princess Olga's diary 27 March 1965

121 Princess Olga's diary 30 March 1965

122 Princess Olga's diary 18 April 1965

123 Princess Olga's diary 11 March 1965

124 Princess Olga's diary 21 March 1965

125 Princess Olga's diary 22 March 1965

126 Princess Olga's diary 31 March 1965

127 Princess Olga's diary 5 May 1965

128 Princess Olga's diary 13 June 1965

129 Princess Olga's diary 10 July 1965

130 Princess Olga's diary 13 July 1965

131 Princess Olga's diary 6 July 1965

132 Letter from Prince Paul to Jacob Hoptner 3 August 1965 Columbia Box 3

133 Princess Olga's diary 11 July 1965

134 Princess Olga's diary 15 October 1965

135 Princess Olga's diary 16 October 1965

136 Princess Olga's diary 16 October 1965

137 Princess Olga's diary 30 October 1965

138 Princess Olga's diary 8 November 1965

139 Princess Olga's diary 16 December 1965

Chapter 23-'So many problems.'

1 Princess Olga's diary 1 January 1966

2 Princess Olga's diary 3 February 1966

3   Princess Olga's diary 7 March 1966

4   Princess Olga's diary 29 March 1966

5   Princess Olga's diary 2 April 1966

6   Princess Olga's diary 16 April 1966

7   Princess Olga's diary 16 June 1966

8   Princess Olga's diary 7 July 1966

9   Princess Olga's diary 2 June 1966

10 Princess Olga's diary 27 June 1966

11 Princess Olga's diary 4 September 1966

12 Princess Olga's diary 13 November 1966

13 Princess Olga's diary 28 November 1966

14 Princess Olga's diary 2 December 1966

15 Princess Olga's diary 13 December 1966

16 Suzy Knickerbocker column Montreal Gazette 6 December 1966 accessed from Google News www.news.google.com 21 November 2013

17 Princess Olga's diary 17 December 1966

18 Princess Olga's diary 5 January 1967

19 Princess Olga's diary 5 March 1967

20 Princess Olga's diary 28 January 1967

21 Princess Olga's diary 6 and 7 March 1967

22 Princess Olga's diary 11 March 1967

23 Princess Olga's diary 13 March 1967

24 Princess Olga's diary 15 March 1967

25 Princess Olga's diary 20 March 1967

26 Princess Olga's diary 10 April 1967

27 Princess Olga's diary 20 April 1967

28 Princess Olga's diary 21 April 1967

29 Princess Olga's diary 29 April 1967

30 Princess Olga's diary 7 May 1967

31 George Chapman obituary in The Telegraph 12 August 2006 accessed from www.telegraph.co.uk 2 September 2016

32 Princess Olga's diary 18 May 1967

33 Princess Olga's diary 20 May 1967

34 Suzy Knickebocker column Montreal Gazette 14 June 1967 accessed from Google News www.news.google.com 4 September 2016

35 Princess Olga's diary 25 June 1967

36 Princess Olga's diary 19 August 1967

37 Princess Olga's diary 22 August 1967

38 Princess Olga's diary 26 August 1967

39 Princess Olga's diary 27 August 1967

40 Princess Olga's diary 11 September 1967

41 Princess Olga's diary 9 November 1967

42 Princess Olga's diary 19 December 1967

43 Princess Olga's diary 12 November 1967

44 Princess Olga's diary 28 November 1967

45 Princess Olga's diary 29 November 1967

46 Princess Olga's diary 6 December 1967

47 The Virgin Islands Daily News 14 December, 1967 accessed through Google News www.news.google.com 20 October 2013

48 Princess Olga's diary 14 December 1967

49 Princess Olga's diary 15 December 1967

50 Princess Olga's diary 16 December 1967

51 Princess Olga's diary 5 March 1968

52 Princess Olga's diary 19 December 1967

53 Princess Olga's diary 9 January 1968

54 Princess Olga's diary 1 February 1968

55 Princess Olga's diary 2 February 1968

56 Princess Olga's diary 16 February 1968

57 Princess Olga's diary 20 February 1968

58 Princess Olga's diary 21 February 1968

Chapter 24-'I am the only one left.'

1 Princess Olga's diary 21 February 1968

2 Princess Olga's diary 4 April 1968

3 E mail 3 May 2011 from Prince Michel of Yugoslavia to the author.

4 Princess Olga's diary 23 April 1968

5 Princess Olga's diary 6 May 1968

6 Princess Olga's diary 3 May 1968

7 Princess Olga's diary 6 May 1968

8 Princess Olga's diary 23 May 1968

9 Princess Olga's diary 29 May 1968

10 Princess Olga's diary 5 June 1968

11 Princess Olga's diary 14 June 1968

12 Princess Olga's diary 17 July 1968

13 Princess Olga's diary 18 July 1968

14 Princess Olga's diary 20 July 1968

15 Princess Olga's diary 21 July 1968

16 Interview with the Duke of Kent May 2011

17 Princess Olga's diary 1 August 1968

18 Princess Olga's diary 9 August 1968

19 Princess Olga's diary 14 August 1968

20 Princess Olga's diary 25 August 1968

21 Princess Olga's diary 26 August 1968

22 Beaton in the Sixties op.cit., p375

23 Interview with the Duke of Kent May 2011

24 Princess Olga's diary 27 August 1968

25 Princess Olga's diary 29 August 1968

26 Princess Olga's diary 30 August 1968

27 Princess Olga's diary 30 August 1968

28 Princess Olga's diary 31 August 1968

29 Princess Olga's diary 7 September 1968

30 Written response by Princess Elizabeth of Yugoslavia to the author by e mail 2 June 2011.

31 Interview with Archduchess Helen of Austria May 2011

32 Telephone interview with Vincent Poklewski Koziell 16 June 2011

33 RA MDKD/OUT/FOX Princess Olga to Kate Fox September 28 1946

34 The Glasgow Herald 26 October 1968 accessed from Google News www.news.google.com 20 September 2016

35 Princess Olga's diary 31 October 1968

36 Princess Olga's diary 26 November 1968

37 Princess Olga's diary 27 November 1968

38 Princess Olga's diary 2 December 1968

39 Princess Olga's diary 6 December 1968

40 Princess Olga's diary 24 December 1968

41 Princess Olga's diary 27 February 1969

42 Princess Olga's diary 12 March 1969

43 Princess Olga's diary 17 March 1969

44 Princess Olga's diary 24 May 1969

45 Princess Olga's diary 20 March 1969

46 Princess Olga's diary 25 March 1969

47 Princess Olga's diary 31 March 1969

48 Princess Olga's diary 21 April 1969

49 The Owosso Argus-Press 25 April 1969 accessed from Google News www.news.google.com 17 October 2013

50 Princess Olga's diary 16 May 1969

51 Princess Olga's diary 11 June 1969

52 Princess Olga's diary 17 June 1969

53 Princess Olga's diary 29 June 1969

54 Princess Olga's diary 15 August 1969

55 Princess Olga's diary 18 August 1969

56 Princess Olga's diary 23 August 1969

57 Princess Olga's diary 18 September 1969

58 Princess Olga's diary 11 December 1969

59 Princess Olga's diary 21 September 1969

60 Princess Olga's diary 27 October 1969

61 Princess Olga's diary 5 December 1969

62 Princess Olga's diary 13 December 1969

63 Princess Olga's diary 20 January 1970

Chapter 25-Failing Health.

1 Princess Olga's diary 14 March 1970

2 Princess Olga's diary 13 April 1970

3 Princess Olga's diary 7 April 1970

4 Princess Olga's diary 28 May 1970

5 Princess Olga's diary 29 May 1970

6 Princess Olga's diary 11 June 1970

7 Princess Olga's diary 5 November 1970

8 Princess Olga's diary 8 November 1970

9 The Morning Record November 13 1970 accessed from Google News www.news.google.com 23 July 2013

10 Princess Olga's diary 16 February 1971

11 Princess Olga's diary 30 March 1971

12 Princess Olga's diary 13 February 1971

13 Princess Olga's diary 13 May 1971

14 Princess Olga's diary 16 May 1971

15 Princess Olga's diary 31 May 1971

16 Princess Olga's diary 5 June 1971

17 Princess Olga's diary 6 June 1971

18 Princess Olga's diary 18 June 1971

19 Princess Olga's diary 15 July 1971

20 Princess Olga's diary 5 August 1971

21 Beaton, Cecil *The Unexpurgated Beaton* Weidenfeld and Nicolson, London 2002 p188

22 Princess Olga's diary 26 September 1971

23 Princess Olga's diary 4 October 1971

24 Princess Olga's diary 26 October 1971

25 Princess Olga's diary 28 October 1971

26 Princess Olga's diary 9 November 1971

27 Princess Olga's diary 18 March 1972

28 Princess Olga's diary 11 November 1971

29 Princess Olga's diary 1 January 1972

30 Princess Olga's diary 13 February 1972

31 Princess Olga's diary 14 January 1972

32 Princess Olga's diary 7 February 1972

33 Princess Olga's diary 31 March 1972

34 Princess Olga's diary 30 April 1972

35 Princess Olga's diary 28 April 1972

36 Princess Olga's diary 1 May 1972

37 Princess Olga's diary 4 May 1972

38 Princess Olga's diary 21 June 1972

39 Princess Olga's diary 19 June 1972

40 Princess Olga's diary 29 June 1972

41 Princess Olga's diary 1 July 1972

42 Princess Olga's diary 1 July 1972

43 Princess Olga's diary 19 July 1972

44 Princess Olga's diary 29 August 1972

45 Princess Olga's diary 2 November 1972

46 Princess Olga's diary 3 November 1972

47 Princess Olga's diary 11 December 1972

48 Princess Olga's diary 16 December 1972

49 Princess Olga's diary 30 December 1972

50 Interview with Prince Alexander of Yugoslavia April 2011

51 Interview with Princess Alexander of Yugoslavia 8 April 2011

52 Princess Olga's diary 30 December 1972

53 Princess Olga's diary 4 January 1973

54 Princess Olga's diary 20 January 1973

55 Princess Olga's diary 26 January 1973

56 Princess Olga's diary 31 January 1973

57 Princess Olga's diary 6 February 1973

58 Princess Olga's diary 7 February 1973

59 Princess Olga's diary 22 February 1973

60 Princess Olga's diary 7 June 1973

61 Princess Olga's diary 3 March 1973

62 Princess Olga's diary 17 April 1973

63 Princess Olga's diary 24 May 1973

64 Princess Olga's diary 1 June 1973

65 Princess Olga's diary 29 July 1973

66 Princess Olga's diary 30 July 1973

67 Princess Olga's diary 12 June 1973

68 Princess Olga's diary 13 June 1973

69 Princess Olga's diary 15 June 1973

70 Princess Olga's diary 23 June 1973

71 Princess Olga's diary 24 June 1973

72 Princess Olga's diary 30 June 1973

73 Princess Olga's diary 7 August 1973

74 Princess Olga's diary 10 September 1973

75 Princess Olga's diary 26 September 1973

76 Princess Olga's diary 17 September 1973

77 Princess Olga's diary 1 October 1973

78 Princess Olga's diary 17 October 1973

79 Princess Olga's diary 6 November 1973

80 Princess Olga's diary 29 October 1973

81 Princess Olga's diary 1 November 1973

82 Princess Olga's diary 6 November 1973

83 Interview with Princess Alexander of Yugoslavia 8 April 2011

84 Interview with Archduchess Helen of Austria May 2011

85 Interview with Princess Alexander of Yugoslavia 8 April 2011

86 Princess Olga's diary 17 November 1973

87 Interview with Princess Alexander of Yugoslavia 8 April 2011

88 Princess Olga's diary 1 December 1976

89 Princess Olga's diary 19 February 1974

90 Princess Olga's diary 19 February 1974

91 Princess Olga's diary 5 April 1974

92 Princess Olga's diary 17 April 1974

93 Princess Olga's diary 8 July 1974

94 Princess Olga's diary 12 July 1974

95 Princess Olga's diary 25 July 1974

96 Princess Olga's diary 8 September 1974

97 Princess Olga's diary 27 August 1974

98 Princess Olga's diary 27 September 1974

99 Princess Olga's diary 29 September 1974

100 Princess Olga's diary 3 October 1974

101 Princess Olga's diary 12 October 1974

102 Princess Olga's diary 13 October 1974

103 Princess Olga's diary 14 October 1974

104 Princess Olga's diary 14 October 1974

105 Princess Olga's diary 15 October 1974

106 Princess Olga's diary 17 October 1974

107 Princess Olga's diary 22 October 1974

108 Princess Olga's diary 11 November 1974

109 Princess Olga's diary 12 November 1974

110 Princess Olga's diary 17
November 1974
111 Princess Olga's diary 23
November 1974
112 Princess Olga's diary 24
December 1974
113 Princess Olga's diary 9 April
1975
114 Princess Olga's diary 29 April
1975
115 Princess Olga's diary 29 October
1975
116 Princess Olga's diary 22 April
1975
117 Princess Olga's diary 7 April
1975
118 Princess Olga's diary 16 June
1975
119 Princess Olga's diary 19 July
1975
120 Princess Olga's diary 16 August
1975
121 Princess Olga's diary 3 September
1975
122 Princess Olga's diary 6 September
1975
123 Interview with Archuchess Sophie
of Austria, Princess of Windisch-
Graetz 21 May 2015
124 Princess Olga's diary 10
November 1975
125 Princess Olga's diary 25 October
1975
126 Princess Olga's diary 1 October
1975
127 Princess Olga's diary 15
December 1975
128 Princess Olga's diary 13
December 1975

Chapter 26-Alone.

1   Princess Olga's diary 4 February
1976
2   Princess Olga's diary 7 February
1976
3   Princess Olga's diary 9 February
1976
4   Princess Olga's diary 18 March
1976
5   Princess Olga's diary 16 June
1976
6   Princess Olga's diary 13 April
1976
7   Princess Olga's diary 5 June 1976
8   Princess Olga's diary 9 June 1976
9   Princess Olga's diary 10 June
1976
10 Princess Olga's diary 18 June
1976
11 Princess Olga's diary 26 June
1976
12 Princess Olga's diary 14 July
1976
13 Princess Olga's diary 20 July
1976
14 Princess Olga's diary 17 August
1976
15 Princess Olga's diary 14 and 16
August 1976
16 Princess Olga's diary 5 September
1976
17 Princess Olga's diary 6 September
1976
18 Princess Olga's diary 14
September 1976
19 The Montreal Gazette 20
September 1976 accessed from
Google News www.news.google.
com 17 March 2013
20 Princess Olga's diary 20
September 1976
21 Interview with the Duke of Kent
May 2011
22 Princess Olga's diary 20
September 1976
23 E mail 3 May 2011 from Prince
Michel of Yugoslavia to author.
24 Princess Olga's diary 21
September 1976
25 Princess Olga's diary 22
September 1976

26 Interview with Princess Alexander of Yugoslavia 8 April 2011

27 Princess Olga's diary 24 September 1976

28 Princess Olga's diary 30 September 1976

29 Princess Olga's diary 28 September 1976

30 Princess Olga's diary 7 October 1976

31 Interview with Archuchess Sophie of Austria, Princess of Windisch-Graetz 21 May 2015

32 Princess Olga's diary 26 October 1976

33 Princess Olga's diary 23 November 1976

34 Princess Olga's diary 24 November 1976

35 Princess Olga's diary 7 December 1976

36 Princess Olga's diary 14 December 1976

37 Princess Olga's diary 16 December 1976

38 Princess Olga's diary 22 December 1976

39 Princess Olga's diary 25 December 1976

40 Princess Olga's diary 31 December 1976

41 Princess Olga's diary 14 February 1977

42 Princess Olga's diary 15 February 1977

43 Princess Olga's diary 17 February 1977

44 Princess Olga's diary 27 April 1977

45 Interview with Archduchess Helen of Austria May 2011

46 Interview with Archuchess Sophie of Austria, Princess of Windisch-Graetz 21 May 2015

47 Interview with Princess Barbara of Yugoslavia 8 April 2011

48 Princess Olga's diary 24 June 1977

49 Princess Olga's diary 17 April 1977

50 Princess Olga's diary 17 June 1977

51 Princess Olga's diary 8 May 1977

52 Princess Olga's diary 27 May 1977

53 Princess Olga's diary 4 June 1977

54 Princess Olga's diary 17 July 1977

55 Princess Olga's diary 10 July 1977

56 Princess Olga's diary 27 July 1977

57 Princess Olga's diary 29 August 1977

58 Princess Olga's diary 30 August 1977

59 Neil Balfour to Alexander Macmillan 10 October 1977 Columbia Box 6

60 Princess Olga's diary 11 September 1977

61 Princess Olga's diary 13 September 1977

62 Princess Olga's diary 18 September 1977

63 Princess Olga's diary 20 September 1977

64 Princess Olga's diary 25 September 1977

65 Princess Olga's diary 2 October 1977

66 Princess Olga's diary 14 October 1977

67 Interview with Archuchess Sophie of Austria, Princess of Windisch-Graetz 21 May 2015

68 Ibid.

69 Princess Olga's diary 26 November 1977

70 Princess Olga's diary 30 November 1977

71 Princess Olga's diary 2 December 1977
72 Princess Olga's diary 13 December 1977
73 Princess Olga's diary 24 December 1977
74 Princess Olga's diary 31 May 1978
75 Princess Olga's diary 11 June 1978
76 Lane, Ken *Princess Michael of Kent* Robert Hale London 1986 p94
77 Princess Olga's diary 29 June 1978 (wrongly entered by her-should have been entry for 30 June)
78 Princess Olga's diary 30 June 1978 (wrongly entered by her-should have been entry for 1 July)
79 Lane, Ken op.cit., p94
80 Princess Olga's diary 30 June 1978 (wrongly entered by her-should have been entry for 1 July)
81 Lane, Ken op.cit., pp 95-96
82 Princess Olga's diary 5 July 1978
83 The Times, Monday, 3 July 1978
84 Princess Olga's diary 2 July 1978
85 Princess Olga's diary 19 August 1978
86 Princess Olga's diary 15 November 1978
87 Princess Olga's diary 11 September 1978
88 Princess Olga's diary 16 October 1978
89 Princess Olga's diary 6 November 1978
90 Princess Olga's diary 5 December 1978
91 Princess Olga's diary 6 December 1978
92 Princess Olga's diary 8 December 1978
93 Princess Olga's diary 25 December 1978
94 Princess Olga's diary 1 January 1979
95 Princess Olga's diary 4 January 1979
96 Princess Olga's diary 19 January 1979
97 Princess Olga's diary 21 January 1979
98 Princess Olga's diary 31 January 1979
99 Princess Olga's diary 11 February 1979
100 Princess Olga's diary 13 February 1979
101 Princess Olga's diary 11 March 1979
102 Princess Olga's diary 29 March 1979
103 Princess Olga's diary 10 April 1979
104 Princess Olga's diary 7 July 1979
105 Princess Olga's diary 9 July 1979
106 Princess Olga's diary 12 July 1979
107 Princess Olga's diary 30 August 1979
108 Princess Olga's diary 27 August 1979
109 Princess Olga's diary 23 October 1979
110 Princess Olga's diary 26 December 1979

Chapter 27-'Mental Drowning'

1 Princess Olga's diary 19 May 1982
2 Princess Olga's diary 2 June 1982
3 Princess Olga's diary 16 December 1982
4 Princess Olga's diary 27 February 1982
5 Princess Olga's diary 10 May 1982

6 Princess Olga's diary 21 February 1984

7 Princess Olga's diary 21 June 1982

8 Princess Olga's diary 22 June 1982

9 Princess Olga's diary 13 May 1982

10 Princess Olga's diary 21 August 1982

11 Princess Olga's diary 3 April 1982

12 Princess Olga's diary 21 September 1982

13 Princess Olga's diary 27 September 1982

14 Princess Olga's diary 9 October 1982

15 Princess Olga's diary 19 November 1982

16 Princess Olga's diary 28 November 1982

17 Princess Olga's diary 2 December 1982

18 Interview with the Duke of Kent May 2011

19 Interview with Princess Alexander of Yugoslavia 8 April 2011

20 Interview with Archuchess Sophie of Austria, Princess of Windisch-Graetz 21 May 2015

21 Interview with Archduchess Helen of Austria May 2011

22 Princess Olga's diary 12 January 1984

23 Princess Olga's diary 5 January 1984

24 Princess Olga's diary 13 January 1984

25 Princess Olga's diary 16 and 18 January 1984

26 Princess Olga's diary 25 January 1984

27 Princess Olga's diary 14 April 1982

28 Princess Olga's diary 14 June 1984

29 Princess Olga's diary 25 June 1984

30 Princess Olga's diary 1 July 1984

31 Princess Olga's diary 16 September 1984

32 Princess Olga's diary 29 October 1984

33 Princess Olga's diary 7 October 1984

34 Princess Olga's diary 19 November 1984

35 Diary 'notes' section for end of November 1984

36 Sotheby's Monaco "Bel Ameublement" catalogue details for 23 and 24 June 1985 accessed from http://primo.getty.edu/primo_library/libweb/action/dlDisplay.do?vid=GRI&afterPDS=true&institution=01GRI&docId=GETTY_ALMA2112967 8970001551 06 May 2015

37 Princess Olga's diary 4 January 1986

38 Princess Olga's diary 19 January 1986

39 Princess Olga's diary 23 January 1986

40 Princess Olga's diary 23 February 1986

41 Princess Olga's diary 21 February 1986

42 Princess Olga's diary 7 March 1986

43 Princess Olga's diary 26 April 1986

44 Princess Olga's diary 14 July 1986

45 Princess Olga's diary 1 April 1986

46 Princess Olga's diary 17 November 1986

47 Princess Olga's diary 28 May 1986

48 Princess Olga's diary 18 February 1988

49   Princess Olga's diary 25 May 1988

50   Interview with Archduchess Helen of Austria May 2011

51   Princess Olga's diary 21 May 1988

52   Princess Olga's diary 29 February 1988

53   Princess Olga's diary 25 May 1988

54   Princess Olga's diary 30 May 1988

55   Princess Olga's diary 8 June 1988

56   Princess Olga's diary 20 August 1988

57   Princess Olga's diary 25 August 1988

58   Interview with Prince and Princess Alexander of Yugoslavia 8 April 2011

59   Interview with Archduchess Helen of Austria May 2011

60   Interview with Princess Alexander of Yugoslavia 8 April 2011

61   Interview with Archduchess Helen of Austria May 2011

62   Interview with Princess Alexander of Yugoslavia 8 April 2011

63   Ibid.

64   Ibid.

65   My Will written on May 2 1943 at rear of 1943 diary.

66   Interview with Prince Alexander of Yugoslavia 8 April 2011

67   Details provided on the European Royal Message Board July 2012

68   Interview with Archduchess Helen of Austria May 2011

69   Kosta Petrov Youtube interview with Princess Elizabeth uploaded 21 January 2012 http://www.youtube.com/watch?v=fKywWOFuvIo

70   Jelisaveta Majesty Magazine Vol. 37 No. 3 p32

71   Serbian Orthodox Church Official website http://www.spc.rs/eng accessed 27 December 2016

Bibliography

Aronson, Theo *Crowns in Conflict*, Salem House Publishers, New Hampshire, 1986

Balfour, Neil and Mackay, Sally *Paul of Yugoslavia*, Canada Wide Magazines and Communications Ltd, 1996

Battiscombe, Georgina *Queen Alexandra* Constable and Company, London, 1969

Beaton, Cecil *The Unexpurgated Beaton* Weidenfeld and Nicolson, London 2002

Beaton in the Sixties: The Cecil Beaton Diaries as He Wrote Them, 1965-1969 Alfred A. Knopf 2004

Beech, Arturo *Dear Ellen...*Eurohistory and Richmond House Books, 2011

Bertin, Celia *Marie Bonaparte*, Harcourt, Brace, Jovanovich, New York, 1982

Bonus, Wendy *The Faberge Connection: A memoir of the Bowe Family* iUniverse, Bloomington, 2010

Broadberry Stephen and O'Rourke Kevin, *The Cambridge Economic History of Modern Europe: Volume 2, 1870 to the Present*, Cambridge University Press.

Brugere, Raymond, *Veni Vidi Vichy* Calmann-Levy, Varves, France 1944

Bulow, Bernhard Prince von, *Memoirs 1897-1903* Putnam, London, 1931

Channon, Henry (James, Robert Rhodes. Ed.) *Chips: The Diaries of Sir Henry Channon* Weidenfeld and Nicolson, London, 1967.

Christmas, Captain Walter *King George of Greece* McBride Nast and Company, New York, 1914

Christopher, Prince *Memoirs of HRH Prince Christopher of Greece*, Hurst and Blackett, London, 1938

Churchill, Winston S., *The Grand Alliance (The Second World War Volume III)* Mariner Books (an imprint of Houghton Mifflin), Boston, 1986

Hoptner, Jacob B. *Yugoslavia in Crisis,* Columbia University Press, New York, 1962

Cohen, Philip *Serbia's Secret War,* Texas A&M University Press, 1996

D'Este, Carlo *Warlord: A Life of Churchill at War 1874-1945,* Allen Lane, London, 2009

Dimitrakis Panagiotis *Greece and the English: British Diplomacy and the Kings of Greece* I.B Tauris Ltd London 2009

Duff, David *Alexandra Princess and Queen* Sphere Books Ltd., London, 1981

Ellis, Jennifer *The Duchess of Kent* Odhams Press, London, 1952

Field, Leslie *The Queen's Jewels* Weidenfeld and Nicholson, London, 1987

Forbes, Grania *My Darling Buffy-The Early Life of the Queen Mother* Headline Richard Cohen Publishers, London, 1999

Higham, Charles *Wallis The Secret Lives of the Duchess of Windsor,* Sidjwick and Jackson, London 1988

Irving, David *The War Path,* 2003, accessed from http://www.fpp.co.uk/books/WarPh/WarPath.pdf

Jelavich, Barbara, *History of the Balkans: Twentieth Century,* Cambridge University Press, 1983

King, Stella *Princess Marina: Her Life and Times* Casell, London, 1969

Lampe, John R. *Yugoslavia as History: Twice There Was a Country,* Cambridge University Press, 2000

Lane, Ken *Princess Michael of Kent* Robert Hale London 1986

Maček, Vladko *In the Struggle for Freedom,* R Speller and Sons, New York 1957

Massie, Robert K, *Nicholas and Alexandra* Victor Gollancz, London, 1968

McLean, Roderick R. *Royalty and Diplomacy in Europe 1890-1914,* Cambridge University Press, 2007

Muylunas, Andrei and Mironenko, Sergei *'A Lifelong Passion-Nicholas and Alexandra Their Own Story,'* Weidenfeld and Nicolson, London, 1996

Nicholas, Prince *My Fifty Years* Hutchinson and Co., London, 1926

Pakula, Hannah *The Last Romantic-A Biography of Queen Marie of Romania,* Weidenfeld and Nicolson, London, 1985

Parrot, Cecil *The Tightrope* Faber and Faber, London, 1975

Onslow, Sue *Britain and the Belgrade Coup of 27 March 1941 Revisited* eJournal of International March 2005 accessed from www.researchgate.net/publication/30522529

Peter, King *A King's Heritage,* Putnam, New York, 1954

Ramet, Sabrina *The Three Yugoslavias: State-Building and Legitimation, 1918-2005,* Indiana University Press, 2006

Ristelhueber, René *A History of the Balkan Peoples* Twayne Publishers, Woodbridge, 1971

Rothwell, Victor *Anthony Eden: A Political Biography,* Manchester University Press, 1992

Shawcross, William *Queen Elizabeth the Queen Mother: The Official Biography,* Macmillan, London, 2009

Sotirovic, Vladislav B. *Creation of the Kingdom of Serbs, Croats and Slovenes,* Vilnius University Press, 2007

Stojadinović, Milan *La Yougoslavie Entre Les Deux Guerres,* Nouvelles Editions Latines, Paris, 1979

Thorpe, D.R *Supermac: The Life of Harold* Macmillan Chatto and Windus 2010

Tucker, Spencer & Roberts, Priscilla *World War I* ABC-CLIO, Santa Barbara, 2005

Vassili, Count Paul *Behind the Veil at the Russian Court* Reprint Series, Forgotten Books, 2010

Van Creveld, Martin *Hitler's Strategy 1940-1941 The Balkan Clue,* Cambridge University Press, 1973

Van der Kiste, John *Kings of the Hellenes,* Sutton Publishing, Stroud, 1994.

Vickers, Hugo *Alice Princess Andrew of Greece,* Penguin Books, London, 2001

Wheeler-Bennett John *King George VI: His Life and Reign,* Macmillan, London, 1958

Zeepvat, Charlotte *From Cradle to Crown,* Sutton Publishing, Stroud, 2006.

Newspaper Websites:

www.archive.catholicherald.co.uk
www.news.google.com www.independent.co.uk
www.novsti.rs www.nytime.com www.select.nytimes.com
www.trove.nla.gov.au

Reference Websites

Alexander Palace Royal Forum www.forum.alexanderpalace.org

Australian Women's Weekly www.trove.nla.gov.au

British Parliamentary proceedings www.theyworkforyou.com/debates/

CIA website www. cia.gov/library/

www.economist.com

European Royal Message Board https://members3.boardhost.com/EuropeanRoyals/

Goering's testimony Nuremberg trials: http://goring.tripod.com/goo28.html

Greek Royal Family website www.formerkingofgreece.org

Ladies Home Journal www.tkinter.smig.net

Serbian Orthodox Church www.spc.rs/eng

Serbian Royal Family www.dvor.rs

Reference Books

Documents on German Foreign Policy {DGFP], HM Stationary Office, 1956, London

Foreign Relations of the United States Diplomatic Papers, Government Printing Office, 1957, Washington.

Unpublished Sources

Olga, Princess *Lest Memory Fails*.

Princess Olga's diaries.

Princess Olga's private family correspondence.

Index

About the Author

Robert Prentice has been a regular contributor to Britain's "Majesty" magazine for over a decade, as well as to numerous Facebook pages dedicated to royalty including Royalty Digest, Royal History, The World's Best Royals. He contributes articles for his own Royal Blog royaltyrobertwriter.home.blog/ He has been an occasional commentator on BBC Radio Scotland and BBC Scotland television news programmes.

CPSIA information can be obtained
at www.ICGtesting.com
Printed in the USA
BVHW060112250321
603355BV00002B/46

9 781839 754425